ODYSSEY, BOOK 1

Homer

Odyssey, Book 1

Edited with an Introduction,
Translation, Commentary, and Glossary
by
SIMON PULLEYN

OXFORD
UNIVERSITY PRESS

OXFORD
UNIVERSITY PRESS

Great Clarendon Street, Oxford, OX2 6DP,
United Kingdom

Oxford University Press is a department of the University of Oxford.
It furthers the University's objective of excellence in research, scholarship,
and education by publishing worldwide. Oxford is a registered trade mark of
Oxford University Press in the UK and in certain other countries

Published in the United States of America by Oxford University Press
198 Madison Avenue, New York, NY 10016, United States of America

British Library Cataloguing in Publication Data
Data available

Library of Congress Control Number: 2017964400

ISBN 978-0-19-878880-5 (hbk.)
ISBN 978-0-19-882420-6 (pbk.)

Printed and bound by
CPI Group (UK) Ltd, Croydon, CR0 4YY

omnibus qui me
docuerunt atque erudierunt

Preface

The *Odyssey* is one of the greatest poems ever made. Nothing written about it could possibly exhaust the stock of things one might say. Yet this book consists of a lengthy introduction, a Greek text, a critical apparatus, an English translation, a detailed commentary, and a full vocabulary. What is it all for? The modest goal is simply to offer pointers to enrich the experience of reading *Odyssey* Book 1, whether the reader be a relative newcomer to Homer or a more experienced traveller.

If one listens to a great piece of music, one does not typically ask, 'What does this *mean*?' People are less hesitant to ask this of a poem. It must *mean* something, we think, as though all verbal artistry were just so much window dressing—idiom, imagery, and metre just a convenient sauce with which to serve up 'ideas'. But we reach our greatest maturity as readers when we stop trying to read the poem like that and instead allow the poem to read us. Do you identify with Odysseus? Perhaps you miss the ways in which you are more like one of his companions. Do you sympathize with Calypso? Perhaps you are more like Penelope. Do you feel indignation at the behaviour of the suitors? Perhaps you forget the beggar whom you just ignored in the street. At any rate, the experience of reading a poem ought to be more than marshalling a series of propositions.

But our access to the epics is not straightforward. They are the product of an age that had in many respects already vanished by the time that Homer was at work. Pointers are needed simply to orient oneself in that world. In the *Iliad*, for example, Achilles is monumentally angry at the loss of his concubine Briseis. What does it mean when he says τὴν ἐκ θυμοῦ φίλεον? Does φιλέω map neatly onto 'love'? Did he love her romantically in the way that Romeo and Juliet loved each other? Or was it more visceral, after the fashion of D. H. Lawrence? What is θυμός? Does he mean 'I felt romantic affection for her from the bottom of my heart' or 'I counted her with all my vital spirit among those close to me?' What of the fact that she is unfree, captured in war and sharing his bed through necessity? If we could go back in time to the relevant periods and make a sociological study of sexual politics, how far would this help in interpreting a literary work of art?

Moving to the *Odyssey*, we might consider the scene in Book 1 where Telemachus is being stand-offish about his father and rude about his mother. We cannot help at least sometimes glancing at this through the lens of other things we know—from 'Woman, what have I to do with thee?'[1] to *Hamlet*. This is natural; it is hard to say that some reactions are 'allowed' and others excluded because 'anachronistic'. That said, it is not unreasonable at least to wonder what might have been the reactions of the original audience.

Those of us who are trained in philology (in the broad sense) are accustomed to using all kinds of sharp-looking instruments to help us get inside the texts. We have papyrology and palaeography to help us to read and correct versions of the poem that survive from the Hellenistic period and the Middle Ages; we have the resources of archaeology to help us to understand references to the material world; we have historical anthropology to throw light on the cultural world of the archaic bards; we have comparative philology and linguistics that can clarify the surface meaning of a word or phrase. But language is not simply a tool for pointing things out or making arguments and great literature does not exist so much to *inform* us as to *form* us. It is no part of my task to dictate the outcome of that experience; but I am bound to try to elucidate the often opaque and unusual language in which the poems are couched, to draw attention to features of execution, style, and plot that seem to me, at least, to be worthy of comment and to offer a view on what the original text looks like and how we might construe it in modern English.

Some pedagogues will throw up their hands in horror at a commentator who also provides a translation. Their students, they say, will 'cheat' by looking at the translation before having wrestled sufficiently with the Greek. I credit readers with more maturity than this: it is perfectly open to them to put a piece of paper over the right-hand page and use the translation as a secondary check rather than a primary shortcut. In any event, in the age of the smartphone, the reader who wants a translation does not even need to go to a bookshop. I would rather the translation were mine and reflected the considered views that I have formed in the commentary as to how the Greek is to be construed. It has been customary in the past for writers who do not provide a translation nevertheless to translate in the commentary those words and phrases which seem to them to present particular difficulty. I have chosen to unburden the commentary of such content and at the same time not to guess which phrases are difficult and which are not. The reader can now see how I take the entire text with no omissions. I ought to say that the translation makes no pretence to literary merit; it is certainly not intended as a rival to the many freestanding translations of the entire poem that are readily available. It is designed to help

---

[1] John 2:4.

the reader to construe the Greek on the facing page and to reflect, as far as possible, effects of word order and sound in the original.

Much of the commentary uses the techniques of comparative linguistics and historical syntax to gloss individual words or to construe longer phrases. What is being unfolded here is the surface meaning. When we are told that Athena flew away ὄρνις ... ὣς ἀνόπαια, what does ἀνόπαια signify (*Od.* 1.320 n.)? Should one read ἀνόπαια or ἀν᾽ ὀπαῖα? The differing arguments are canvassed in the commentary and a view is taken. This view might not commend itself to all readers, who might weigh the evidence differently. But, because reasons and sources are given, the reader can form a judgement rather than being told what to think. All of this only looks at the surface meaning. It is for readers now, as the audience then, to reflect on what they think the poet meant and just how Athena took her leave and what that means about her.

This does not mean that a person who writes about Homer is absolved from scholarly inquiry and engagement with technical matters that might not be congenial to her or all her readers. Such matters might be judged by some as too 'taxing' for the readership. I prefer not to patronize my readers. The book is aimed at anyone from advanced students in the upper forms of schools through undergraduates and on to professional scholars. It is hoped that there is something here for people at all levels. It is true that readers who need to rely heavily on the glossary might not yet be in a position to evaluate arguments based on comparative linguistics; but that is not a justification for suppressing such information. Some readers will want more of some kinds of analysis and less of others; that is inevitable and I make no apology for pursuing some avenues that might not seem altogether fashionable. The more technical terms used within the field of linguistics and philology are listed and explained in a section at the end of the book. With regard specifically to etymology, of which there is a good deal in the commentary, there are three ways in which it helps. First, it might throw light on words which occur only once and for which we have no parallels save for cognates in other languages. Second, we might assume that we know what a word like ἱερός means because we have studied a lot of classical Greek; but Homer is a good deal older and we cannot assume that what is true of, say, Euripides also holds good for the epics. A glance outside Greek can often correct our views. Finally, although etymology badly applied may be criticized as a fallacious search for origins cut loose from the historical context of the epic, we do not have to apply it badly. If we think that a word X originally meant Y but that Homer was ignorant of this and used it instead to mean Z, that is an interesting fact about the early history of reception. Even as early as the formative period of the epics, the original meaning of many words had been forgotten or re-interpreted in interest-ing ways.[2]

In the end, all this is put before the reader in the hope that it will allow her to engage in a closer reading with this poem, which is as breathtaking in its overall sweep and conception as it is beautiful and subtle in the details of its execution. To that end, the commentary does not hesitate to point to what might be thought by some to be more purely 'literary' con-cerns. The choice is inevitably personal. Readers of great literature find that new insights occur with every reading. I do not aim to serve up such insights ready to wear, but I do hope to have provided enough raw mater-ials for the reader to make some sort of serviceable garment.

I am grateful to the following who have answered queries and otherwise given their help: Armand d'Angour, Michele Bianconi, François de Blois, Johnny Cheung, Stephen Colvin, James Diggle, Ahuvia Kahane, Jane-Frances Kelly, Stuart Kelly, Geoffrey Khan, David Kovacs, Gabe Moss, Richard Parkinson, John Penney, Philomen Probert, Nicholas Richardson, Graham Shipley, Elizabeth Tucker, Matthew Ward, Mark Weeden, Andreas Willi. Needless to say, the errors that remain are not to be laid at their door. Stephanie West very generously allowed me to see the text of Book 1 prepared by the late Martin West as part of his new Teubner edition of the *Odyssey*. The staff of the library of the Institute of Classical Studies in London have been a source of unfailing help and support: I am particu-larly grateful to Christopher Ashill, Ryan Cooper, Flor Herrero Valdes, Paul Jackson, Naomi Rebis, Louise Wallace, and Sue Willetts. In my paro-chial ignorance, I once thought that it was impossible to recreate the Bodleian–Ashmolean axis outside Oxford; but the fact that one can step from the Institute of Classical Studies to SOAS to the Warburg to UCL in more or less a straight line and practically no time at all has been a revela-tion and a joy to me. Long may these institutions flourish. Geoff Caseley introduced me to Classics when I was a schoolboy; forty years later I con-tinue to benefit from his νημερτέα βουλήν, always gently offered. It was his suggestion that I should undertake this commentary in the first place. I am grateful to Hilary O'Shea, now retired from Oxford University Press, for accepting this book; to Charlotte Loveridge for so graciously counten-ancing its resurrection after it had lain fallow for some years; to Georgina Leighton for unflagging help and support at every stage; and to Matthew Humphrys and Viki Kapur for seeing it through the production process. The two anonymous Press readers made many helpful and penetrating suggestions and saved me from many blunders. Timothy Beck did an

---

[2] Katz (2010) gives a spirited and principled defence of the etymological approach, together with a plea for 'pre-ception' as a freestanding element of intellectual history.

outstanding job in copy-editing a very fiddly typescript: with a rare combination of insight, learning, and tact he saved me from numerous errors and made many suggestions for improvements. Kathleen Fearn, with her keen eye for consistency and style, made a number of much-needed interventions at the proof-reading stage as a result of which the text looks and reads much better. I dedicate this book to all those who have taught me and continue to do so. Invidious as it is, I make special mention of Jasper Griffin and the much-missed Oliver Lyne, with both of whom I had tutorials on Homer at Balliol in the 1980s and who are continually present to my mind as I work all these years later. Nicholas Richardson was my *Doktorvater*; I have never ceased to admire his remarkable acumen and patient kindness. In particular, he read a revised draft of the translation and made me think again about a good many points. I am conscious that I have done things rather differently from these three scholars; I can only hope that the overall product is not unworthy of them. This commentary, abandoned once, would not have been resumed but for the encouragement of my wife Jane and it could never have been finished without her unstinting love and support.

Contents

Abbreviations

Greek authors and their works are generally cited using the same abbreviations as Liddell and Scott's *Greek–English Lexicon*, 9th edn.

Latin authors and their works are generally cited using the same abbreviations as the *Oxford Latin Dictionary*, 2nd edn.

Where an author and/or work is not cited in one of the above, the abbreviation used follows the style of the *Oxford Classical Dictionary*, 4th edn.

Journals are abbreviated according to the practice of *L'Année philologique*. If a journal is not indexed in that publication, its name is given in full.

Attention is drawn to the following:

Allen	Allen 1912
DELG	Chantraine et al. 1999
DF	Davies and Finglass 2014
DK	Diels and Kranz 1964
FGrH	Jacoby 1923–58
IEG	M. L. West 1989–92
LfgrE	Snell et al. 1955–2010
MW	Merkelbach and West 1967
Pf.	Pfeiffer 1949–53
RV	Rig Veda
TrGF I	Snell 1986
TrGF IV	Radt 1999

Map 1. Greece and the Aegean.
The Ancient World Mapping Center 2017.

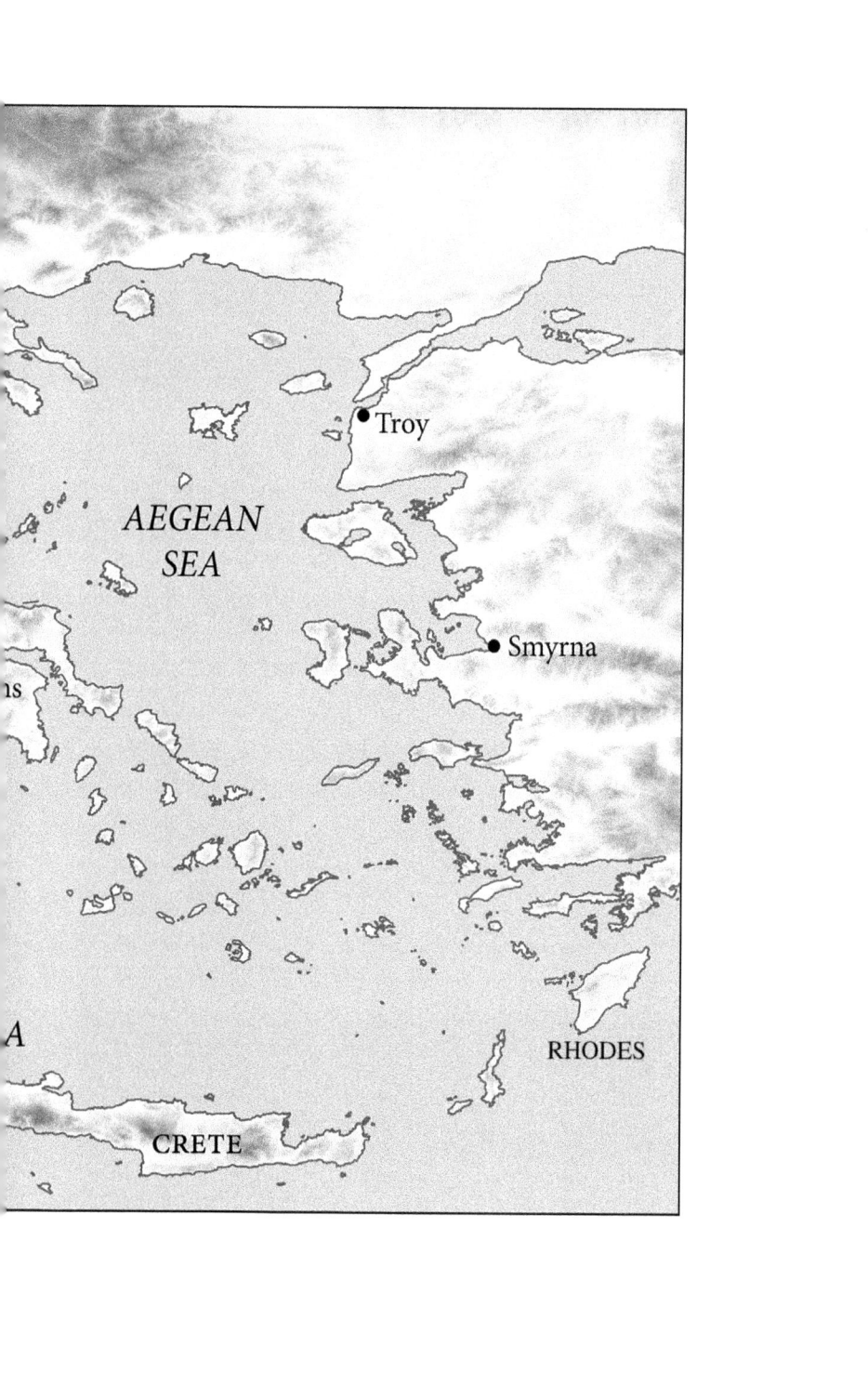

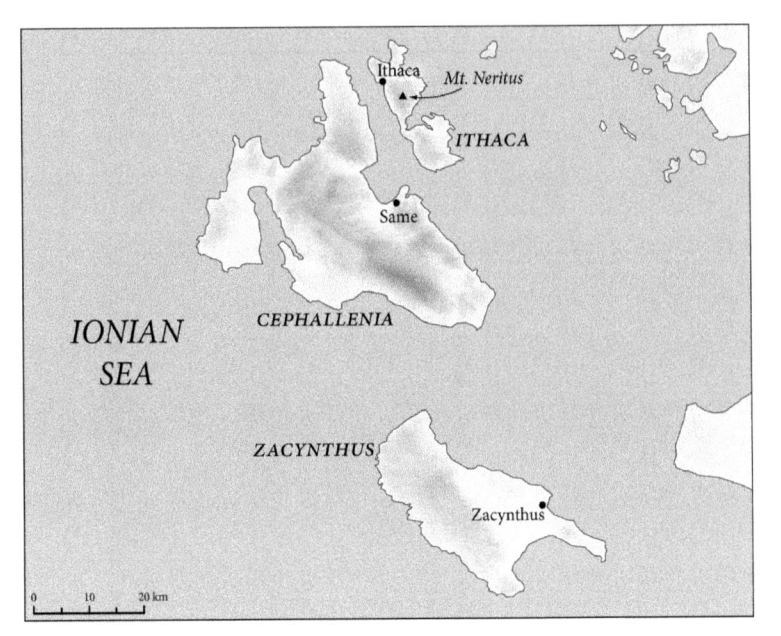

Map 2a. Ithaca and islands: the older view.

The Ancient World Mapping Center 2017.

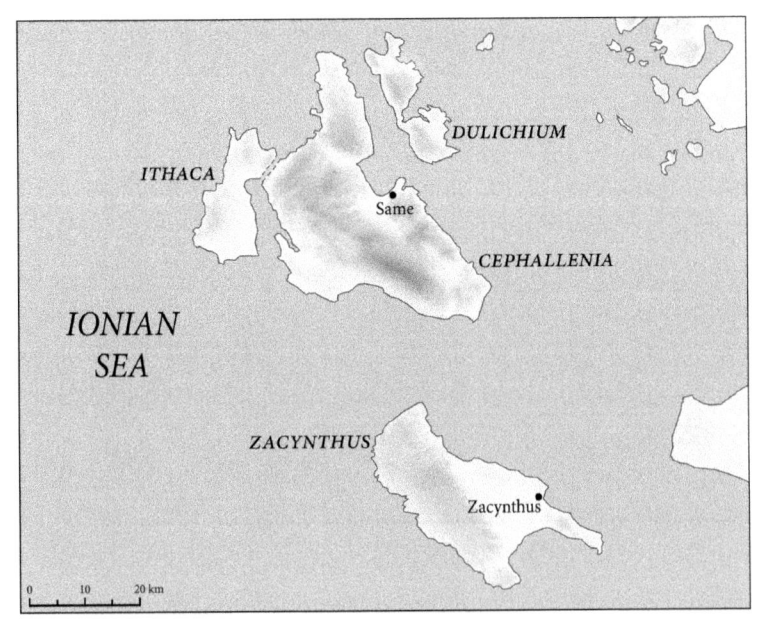

Map 2b. Ithaca and islands: Bittlestone's view.

The Ancient World Mapping Center 2017.

Introduction

THE APPEAL OF THE *ODYSSEY*

In Clint Eastwood's great Western, *Unforgiven*,[1] we meet a young man called The Kid. He aspires to be a tough guy. To prove himself, he casually shoots dead in cold blood a defenceless man whose pants are down. Hit suddenly by the realization that this was not, after all, so heroic a deed, he tries to drown the memory in drink. He turns to his older associate, and seasoned gun-slinger, Bill Munny:

> Kid: *Jesus Christ! It don't seem real. Guy ain't gonna never breathe again ever. Now he's dead, and the other one too, all on account of pullin' a trigger.*
> Bill: *It's a hell of a thing, killin' a man. You take away all he's got and all he's ever gonna have.*[2]
> Kid: *Yeah. Well, I guess they had it comin'.*
> Bill: *We all have it comin', kid.*[3]

To mention Homer in the same breath as a Western film might appear to be an ill-judged attempt at novelty, the desperate last pitch of a hopelessly out-of-touch lecturer in a David Lodge novel. But there is a direct line between this scene and the episode at the end of the *Iliad* where the youthful Achilles gives the aged Priam the benefit of his considered opinion on life: no human being can avoid suffering.[4] A young but already hardened killer looks back coolly on a lifetime of slaughter and sees that what once he took for glory amounts to dust and ashes. Anybody's fortunes might at any moment turn towards disaster: Priam, ruler of a great city, has now suffered irreparable loss, both of his rule and of the lives of those close to him.[5] Such reversal is the very marrow of Greek tragedy; not without reason did Plato call Homer the 'pathfinder of tragedy'.[6] Whereas Achilles was once prepared, like his comrades, to accept a short life in return for imperishable glory,[7] he now sees himself as just 'sitting' at Troy and causing grief to Priam and his children.[8] As he says all this, and pointedly encourages Priam to eat, there lies outside in the dirt the corpse of Hector that he has

---

[1] Directed by Clint Eastwood, screenplay by David Webb Peoples, released by Warner Bros., 7 August 1992.

[2] Cf. *Il.* 9.406–9.   [3] Cf. *Il.* 9.318–20.

[4] *Il.* 24.527–33.   [5] *Il.* 24.543–9.

[6] Pl. *R.* 598 d–e; Macleod 1982: 1–8.   [7] *Il.* 12.322–8 (Sarpedon to Glaucus).

[8] *Il.* 24.541–2.

deliberately defiled. But Achilles has now seen beyond the outlook that once informed all his actions.[9] He might have killed countless enemies, he might have weathered the loss of many comrades; but what changes everything is the death of somebody close to him. His grief recalls that of Gilgamesh after the death of Enkidu.[10] The *Iliad* mesmerizes us by the unblinking way in which it presents the stark opposition between life and death.[11]

Just as *Unforgiven* makes it hard to imagine another Western along traditional lines, it is hard to see where the genre of martial poetry about Troy can go after the scene in Achilles' hut. Where it in fact goes in the *Odyssey* is far away from the towers of Ilium. By the start of the poem, long years have passed. The very first word of the epic proclaims its subject: a man. He is not named for another twenty lines; but he is Odysseus, commander of one contingent of that mighty Achaean host that, having sacked Troy, had at last set sail for home. In the *Iliad*, Achilles slyly vilifies Odysseus as a master of double-talk,[12] even if others admire his strata-gems[13] and rhetoric.[14] The very qualities that repel Achilles are the ones that keep Odysseus alive and bring him safely home to take vengeance upon those who had sought to take his wife and property.

The world of the *Odyssey* is utterly different from that of the *Iliad*—so much so that some critics have thought that the two poems cannot be the work of the same mind. Certainly the inwardness of Odysseus, his cunning and his trickiness, contrast sharply with the frankness of speech and cleanness in combat[15] of great heroes such as Achilles, Hector, Ajax, Glaucus, and Sarpedon. But that is not all. Whereas the *Iliad* was claustro-phobically limited in time and space to a short period in the tenth year of the siege before the walls of Troy, the *Odyssey* is drawn on a canvas of astonishing breadth. We begin on Ithaca, home of Odysseus, where his son Telemachus receives a visit from a goddess in disguise. He moves on to Pylos[16] and then Sparta,[17] receiving much news by way of narrative flashback. This device, used sparingly in the *Iliad*,[18] is essential to the structure of the *Odyssey*. The embedding of story within story is one of the chief beauties of the poem and a feature of no small sophistication.[19] Only

---

[9] This awareness had already dawned when he received the Embassy: *Il.* 9.318–20.
[10] George 1999: 62–9.   [11] Griffin 1980: 81–102.   [12] *Il.* 9.312–13.
[13] *Il.* 3.200–2.   [14] *Il.* 3.216–24.
[15] The poisoned arrows attributed to Odysseus in the *Odyssey* would be unthinkable in the *Iliad*; cf. *Od.* 1.261–2 n.
[16] *Od.* 3.4–5.   [17] *Od.* 4.1.
[18] e.g. Phoenix's life-story and the episode of the Calydonian boar (*Il.* 9.434–605); Nestor's account of disputes over cattle raids (*Il.* 11.670–803).
[19] De Jong 2001.

in Book 5 do we meet Odysseus, trapped on the island of Ogygia by the exotic, alluring, and immortal Calypso. When at last he gets away, Odysseus is launched into a series of adventures that take him ultimately to Scheria[20] where he meets the Phaeacians who live in a fabulously detached world.[21] There he narrates in flashback his adventures with the Cicones who ate six of his companions,[22] with the hippy allurements of the Lotus Eaters,[23] with Polyphemus who ate another six of the companions,[24] with the Laestrygonians who ate one more and were responsible for the loss of eleven ships as well,[25] with the witch Circe who turned his men into pigs,[26] with the perilous blandishments of the Sirens,[27] with the monstrous man-eating Scylla and the deadly whirlpool Charybdis,[28] and more besides. There is an extended description of a visit to Hades.[29] It is hard in a world that is accustomed to Dante (or *Tomb Raider*)[30] to appreciate what an astonishing episode this is. Going to Hades is usually a one-way trip; but resourceful, enduring Odysseus goes there and meets many significant figures from his past and from the fantastical world of myth.

There is a sophisticated self-consciousness in the way that Homer not only shows us bards like himself at work (Phemius[31] and Demodocus[32]) but also portrays Odysseus in the same light, spinning tales both on Scheria[33] and back home on Ithaca.[34] There is very considerable psychological subtlety in the way that Odysseus narrates extended stories to Eumaeus[35] and Penelope,[36] mixing truth and falsehood like the Muses,[37] testing the loyalty of his family and retainers at the same time as making himself into a poetic narrator of no small virtuosity.

A Greek proverb says πόλλ᾽ οἶδ᾽ ἀλώπηξ, ἀλλ᾽ ἐχῖνος ἓν μέγα ('the fox knows many things, but the hedgehog one great thing').[38] To follow the image, we might say that the *Iliad* is the hedgehog: its great theme is the overwhelming tragedy of the human condition, explored in scenes of incomparable verbal artistry and unbearable pathos. The *Odyssey* is more

---

[20] *Od.* 6.3, 8, 195. Homer never uses the name Phaeacia for the territory of the Phaeacians.
[21] *Od.* 6.201–5.   [22] *Od.* 9.60–1.   [23] *Od.* 9.96–7.
[24] *Od.* 9.289–90, 311, 344.   [25] *Od.* 10.116, 132; cf. Stanford 1959: 371.
[26] *Od.* 10.237–40.   [27] *Od.* 12.165–200.   [28] *Od.* 12.234–59.
[29] *Od.* 11 (the *Nekyia*).
[30] *Tomb Raider: Underworld*, released by Eidos Interactive 2008.
[31] *Od.* 1.153–5, 325–52.   [32] *Od.* 8.261–369, 471–541.
[33] The mention of κηληθμός (*Od.* 11.334; 13.2) is bound up with the notion of poetry as a spell or charm (cf. *Od.* 1.337 n.).
[34] *Od.* 17.518–21.
[35] *Od.* 14.192–359.   [36] *Od.* 19.165–202, 221–48, 262–307, 336–48.
[37] *Od.* 19.203; for his likeness in this respect to the Muses, cf. Hes. *Th.* 27–8.
[38] Zen. 5.68 = Archil. fr. 201 W.

like the fox, showing us a vivid panorama of many kinds of things. Whilst
the cunning and endurance of Odysseus are major themes, there is also
a palpable fascination for exploring the endlessly varied marvels and
strangeness of the bigger world away from Troy. The *Iliad* might be said
to be a tragic poem; the *Odyssey* is not. The *Iliad* has a chillingly bleak
outlook that leaves little for our comfort but moves us to great admiration
for human dignity in the face of divine inscrutability and whim; in the
Odyssey, we are supposed to think that things have in the end somehow
been put to rights (even if the deadly and merciless justice meted out by
Odysseus and his son might not quite square with our modern sensibil-
ities). The *Iliad* deals with reversal of fortune and irreparable loss; the
Odyssey is the archetypal poem about a hero on a quest. In that sense, it
might be said to be the ultimate precursor of the European novel. George
Steiner once proposed an imaginary society in which secondary writing
about literature should be prohibited because the highest form of reflection on literary art is more literary art.[39] Following that line of thought,
one might see Virgil's *Aeneid*, Dante's *Divine Comedy*, and Joyce's *Ulysses*
as more compelling responses to the *Odyssey* than much of the ink spilled
by those of us who write books like the one you are reading. Its purpose,
however, is not to furnish people with judgements rendered incontrovert-
ible by the scientific investigations upon which they rest, but to assist
readers to form their own views through the close reading of a work of
genius produced in a milieu very different from our own but nevertheless
speaking to us freshly about things that matter.

Suggested reading: Griffin 1980; 1987.

STRUCTURE

The *Odyssey* is, in the words of the Psalmist,[40] 'fearfully and wonderfully
made'. It is right that we feel admiration for the skill of a poet who,
composing without the aid of writing,[41] manages to weave the narrative so
subtly. The poem begins by announcing its theme: a man who has travelled far and both seen and suffered much. Odysseus is, however, not
named until *Od.* 1.21. This slight postponement mirrors the way that we
do not see Odysseus himself until Book 5. Much play is made elsewhere in

---

[39] G. Steiner 1989: 4–21, esp. 12–13.   [40] Ps. 139:14.
[41] For the debate on this question, see below, pp. 38–9.

Book 1 of who will utter the name of Odysseus and in what circumstances.[42] So we see a theme introduced, allowed to drop into the background, taken up later in Book 1, and partially submerged again until Book 5. But this too is artful, for when Telemachus goes to Pylos and Sparta for news of this father, Odysseus is ever in our minds. On one level, we have a story about a young man going on a journey; on another, we have Nestor and Menelaus giving yet more indirect pointers to the character and exploits of the hero of the poem who is deliberately being kept in the shadows. It is hard not to think that this occultation of the name and person of Odysseus in the early part of the poem is meant to mirror the concealment of his true identity that allows him to return to Ithaca unrecognized and work his revenge on the suitors. The same cleverness on the part of Odysseus—and the poet, of course—is what famously allows him to persuade Polyphemus that his name is Οὖτις ('Nobody'),[43] so that the other Cyclopes do not come to help when they hear that Nobody has attacked Polyphemus.[44]

The action of the poem begins with the gods together on Olympus. Although all but Poseidon are said to be present, the scene is a delicate two-handed exchange between Athena and her father Zeus. As in the *Iliad*, where Thetis goes to Olympus to supplicate Zeus in aid of her son's cause, we might expect Athena to launch into an immediate appeal to help Odysseus. In fact, Zeus begins with a speech expressing frustration at mortals who lay at the feet of the gods the blame for the consequences of their own wrongdoing. This is an interesting and characteristic misdirection. Athena has to say, in effect, 'I agree entirely with all that you say— down with mortal sinners! But what worries me is the innocent suffering of Odysseus.'[45] It is decided that Hermes ought to go to Ogygia to deal with Calypso and that Athena herself will visit Ithaca to encourage Telemachus and propose the mission to Pylos and Sparta.[46]

The *Odyssey* as a whole can be said to fall into three distinct movements:[47] (1) the so-called Telemachy[48] in Books 1–4 with part of Book 15,[49] (2) the Wanderings of Odysseus in Books 5–12, (3) the Homecoming in Books 13–24. Whilst the Wanderings are plainly a necessary precursor to the Homecoming, the Telemachy has been described as an 'inorganic appendage'.[50] To the extent that it could be removed from the poem without seriously damaging the main thrust of

---

[42] *Od.* 1.163 n.   [43] *Od.* 9.366.
[44] *Od.* 9.408, 410–12.   [45] *Od.* 1.46–8.
[46] *Od.* 1.81–95.   [47] M. L. West 2014: 94–5.
[48] This deals with the giving of divine encouragement to Telemachus by Athena and his doings and travels thereafter. The name is not meant to imply that it had a prior existence as a free-standing poem.
[49] *Od.* 15.1–300.   [50] M. L. West 2014: 95.

the narrative of the returning hero, this is true. But the poem as a whole is far better for having the Telemachy. It contains much that is good: we see at length how a young man finds his feet, learns to deal with tricky adults at home, goes on a big and risky journey, and meets grand old men who have survived the Trojan War. We are also able to contrast the Wanderings and Homecoming of Odysseus with the fortunes of Nestor and Menelaus as told in dramatic narrative by the protagonists themselves to Telemachus. They have striking tales of adventure and loss to recount, but both are now safely at home enjoying the sort of settled life which in the *Iliad* is barely even contemplated.[51] The postponement to Book 5 of Hermes' trip to Ogygia seems a small price to pay for all of this. It is true that, just before his departure, there is an awkward scene where Athena once again addresses Zeus with a complaint that everyone has forgotten Odysseus who is still detained by Calypso.[52] In fact the matter had already been settled in Book 1.[53] It might have been possible to present the departure of Hermes without the need to have a scene of him being summoned and despatched by Zeus. For example, it is decided in Book 5 that Athena should save Telemachus from the suitors;[54] because of the Wanderings and Homecoming, this cannot be narrated until Book 15. But then there is no council on Olympus; we simply have the announcement that Pallas Athena went to Sparta to remind Telemachus that it was time to go home.[55] The Telemachy is surely a new addition to older material. But the poem is not spoiled just because of these slight wrinkles in the narrative texture.[56]

Let us return to Book 1. Athena disguises herself as a man called Mentes in order to come to earth and mix with Telemachus and the other inhabitants of Odysseus' palace.[57] We are accustomed from the *Iliad* to gods who take on the likeness of named human beings.[58] In this context the device is another facet of the pervasive theme of cunning and guile: Athena disguises herself, Odysseus conceals his name,[59] Athena disguises Odysseus.[60] Within the economy of Book 1, the arrival of a disguised guest also allows the poet to contrast the hospitality of Telemachus with the improper behaviour of the suitors.[61] The suitors assume that Mentes is a person of no importance to them and so ignore him; Telemachus knows

---

[51] Except obliquely in the Shield of Achilles: *Il.* 18.490–508.   [52] *Od.* 5.11–15.

[53] *Od.* 1.64–79.   [54] *Od.* 5.25–7.   [55] *Od.* 15.1–3.

[56] To say that the Telemachy is a later part of the poem is not to accept that Homer had already composed the Wanderings and the Homecoming in the form in which we now have them and later added the Telemachy. All that is meant is that the Telemachy is the most recent of the elements to be fashioned before the act of monumental composition that produced the entire *Odyssey* in the order and form in which we now have it.

[57] *Od.* 1.105 n.

[58] e.g. *Il.* 2.790–5 (Iris); 3.386–9 (Aphrodite); 24.406–7 vs. 460–1 (Hermes).

[59] *Od.* 9.366.   [60] *Od.* 13.430–8.   [61] *Od.* 1.113–43, 120 nn.

that all strangers are worthy of welcome. The character of Mentes finds a curious doublet in another persona adopted by Athena, namely Mentor, a friend of Odysseus whose true person appears[62] only moments before his likeness is borrowed.[63] Using our linguistic knowledge of Greek nominal compounds, we may form a view about which of Mentes and Mentor was the earlier conception.[64] We may accuse the poet of not trying very hard over names; we may think there has been some sloppiness of execution. At all events, Telemachus is provided with two companions whose very names show that they are there to tutor the young man as he finds his position in the world.[65] We see this unfold over Books 2–4.

The lies told by Mentes about his provenance and history are really programmatic for the rest of the poem. We know that Odysseus is a consummate trickster; Athena is the same.[66] A little of this rubs off on Telemachus, who learns very quickly to be economical in what he tells the suitors.[67] There are countless points when just a slight linguistic evasion is enough to avert their suspicion. These misdirections by characters are echoed by similar ploys on the part of the poet, of course. To judge from the proem, one might think that the episode of the eating of the oxen of the Sun on Thrinacia would bulk large in the poem—it does not, albeit the consequences are severe. The opening scenes lead one to expect the immediate rescue of Odysseus, but this is postponed until Book 5. The tale of the poisoned arrows leads one to expect that these might be used against the suitors—they are not. Some critics might view these as mere failure to tidy up the narrative, parts of other stories poorly integrated in view of what actually happens; others see this as deliberate and artful narration, possibly of a kind that audiences liked and expected. The judgement is in the end one that the reader must make.

We have seen how, across the early books of the poem, the figure of Odysseus is allowed to fade in and out according to the poet's purpose. Within Book 1, a similar device is used with regard to Phemius. He begins his song at line 123; but this is allowed to fade into the background until line 325 while Mentes and Telemachus talk to each other.[68] Again, this is a kind of misdirection: the bard strikes up on the lyre but we do not hear the song. When we have perhaps forgotten about the song, it is reintroduced and made the subject of quite a self-conscious discussion about poetic freedom.[69] But there is more at issue in the song of Phemius. There is

---

[62] *Od.* 2.224–5.   [63] *Od.* 2.267–8.   [64] See *Od.* 1.105 n.
[65] The root *men–* that underlies both of these names is also present in the word Μοῦσα (*Od.* 1.1 n.). The idea of mental activity, in particular remembering and reminding, appears to be present in all three words.
[66] *Od.* 13.296–310.   [67] *Od.* 1.412–19, 414, 415–16 nn.
[68] Thomas 2014: 89–91.   [69] *Od.* 1.337–55, 347, 352 nn.

deliberate ambiguity as to whether the bard sings of the death of Odysseus. The suitors might take the poem in one way, Telemachus in quite another.[70] We see within Book 1 the poet deliberately showing us not only how he can misdirect his living audience but how Phemius might be doing the same to the suitors as the imaginary audience of a poem within a poem.

Phemius himself is part of a complex narrative arc that spans almost the entire poem. When he is introduced, we are told that he sang for the suitors ἀνάγκῃ ('under compulsion').[71] In Book 22, he comes close to death at the hands of Odysseus. He pleads for his life:[72] Homer reminds us that Phemius sang ἀνάγκῃ,[73] and Phemius picks up and uses the same verbal cue.[74] This is part of the broader device of narrative foreshadowing where the doom of the suitors that comes towards the end of the poem is alluded to at the very beginning. In part, this is done quite explicitly, as when Mentes says that Telemachus must kill the suitors even if he cannot find his father.[75] Elsewhere the reference is ironic, as when Telemachus says that the suitors would pray to be lighter on their feet if Odysseus were back.[76] Wrapped up in that is also a reflection on the difference between dancing—their current occupation—and running for one's life.[77] Sometimes the reference is altogether more oblique: the reference to there being in the palace spears belonging to Odysseus,[78] or the contrast between the ease of the suitors' current life[79] and the difficulty they are going to have in getting away from Odysseus.

When Mentes first arrives, he talks about Laertes so that we expect that it is Laertes that he has come to see. Indeed, when Mentes says the words σὸν πατέρα ('your father'),[80] they come as a surprise since we expect him to mention his grandfather, not Odysseus. Laertes is mentioned again at the end of the book in the context of explaining how he had bought Eurycleia as a slave.[81] If Book 24 as we have it is genuine,[82] then it represents another example of the long narrative arc. Laertes was mentioned in Book 1 as living a wretched life on his lands and never coming into town.[83] There is specific reference to the ground of his vineyard (ἀλωή).[84] It is precisely in this location, described by the same word, that Odysseus finds his

---

[70] _Od._ 1.347 n.; Thomas 2014: 94–101.   [71] _Od._ 1.154.
[72] _Od._ 22.344–60.   [73] _Od._ 22.330.   [74] _Od._ 22.353.
[75] _Od._ 1.296.   [76] _Od._ 1.164–5 n.   [77] Thomas 2014: 91–3.
[78] _Od._ 1.128 n.   [79] _Od._ 1.160 n.   [80] _Od._ 1.195.
[81] _Od._ 1.430–1.
[82] This was disputed already in antiquity, it being thought by Aristarchus and Aristophanes of Byzantium that the true end of the poem was 23.296. The literature on both sides is summarized by Fernandez-Galliano 1992: 342–5. The argument for non-authenticity has been made most recently by M. L. West 2014: 294 n. 327; cf. S. R. West 1989.
[83] _Od._ 1.189–93.   [84] _Od._ 1.193.

father in Book 24.[85] For all the difficulties in the language and ethos of Book 24, it is hard to regret the scene where Odysseus is reunited with his father.[86] The theme of Odysseus' trickiness is carried to the bitter end and the story about the arrangement of the trees echoes the secret of the construction of Odysseus' bed.

It is widely believed that the twenty-four books into which the *Odyssey* is divided were the product of the intervention of later ages— probably connected with how much text would fit on a papyrus roll.[87] It is thus problematic to talk about the internal structure of Book 1 by itself as though Homer thought of it as a discrete artistic entity containing 444 lines. That said, the book does end with Telemachus going to bed before the assembly that takes place next morning. These alternations of night and day undeniably mark natural turning points in the narrative, together with things like arrival and departure. To this extent, we might ask how Homer chooses to structure the first day of narrated events on Ithaca. We begin with the news that Troy has fallen and that every other survivor has reached home, apart from Odysseus himself, whose comrades have perished and who is stranded with Calypso after an unspecified number of years.[88] A great deal of information is disposed of in a very few lines. The narrative pace then changes and becomes much slower for the council on Olympus and the visit of Athena to earth that takes up most of the book. There are obvious ways in which the crimes of Aegisthus are likened to those of the suitors. This idea is introduced by Zeus towards the beginning of the day[89] and picked up by Athena towards the evening to encourage Telemachus to kill the suitors.[90] The figure of Clytemnestra is also in the background, with all the overtones her figure brings in terms of how Telemachus might feel about his own mother.[91]

There are other structural schemes that can also be discerned in the way that the overall narrative of the *Odyssey* is arranged. One of these involves seeing the epic as six groups of four books. This cannot be original because the division of the epic into books is not original to the

---

[85] *Od.* 24.226. This correspondence might be thought to argue for the authenticity of Book 24.

[86] We might also reflect on the theme of fathers and sons that runs through Book 24 of the *Iliad*.

[87] The bibliography is collected in Heiden 1998: 68 n. 2. A case for an original division into twenty-four books by the original monumental composer has been made by Goold 1960: 287–9 and Heiden 2000.

[88] *Od.* 1.1–16.   [89] *Od.* 1.35–42, 46–7.

[90] *Od.* 1.298–300.   [91] See *Od.* 1.298 n.

monumental composer so that what follows tells us more about the perceptions of those critics who divided the *Odyssey* into books in the first place: (1) Books 1–4 deal with Telemachus, (2) Books 5–8 cover matters on Scheria, (3) Books 9–12 contain Odysseus' narration of his adventures, (4) Books 13–16 involve Odysseus returning home and establishing connexions with people who matter to him, (5) Books 17–20 involve disguise and preparation, (6) Books 21–24 represent the culmination of the story: the contest of the bow, the slaughter of the suitors, the reunion of Odysseus and Penelope, and the final wrapping up of loose ends.

Perhaps more revealing than this, since it does not depend on the division of the poem into books, is the fact that the poem can be split into two halves that correspond remarkably closely with each other. We may use book numbers to chart these correspondences, but they do not of themselves depend on the division of the epic into books. If the book divisions were removed, the overall order of events would remain the same. We can see this most clearly in the following table:[92]

Books 1–4	Books 13–16
a. Ithaca	a. Ithaca
b. Athena with Telemachus	b. Athena with Odysseus
c. Suitors are bad hosts	c. Eumaeus is a good host
d. Telemachus goes away	d. Telemachus comes back
e. Suitors plot to kill Telemachus	e. Telemachus (with father) plots to kill suitors

Books 5–8	Books 17–20
a. Journey to Alcinous' palace	a. Journey to Odysseus' palace
b. Contest with young Phaeacians	b. Conflict with beggar and suitors
c. Who will marry Nausicaa?	c. Who will marry Penelope?
d. Identity of Odysseus concealed	d. Identity of Odysseus concealed

Books 9–12	Books 21–4
a. Odysseus identifies self; becomes singer	a. Odysseus identifies self; strings bow
b. Odysseus narrates adventures to Phaeacians	b. Odysseus wins confidence of Penelope[93]
c. Odysseus wins support of Arete	c. Recounts adventures to Penelope
d. Underworld/mother/heroes	d. Underworld/heroes/father

[92] What follows is an adapted re-presentation of material that derives from Tracy 1997: 372–3.

[93] The second and third items in Books 21–4 are inverted with respect to the order of events in Books 9–12.

Both within individual episodes (which might or might not coincide with the boundaries of the later divisions into books) and within the epic as a whole, we can see numerous thematic parallels that might involve likeness or contrast. These are so consistently detectable that they can scarcely be attributed either to chance or to the activities of later critics. In particular, the correspondences that are apparent when one divides the poem into two halves reveal the greatest degree of deliberation in arrangement.

In the end, everything hinges around the visit to the Underworld in Book 11. As the Mesopotamian hero Gilgamesh goes to see Utana-Pishtim, survivor of the Flood, and learns the great truths about life and death, so Odysseus learns his destiny from Teiresias.[94] The *Iliad* is an almost unbearably concentrated narrative of death and loss; the *Odyssey* is about life—it might be complex and challenging but it is also breath-taking in the possibilities that it offers and which are exemplified in a man like Odysseus. When Achilles says that he would rather occupy the lowest and most servile station on earth rather than be king over all the dead,[95] he clearly repents of the choice that he made in the *Iliad* for early death and heroic glory.[96] In place of that warrior ethic, articulated also by others in the *Iliad*,[97] we have in the *Odyssey* a man who tries to prolong life on earth because that is all that is really worth having. Odysseus lives it to the full.

Suggested reading: Thornton 1970; Tracy 1997; Thomas 2014.

STYLE

When we buy any desirable new electronic gadget, we do not generally worry too much about reading the instructions. We have owned such things before, they mostly work in the same way as each other, and we want to get on with enjoying our purchase. The same is true of literature. When we buy an edition of a nineteenth-century novel, we tend to skip the introduction and get on with the text. If we apply this approach to Homer, how should we fare?

Poetic Texture

So far as the Greeks were concerned, Homer was undoubtedly a poet: he composed in the dactylic hexameter and used a form of language that

---

[94] *Od.* 11.100–37.   [95] *Od.* 11.489–91.   [96] *Il.* 9.410–16.
[97] *Il.* 12.322–8.

differed from ordinary speech. But the first thing that strikes the new reader of Homer is usually how much repetition there is. This is rather different from what we are used to if we think of poetry as spare and taut and boiled down—the *Odyssey* is not like a Japanese *haiku*, nor is it like Donne or Eliot or Pound. Even allowing for the fact that narrative verse has a different consistency, Homer is not like Tennyson or Coleridge. For example, Agamemnon gives a lengthy account in thirty-four lines of the gifts that he will make to Achilles if the latter returns to the fight; Odysseus repeats this almost verbatim to Achilles barely a hundred lines later.[98] But this is just an extreme case of a general tendency to repetition. Whenever a Homeric character starts to speak, we regularly find τὴν δ' ἀπαμειβόμενος προσέφη ('in answer to her spoke . . .')[99] or τὸν δ' αὖτε προσέειπε ('s/he addressed him in turn')[100] or τὸν δ' ἠμείβετ' ἔπειτα ('then . . . answered him').[101] When people have finished a meal, we frequently find αὐτὰρ ἐπεὶ πόσιος καὶ ἐδητύος ἐξ ἔρον ἕντο ('but when they had put off the desire for drink and food').[102] At the break of dawn, we find ἦμος δ' ἠριγένεια φάνη ῥοδοδάκτυλος Ἠώς ('and when early-born rosy-fingered dawn appeared . . .').[103] Greeks are sometimes called Ἀχαιοί and given the epithet μεγάθυμοι ('great-spirited')[104] or ἐϋκνήμιδες ('well-greaved');[105] Achilles is πόδας ὠκύς ('swift of foot') even when standing still addressing an assembly.[106] These are not isolated occurrences, chosen for the purposes of illustration; they are a fundamental and thoroughgoing feature of both Homeric epics.

There is some hesitation among observers over what counts as repetition: does one mean verbatim reproduction or are we also to take account of phrases which are broadly similar in shape but where the grammatical case or some other component has changed? For example, looking at the first twenty-one lines of the *Odyssey*, we can see that ἔνθ' ἄλλοι μὲν πάντες[107] recurs nine times in Homer in precisely this form.[108] It is obviously a useful device for describing what 'everyone else' is doing. The phrase ἐν πόντῳ πάθεν ἄλγεα ὃν κατὰ θυμόν is different.[109] ἐν πόντῳ πάθετ' ἄλγεα occurs at *Od.* 10.458. The verb there is middle rather than active; but one senses that the expressions are structurally akin. The

---

[98] *Il.* 9.122–56 ≈ 264–98.   [99] *Od.* 1.63; 4.147; or τὸν κτλ. *Od.* 4.168, 203.
[100] *Od.* 1.178, 221.   [101] *Od.* 1.44, 80, 314.
[102] *Od.* 1.150; 3.67, 473; 4.68.   [103] *Od.* 2.1; 3.404, 491; 4.306, 431.
[104] *Il.* 1.123, 135; *Od.* 24.57.   [105] *Il.* 1.17; 2.331; 3.86, 304.   [106] *Il.* 1.58.
[107] *Od.* 1.11.
[108] Adam Parry 1971: 303. He took a hard line on the impossibility of Homer having scope for a distinctive style: for him, all epic language was formulaic (1971: 270, 317). See on Origins, pp. 36–40.
[109] *Od.* 1.4.

sub-unit πάθεν ἄλγεα occurs at *Il.* 24.7; this is an exact repetition. Perhaps it is an older formula that has been expanded in the *Odyssey* to deal with maritime woes. πάθ᾽ ἄλγεα ὃν κατὰ θυμόν occurs at *Od.* 13.90. There is no mention of the sea, but one might conclude that πάθ᾽ ἄλγεα ὃν κατὰ θυμόν is closely related to *Od.* 1.4 even though we find πάθεν instead of πάθ᾽. If we look at the even smaller unit ὃν κατὰ θυμόν, we find it verbatim in four other places in Homer, always in the *Iliad*.[110]

As we shall see in later sections,[111] the poem is like this because it was fashioned within a tradition of oral poetry that used these formulae as an aid to composition. But does this mean that our literary appreciation of it has to proceed in a different manner from that of, for example, Horace's *Odes*? The latter is chosen because we know that Horace composed in writing, had leisure to choose his words, change them, and shape the overall structure of his books of lyric poetry. Whatever else is true of Homer, we know that he did not compose in this way. So the question is whether we need some sort of oral poetics to help us to understand his work.

Imagine, for example, that one comes across the expression γλαυκῶπις Ἀθήνη ('owl-eyed Athena'; *Od.* 1.44). One might, whether anachronistic-ally or not, form the view that the owl is a bird of wisdom and that this choice of epithet is significant at the start of a speech where Athena uses rhetorical craft and skill to persuade Zeus that it is time to intervene to help Odysseus. As a literary judgement, it is unobjectionable: it is scarcely far-fetched, one might think, to take the adjective in this way. But if some-one were to point out that the phrase γλαυκῶπις Ἀθήνη appears 78× in Homer, one might hesitate for a moment. Do we wish to revise our ori-ginal judgement? Maybe not: perhaps wisdom is her perpetual quality, just as it is for the owl. But whenever her name appears in the same pos-ition but in the genitive case (4×), it is always in the form Ἀθηναίης, coupled with the epithet ἀγελείης ('driver of spoil'; e.g. *Od.* 16.207). Under those metrical and syntactical constraints, it would seem, the goddess can never be owlish.

Similarly when we read that Odysseus went to Ephyra θοῆς ἐπὶ νηός ('on board a swift ship'; *Od.* 1.260), we might fancy that a swift ship was appro-priate for the rapid and discreet accomplishment of this risky and morally doubtful mission. The phrase θοῆς ἐπὶ νηός ('on board a swift ship') occurs only twice in Homer—so one might be inclined to attach some signifi-cance to the epithet. But when, in the same position, ships need to be in the accusative case (9×), they are also described as swift. If one is struck by the

---

[110] *Il.* 1.429; 13.8; 23.769; 24.518.   [111] See pp. 36–40.

significance of a ship being 'dark-prowed',[112] one might be troubled to discover that, in eleven out of twelve instances, the epithet is in the genitive. Ships in the nominative or dative case never have dark prows. All of this makes one wonder how much meaning to read into any given instance. How can we judge when the choice of word is deeply telling or when we might be making a mountain out of a cliché?

There is no definitive way to tell whether a literary effect depending on epithets (or anything else) is 'there'. To a large extent, significance is where you find it;[113] but some conclusions are more plausible than others. When Priam visits Achilles to recover the body of Hector, the old king kisses the hands of the young warrior. The poet describes them as δεινὰς ἀνδροφόνους, αἵ οἱ πολέας κτάνον υἷας ('terrible, man-slaying ones that had slain many of his sons').[114] At one level, it is banal to describe as 'man-slaying' the hands that slew Priam's son. Upon closer study, we find that the epithet is used only twice elsewhere of the hands of Achilles, when he lays them upon the breast of his friend Patroclus, killed by Hector.[115] Surely this prefigures the scene where the man-slaying hands will have slain the very person who slew Patroclus. But there is more. ἀνδρόφονος is found 15× in the *Iliad*, of which eleven instances are applied to Hector himself in the formula Ἕκτορος ἀνδροφόνοιο.[116] In the traditional diction of the bards, this word was especially associated with Hector. Its transference to Achilles surely makes us think that man-slaying Hector has met his match in man-slaying Achilles who has, one might say, taken his epithet as well as his life. Its first application to the hands of Achilles when mourning Patroclus might be thought significant, the poet wresting Hector's epithet from him while he yet lives.[117]

In the *Odyssey* ἀνδρόφονος occurs only once. It is used to describe the poison that Odysseus sought in Ephyra in order to anoint his arrows.[118] Does the reader who comes to the *Odyssey* aware of the formulaic conventions of the *Iliad* perceive something significant here? Perhaps a contrast is being drawn between the tragic nobility of Hector on the one hand and the underhand use of poisoned arrows, not a feature of the *Iliad* where even non-toxic archery is frowned upon as beneath heroic dignity.[119] The *Iliad* has in it heroes like Hector who fight cleanly; the *Odyssey* has in it a

---

[112] e.g. *Il.* 15.693.   [113] Currie 2016: 29–30.   [114] *Il.* 24.479.
[115] *Il.* 18.317; 23.18.
[116] *Il.* 1.142; 6.498; 9.351; 16.77, 840; 17.428, 616, 638; 18.149; 24.509, 724. The other instances refer to the hands of Achilles (*Il.* 18.317; 23.18, already discussed), Ares (*Il.* 4.441), and Lycurgus (*Il.* 6.134).
[117] *Il.* 18.317; Hector is dead by the time it is used again at *Il.* 23.18. Sacks (1987) 175 n. 56 touches on this.
[118] *Od.* 1.261.   [119] See *Od.* 1.261–2 n.

hero like Odysseus who lives by cunning: poisoned arrows and verbal deception—a different world.

Imagery

> The first person who compared painting and poetry with one another was a man of delicate feeling who was conscious that both art forms had a similar effect on him. Both of them, he sensed, present to us things absent as though they were present, appearance as reality; both deceive, and the deceit of both is pleasing.[120]

Lessing probably had in mind Horace,[121] or possibly Simonides before him.[122] Plainly all language has the capacity to make present that which is absent. If I say, 'a man opened his newspaper' a mental image is produced; but we should not call it poetic. Something is lacking.

What Lessing calls the 'deceit' of poetry is much in evidence in Homer. The poet uses words so as to conjure into the mind of the audience things, persons, and places either far removed from or utterly outside normal human experience. The robotic golden dogs of Alcinous,[123] the monstrous Cyclopes,[124] and the realm of Hades all come into the category of things that nobody has seen; they live through the narrator. Amongst things closer to reality but still removed from ordinary life, we think of the palace of Menelaus in Sparta with its fabulous wealth[125] or of the contest of the bow in the palace of Odysseus.[126]

The imagery of Book 1 does not dwell in depth on the fantastic elements of Homer's invention. Instead, language is used with restraint to hint at the breadth of the world yet to be unfolded to us. In the first twenty lines, we glance at the sacked city of Troy, the oxen of Hyperion, and the caves of Calypso. We are told that Poseidon has gone to visit the Ethiopians, which prompts a compressed evocation of their fantastic location at the edges of the world. At the council of the gods on Olympus, the big picture is lacking: the ambrosial locks of Zeus do not roll forward, Olympus does not quake,[127] Hephaestus does not bustle about serving wine.[128] We hear that

---

[120] Lessing 1767: 3 (translation mine).   [121] *AP* 361.
[122] Plu. *Mor.* 346f; *Rhet. Her.* 4.28.39.   [123] *Od.* 7.91–4.
[124] Although it is curious that the poem nowhere explicitly states that the Cyclops has only one eye: *Od.* 1.69 n.
[125] *Od.* 4.71–5.   [126] *Od.* 19.572–81.
[127] *Il.* 1.528–30. ΣA remark that this passage inspired the famous statue of Zeus at Olympia by Phidias—an example of poetry influencing art.
[128] *Il.* 1.596–600.

most of the gods were present,[129] but they pass out of view and the focus contracts to Zeus and Athena. Their talk ended, we pass to a surprisingly detailed account of Athena's preparing for her visit to earth: the golden sandals, the mighty spear with which she lays low mortal men, the darting movement from the mountain peaks, the effortless transformation of the immortal goddess into the guise of a mortal man who, nevertheless, still has that spear.[130] This is a clever adaptation of the traditional arming scene familiar from the *Iliad*: plainly some dilation on apparel and weapons was a feature of martial poetry. It is a different kind of fray that the Athena joins on Ithaca: she arms herself, but must use words for weapons when rousing Telemachus to action. So it is to speech that we must now turn.

Speech

One of the glories of the epics is speech, where characters are given language that is partly traditional and party innovative. The overall result can be quite subtle. The scene between Mentes and Telemachus is in many ways traditional—a visitor is welcomed and fed and only then asked for news. When Mentes starts to say who he is, he does so in purely formulaic language: τοίγαρ ἐγώ τοι ταῦτα μάλ᾽ ἀτρκέως ἀγορεύσω ('therefore I will tell you everything accurately').[131] But what he goes on to say is a tissue of lies; the audience reflects on the irony of promising truth and delivering falsehood—something that becomes typical of the *Odyssey* as a whole.[132] It is also striking that when the young, inexperienced Telemachus first says these words, he actually does tell the truth.[133] He soon learns to be more economical with the truth, but interestingly does not use this formula when lying to Antinous.[134]

The speeches are deliberately structured in a sophisticated manner. One of the themes of the poem is the concealment of the name of Odysseus.[135] This is partly a device used by the man himself to save his skin; partly it is a literary device linked with postponing the appearance of the main character until Book 5. But within the structure of Book 1, Telemachus cannot at first bring himself to utter his father's name. He repeatedly uses pronouns such as κεῖνος ('that man') or αὐτός ('him') instead.[136] Telemachus is disheartened: feeling abandoned by his father, he wonders if he is even truly his son. Mentes, by contrast, introduces Odysseus' name and gradually uses it more and more. By the end of his

[129] *Od.* 1.27. [130] *Od.* 1.96–105. [131] *Od.* 1.179.
[132] *Od.* 14.192 ff. (lying to Eumaeus). [133] *Od.* 1.214.
[134] *Od.* 1.413–19. [135] *Od.* 1.1 n. [136] *Od.* 1.163 n.

third (and penultimate) speech, he has spoken it six times.[137] Telemachus follows this lead and begins to use the name.[138] This is psychologically satisfying: the older adviser encourages the young man to have confidence in his lineage and in himself. It is also proof of the cunning of Athena who knows how to accomplish the plan she described to Zeus at the outset.

There is also verbal sparring between the newly emboldened Telemachus and his mother. He tells Penelope quite bluntly to let Phemius sing whatever he likes because bards must follow their own paths.[139] She is amazed at the prudence of his speech.[140] Penelope is not a downtrodden woman from an archaic society who had to obey her son no matter how juvenile. She is a queen, a woman of character and stratagem. That she withdraws so meekly is a mark of the change that has come over her son in a short time. All of this is worked out in speeches. The narrator says almost nothing about character in his own voice, preferring to fade into the background and let the characters do the work—one of the ways in which epic prefigures tragedy.

The speeches with which the book ends are a series of carefully constructed confrontations with the suitors. This is the first test of Telemachus' mettle against those who threaten his livelihood and life. He begins peaceably with the invitation to food and pleasure but moves suddenly to a strong attack on the suitors for eating him out of house and home.[141] The narrator has shown us the arrogance of the suitors;[142] Telemachus has complained of it to Athena;[143] now he has the courage to name it to their faces and to hint that the gods will see that justice is done.[144]

Also at this point, and again through speech, there begins the differentiation of the characters of some of the suitors. They are filled with consternation at Telemachus' words. The first who speaks is Antinous, in a compressed rebuke of only four lines: if the gods have done anything, it is to teach Telemachus to talk like an arrogant young puppy.[145] Telemachus responds with ten lines, defending his position and promulgating the lie that Odysseus is dead. This deliberate misdirection is programmatic of what will happen when Odysseus returns in disguise to take revenge. Eurymachus is shrewder. He brushes away the arrogant threats of Antinous but focuses on precisely this lie. Who was the stranger and did he bring news of Odysseus?[146] This is the cue for a very short speech where Telemachus says that he is not disposed to believe anything he hears about his dead father. The stranger was a guest-friend, in search of

---

[137] *Od.* 1.196, 207, 212, 253, 260, 265.
[138] *Od.* 1.354 n.   [139] *Od.* 1.349.   [140] *Od.* 1.360–1.
[141] *Od.* 1.375.   [142] *Od.* 1.107–8, 119–20.   [143] *Od.* 1.160, 243–51.
[144] *Od.* 1.378–80.   [145] *Od.* 1.383–7.   [146] *Od.* 1.400–11.

hospitality. The speech is rounded off with a repetition of the lines which,[147] in the mouth of Mentes, were a lie but which Telemachus is content to retell to Eurymachus, himself knowing them to be a lie since his visitor was an immortal.[148]

Vocabulary

We have looked at Homer's style in terms of formulaic artistry, imagery, and rhetoric. Although formularity is a natural focus for thinking about epic language, we ought not to ignore individual words, whether as part of repeated formulaic systems or not. Whilst we have no samples of everyday spoken Greek against which to compare the epics, it is uncontroversial to say that the language of the epic is different—marked off by archaism, dialect, or just rarity. The formulaic economy tended to preserve odd words when not only the vernacular of the bards but also the language in which they were composing had moved on.

Observers since antiquity have been struck by the so-called *hapaxes* in Homer, words that occur only once. The 'absolute' *hapax* is one which appears only once in all of Homer (i.e. both epics taken together) and never again in the recorded history of Greek except for quotations. A 'Homeric *hapax*' is a word which, whilst found only once in Homer, is used by later Greek writers. One may also distinguish words that are found once in one of the epics but recur more often in the other. Given that so much of Homer's language is formulaic, it is surprising to find that Homeric hapaxes are quite common. They account for about 35 per cent of the discrete items of vocabulary in the *Iliad* and 33 per cent in the *Odyssey*. This is not to say that, of the words on the page, 34 per cent on average are *hapaxes*; if one looks at the actual word count, only about 2 per cent of the total words used are *hapaxes*. Even then it is striking that they occur on average about once in every ten lines.[149]

Some of these words might be features of ordinary language which, by the laws of chance, happen to figure only once in Homer. περιφραζώμεθα (76 n.) is transparent in meaning and rather prosaic in sense; it is hard to see it as a Homeric coinage or to suppose that the audience perceived anything special about it. The same is true of μέθημαι (118 n.). The noun βοητύς (369 n.) is plain enough in meaning but was probably created specially to end a line whose beginning was itself unique. Other words have the feel of exoticism, especially when their meaning is opaque—e.g. ἐπαλαστέω (252 n.)

---

[147] *Od.* 1.180–1.   [148] *Od.* 1.420.
[149] These references are derived from the tables in Kumpf 1984: 203–7.

and ἀνόπαια (320 n.). It is possible that some were already obscure to the poet and, by extension, to the audience; their deployment is a feature of the high style. Just as Nestor bemoans the loss of an era when men were real men,[150] so the bard might hark back to a time when the tradition could deploy words that nobody in his own day understands. Like many *hapaxes* δουροδόκη (128 n.) and ἐπίστροφος (177 n.) are compounds; they have transparent meanings but were perhaps fashioned purely for their contexts. Some *hapaxes* come in little runs, usually where the description of a particular scene requires it. Thus γραῖα (438 n.), πυκιμηδής (438 n.), ἀνακρεμάννυμι (440 n.), and ἐπερύω (441 n.) are all *hapaxes* in the scene where Telemachus goes to his bedroom. They are not the result of a unique technical description: the vocabulary for parts of a lock occur elsewhere. It is simply that this kind of scene is not typical. Maybe the words were in vernacular use, we do not know; the poet seems at these points to be stepping outside the formulaic system. The effect is not a passage of staggering high style; it is just a change in texture and a step away from tradition. ἐπικλείω (351 n.) and ἀμπιφέλομαι (352 n.) occur together as part of a unique discussion of poetic reputation and so it is not surprising that they are *hapaxes*.

Besides all of that are what we might call lexical rarities—items not unique but rare, whose deployment is similarly a mark of a high style: ἑρπύζω (193 n.), κειμήλιον (312 n.), θελκτήριον (337 n.), παλίντιτος (379 n.).

Versification

'Down in a deep, dark dell sat an old cow munching a beanstalk.' This not particularly useful mnemonic was taught to generations of English schoolchildren to get across to them the basic shape of Homer's metre (see pp. 45–51 for a better account). The exigencies of metre might prohibit certain words and phrases, but we have seen that the poet nevertheless has considerable freedom of choice. But poetry is not just about vocabulary; we cannot appreciate it without looking also at the shape of the verse.

At the most obvious level, there are verses where the thought is not co-extensive with the line but runs over to the next. This phenomenon is called *enjambment*. At one level, this is simply a device to create variety; if every line were a complete thought, it would be rather like reading Longfellow's *Hiawatha*.[151] But individual examples are about emphasis as well as variety. In line 1 μάλα πολλά ends the verse but not the thought and we have to wait for the first word of the next verse to discover what it is

[150] *Il.* 1.260–72.   [151] M. L. West 1971 shows what this might be like.

that the man did: πλάγχθη ('he wandered'). The same effect is found between lines 8 and 9: what did the companions do to the oxen of Hyperion? ἤσθιον ('they ate') them—once again an emphatic word is held over for effect. In both cases, the word in run-over comes before a slight break in sense (πλάγχθη, ἐπεί (2) and ἤσθιον· αὐτάρ (9)) so that we pause on it, albeit briefly, which adds emphasis to the word. The device can be used to great effect in speeches. At line 241, Telemachus' assertion that his father has been snatched away is co-extensive with the verse: as the line ends, so the thought. The idea is starkly put with a metrical full-stop, as it were; there is no invitation to consider alternatives. 'He' is gone.[152] But when Telemachus describes what this means to him personally, the thought runs over the line just as do the consequences of his loss:

> ἐμοὶ δ᾽ ὀδύνας τε γόους τε
> κάλλιπεν· οὐδέ τι κεῖνον ὀδυρόμενος στοναχίζω
> οἶον, ἐπεί ...　(242–4)

The verb of leaving acquires emphasis by running over from the previous line; it leaves behind the verse where the thought began and acquires further emphasis by being placed before a sense-break. The same is true of the fact that Telemachus says that he does not mourn him only: just as there are other troubles, so the thought overruns the line in which those first troubles might have been contained.

In other places, the structure of the line is broken up for rhetorical effect into three or four units called *cola* (or limbs, which are units of sense and not discrete metrical entities). Thus line 23 falls into three such units as marked:

> Αἰθίοπας, | τοὶ διχθὰ δεδαίαται, | ἔσχατοι ἀνδρῶν.

Each limb adds a little more information about the Ethiopians. In some cases, each colon has more syllables than the preceding, the overall effect being of a rhetorical crescendo. An example is line 137:

> καλῇ | χρυσείη, | ὑπὲρ ἀργυρέοιο λέβητος.

Each colon adds one more facet of the scene—the jug was beautiful, the jug was golden, and below it was a bowl made of silver.[153] In a similar way, line 100 falls into four cola:

> βριθὺ | μέγα | στιβαρόν, | τῷ δάμνησι στίχας ἀνδρῶν.

---

[152] On Telemachus' inability to name his father, see 163 n.
[153] Cf. *Od.* 1.131.

The first three words lack any connectors; this harsh asyndeton making the description all the more arresting: the spear was heavy—big—strong. Then the fourth colon describes how it is used.

Within the line, variations of tempo are achieved by altering the preponderance of light and heavy syllables. In a context where there is motion, the thought is underlined by the use of tripping dactyls (— ‿‿) to the fullest extent allowed. So when Eurycleia leaves Telemachus at the end of the book, we find (441):

$$— ‿‿ —‿ ‿—‿ ‿ — ‿‿—‿ ‿ ——$$

βῆ ῥ᾽ ἴμεν ἐκ θαλάμοιο, θύρην δ᾽ ἐπέρυσσε κορώνῃ.

This does not mean that every dactylic line accompanies or implies tripping movement, only that there can be a happy coincidence of content and form. By the same token, a heavily[154] spondaic line might by its ponderousness add solemnity to what is being said. Thus, when Eurycleia is introduced, it is with full patronymics that take up the entire line and represent four spondees out of a possible six:

$$— — — — —‿ ‿— — — ‿‿ —‿$$

Εὐρύκλει᾽, Ὦπος θυγάτηρ Πεισηνορίδαο.

Conclusion

Whilst we speak of this or that 'effect', one cannot suppose that there was a tool-box which told bards to use dactyls for one effect, spondees for another, enjambment for a third, and an ascending tricolon for something else. All we can do is be attentive to the overall prosodic texture of the verses, to see how variety is achieved and to wonder whether there might sometimes be coincidences of form and content. But, just as matters of verbal allusion must ultimately be matters for individual judgement (literary criticism not being mathematics), so the existence of these effects must to some extent depend on what the individual reader now finds. The most that the commentator can do is to provide suggestions and, where appropriate, parallels.

Suggested reading: M. W. Edwards 1997; Kahane 2012, ch. 4.

---

[154] Lines with six spondaic feet are vanishingly rare in Homer: 0.02 per cent overall (Dee 2004: xvi). This is not least because the fifth foot is almost always a dactyl.

THE WORLD OF THE *ODYSSEY*

Bygone school-texts of the *Odyssey* often sported diagrams attempting to reconstruct the palace of Odysseus from the indications given in the text, what the furniture looked like and so forth. This is a perfectly reasonable endeavour—the world described by the poet presumably had some definite material and social contours and would have to be something to which the audience could relate in its imagination. But both epics come at the end of a very long tradition. Just as their language preserves features of high antiquity beside demonstrably newer forms, so their material and social world is not a snapshot of one period. In the *Iliad*, heroes almost always use bronze weapons; but there are references to iron for agricultural and industrial tools. This situation was unknown in the world revealed to us by archaeology, where the replacement of bronze by iron began in the military sphere. In the same way, warriors are described as using chariots, but only for transport; the tradition seems unaware that people once used to fight from them.[155]

This only appears to be a problem if we mistake what the epics were and conclude that they were a bad attempt at history. One cannot judge lengthy poems by the same standards as a monograph in historical anthropology. That said, the epics are not a careless antiquarian congeries. Even if we allow for some throwbacks to the Bronze Age,[156] the world they depict is fundamentally post-Mycenean.[157] It has a sociological coherence,[158] describing 'what *some* late eighth-century Greeks thought the heroic world *ought* to have been like.'[159] That world was probably located in their collective imaginative recall of the late ninth and early eighth centuries.[160]

Political Life

The world of the *Iliad* is one of aristocratic warriors far from home. Such glimpses as are afforded of the lower orders (shepherds,[161] carpenters,[162] smiths,[163] dyers,[164] agricultural labourers[165]) are confined to the similes or the Shield of Achilles or appear as incidental to descriptions of something else. The *Odyssey* gives a surface impression of a more settled and ordinary world, but this is truer of the second half than the first. The proem tells us that Odysseus visited many ἄστεα ('cities'); he did not. Most

---

[155] Murray 1993: 36.   [156] Bennet 1997.   [157] M. I. Finley 1981: 232.
[158] M. I. Finley 1977: 153.   [159] I. Morris 1997: 558.
[160] Raaflaub 1997: 628.   [161] *Il.* 4.455.   [162] *Il.* 23.712.
[163] *Il.* 12.295.   [164] *Il.* 4.141.   [165] *Il.* 18.566–7; 21.257.

of the beings he meets on his travels, apart from the Phaeacians (*Od.* 7.14) and Cicones (*Od.* 9.40), do not live in cities: Calypso, Circe, the Cyclopes, the Lotus Eaters, the Sirens, Scylla, the inhabitants of Hades. The Phaeacians are the most notable exception: although their world is in many ways fantastical (immortal robotic guard-dogs made from gold and silver,[166] ships endowed with minds that know their own way and have neither rudder nor helmsman[167]), they nevertheless have government that is similar to that of other societies.[168] They also have some marks of urbanization. Odysseus asks Nausicaa who are the people οἳ τήνδε πόλιν καὶ γαῖαν ἔχουσιν ('who possess this *polis* and land').[169] By πόλις he seems to mean the entire community—the town itself, which he calls ἄστυ,[170] and the surrounding territory to the sea. Nausicaa talks of the physical town as a πόλις with fortifications.[171] All of this is presumably a glance at a proto-*polis* in the Greek Dark Age.[172]

The physical and political world of Ithaca is nevertheless the most fully described in the poem. Towards the end of Book 1, Telemachus announces that he is calling an assembly to tell the suitors publicly to leave his house.[173] This provokes Antinous to express the hope that Telemachus will never become βασιλεύς, an office that he says belong by heredity to Telemachus' family.[174] Eurymachus by contrast separates out the question of who shall be βασιλεύς from that of who shall be master of the house and all it contains: the latter must in his view be Telemachus, whereas the identity of the former is in the lap of the gods.[175] This implies that the office and the household are distinct objects of ownership; perhaps so, but they happened to coincide in the person of Odysseus and their proposed separation seems to have more to do with Eurymachus' trying to distance himself from Antinous than with any real-life distinction. Perhaps the situation was always rather fluid. If Telemachus had been older and more robust, this apparent power vacuum might never have occurred.

In the Mycenean texts, the word *qa-si-re-u* is formally identical with alphabetic Greek βασιλεύς. In the Mycenaean world he was a local official, probably not appointed by the palace but recognized by the community.[176] In classical Greek usage he was a monarch. In Homer, however, the word is in flux. Alcinous is one βασιλεύς among thirteen.[177] On Ithaca too there are 'many' βασιλῆες;[178] perhaps they are identical in number with

[166] *Od.* 7.91–4.   [167] *Od.* 8.556–63.
[168] *Od.* 8.390–1; M. I. Finley 1977: 156.   [169] *Od.* 6.177.
[170] *Od.* 6.178.   [171] *Od.* 6.262–7; Murray 1993: 63.
[172] Raaflaub 1997: 646.   [173] *Od.* 1.372–4.   [174] See *Od.* 1.387 n.
[175] *Od.* 1.400–4.   [176] Bennet 1997: 521.   [177] *Od.* 8.390–1.
[178] *Od.* 1.394–5.

the twelve suitors said to come from the island.[179] Amid much controversy,[180] it has been well said that Homeric βασιλῆες are really just noblemen whose attributes do not differ significantly among themselves.[181] In
any given case, one might enjoy an uneasy and contested supremacy—
Agamemnon at Troy, for example, and the apparent vacancy on Ithaca. In
such a case, we might call him in English a 'chief'.

The assembly that Telemachus calls takes place at the start of *Odyssey*
Book 2, like the assembly of the Greek host in the same book of the *Iliad*.
He instructs the heralds to call 'the long-haired Achaeans'[182] to the place of
assembly. This done, he walks into the assembly with a spear in his hand
and accompanied by his dogs.[183] Although Homer says that all the people
were present,[184] we may be sure that slaves and women were excluded.
Telemachus takes his father's seat among the elders—and they yield to
him.[185] The first to speak is the aged Aegyptius, who points out that there
has been no assembly since Odysseus left. This might imply that Odysseus
alone enjoyed the right to summon one. Has Telemachus heard news of an
approaching army? Or is there some other public matter that he wishes to
air?[186] Telemachus stands up to speak and the herald places the sceptre in
his hands; we recall that this was a significant object in the assembly in
Book 2 of the *Iliad*, symbolizing royal power and prerogatives.[187] When
he finishes speaking, he bursts into tears and casts the sceptre to the
ground. Plainly a contrast is intended between the confident and indignant Achilles in Book 1 of the *Iliad* and the young and emotional Telemachus
struggling to assert his authority. The allusion was not lost on ancient
readers.[188] The scene is thus carefully worked out. But what is its political
significance? There is no deliberation or voting of the kind that we find in
classical Athens. There is no sense that Telemachus is consulting the people
or seeking their approval. He is making public his grievance against the

---

[179] *Od.* 16.251.The ghost of Amphimedon calls Antinous a βασιλεύς (*Od.* 24.179).
Telemachus says the same of him and Eurymachus (*Od.* 17.64–5); the evident mockery
need not extend to their status (Lenz 1993: 203 n. 97).

[180] Raaflaub 1997: 634 n. 46.

[181] Murray 1993: 38.

[182] *Od.* 2.6–7; by which is meant simply every male person entitled to attend.

[183] A peculiar formulaic aberration: whenever a line begins οὐκ οἶος/οὐκ οἴη, it
otherwise always ends with a reference to the subject being accompanied by attendants
of some kind (*Il.* 2.745, 822; 3.143; 24.573; *Od.* 1.331; 6.84; 18.207; 19.601). This change
draws attention to how isolated Telemachus really is—he has no satellites but his dogs.

[184] The same λαοί whom Nestor has in mind when he asks whether it is their hatred
of Telemachus that stops them from dealing properly with the suitors (*Od.* 3.214–15).

[185] *Od.* 2.14; cf. *Il.* 18.503–4.   [186] *Od.* 2.25–34.

[187] *Il.* 2.101–8; Griffin 1980: 9–13.   [188] ΣbT on *Il.* 1.245.

suitors, declaring that they must leave and warning them of public opinion and the judgement of the gods.[189]

Whilst at the public level there are competitive noblemen and public assemblies, the basic unit of society is the οἶκος ('house'). Telemachus repeatedly refers to the damage being done by the suitors to the wealth of the οἶκος.[190] He also makes it clear to his mother[191] and to Antinous[192] that he has and will have overall power in the οἶκος. Whatever the position concerning who will be chief, he asserts his power over and within the household unit.

Slaves

In the same breath, he mentions his ownership of the slaves, who are simply chattels, the booty of war brought home by Odysseus.[193] This power is absolute and extends to life and death. The female slaves who have been helping the suitors and sleeping with them are hanged mercilessly in a death chosen to be especially 'filthy', as Telemachus puts it.[194] The nurse Eurycleia is an interesting case. She is a great support to both Telemachus and Odysseus; she is instrumental in the killing of the suitors and rejoices at it. But she too was a spoil of war, bought by Laertes for an extraordinary price when she was only a young woman.[195] We are told that Laertes did not have sex with her because he feared the anger of his wife—the poet takes it for granted that, absent that restraint, she would have been his for the taking.[196] Apart from the δμῶες, other unfree staff are called ἀμφίπολοι[197] and κοῦροι;[198] the θεράπων[199] and the οἰκεύς[200] are not necessarily slaves.

Eumaeus remarks that, on the day a man becomes a slave, he loses half his manhood.[201] But the role of the slave is not altogether the worst that can be imagined.[202] When the ghost of Achilles tells Odysseus that he would rather have the most menial role among the living than be king of all the dead, the example he gives of the former is not a slave but a worker for hire.[203] Eurycleia is plainly a valued retainer. Eumaeus excites warm feelings. He and Philoetius are promised handsome rewards if they serve Odysseus well against the suitors: they will have wives, goods, and houses near that of their master.[204]

---

[189] *Od.* 2.51–79. [190] *Od.* 1.232, 248, 251, 258.
[191] *Od.* 1.359. [192] *Od.* 1.397.
[193] *Od.* 1.398. [194] *Od.* 22.462–73. [195] *Od.* 1.431 n.
[196] *Od.* 1.433 n. [197] *Od.* 1.191 n. [198] *Od.* 1.148 n.
[199] *Od.* 1.109 n. [200] *Od.* 1.398 n. [201] *Od.* 17.322–3.
[202] Raaflaub 1997: 638. [203] *Od.* 11.489–91, the verb being θητευέμεν.
[204] *Od.* 21.213–15.

Women

In E. M. Forster's *Maurice*, Clive Durham advises Fetherstonehaugh to
re-read Sophocles' *Ajax* keeping his eye on the characters.[205] The same
might be said of the women in Homer. They were not called into being
chiefly to generate questions for later examination papers in Gender
Studies. We can look at them like that, if we choose, for the purposes of
historical and anthropological investigation. But for literary appreciation,
it is unhelpful. There are those who suppose that history is key to literature. For example: Romans thought that widows ought to remain chaste
(*univira*);[206] Virgil was a Roman; therefore we may conclude that Dido is
open to censure for loving Aeneas after the death of her husband Sychaeus.
It is one more reason why she is the first of many bad Carthaginians.[207]
Any sense we might have of Virgil inviting sympathy for Dido is to be
subordinated to this overarching historical determinant. The same sort of
thing is easily done with Homer. This was an archaic society; everyone
knows that women at that time were less powerful than men; thus
Penelope is just an extreme example of the type of the useful wife[208] rather
than an engaging character on her own account.

The first female character mentioned in the poem is the Muse. We do
not know her name. But she knows the story and the invocation is necessary if Homer is to tell us what there is to know. It is striking that, in a
patriarchal society, the resources of memory and omniscience[209] should
be thought to reside with female figures.[210] It is perhaps not unsurprising
that there are other goddesses distinguished by their cleverness. Chief
among these is, of course, Athena. She is the first female character whose
actions and words are portrayed in the poem as she speaks in counsel with
Zeus. Her bravery and initiative are unusual even among the Olympians;
Zeus himself compares her successful interventions in the fighting at Troy
with the failure of Aphrodite.[211] She is plainly the great promoter and
defender of Odysseus. But there is a more interesting dynamic at work.
The man whom she admires and helps is married. But for this, and for her
own abstinence from the works of Aphrodite, one feels that they would be
a perfect match.[212] Athena almost says as much when she takes on the
form of a beautiful woman, strokes Odysseus with her hand, and tells
him that they excel all others of their kind in respect of their counsel and

---

[205] Forster 1972: 39.   [206] Hor. *Carm.* 3.14.5; Balsdon 1966: 185.
[207] Horsfall 1990: 134; differently Rudd 1990: 154–61.
[208] *Od.* 6.182–5; cf. Hes. *Op.* 702–5.   [209] *Il.* 2.485.
[210] *Od.* 1.1 n.; cf. Doherty 1995.   [211] *Il.* 5.428–30.
[212] Cf. *Od.* 1.199 n.; Murnaghan 1995: 72–4.

cunning.[213] It is thus interesting how the character of Penelope, the mortal wife of Odysseus, is presented as being very similar to Athena.[214] The character of Penelope gains from this: anyone who can live with Odysseus must be extraordinary. Her cunning is constantly emphasized—not only by the suitors, who resent her stratagem with the web,[215] but also by the poet who depicts her interrogating Odysseus with the same measure of lies and trickery as he himself would use.[216]

The epithet περίφρων is used 50× of Penelope in the *Odyssey*; whilst it is not unique to her, it is used only 4× for Eurycleia[217] and 1× for Arete.[218] It is striking that all these characters are female. Plainly this distribution says something about the fascination of the poet with clever women; but it also underlines Penelope's pre-eminence among them. There are few other epithets associated with Penelope (ἐχέφρων 5×;[219] ὀδυρομένη 8×;[220] γοόωσα 5×[221]). This suggests that she is not well integrated into the epic tradition. It seems likely that her character started life as the type of the good but obscure wife; then Homer saw the opportunity to make much more of her.[222] Even if we do not have to accept Finley's view that the poem is almost as much of a *Penelopeia* as it is an *Odysseia*,[223] there is no doubt that Penelope plays a huge role. Her name is mentioned in almost every book.[224] But she is not simply a sort of Greek analogue for the Queen of Sheba, who turns out to be such a good match for wily King Solomon.[225] She is also a wife who grieves,[226] prompt to tears not simply for her own loss but from a genuine affection for her husband.[227] Before we are tempted to lay too much stress on the 'otherness' of the Greeks, this conjugal love is to be borne in mind, even if it never quite reaches the affective power with which the relationship between Hector and Andromache is so succinctly but poignantly drawn in the *Iliad*.[228] Within

---

[213] *Od.* 13.291–302. Skill and craft (τέχνη) are very much attributes of Athena (e.g. *Od.* 6.232–5; 7.109–11); it is not surprising if she responds to it in others. It seems that, even then, clever was the new sexy.

[214] *Od.* 19.325–6 (Penelope) ~ *Od.* 13.298–9 (Athena).   [215] *Od.* 2.93–110.

[216] *Od.* 23.107–10, 177–81, 206.   [217] *Od.* 19.357, 491; 20.134; 21.381.

[218] *Od.* 11.345.   [219] *Od.* 4.111; 13.332, 406; 16.130, 458; 17.390; 24.198, 294.

[220] *Od.* 4.800, 828; 13.379; 14.129; 18.203; 19.46, 513, 517.

[221] *Od.* 4.721, 800; 19.210, 264, 513.   [222] Gilchrist 1997: 112.

[223] J. H. Finley 1978: 3 based on *Od.* 24.192–202.

[224] Gilchrist 1997: 318–19 lists all such mentions.

[225] Toy 1907; Pritchard 1974.

[226] *Od.* 4.721, 800, 828; 13.379; 14.129; 18.203; 19.46, 210, 264, 513, 517.

[227] *Od.* 1.336; 11.181–3; 23.207. Odysseus himself weeps (*Od.* 23.232); but it was proverbial in Greek that good men were prone to tears—ἀγαθοὶ δ᾽ ἀριδάκρυες ἄνδρες (Zen. 1.14.1).

[228] *Il.* 6.482–96, where great emotional meaning is loaded into apparently small visual details drawn in compressed but arresting language: δακρυόεν γελάσασα (*Il.* 6.484) and ἐντροπαλιζομένη (*Il.* 6.496).

the narrative economy of Book 1, we see only some foreshadowing of all this. Penelope has been listening to the song of Phemius from her quarters upstairs.[229] She is pained by the details, perhaps because she fears that he will narrate the death of Odysseus.[230] She has enough confidence and authority to come downstairs and command Phemius to change subject,[231] a right that presumably otherwise belongs to the suitors (who compel him to sing)[232] as it belongs to King Alcinous on Scheria[233] or his guest Odysseus.[234] Against that background, it is remarkable how brusquely Telemachus tells his mother to return to the οἶκος and get on with her woman's work.[235] This gives us a disturbing glimpse of how even an aristocratic woman of her rank is subordinated to the power of her adolescent son, who is still finding his way in the world but who feels himself entitled to talk like this simply because he is male. But then her life is dominated by the needs of men. The suitors are there precisely to contend for her hand. In part, of course, she is outstandingly attractive;[236] but this is not a charmingly romantic story of boy meets girl. Marriage to Penelope appears to be bound up with the question of who will be the next local chief in Ithaca.[237]

Eurycleia has already appeared in the context of slaves but it is worth dwelling on her cleverness. Twice Penelope herself calls her περίφρων.[238] On two other occasions, the omniscient poet uses it of her: once when she is talking to Odysseus[239] and once when she addresses Telemachus.[240] She is plainly a fitting helper for the main characters even if her servile status reduces her overall potential to act within the poem.

In Calypso we find a goddess who, unlike Athena, does not stop short of trying to make Odysseus her husband.[241] Her character is not as fully drawn as that of Penelope. In some ways, she exists as a foil—an obstacle to the homecoming of Odysseus, in which respect she provides some of the material for Dido in the *Aeneid*: both are affectionate, desirable, and powerful, but problematic because they represent the allure of a different destiny. It is noteworthy that, although she is undoubtedly the greater goddess, Athena does not herself engage directly with Calypso. There would be too much risk of an unseemly spat with 'the other woman.' Rather, Athena gets her father Zeus to send Hermes to deal with the

---

[229] *Od.* 1.328.   [230] See *Od.* 1.343 n.   [231] *Od.* 1.340.
[232] *Od.* 1.154.   [233] *Od.* 8.537–8.   [234] *Od.* 8.492.
[235] *Od.* 1.356–9 n.; cf. John 2:4.   [236] *Od.* 18.245–9.
[237] *Od.* 1.400–1 n. Eurymachus separates the two, claiming that only Antinous wanted to rule (*Od.* 22.50–3) whereas the other suitors only wanted the marriage.
[238] *Od.* 19.357; 21.381.   [239] *Od.* 19.491.   [240] *Od.* 20.134.
[241] *Od.* 1.15 n.

matter since it is presented as one of almost cosmic proportions. Calypso is outclassed and says as much.[242]

The character of Circe is almost a doublet of Calypso. She, too, wants to detain Odysseus—albeit in the form of a pig in a sty. When her magical powers are undermined by the *moly*[243] root that Hermes has shown to Odysseus, she changes tack and tries instead the same sort of sexual bland-ishment that keeps Odysseus on Calypso's island.[244] But, if Calypso is lightly sketched in comparison with Penelope, Circe is positively thin compared with Calypso. Her character and motivation are impenetrable: this is perhaps because she exists more at the level of plot than character. She is the type of the folk-tale witch, who threatens to hold back the hero but is overcome and provides some useful help.[245]

It is worth pausing to note that Odysseus does not resist the sexual invitations of Calypso[246] and Circe.[247] There is an evident asymmetry in expectations of sexual fidelity. The faithfulness of Penelope remains a live question until very late in the poem:[248] Telemachus is unsure of it,[249] Athena plays on these fears as late as Book 15;[250] but Odysseus need con-form to no such standards for himself. Whatever it meant for Odysseus to miss his wife,[251] this was just one of the things he missed about Ithaca. There were other reunions to be made—with his son, his retainer Eumaeus, his father (assuming Book 24 is genuine).[252]

It is thus all the more striking that Odysseus sidesteps any kind of sex-ual relationship with Nausicaa when he meets her on Scheria. She is, after all, a mortal and in many ways a far more realistic person for him to desire, were he minded to leave Penelope. Why does he do this? She is not under marriageable age for those days: she already has suitors from her com-munity.[253] Her father recognizes this:[254] he would like Odysseus for a son-in-law.[255] Odysseus deftly passes up this offer without mentioning it.[256] Nausicaa lacks depth of character. The poet presents her as barely on the threshold of adulthood: she and her companions delight in ball games.[257] It is hard to imagine Penelope doing this or Odysseus caring much for her if she did. He values Penelope as a worthy partner. This is an interesting glimpse into the value of a mature relationship in a society where females

---

[242] *Od.* 5.118–40.   [243] *Od.* 10.304–6.   [244] *Od.* 10.334–5.

[245] One might think in this respect of Baba Yaga in Russian folk-tales (Novikov 1977)—although she is much scarier and not at all sexy.

[246] *Od.* 5.227.   [247] *Od.* 10.347.

[248] Zeitlin 1995; Gilchrist 1997: 329–32 collects evidence from all sources on this topic.

[249] *Od.* 1.215–16.   [250] *Od.* 15.20–3.   [251] *Od.* 1.13 n.

[252] See on Structure, pp. 8–9.

[253] *Od.* 6.34.   [254] *Od.* 6.67.   [255] *Od.* 7.313–15.   [256] *Od.* 7.333.

[257] *Od.* 6.100.

were typically married off rather young. We might reflect that the sex with Circe and Calypso, whilst doubtless freely chosen, was not as significant as it might seem at first blush. These were powerful figures who could affect his destiny. When offered sex with a young woman whom he could potentially dominate, he rejects it.

Arete, mother of Nausicaa and wife of Alcinous, is a powerful character. Unlike Penelope, she does not hide in the women's quarters but is found feasting with the nobles.[258] Although she performs the typical work of weaving by the fireplace,[259] she also resolves disputes for the Phaeacians,[260] which makes her unique among Homeric women. It is she whom Odysseus approaches on reaching the palace of Alcinous.[261] In part, this was because Nausicaa advised her that it would be best to avoid potentially irritating her father.[262] But wrapped up in this is the fact that she was a person of substance upon whose good opinion rests his hope of getting home.[263] In receiving the suppliant Odysseus, she not only shows herself as a person of importance but also mirrors the way in which Penelope will receive him, disguised as a beggar, on his return to Ithaca.

Helen is perhaps the most extraordinary female character in the epics. In sharp contrast to Penelope, she is the type of the errant wife. But, when visited by Telemachus, she is living quietly in retirement with her husband Menelaus. The dust has now settled on the Trojan War, which she caused.[264] Already in the *Iliad*, however, Helen was set apart from the other characters by her self-awareness, her grasp of her place as a figure in a larger story. We first meet her in Book 3, weaving.[265] This is a common enough activity for women in archaic societies. But the tapestry itself is far from typical: it depicts all the sufferings of the Trojans in the war.[266] Helen thus becomes a narrator like the poet himself; she might not sing songs, but she produces an enduring artistic representation of human suffering.[267] She stands sufficiently obliquely to the flow of history that she can exhibit the wider view of things to herself and others. In the *Odyssey*, some of this aura remains about Helen. She has a mysterious drug from Egypt, apparently famous for its many drugs.[268] She slips this into the drinks of her guests.[269] Its power is such that it could make one forget even if one had just seen all one's nearest and dearest slain in a war.[270] In other

---

[258] *Od.* 7.136–8, 141.   [259] *Od.* 6.305–6.

[260] *Od.* 7.74.   [261] *Od.* 7.146–52.

[262] *Od.* 6.313–15; advice underlined by Athena, *Od.* 7.75–7. Alcinous rejects the idea that he would have ever looked askance at a stranger, *Od.* 7.309–10.

[263] ἐλπωρή: *Od.* 6.314; 7.76.

[264] *Il.* 3.128, 157, 180; Priam takes a gentler view: *Il.* 3.164–5.

[265] *Il.* 3.125.   [266] *Il.* 3.126–8.   [267] Cf. *Il.* 6.356–8.

[268] *Od.* 4.228–32.   [269] *Od.* 4.220.   [270] *Od.* 4.222–6.

words, Helen has the antidote for the Trojan War. She alone is sufficiently outside history to see the need and to administer the necessary physic. Even her husband Menelaus is among her patients.

Travel and Trade

In the age of Jane Austen, not so very removed in time from our own, travel by horse and carriage was wearisome and most ordinary people did not go outside the county where they lived, much less overseas. For most people, the same remained true well into the twentieth century. In spite of the advent of the aeroplane, foreign travel was prohibitively expensive until the package holiday came into being. Things can scarcely have been different in archaic Greece: most people will not have gone far. But their imaginative literature is the product of an elite, and some poets plainly travelled quite widely for poetic contests[271] and patronage.[272] The epics, in particular, transcend the limits of space, albeit in different ways. The Catalogue of Ships in Book 2 of the *Iliad* describes the places of origin of the many military contingents that were present at Troy. This is perhaps the only real hint of a wider world in a poem whose action otherwise unfolds in an almost claustrophobic atmosphere before the walls of Troy. The *Odyssey*, on the other hand, is drawn on a much larger canvas of geographical imagination (Map 1).[273] The wanderings of Odysseus are surely the earliest core of the poem around which the homecoming and Telemachy coalesced rather later; they show us the much larger world. The *Odyssey* contains many place-names, of which some are apparently still in use today (albeit not necessarily for the same places)[274] and others were the subject of speculation already in antiquity (Maps 2a, 2b). The difficulty is that the poem is not a travelogue; it is a work of imagination that blends the imaginary with the real in ways that are satisfying for the audience but less so for the geographer.[275]

On the way back from Troy, Odysseus and his men pause to pillage Ismarus in Thrace, home to the Cicones who were allies of the Trojans.[276]

---

[271] *Od.* 17.382–6.   [272] Bowra 1964: 355–7.

[273] Map 1 illustrates all places referred to in Book 1 except for Ogygia, which cannot be identified with any certainty (see *Od.* 1.85 n.).

[274] The name and location of Ithaca is perhaps the most pertinent such problem. It is possible that modern Ithaki is not Homer's Ἰθάκη and that the latter was part of what is now called Cephalonia. See *Od.* 1.246–7 n.

[275] Roller 2016: 16–23 gives an excellent account of such geographical reality as might be disengaged from the poem. The identifications of places cited here derive from his work.

[276] *Od.* 9.39–81.

The Lotus Eaters[277] were probably somewhere in North Africa; this would be quite likely if the crew was blown off course in attempting to round Cape Malea.[278] Several ancient writers thought that the place was the island of Meninx (modern Djerba).[279] The land of the Cyclopes has been identified with the island of Lipari north of Sicily.[280] Aeolia has also been identified with Lipari.[281] The Laestrygonians have been placed in the vicinity of Etna.[282] Circe has been placed on the Italian coast between Naples and Rome, in an area still known as Monte Circeo and renowned for magical roots.[283] The Sirens may be placed in the Bay of Naples, perhaps near modern Sorrento.[284] Scylla and Charybdis are placed in the Straits of Messina.[285] Thrinacia is probably Sicily.[286] In general, we can see that the wanderings of Odysseus seem localized to the Western Mediterranean; Calypso advises him to keep certain constellations to the East in order to find his way home by sailing eastwards.[287]

Clearly the tradition knew a great deal about the world not only of Troy and Asia Minor but also of the Western Mediterranean, where Greek colonization had begun in the eighth century BC. But, even in Book 1, the action of which chiefly takes place on Ithaca, the gaze of the poet ranges much wider. The poet says that Poseidon had gone to see the Ethiopians, the most far-flung inhabitants of the planet who dwell in territories to the uttermost East and West. This reflects in part knowledge of a real people in Africa, in part mythical ideas about the places that are farthest away being home to the greatest abundance.[288] Athena alludes to the island of Ogygia where Calypso lives.[289] Mentes tells Telemachus that he is a merchant trading metals to Temese on Cyprus.[290] The world of the archaic Aegean was no stranger to ships and trade at this period,[291] even if most people will not have been engaged in it. There is a glimpse also in this book of a journey made by Odysseus northwards to Ephyra in Thesprotia to get poison for arrows.[292] Throughout the poem we perceive this characteristic interlacing of geography and ideology—there are real places but they are overlain by ideas about the moral qualities of the distant and unknown.[293]

---

[277] *Od.* 9.82–104.   [278] *Od.* 9.80–1.

[279] Eratosth. fr. 105 (Roller); Plin. *Nat.* 5.41; Str. 1.2.17; 17.3.17.

[280] *Od.* 9.105–51; Call. *Hy.* 3.46–9 (Pf.).

[281] *Od.* 10.1–75; Antiochus of Syracuse *FGrH* 555 F 1; Str. 6.2.10.

[282] *Od.* 10.80–132; Hes. fr. 150.25–6 (MW).

[283] *Od.* 10.133–574; Thphr. *HP* 5.8.3; cf. 9.15.1.

[284] *Od.* 12.165–200; Str. 1.2.12–3.   [285] *Od.* 12.426–53; *Th.* 4.24.4–5.

[286] *Th.* 6.2.2.   [287] *Od.* 5.272–7.

[288] *Od.* 1.22, 23 nn.   [289] *Od.* 1.85 n.   [290] *Od.* 1.184 n.

[291] Donlan 1997.   [292] *Od.* 1.259 n.   [293] cf. *Od.* 9.105–15, 174–6.

Physiology and Psychology

We live in a world where the workings of the human body may be known by anyone with the curiosity to find out: the heart pumps blood, the lungs are for oxygenating it, and the brain is where thinking gets done. None of these seemingly self-evident facts was known to the epic tradition. The locus of thought and impulse is variously described as being in the θυμός, φρένες, or κραδίη (together with some other locations).[294] The earliest Ionian medical texts suggest that the brain was thought of as a centre for the production of semen, which was identified with the cerebro-spinal fluid.[295] The function of the heart as a pump was not well understood until Galen; and it was not until Harvey discovered capillaries in the seventeenth century that the picture was complete. The ψυχή, so often translated as 'soul',[296] is more like 'breath' and the μένος that Athena puts into Telemachus is more likely to have been conceived as a vigorous motion than an abstract quality of courage.[297]

One can draw too many conclusions from all of this. Bruno Snell famously observed that Homer has no single word for the living body (σῶμα denotes only a corpse); instead we find the plurals μέλη and γυῖα ('limbs').[298] By the same token, the attribution of mental processes not to a unitary organ but to θυμός, φρένες, or κραδίη, is taken as proof that Homeric people had no sense of a unified personality; there was just a jumble of physiological structures that were open to psychic influences of various kinds.[299] All of this evokes a world of otherness worthy of the palmy days of late Victorian anthropology. As Martin West pointedly observed, the Greeks did not have a singular word for their backsides either: that they used the plural γλουτοί does not mean that they lacked an understanding of the posterior as a unitary entity.[300] One can go too far in supposing that linguistic devices such as this are actually a reflection of the cognitive universe of the speaker. In the same way, although some writers have suggested that Homeric characters do not make real decisions but are the puppets in a divine theatre, this too is an exaggeration and a careful reading of the text shows otherwise.[301] Of course it is legitimate to point to the 'otherness' of Homer, but it ought not to be overstated.

This is all important because, at some level, it is not hard to see reflections of the world we know in the world of the *Odyssey*: uncertain

---

[294] Pulleyn 2000: 36 n. 2; Clarke 1999: 61–83, 122.   [295] Pulleyn 2000: 35 n. 1.
[296] Clarke 1999: 53–60.   [297] *Od.* 1.89 n.; Clarke 1999, 76 n. 33, 110–12.
[298] Snell 1953: 15–16.
[299] Snell 1953: 21; cf. the common expression where a god is said to put an idea into somebody's φρένες (e.g. *Od.* 1.89; 5.427, etc.).
[300] M. L. West 1965: 159.   [301] Gaskin 1990.

adolescents, arrogant aristocrats, plucky mothers, absent fathers—these
are not things confined to the archaic period of ancient Greece. Of course
their values and knowledge and suppositions and prejudices were not
ours; but neither are they aliens from another planet. The reason why we
still read these poems with pleasure and admiration is because they paint
a compelling picture of enduring aspects of the human condition.

The Divine

From the earliest times for which we have evidence, the Greeks were
polytheists. This puts them in company with the Sumerians, Egyptians,
Babylonians, Hittites, Mitanni, and others. The ancient Israelites, by contrast, believed in one god and this belief is found in Christianity and
Islam. In the modern world, the only polytheistic system likely to be
familiar to most people is Hinduism. Most modern readers will either
believe in one god or no gods at all. It is thus hard to enter into the world
of the epics, where things are so different. Herodotus said that Hesiod and
Homer (in that order) had effectively given the Greeks their gods by
defining their different spheres of operation and the cult paid to them.[302]
It seems unlikely that these poets created the gods out of nothing—more
probably, they expanded upon and embellished existing details of cult.
We also find from time to time references to gods and goddesses having
temples and altars in this or that place and confirmed by archaeology.[303]
Nevertheless, one cannot underestimate the influence of the epics on the
Greek religious imagination.

The *Iliad* is far more taken up with the doings of the gods than is the
Odyssey. On the plain before Troy, we see Athena, Hera, Poseidon, Ares,
Apollo, and even Aphrodite taking the field to promote the interests of
their favourites.[304] In the *Odyssey*, the chief interventions are those of
Athena; Poseidon[305] and Hermes[306] are also involved, and Zeus sits in his
managerial heaven. The overall impression is of a poem where the divine
machinery is much less on show and human concerns are the chief preoccupation. In the *Iliad*, the poet himself stops to give a somewhat unexpected account of how the gods do not have blood in their veins but *ichor*,
pointing out that this is the corollary of their consuming not ordinary

---

[302] Hdt. 2.53.

[303] A sanctuary of Demeter at Purasos: *Il.* 2.695–6, Kirk 1985: 230–1; Zeus on Ida: *Il.*
8.47–8, Kirk 1990: 302; Apollo at Troy: *Il.* 5.446, Kirk 1990: 107; Athena at Troy, *Il.* 6.88,
Kirk 1990: 166.

[304] Non-exhaustive examples: Athena and Hera, *Il.* 5.778–9; Poseidon, *Il.* 13.10–30,
59–65; Ares, *Il.* 5.461–3; Apollo, *Il.* 16.788–804; Aphrodite, *Il.* 5.311–51.

[305] *Od.* 1.75; 13.162–4.   [306] *Od.* 5.43–86; 10.277–307.

food and drink but nectar and ambrosia.[307] Elsewhere, there is specific reference to the gods being heavier than human beings, so that a chariot groans under the weight of the goddess Athena.[308] Beyond the power of Athena to change the appearance of Odysseus, the *Odyssey* is not much interested in the special attributes of the gods. In the *Iliad*, they all take part in councils on Olympus;[309] in the *Odyssey*, by contrast, only Athena and Zeus do so.

That the gods of the *Odyssey* are less prominent does not indicate an outbreak of religious scepticism; it simply reflects a difference of emphasis. The idea of not believing in the gods was not really on the menu at this period. One might disrespect or disregard them,[310] but not doubt their existence. The *Odyssey*, for all the prominence it gives to humans, nevertheless takes for granted the existence of a divine machinery. In particular, prayer and sacrifice are much in evidence whenever characters wish to give thanks or seek divine help.[311] In the same way, the gods are guarantors of oaths.[312] All of this is taken for granted as *usage du monde*; the lower prominence given in the poem to the other Olympians demonstrates that the difference between the *Iliad* and *Odyssey* is one of literary and narrative emphasis rather than of fundamental religious orientation.

Book 1 begins with a council of the gods in Olympus. Zeus has a good deal to say about mortal complaints about divine conduct, making it clear that humans suffer deservedly on account of their transgressions.[313] This is something of a contrast to the *Iliad*, where gods promote the interests of this or that side according to personal preferences. Zeus is said to have a 'plan',[314] but that is inscrutable and his visiting of suffering upon the Greeks in response to the supplication of Thetis does not look particularly like the action of the arbiter of cosmic justice.[315] It may be thought that the *Odyssey* is far more concerned with the overall justice of the world. Certainly its overall narrative shape is less like the tragedy of the *Iliad* and more like that of a moralizing folk-tale: the absent master returns to punish the usurpers.[316] But we might be permitted some doubt here. Do Odysseus' men really perish by their own sin? It is true that they were warned not to eat the oxen of the sun, and they did so. But we are also told that they were facing starvation. They had been driven off course by Poseidon, brought

---

[307] *Il.* 5.339–42; Pulleyn 2006: 61–74.   [308] *Il.* 5.837–9.
[309] *Il.* 1.533–5; 8.4; 24.23–32.
[310] *Od.* 9.274–7, but contrast 9.107; cf. *Il.* 9.537.
[311] *Od.* 2.143–5, 262–6; 3.6–9, 40–62, 380–4, 430–63; 4.762–6; 5.445–50; 6.323–7; 7.329–33; 9.528–34; 13.356–60; 17.240–6; 20.60–5, 98–101, 112–19.
[312] *Od.* 2.377–8; 5.184–91; 14.158–64; 17.155–61; 19.303–7; 20.230–4.
[313] *Od.* 1.32–43.   [314] *Il.* 1.5; Pulleyn 2000: 121–2.
[315] *Il.* 1.498–530. Cf. *Od.* 1.379 n.   [316] Lloyd-Jones 1983: 31.

to the brink of death and punished for turning in desperation to their only remaining source of food. The justice of Zeus is not immediately evident in this. The 'filthy'[317] death by hanging of the disloyal maidservants on Ithaca is also an unattractive feature. The idea of merciful forbearance is very common in the epics;[318] the killing of slaves who had sex with the suitors thus seems remarkably harsh. Even if one allows that most of the maidservants did not misbehave in this way,[319] it is hard not to feel uneasy about this treatment of unfree persons whose choice might not have been free.[320] The killing of the suitors itself is, of course, the climax to which the whole story looks. It is foreshadowed as early as Book 1, when Mentes bluntly recommends it.[321] Whilst Antinous is indubitably a nasty man, and whilst the suitors as a group had plotted (albeit in vain) to kill Telemachus,[322] their mass slaughter at the end of the poem causes great tension on Ithaca. Book 24, which I take to be largely original, shows the difficulty of reconciling this action with the values of the larger community left behind on Ithaca.[323] That the intervention of Athena is required to avert civil war does nothing to persuade us of the morality of these killings; it simply solves a problem by an early instance of *deus ex machina*.[324]

Overall, then, although we might say that the *Odyssey* is drawn on a wider geographical and ethnographic canvas than the *Iliad*, with every bit as much psychological sophistication in the portrayal of the characters, it is nevertheless morally and theologically rather simpler in outlook.

Suggested reading: *politics*, Osborne 2004; *women*, Peradotto and Sullivan 1984; *the body*, Clarke 1999; *gods*, Griffin 1980, chs. 5–6.

ORIGINS

We have seen that the Homeric poems contain a significant number of repeated phrases that are generally called formulae. On one reckoning, of the 27,853 verses that make up the *Iliad* and *Odyssey* together, some 9,253

---

[317] *Od.* 22.462.

[318] *Il.* 2.27, 64; 6.407, 431; 7.27; 9.302; 10.176; 11.665; 13.15; 21.147; 24.19, 23, 174; *Od.* 1.19; 3.96; 4.326, 828; 5.450; 6.175; 10.399; 14.389; 17.367; 19.210; 20.202; 23.313.

[319] Of the fifty maidservants in the house (*Od.* 22.421), only twelve had slept with the suitors (*Od.* 22.424).

[320] See *Od.* 1.398 n.   [321] *Od.* 1.294–6.   [322] *Od.* 4.822–3, 842–7.

[323] *Od.* 24.426–38 (Eupeithes evokes sympathy); 454–62 (Halitherses puts the case against the suitors); 463–6 (more than half of the people sympathize with Eupeithes and the suitors).   [324] *Od.* 24.472–548.

are repeated in whole or in part elsewhere.[325] That means that approximately one-third of the poem is formulaic; two-thirds are not. This figure refers to strictly verbatim repetition. On another analysis, taking account of expressions that are similar as well as identical, these proportions are reversed.[326]

On any reading, this state of affairs calls for an explanation. Not only do Virgil, Dante, and Milton not write like this; nor do later writers of Greek hexameter poetry in the epic manner such as Apollonius of Rhodes, Quintus of Smyrna, Nicander of Colophon, or Nonnus of Panopolis. They imitate Homer's turns of phrase but their formulae are more like window-dressing rather than an integrated part of the fabric of their work.[327]

One might simply suppose that repetition is the mark of an archaic taste—a charming peculiarity or curious habit of diction left over from when the world was young. This does not quite satisfy as an explanation. It was not until the middle of the last century that serious attention to the oral poetry of other cultures provided the key. Milman Parry's brilliant studies of the living bardic tradition of (the then) Yugoslavia revealed a similarly widespread system of formulae in South Slavic song.[328] When he came to study the Homeric evidence more closely in the light of this realization, he saw that many formulae run from the beginning of the line to one of a variety of natural pauses that fall around the middle and are called caesurae, or from such a caesura to the end.[329] They exhibit what he called 'extension' and 'simplicity'.[330] By the former, he meant that, for any given person or idea, there is generally a combination of noun and epithet that will fit one of these spaces in the hexameter line before or after the caesura. By the latter, he meant that there tend not to be superfluous alternatives of the same metrical shape. His great insight was to see that this sort of system is precisely what one might want if engaged in improvising a lengthy heroic poem. Parry saw that such a system could not be the work of one person. It was far too complex and elaborate and must have been developed and handed down over many generations. To this extent, it makes sense to call it 'traditional'.

Modern scholars have asked whether the poems themselves are likewise traditional. Did they come into being as the work of many hands over a long period of time? Or was a single creative mind at work? In antiquity, the question did not pose itself in this form. The debate was whether the same person composed both the *Iliad* and the *Odyssey*. Those known as

---

[325] Notopoulos 1960: 180. [326] Hainsworth 1962: 9; 1964: 63.
[327] Adam Parry 1971: 24–9 gives figures for Apollonius of Rhodes.
[328] M. Parry 1933. [329] Adam Parry 1971: 39. [330] M. Parry 1928: 48.

οἱ χωρίζοντες ('the separators') answered that question in the negative.[331] The view that both poems were the work of one and the same person is probably now a minority one among professional scholars—but no less respectable for that. Many others accept the proposition that each poem was the work of one person, but not of the same person.[332] Some people find the difference in ethos between the two poems simply too great for both to be the work of the same person.[333] Others point out that artists can change over their lifetime and that perceived inconsistencies are not proof of separate authorship.[334]

With the Enlightenment the question took on a different inflection: could one say that either poem was in itself a unity or was each just a patchwork of traditional stories?[335] The poems themselves show us the world in which archaic bardic poets worked. Phemius and Demodocus are asked to entertain the gathered company and, to the accompaniment of the lyre,[336] they sing[337] heroic verses about this or that topic, chosen either by themselves[338] or by the audience.[339] But these interludes are brief and cannot be compared with the colossal scale of either the *Iliad* or the *Odyssey*. Either poem, if recited in its entirety, would take days to complete. This has led some scholars to suppose that they were originally composed in the context of a religious festival extending over the necessary period of time.[340] But what happened next?

There is little doubt that many of the episodes concerning the Trojan War and the wanderings of Odysseus will have been treated several times over the centuries by successive bards. There might, of course, have been deviation from one performance to another. But, on Adam Parry's view (which I share), there came in the latter half of the eighth century BC an artistic genius, a monumental composer whom we may call Homer, who took these various episodes and, adding material of his own, fashioned the *Iliad* and *Odyssey* as we have them.[341] They became fixed though being dictated to a scribe at some point soon after the poet decided that they had reached their final form.[342] Some scholars doubt the dictation theory,

---

[331] Pfeiffer 1968: 230 with n. 7.
[332] Rutherford 1992: 2.   [333] M. L. West 2014: 1.
[334] Janko 1982: 82, 191; Macleod 1983: 1.   [335] Pulleyn 1997: 3.
[336] *Od.* 1.153; 8.261–2.   [337] *Od.* 1.154–5; 8.266.   [338] *Od.* 1.346–7.
[339] *Od.* 8.492.
[340] Taplin 1992: 39–41; doubted by Garvie 1994: 17–19 with n. 57.
[341] Adam Parry 1966: 205, repr. 1989: 130.
[342] This theory of dictation is not incompatible with some parts of the poem (such as Book 1) being later, relatively speaking, than others. The act of dictation will have created a single original text; but its constitutent parts were of differing degrees of antiquity.

feeling that the monumental composer(s) must have used writing in order to shape and edit the monumental composition.[343] In either case, this first text is the lost archetype from which all modern texts derive. It is (more or less) this that one is trying to reconstruct when we edit the text of Homer.[344]

Another view says that the poems did not find anything approaching fixity of form until reduced to writing by the Athenian tyrant Pisistratus or his son Hipparchus in the sixth century BC.[345] Adam Parry famously rejected this idea saying that such oral transmission over several centuries, even by skilled poets, would have resulted in a text far inferior to the one that we have.[346] That is a value judgement, but in matters such as these it is salutary to remind ourselves that we rely on our subjective judgements about such things much of the time, even when we think we are being scientific. Griffin makes the telling point that:

> It was the *Iliad* and the *Odyssey* that the Athenians of the sixth century wanted to hear; Solon, or the tyrant Pisistratus, aimed to please by meeting a demand for them, not for the numerous other epic poems that existed at the same time. It is a puzzle how this can have happened, if the two epics did not have the qualities which made them supreme—if in fact they did not really exist in definite form—until their performance at Athens finally brought them into shape.[347]

In the sharpest distinction to all of the foregoing stand those critics who find it quaintly outmoded to think that great art must be the work of a single controlling mind. Just as the faith once put in God reposes nowadays largely in committees, so we are invited to see the epics not as the masterpieces of an individual artist but as the product of numerous generations of bards each contributing their bit. We are asked to rid ourselves of anachronistic notions of the genius of individual authors.[348] The poems are rather like a snowball that starts rolling down a mountain and gets bigger as it accretes new and varied material: virgin snow, sharp twigs, pebbles, dirt, perhaps the odd shiny thing; but they cannot sensibly be called

---

[343] Garvie 1994: 17; M. L. West 2011: 10–14. If Homer himself used writing, he certainly did not avail himself of the opportunities that it offered to go back and remove inconsistencies—Pulleyn 2000: 7–8. The position is summarized by Rutherford 2013: 31–4.

[344] M. L. West 1998b.   [345] Nagy 1995: 166, 174.

[346] Adam Parry 1966, repr. 1989: 104–40. It is important to note that he did not reject the idea of the recension itself (on which, see next section on Transmission).

[347] Griffin 1995: 8.

[348] Seaford 1994: 151–2; a brief but pointed riposte to that stance is Heiden 2006. It is worth reminding oneself that, when Roland Barthes proclaimed The Death of the Author in 1967, he did not mean that there was literally no such thing as an author.

the 'work' of any one 'artist'. The idea of such collective effort has a patina of sophistication; but it does presuppose that the agency of individual artists was unrecognized until it suddenly sprang into being just in time for the works of those poets of the seventh century BC whose names we know.

An extreme—and, it might be thought, minority—version of this view is held by Nagy, who thinks of Homer as a 'multi-text' which did not crystallize into something fixed until the Hellenistic period.[349] Looking at the Ptolemaic papyri, he concludes that the degree of deviation found in them is not such as could be expected if there had been a literate transmission of a poem reduced to writing centuries earlier. In his judgement, the variations go beyond mere scribal error, pointing rather to a continuous process of active composition-in-performance continuing for centuries later than the latest date at which other scholars see the poem as having been created, whether by one poet or two.

Martin West, with whose precise views of the composition of the poems I do not concur, nevertheless sums up the controversy when he says that Nagy confuses composition with transmission.[350] Nagy would say that the distinction is meaningless in the case of Homer: it was composed as it was transmitted and this is proved by the alleged variants in the papyri. West finds the variations less striking than Nagy, and less striking than those found in written versions of other oral poems such as the *Chanson de Roland*. My view, not held in isolation, is that the variations found in the papyri do not go beyond what we might expect from centuries of written transmission. We will pursue this further in the next section.

Suggested reading: Janko 1992: 8–19; Rutherford 2013: 19–34; M. L. West 2014.

TRANSMISSION

Once the text of the epics was reduced to writing, as I think not later than 700 BC,[351] its transmission must have become subject to the same risks of scribal error and interference as any other. Like our earliest inscriptions, it will have been written in capital letters, probably with lines written from right to left alternating with those written from left to right.[352] At this period, there was no single Greek alphabet; rather, there was considerable

---

[349] Nagy 1996: 42.
[350] M. L. West 2002; Finkelberg 2000: 5 with earlier literature.
[351] Janko 1992: 37–8; Haslam 1997: 81 with n. 68.
[352] Powell 1991: 65, 120–1.

geographical variety in both the forms and usage of individual letters.[353] Considerations of dialect and geography suggest that the earliest text was probably written down in Ionia.[354]

As was mentioned in the preceding section, our sources indicate that in the sixth century BC the Athenian tyrant Pisistratus and his son Hipparchus somehow intervened in the process of textual transmission. The motive was apparently the desire to have a uniform edition for rhapsodic performers at the Panathenaic festival.[355] But we have to be clear about what was *not* done. First, as I have argued, this was not the occasion on which the texts were reduced to writing for the first time: that happened shortly after the act of monumental composition; it stretches belief to suppose that the epics could have survived in their current quality over a century or more of oral tradition.[356] Second, and consequently, the Pisistratids cannot have pieced together the *Iliad* and *Odyssey* from scattered books.[357] There must already have been complete texts of each epic in circulation. Third, they did not engage in a wholesale reworking of an earlier text to reflect Athenian ideological concerns: there are too many missed opportunities in the text.[358] Such a recension would explain the general 'veneer' (no more)[359] of Atticism in our manuscripts.[360] For this reason, it is sometimes suggested that all our manuscripts derive ultimately from this Attic recension.[361] But this is not the same as suggesting that there were no complete texts of Homer before this or that nothing got into the later tradition that did not flow through the Attic channel.

Spoken Greek differentiated three classes of e-vowels: short (ϵ), long close ($\epsilon\iota$),[362] and long open (η) with three corresponding o-vowels (o, ov, ω). The extent to which these distinctions were reflected in the local scripts of archaic Greece differs from place to place.[363] Nevertheless, Attic script used a single sign (E) for all varieties of e-vowel and a single sign (O) for all types of o-vowel.[364] Likewise it did not write doubled consonants.[365] Thus, to the extent that texts were copied out in Athens, they will not have shown these features—even though Eastern Ionic scripts did mark two

---

[353] Jeffery 1990; Colvin 2007: 18–19.   [354] Chantraine 1958: 5.

[355] Pl. *Hipparch.* 228b; cf. (mentioning no names) Lycurg., *In Leoc.* 102; Isoc. *Paneg.* 159.

[356] Adam Parry 1966: 216, repr. 1989: 139; Janko 1992: 37; Griffin 1995: 8.

[357] Despite Cic. *De orat.* 3.137.   [358] Janko 1992: 32, 133–4 (on *Il.* 13.689–91).

[359] S. R. West 1988: 38 n. 15.

[360] Janko 1992: 35 points to δέχομαι, μείζων, ἐνταῦθα, οὖν, χίλιοι, ἀφικάνω instead of Ionic δέκομαι, ἐνθαῦτα, μέζων, ὦν, χείλιοι, ἀπικάνω.

[361] Chantraine 1958: 5; S. R. West 1988: 36–40.

[362] The so-called 'spurious diphthong', since in such cases no inherited *i* is present.

[363] Jeffery 1990.   [364] Immerwahr 1990: 1–19.   [365] Ibid. 169.

kinds of long-e and two kinds of long-o from an early date[366] and also wrote double consonants.[367] It has been suggested that the existence of texts of Homer in Ionic script was a chief driver for the Euclidean reform of 403 BC when Athens moved from Attic to Ionic writing.[368] There was thus ample scope for confusion when the local texts were transcribed into Attic in the sixth century BC and when these Attic versions were transcribed into Ionic after 403 BC. It might be that fewer textual problems are to be solved by reference to this this so-called μεταχαρακτερισμός than is sometimes said;[369] but it does explain some.[370]

Whatever went on in sixth-century BC Athens, it is impossible, absent the printing press, to produce a stable text that will not succumb once more to the errors inherent in the process of copying by hand. To judge from the earliest papyri, such variation was rife.[371] As well as the expected variant readings, a number of 'plus' verses also crept in. But these interpolations are of a fairly modest kind and do not indicate that either epic was subject to re-composition and expansion in performance after 700 BC.[372] The degree of textual variation fell radically as a result of the work of Aristarchus of Samothrace (c.217–145 BC) working in the Library and Museum founded by Ptolemy I in Alexandria in 307 BC and enlarged by Ptolemy II in 283 BC.[373] He was not the first person in that institution to undertake serious work on the text: Zenodotus of Ephesus (c.330–260 BC) and Aristophanes of Byzantium (c.257–180 BC) were there before him. But there is no doubt that the papyri that postdate him show far fewer plus-verses and this was in general terms a significant act of textual stabilization.[374]

We know of the activities of these Alexandrian scholars principally from marginal notes found in medieval manuscripts which refer to them by name. Such notes are known collectively as *scholia* even though, as a group, they are very diverse, ranging from literary and aesthetic judgements to exegesis of linguistic and textual points.[375] The modern study of these sources was launched in 1788 when François Villoison published a tenth-century AD manuscript that he had discovered nine years earlier in the library of San Marco in Venice.[376] The so-called Venetus A has copious marginal annotations that clearly go back to the Alexandrian period. Other manuscripts and papyri have scholia, some of which come from

---

[366] Buck 1910: 16–17.   [367] Ibid. 165.
[368] Janko 1992: 37; Colvin 2007: 56.   [369] S. R. West 1988: 39 n. 18.
[370] Horrocks 1997: 194–5.   [371] S. R. West 1967.
[372] Finkelberg 2000: 5 with earlier literature.   [373] Pfeiffer 1968: 96–104.
[374] It is something of a mystery how Aristarchus fits into the process since the proportion of his reported readings in the text is very low. At the same time, he clearly did fix the number of verses. See Haslam 1997: 84–5.
[375] N. G. Wilson 1984; Pontani 2005.   [376] Villoison 1788; Nagy 1997: 101–2.

different sources and represent different kinds of scholarly effort ranging from glossing individual words to discussing entire lines and scenes. For the *Odyssey*, there are almost no manuscripts prior to AD 1201, except for F (tenth century AD) and G (eleventh century AD), and these have practically no scholia.[377] There is nothing comparable to the scholia found in the Venetus A or the Townleian manuscript of the *Iliad*. What there is tails off in quantity very markedly in the second half of the poem; by contrast, they are at their fullest for Book 1. The scholia are interesting not only for what they tell us about the scholarly methods of Alexandrine librarians but also because they transmit textual and literary judgements.[378] We are not bound to adopt what we find in the scholia simply because they are old; nevertheless, they do contain valuable insights and these are cited from time to time in the commentary with the symbol *Σ*.

In producing a text, then, a modern editor is faced with many different kinds of evidence. There are:

(a) papyri from antiquity, none earlier than the third century BC and all of them fragmentary;

(b) quotations in ancient writers of lines from Homer, often different from what we have in later manuscripts, either because the later manuscripts are faulty or because the ancient author was misremembering or reading a lost or faulty text;

(c) scholia (see above);

(d) medieval manuscripts, by which is meant documents recorded in codex form on parchment or vellum which contain some or all of the *Iliad* and *Odyssey* and none of which is earlier than the tenth century AD with most being several centuries later.

There are considerably fewer papyri and manuscripts of the *Odyssey* than of the *Iliad*, a reflection of their relative prestige in antiquity and the taste of those setting the ancient school curricula.

The editor of, say, Virgil has a task which editors know how to undertake. One must make a survey of all the surviving evidence of the kinds mentioned above and decide for every word which is most likely to have been what Virgil wrote. The work is demanding and difficult. But we know who Virgil was and when he wrote. It makes sense to talk of trying to reconstruct 'the original text' as he *wrote* it. The origins of Homer are lost in the eighth century BC and even the most optimistic editor would

---

[377] Pontani 2007: xi.
[378] As Richardson 1980 discusses in detail for the class of exegetical scholia to the *Iliad*.

not try to reconstruct 'what Homer sang'. That would involve, for example, never printing Book 10 in texts of the *Iliad* and, according to some scholars, omitting some of Book 23 of the *Odyssey* and all of Book 24. The best we can hope for is to reconstruct the text as it was after the last great stage of creative activity.[379] Plainly this view is premised on the belief that the poems were committed to writing shortly after their creation and that we are not dealing with a so-called 'multi-text'.

The text presented in this edition is not based on a fresh examination of papyri and manuscripts. The texts of Allen, von der Muehll, and Van Thiel report variants found in those kinds of sources.[380] Stephanie West kindly showed me the late Martin West's text and apparatus for *Odyssey* 1 in advance of its publication; I had by then already established my text and apparatus, but have changed my mind in perhaps a handful of places having seen his work. He was also able to give a much fuller account of the papyri than earlier editors. I have taken these editions and their apparatuses as a reliable indication of what is in the original sources and have printed what seems to me to be the best reading having regard to questions of etymology, dialect, morphology, syntax, and so forth. The reason for these decisions is discussed in the commentary where appropriate; but the commentary has not been burdened with an explanation of every textual choice. With respect to questions of spelling and accentuation, I have tended to follow the conventions adopted by Martin West in the introduction to his edition of the *Iliad*.[381] No attempt has been made to attribute readings to this or that named ancient or medieval source. Readers of an edition such as this chiefly need to know what the variants are and whether they come from an ancient or medieval source. Those who wish to pursue individual readings may look at the larger editions already mentioned. I have adopted here the kind of apparatus used by Colin Macleod in his edition of *Iliad* 24 and since then by many other contributors to the Cambridge University Press 'Green and Yellow' series. The apparatus states the reading in the text and records deviations. A variant from a medieval manuscript is marked **a**, a variant from a second medieval manuscript is marked **b**, and so on. Anything from a papyrus is marked **p**; where more than one papyrus variant exists, **p2** is used and so on. Readings from ancient authors including scholiasts (collectively testimonia) are marked **T**. Emendations by modern scholars are indicated by giving the name of the proposer. **MSS** means that all the medieval manuscripts agree on a reading; **MSS*** means that most of the medieval manuscripts agree on

---

[379] M. L. West 1998b: 95.   [380] Allen 1917–19; Muehll 1962; van Thiel 1991.
[381] M. L. West 1998a: xvi–xxxvii.

a reading but variants exist and are cited in the apparatus. 'ath.' in the apparatus means 'athetized'—this refers to a habit of Hellenistic scholars of marking by a horizontal line in their text lines which they felt were not genuine but which they nevertheless forbore to delete altogether. We know, however, from the expression οὐ γράφει in the scholia that there were lines that Aristarchus, for example, 'does not write' in his text. These silent deletions might affect the entire later tradition so that our only knowledge of the deleted line comes from the chance testimony of another scholiast.

Space forbids a lengthy discussion of the techniques to be used and principles followed in editing a text. But it is important to say in this context that, just because a reading is old, it need not be authentic. The papyri are not automatically to be preferred to the manuscripts, even if the former are often a millennium or more earlier. It is quite conceivable that a later manuscript relies on a text now lost that is nevertheless less corrupt than that represented in a papyrus.

Suggested reading: Janko 1992: 20–38; Haslam 1997; M. L. West 1998b.

METRE

Metre (from Gk. μέτρον, 'measure') is a way of imposing a rhythmical pattern on words. In English poetry, the organizing principle within the line is the number of syllables and the pattern of stresses. In some poetry, but by no means all, rhyme may also be a feature. Thus, for example, here is a four-line stanza with a rhyme scheme of ABAB, a syllable count of 8686, and stress on every second syllable (iambic):

> Intó my heárt an aír that kílls
> From yón far coúntry blóws:
> What áre those blúe remémbered hílls,
> What spíres, what fárms are thóse?

A. E. Housman, *A Shropshire Lad*, XL

In Greek poetry, by contrast, there is no rhyme and the organizing principle is not stress but the patterning of heavy and light syllables (— and ⏑ respectively). The epic was composed in dactylic hexameters, a line of six feet (or *metra*). The first five may be dactyls (— ⏑⏑) or spondees (— —), although a spondee in the fifth foot is unusual. The last foot must be a spondee or a trochee (— ⏑). The full scheme is thus as follows:

$$\begin{array}{cccccc} 1 & 2 & 3 & 4 & 5 & 6 \end{array}$$
$$-\smile\smile\,|-\smile\smile\,|-\smile\smile\,|-\smile\smile\,|-\smile\smile\,|-\times^{382}$$

The shortest possible syllable is a single vowel (V). The sequence VV (unless it is a diphthong)[383] is analysed as two syllables of the shape V-V. Where consonants (C) are involved, the sequence VCV is treated as V-CV and VCCV is generally treated as VC-CV (but see below on plosive and liquid). Any syllable ending in V is an open syllable; any syllable ending in C is closed.

A syllable is light for metrical purposes if it is open and contains a vowel that is phonetically short. An open syllable that contains a phonetically long vowel or a diphthong is *prima facie* heavy (but see on 'correption' below). A closed syllable is always heavy, even if it contains a phonetically short vowel.

For the purposes of syllabification, words are treated as a continuous stream. Thus, if a word ends in a short vowel, but the following word begins with two plosives,[384] the syllable will be treated as closed and so metrically heavy: thus ἐπὶ χθονί (*Od.* 1.196) is treated as ἐ–πιχ–θο–νι. Similarly a short vowel followed by a single plosive at the end of a word becomes part of a heavy syllable if the following word begins with another plosive, e.g. νῆσος δενδρήεσσα (*Od.* 1.51) is treated as νη–σōσ–δεν–δρη–εσ–σα.

Although it is conventional to talk of long and short syllables in metre, it is preferable to think in terms of heavy and light. This is because it is essential to distinguish clearly between vocalic length and syllabic weight. In the word ἐσ–τί for example, the first syllable is heavy because it is closed; but the vowel is phonetically short, pronounced as [ɛ] like the first vowel in English *editor* not [ɛ:] as in *heir*. Had the vowel itself been long, the word would eventually have come to be written as *ἤστί. This is the mischief of the old nostrum that 'a vowel is long if followed by two consonants' and the related idea of a vowel being 'long by position.' A short vowel is always short; it does not become long because of its position.

---

[382] The symbol × is known as *anceps* and represents a space in the metre that may be occupied by a heavy or a light element.

[383] A diphthong would count simply as V.

[384] A plosive is a consonantal sound that completely obstructs the egressive air stream, e.g. [p], [b], [t], [d], [g]. It is not correct to say that a short vowel is always part of a metrically heavy syllable if it is followed by just any two *consonants*. A sound such as [l] or [r] might loosely be classified as a consonant, but it does not completely obstruct the air stream. The combination [pr] or [tr] in Greek is sometimes treated as though it were two plosives and sometimes not. See below on 'Plosive and Liquid (or Nasal)'.

The operation of all these principles might be seen by the following analysis of *Od.* 1.11 where vocalic length and syllabic length are indicated on separate lines:

ἔνθ' ἄλλοι μὲν πάντες, ὅσοι φύγον αἰπὺν ὄλεθρον

Syllabic division	εν-θαλ-λοι-μεν-παν-τε-σο-σοι-φυ-γο-ναι-πυ-νο-λεθ-ρον
Syllabic weight	— — — — — ◡ ◡ — ◡ ◡ — ◡ ◡ — —[385]
Vocalic length	◡ ◡ — ◡ ◡ ◡ ◡ — ◡ ◡ — ◡ ◡ ◡ ◡

Digamma

It will not be possible to scan some lines correctly unless one bears in mind the digamma. This refers to a consonant [w] which existed in Proto-Indo-European. The decipherment of Linear B shows that the sound also survived in Mycenaean. Some Greek dialects preserved the sound well into the classical period and it is attested in inscriptions where it is written with the graph ϝ (which looks like two capital letters Γ one on top of the other, whence the name digamma). The Ionian vernacular of the epic bards started to lose the sound at a time which cannot be given an absolute date with any precision.[386] By this time, there was already a good number of formulae that would only scan properly if this sound were present. These were preserved in the artificial language of the epics even though digamma was no longer used in everyday speech. The bards continued to create new formulae, however, and some of these required inherited [w] to be ignored for the line to be metrical. The result was that the same word might sometimes be treated as beginning with digamma and sometimes not.[387] There are approximately 350 cases where a concealed digamma operates to make the preceding short vowel heavy (e.g. εἶπες ϝέπος, *Il.* 1.108).[388] One cannot tell where to expect an inherited digamma without the use of comparative historical grammars and

---

[385] The last syllable is heavy because closed. In some metres, one has to look to the word that begins the following line (*synapheia*) to decide the matter. This does not apply to dactylic hexameters (M. L. West 1997b: 221).

[386] Janko 1982: 87–91.

[387] οἶνος must originally have been ϝοῖνος, as its Lat. cognate *vinum* shows. The digamma is treated as present in the formula μελιηδέα οἶνον (*Od.* 14.78) but not in μελιηδέος οἶνου (*Od.* 3.46).

[388] Chantraine 1958: 117.

dictionaries.[389] It is from time to time proposed that life would be simpler if texts were printed that showed digamma when present. Whilst this would favour simplicity, it would not necessarily make for accuracy since there are numerous cases where the presence of digamma is controversial and an alternative reading is available that assumes no digamma. Some such instances are discussed in the commentary.[390]

Digraphs

The letters ζ, ξ, ψ are digraphs—they indicate not one but two sounds: respectively σδ, κσ, πσ. This means that a preceding syllable will always be treated as closed. If it contains a short vowel, it will never the less be metrically heavy: e.g. χαῖρε̄, ξεῖνε (*Od.* 1.123). The letters θ, φ, and χ are not treated in the same way because each represents only a single sound—the aspirated variants of τ, π, and κ respectively.

Plosive and Liquid (or Nasal)

Based on what has been said already, we should expect a sequence such as φρ or βρ to be treated as closing a preceding syllable and making it metrically heavy if it contained a short vowel. This is sometimes the case: e.g. ἀγαθᾰ̈ φρονέων (*Od.* 1.43), sometimes not e.g. ἐστὶ βροτῶν (*Od.* 1.66). The circumstances in which the preceding syllable may be treated as released[391] rather than closed are confined to situations where a plosive is followed by a so-called liquid (λ, ρ) or nasal (μ, ν). The term liquid was coined in antiquity, perhaps to describe precisely this ambivalent behaviour.[392] A sequence containing a voiced plosive (β, δ, γ) or a nasal is more likely to be treated as closing the previous syllable than releasing it. The release is hardly ever found with nasals before the fifth century and never at any period in the case of γμ, γν, δμ, δν. Homer never treats βλ or γλ as syllable releasing.[393]

Lengthening by Continuant (or Nasal)

A continuant is a sound which partially occludes the air stream and so includes those written as λ, ρ, σ. These, together with the nasals μ and ν,

---

[389] Such as Chantraine 1958; Chantraine et al. 1999.
[390] e.g. on *Od.* 1.19, 110.
[391] In technical terminology, release is the opposite of closure: that which does not close a syllable is said to release it.
[392] W. S. Allen 1987: 39–40.   [393] M. L. West 1982a: 16–17.

sometimes have the unexpected effect of closing the preceding syllable so that, if it contains a short vowel, it is treated as metrically heavy: e.g. ἐνὶ μεγάροισιν (*Od.* 1.27) is treated as though it were ἐνὶ μμεγάροισιν. This phenomenon appears to overlap, at least partly, with the uncertainty over the weight of liquids discussed above.

Elision

A final vowel is regularly struck out before a vowel or diphthong at the start of the following word: e.g. δ᾽ ὅ γ᾽ ἐν (*Od.* 1.4). In the comparatively rare cases where this does not happen, we have apparent or actual hiatus (see below).

Correption

A phonetically long vowel or a diphthong may be treated as metrically light when followed by a short vowel: e.g. νήπιοι, οἵ (*Od.* 1.8). There are about 160 places where a concealed digamma prevents correption of a long vowel or diphthong: e.g. δὴ ἔτος (*Od.* 1.16).[394]

Synizesis

Sometimes two vowels, or a vowel and a diphthong, are slurred together and treated as one syllable: e.g. δατέοντο (*Od.* 1.112).

Hiatus

It is possible, but very unusual, for two vowel sounds to stand next to each other without elision, correption, or synizesis occurring. There are more than 2,300 examples of a digamma preventing the elision of a short vowel in what without the digamma would look on the page like hiatus (e.g. ἄλγεα ϝὸν, *Od.* 1.4).[395]

Caesura

There are rhythmically mandated pauses (*caesurae*) within the epic hexameter. They occur only at the end of a word within a foot. The caesura must have been for the bards far more significant than the boundaries between feet. Many formulae are designed to run from the start of the line to the

---

[394] Written ϝέτος in *SIG* 9.2 (sixth century BC); cf. Lat. *vetus*.
[395] Statistics are in Chantraine 1958: 117–18.

caesura or from the caesura to the end.[396] In the scheme below, divisions between feet are marked with | and caesurae with //. The latter may occur in one of three positions, as follows.

(i) After the first heavy element of the third foot (penthemimeral or 'masculine' caesura):

πλάγχθη, ἐ|πεὶ Τροί|ης // ἱε|ρὸν πτολί|εθρον ἔ |περσε (*Od.* 1.2).

(ii) After the first light element in a dactylic third foot (trochaic or 'feminine' caesura):

ἄνδρα μοι | ἔννεπε, | Μοῦσα, // πο|λύτροπον, | ὃς μάλα | πολλά (*Od.* 1.1).

(iii) After the first heavy element of the fourth foot (hephthemimeral caesura):

ἀρνύμεν|ος ἥν | τε ψυ|χὴν // καὶ | νόστον ἑ|ταίρων (*Od.* 1.5)[397]

Over 98 per cent of lines fall into one of types (i) or (ii), with (ii) being commoner than (i) by a ratio of 4:3.[398] Type (iii) is much rarer: its frequency in the *Odyssey* is 9× in every thousand lines.[399]

A caesura may coincide with an elision:

ὣς εἰ|πὼν ἡ|γεῖθ', // ἦ | δ' ἕσπετο | Παλλὰς Ἀ|θήνη (*Od.* 1.125).

If there is more than one word-end where the caesura might fall, its actual position is best determined by sense. In the following line, a hepthemimeral caesura might theoretically be placed after ἐνί; but it would be absurd for the singer to pause between a preposition and its noun, so that it makes much better sense to mark the caesura after ἐσθλόν:

ὀσσόμε|νος πατέρ' | ἐσθλὸν // ἐ|νὶ φρεσίν, | εἴ ποθεν | ἐλθὼν (*Od.* 1.115).

Bucolic Diaeresis

Where the end of a dactylic fourth foot coincides with the end of a word, the phenomenon is known as the bucolic diaeresis (or caesura). This is marked below with a superscript [B]:[400]

ἄνδρα μοι | ἔννεπε, | Μοῦσα, // πο|λύτροπον, |[B] ὃς μάλα | πολλά (*Od.* 1.1)

---

[396] M. L. West 1982b: 293.

[397] A caesura cannot stand before an enclitic such as τε, μιν, ποτε, etc. because enclitics are thought of as following immediately upon the preceding world as a single utterance. Thus, in this line, although there is a word break after τε, the caesura cannot fall there.

[398] M. L. West 1997b: 222–3.   [399] M. L. West 1982a: 36.

[400] M. L. West 1982b: 292.

This break is not an alternative to one of the three types of caesurae mentioned above. Whereas the diaeresis appears at the end of a foot, the caesura must fall within a foot. As we saw above above, *Od.* 1.1 has a trochaic caesura in the third foot. The bucolic diaeresis is simply a further prosodic feature, exhibited by some 47 per cent of lines in Homer.[401] It is the consequence of there being a number of words or word-groups of the shape ⏑ — ⏑ ⏑ or ⏖ —⏑⏑ which sit neatly after a third-foot caesura and have as their necessary by-product a word-end at the end of the fourth foot.[402] Ancient metricians varied in their evaluation of the merits of such breaks; such reactions must have been subjective even then.

Suggested reading: M. L. West 1982a: 35–9; 1997b.

DIALECT AND GRAMMAR

Before the advent of powerful centralizing influences such as radio and television, people's spoken language tended to vary considerably according to region. Even in the modern world, where the 'received pronunciation' of BBC English has exercised a strong homogenizing influence in the UK, regional differences in phonetics, morphology, syntax, and lexicon are still widespread. While a speaker of Southern English realizes 'grass' and 'last' as /grɑːs/ and /lɑːst/, they are realized in the North as /græs/ and /læst/. Where a Londoner asks 'How are you?' a person in Somerset might ask 'Ow be ye?', the differences now going beyond the phonetic level. Speakers of English in southern Pennsylvania say 'bucket' whereas those in the north say 'pail'. Such phenomena can be indicated on a map by lines ('isoglosses') demarcating the places where they are found and part of the business of dialectology is to determine how far these features or bundles of features form coherent dialectal groups.

So it was in Greece, but the task of the dialectologist is made more difficult by the fact that there are no living Greeks left to inform us about ancient pronunciation and we are left to make deductions from written records from various different places. The problem becomes even more difficult when one tries to take account of change over time. Inscriptions show us, for example, that Laconians (among others)[403] used a conditional modal particle κᾱ (cf. Attic ἄν).[404] Laconian is part of a larger dialect grouping called Doric, which is perhaps most familiar to us from the choral

---

[401] M. L. West 1982a: 154. [402] M. L. West 1982b: 294.
[403] Thumb 1932: 53. [404] Solmsen 1905: 50–1; Buck 1910: 226; Colvin 2016.

lyric of Alcman, Pindar, and Bacchylides. And yet in none of these lyric poets do we find κᾱ but always κε (doubtless under the influence of epic).[405] This is just one example of many ways in which the literary language was fashioned as a supra-regional entity, no longer able to be tied to the speech habits of one place and preserving prestigious elements from epic.

The same is true of the language of the epics, only to a far greater degree. Karl Meister called it a *Kunstsprache*[406]—an artificial literary amalgam of items from different times and places that represents the real speech of no one group. For example, the second-declension genitive in −οιο is old, being plainly attested in the Mycenaean tablets. In time, it was replaced by the newer form in −ου. Both are found in Homer. This is unexpected since, when such changes happen, they apply uniformly unless some other factor is at work to prevent this. In the case of epic, various formulae had been formed when the ending −οιο was current; they could not be remade with −ου since that would be unmetrical. Thus we find an ancient morpheme preserved in the poetic language which has nevertheless continued to make formulae and so has adopted the newer −ου as well.

The epic dialect is also artificial in the narrower sense that it contains words that cannot be accounted for by the usual processes of historical change, are not attested in any dialect, and must have been pure invention by the bards. Such creations are motivated by the need to adapt words from the spoken language to the metre of the epic. Perhaps the best-known example of this is the phenomenon of διέκτασις ('stretching'), e.g. φόως (*Od.* 5.2) beside φάος (*Od.* 3.335). In the spoken language, original φάος had contracted to φῶς (cf. the mature Ionic of Hdt. 2.62.9). But this new form, whilst by no means impossible to fit into a hexameter, was formulaically less convenient. So the bards arbitrarily invented φόως by inserting before the long vowel that resulted from contraction a short vowel of the same colour.[407] By a different method they created εὐρέα πόντον (*Od.* 24.118); the expected accusative of this adjective is εὐρύν (*Od.* 1.67).[408] Athematic ἡνιοχῆα, −ῆες (*Il.* 5.505; 8.312, etc.) are surprising beside the expected thematic ἡνίοχος (*Il.* 11.280).[409] Considerable licence is apparent in the lengthening of vowels (e.g. δῡναμένοιο, *Od.* 1.276 n.).[410] There is also a tendency for words to be refashioned by bards to fit new contexts: for example, the verb εἴβω is a decapitated form of λείβω ('pour', 'let flow'), created due to metrical necessity when older formulae were adapted

---

[405] Palmer 1980: 124.   [406] Meister 1921.

[407] Adam Parry 1971: 350–1.

[408] Probably a creation by analogy with εὐρέϊ πόντῳ: Chantraine 1953: 97.

[409] Ibid. 232–3.

[410] The classic study is Wyatt 1969; cf. Chantraine 1953: 94–112.

to new contexts.[411] ὀκρυόεις ('chilling') is a doublet of κρύοεις and probably arose by reanalysis of a sequence that was once ἐπιδημίοο κρυόεντος (*Il.* 9.64). When ἐπιδημίοο became ἐπιδημίου, ὀκρυόεντος was adopted to restore the metre.[412]

It seems indisputable that the bulk of the epics was formed in Ionic, which suggests that the poems took their final shape in those parts of Asia Minor that had been colonized by Ionian Greeks in the tenth century BC. We also find archaic forms from the Bronze Age speech of the Peloponnese (whose historical representatives are sometimes called Achaean) such as ἦμαρ ('day'; Ionic ἡμέρη will not scan), αἶσα ('fate', 'portion'), δῶμα ('house'), πτόλις ('city'). In addition, we find Aeolic forms such as πίσυρες ('four') and ποτί (Ionic πρός). These Aeolicisms might be explained by thinking of the geography of coastal Asia Minor. A town such as Smyrna is at the very junction of the Ionic and Aeolic dialect communities. It is not hard to imagine a fundamentally Ionic (East Greek) tradition acquiring Aeolic influences in this way, and Smyrna was reputedly one of the birthplaces of Homer in antiquity.[413] That said, others have thought in terms of the epic having originally been composed in Aeolic, followed by a gap in time and then a wholesale re-working into Ionic by bards speaking that dialect and retaining Aeolic forms only where absolutely necessary to preserve old established formulae.[414] The topic remains highly controversial.[415]

We can thus see that questions of dialect have a bearing on questions of how and where the poems came into being. But the more immediate problem for most students of Homer is that the language looks unfamiliar and extremely irregular compared with the Attic of classical Athens that is learned first by most people who study any Greek at all. Apart from the unfamiliar vocabulary (see *Glossary* at the end of this book), there are many inflected forms of nouns and verbs that take some getting used to.

What follows is a summary of the chief features that the reader will encounter. Fuller accounts may be had from the suggested reading at the end of this section.

Phonology

Vowels

Epic has η where Attic has the so-called 'pure' long alpha, i.e. after the vowels ι and ε or the resonant ρ: ἀγγελίην (*Od.* 1.408), γενέην (*Od.* 1.222), ἀγορήν (*Od.* 1.90). We sometimes find ο replaced by a long vowel that is

---

[411] Haslam 1976: 201–7.   [412] Leumann 1950: 49–50.
[413] B. Jones 2012.   [414] Janko 1982: 89–93; Janko 2012.
[415] Horrocks 1997: 214–17.

written as ου:[416] οὔνομα (*Od.* 6.194) beside ὄνομα (*Od.* 9.16), πουλύς (*Od.* 4.709) beside πολύς (*Od.* 4.566). Whereas Attic writes φιλεῖ and χρυσῇ, epic often (but by no means always) leaves the vowels uncontracted: φιλέει (*Od.* 8.309 (pres.)) vs. φίλει (*Od.* 10.14 (impf.)), χρυσέη (*Od.* 7.90) vs. χρυσῆς (*Od.* 4.14). In a similar way, the genitive ending –οιο is found beside a newer form –ου suggesting an unattested intermediate form in *–οο that has undergone contraction.[417]

Consonants

In addition to forms like πόλεμος (*Od.* 1.12) and πόλις (*Od.* 1.170) familiar from Attic, epic has πτόλεμος (*Od.* 8.183) and πτόλις (*Od.* 2.383). These are convenient for metrical purposes since a preceding short vowel will scan as a heavy syllable, but unlike φόως they are not purely an invention of the bards. Such forms are attested in Linear B, Thessalian, and Arcado-Cypriot. Many forms exhibit a single or double consonant depending on metrical convenience: Ὀδυσ(σ)εύς (*Od.* 1.57 vs. 2.246), Ἀχιλ(λ)εύς (*Od.* 3.106 vs. 11.478), ὅ(π)ως (*Od.* 1.57 vs. 270), φράσσεται (*Od.* 1.205) vs. ἐπεφράσατο (*Od.* 8.94). Words such as θράσος (*Il.* 14.416), κρατερός (*Od.* 4.11), and κραδίη (*Od.* 1.353) alternate with θάρσος (*Od.* 1.321), καρτερός (*Od.* 4.242), and καρδίη (*Il.* 2.452). The inherited Proto-Indo-European *w is known to have survived into historical times since it is found in inscriptions written as ϝ (digamma). In the epic, [w] is sometimes treated as though it is present and sometimes ignored. This reflects the time depth over which the bardic tradition evolved—the dialect of the Ionian bards of the eighth century had already lost this sound, but they retained it where it was metrically necessary or useful whilst forming other expressions that ignored it. For more on this, see the section on Metre, pp. 47–8.

The 'Article'

The forms ὁ, ἡ, τό, which in Attic are used as a definite article, tend in epic to be simply demonstrative pronouns ('this one', 'that one'). This is histor-ically what they were in Proto-Indo-European. But we can nevertheless see instances where the pronoun is used in such close proximity to a

---

[416] This might have arisen in words where o was lengthened in Ionic to compensate for the loss of digamma after a resonant (e.g. μοῦνος < μόνϝος). Wyatt (1969: 71) proposes a different origin: ἀνώνυμος was taken as built on *ὤνομα, later Ionicized as οὔνομα.

[417] The existence of such a stage is certain, as we can see from phrases such as ἀνεψιοῦ κταμένοιο (*Il.* 15.554) which will not scan as it stands in the text. The expression must have been formed at a stage when the noun was *ἀνεψίοο. It is striking that the participle has been retained in the older form so that this one expression contains examples of the same morpheme at two different stages of its development.

noun—perhaps originally appositionally—that it is indistinguishable from the definite article.[418]

Nouns

First declension

Masculine nouns may have gen. sg. in $-\bar{a}o$ or $-\epsilon\omega$, rarely $-\omega$.

Feminine nouns may have gen. pl. in $-a\omega\nu$ or $-\epsilon\omega\nu$ and dat. pl. in $-\eta s$ or $-\eta\sigma\iota(\nu)$.

Second declension

Any noun may have gen. sg. in $-o\iota o$ as well as $-o\nu$.
Gen. or dat. dual is in $-o\iota\ddot{\iota}\nu$ not $-o\iota\nu$.
Dat. pl. often ends in $-o\iota\sigma\iota(\nu)$ as well as $-o\iota s$.

Third declension

Gen. of s-stems such as $\xi\acute{\iota}\phi os$ are uncontracted: $\xi\acute{\iota}\phi\epsilon os < {}^{*}\xi\acute{\iota}\phi\epsilon\sigma os$ (Attic $\xi\acute{\iota}\phi o\nu s$).

Dat. pl. may end in $-\sigma\iota(\nu)$, $-\sigma\sigma\iota(\nu)$, $-\epsilon\sigma\iota(\nu)$, $-\epsilon\sigma\sigma\iota(\nu)$.

The ι-stems behave differently from Attic: gen. sg. $\mu\acute{a}\nu\tau\iota os$, dat. sg. $\mu\acute{a}\nu\tau\iota$, $\mu a\nu\tau\epsilon\ddot{\iota}$; nom. pl. $\mu\acute{a}\nu\tau\iota\epsilon s$, gen. pl. $\mu a\nu\tau\acute{\iota}\omega\nu$.

In classical Attic a sequence ηo or ηa undergoes a treatment whereby the vowels swap length (quantitative metathesis) and appear instead as $\epsilon\omega$ and $\epsilon\bar{a}$: thus $\pi\acute{o}\lambda\epsilon\omega s$ instead of earlier $\pi\acute{o}\lambda\eta os$, $\beta a\sigma\iota\lambda\acute{\epsilon}\bar{a}$ instead of $\beta a\sigma\iota\lambda\tilde{\eta}a$. In Homer the older forms are found.

Adjectives

Old comparatives in $-\iota\omega\nu$ and superlatives in $-\iota\sigma\tau os$ are much commoner than in classical Attic, where the newer forms in $-\tau\epsilon\rho os$ and $-\tau a\tau os$ had taken hold.

Adjectives in $-\nu s$ have their feminine in $-\epsilon\eta$ or $-\epsilon a$ as well as in $-\epsilon\hat{\iota}a$.

Personal Pronouns

Some personal pronouns are found in some cases with the accent (tonic) and in others without it (enclitic). Forms that exhibit this behaviour are marked with an asterisk (*) below.

---

[418] Chantraine 1953: 164.

Singular

	1st person	2nd person	3rd person
nom.	ἐγώ(ν)	σύ, τύνη	ὁ, ὅδε, οὗτος, ἐκεῖνος
acc.	ἐμέ, με	σέ, σε	ἕ*, ἑέ, αὐτόν, μιν
gen.	ἐμεῖο, ἐμέο, ἐμεῦ, ἐμέθεν, μευ	σεῖο, σέο, σεῦ*, σέθεν, σεο, τεοῖο	εἷο, ἕο*, εὗ*, ἕθεν*
dat.	ἐμοί, μοι	σοί*, τοι, τεΐν	ἑοῖ, οἷ*

Dual

	1st person	2nd person	3rd person
nom./acc.	νώ, νῶϊ, νῶϊν	σφώ, σφῶϊ	σφωε
gen./dat.	νῶϊν	σφῶϊν, σφωϊν	σφωϊν

Plural

	1st person	2nd person	3rd person
nom.	ἡμεῖς, ἄμμες	ὑμεῖς, ὕμμες	οἱ, οἵδε, οὗτοι, ἐκεῖνοι
acc.	ἡμέας, ἤμεας, ἦμας, ἄμμε	ὑμέας, ὕμμε	σφέας*, σφε, σφας
gen.	ἡμέων, ἡμείων	ὑμέων, ὑμείων	σφείων, σφῶν, σφεων
dat.	ἡμῖν, ἥμιν, ἧμιν, ἄμμι(ν)	ὑμῖν, ὕμμιν, ὕμμι(ν)	σφίσι(ν)*, σφι(ν)

Possessive Adjectives

The following differ from the usual forms in Attic:

2 sg. τέος
3 sg. ἑός, ὅς
1 pl. ἁμός
2 pl. ὑμός
3 pl. σφός

Indefinite Pronoun τις

This is inflected mostly as in Attic. The following exceptions are worthy of note:

gen. sg. τέο*, τευ*
dat. sg. τεῳ, τῳ
gen. pl. τέων

The interrogative form τίς differs in having the tonic accent where the indefinite is enclitic.

Suffixes

The following may be added to nouns:

–δε, –ζε, –σε 'towards': added to the accusative, e.g. οἶκόνδε ('homewards');

–θε(ν) 'from': οἴκοθεν ('from home');

–θι 'at': οἴκοθι ('at home');

–φι(ν) 'with' or 'by' (instrumental) or 'at' (locative) or sometimes 'from': ἶφι ('by force'), θύρηφι ('at the door'), ποντόφι ('from the sea').

Verbs

The augment is often omitted, e.g. πλάγχθη (*Od.* 1.2 n.).

Reduplication is found in non-present tenses other than the perfect, e.g. ἔτετμε (*Od.* 1.218), πέφραδε (*Od.* 1.273).

Infinitives (in addition to forms familiar from Attic) may end in –μεναι, –μεν, –ναι.

The endings –αται and –ατο are found in the 3 pl. as well as –νται and –ντο.

Many endings are uncontracted: –σαο for –σω (aor. med.); –εαι, –ηαι for –ῃ, –εο for –ου.

Tmesis

In classical Attic, we are familiar with compound verbs such as κατ–εσθίω ('to eat up'; e.g. Eur. *Cyc.* 341). Such forms are also found in Homer. But it is also very common to find the first element (the 'preverb') separated from the verb by intervening words and sometimes not even in the same line (e.g. κατὰ βοῦς . . . | ἤσθιον; *Od.* 1.8–9). Grammarians refer to this as *tmesis* ('cutting'); but that is misleading in that it suggests that the epic bards severed an existing compound. It seems rather that tmesis was the original state of affairs and that the joining of preverb to verb came later. Tmesis is found in Vedic and Hittite texts of high antiquity but is absent from the Mycenaean texts in Linear B, dated to around 1200 BC, which means that the coalescence had taken place by then within Greek. Its presence in Homer must therefore represent the preservation of a highly archaic phenomenon, which in turn points up the antiquity of the linguistic tradition inherited by Homer.[419]

Short-vowel subjunctives

In Attic, there is a distinction between indicative forms with a short vowel and subjunctive forms with a long one: λύει vs. λύῃ, λύεται vs. λύηται, λύομεν vs. λύωμεν, λύονται vs. λύωνται. This highly regular state of affairs is the result of some remodelling of the paradigm. If we look at an old athematic form such as εἶμι ('I shall go'), the 1 pl. pr. ind. act. is ἴμεν ('we go'). We can see that the ending –μεν is added to directly to the root with no thematic vowel. The inherited Proto-Indo-European subjunctive marker was ᵉ/ₒ. So the original subjunctive was ἴομεν (e.g. *Il.* 2.526). Homer preserves a good many such athematic short-vowel subjunctives besides the newer forms with a long vowel (e.g. ἅλεται, *Il.* 11.192 vs. ἅληται, *Il.* 21.536). The long vowel arose originally in the thematic forms, which have a stem vowel ᵉ/ₒ (i.e. identical to the subjunctive marker) between root and ending. This coalesces with the subjunctive marker to form a long vowel: thus *bheugh* + *o* (thematic) + *o* (subjunctive) + *men* > φεύγωμεν (*Il.* 9.27). The ending could then be reanalysed as –ωμεν in all cases and applied to athematic forms to give, e.g. παύσωμεν (*Il.* 7.29).

Irregular verbs

Even in classical Greek, it is hard to speak of irregular verbs since this implies that there are others that are perfectly regular. Even λύω is not quite that, if one recalls that the root vowel is not stable but changes its length in some parts of the paradigm. Nevertheless, the parts of εἰμί ('I am') and εἶμι ('I shall go') can cause difficulty in Homeric Greek because of their irregularities and so are set out in some detail below. n/a means 'not attested'.

εἰμί ('I am')

Present

	Indicative	Subjunctive	Optative	Imperative
1 sg.	εἰμί	ἔω	εἴην	none
2 sg.	εἶς, ἐσσί	n/a	εἴης, ἔοις	n/a
3 sg.	ἐστί	ἔῃ	εἴη, ἔοι	ἔστω

---

[419] Hajnal 2004; Haug 2012.

	Indicative	Subjunctive	Optative	Imperative
2 du.	ἐστόν	n/a	n/a	n/a
3 du.	n/a	n/a	n/a	ἔστων
1 pl.	εἰμέν	n/a	εἶμεν	none
2 pl.	ἐστέ	n/a	εἶτε	ἔστε
3 pl.	εἰσί, ἔασι	ἔωσι, ὦσι	εἶεν	ἔστων

Present participle: ἐών, ἐοῦσα, ἐόν
Present infinitive: ἔμμεναι, ἔμεν, εἶναι

Imperfect indicative

	Singular	Dual	Plural
1st	ἦα, ἔα, ἔην	n/a	ἦμεν
2nd	ἦσθα, ἔησθα	n/a	ἦτε
3rd	ἦν, ἦεν, ἔην, ἤην	ἤστην	ἦσαν, ἔσαν

Future indicative

	Singular	Dual	Plural
1st	ἔσ(σ)ομαι	n/a	ἐσόμεσθα, ἐσσόμεθα
2nd	ἐσ(σ)εαι, ἔσῃ	ἔσεσθον	ἔσεσθε
3rd	ἐσσεῖται, ἔσ(σ)εται, ἔσται	ἔσεσθον	ἔσ(σ)ονται

Future participle: ἐσ(σ)όμενος, −η, −ον
Future infinitive: ἔσ(σ)εσθαι

εἶμι ('I shall go')

Present

	Indicative	Subjunctive	Optative	Imperative
1 sg.	εἶμι	ἴω	n/a	none
2 sg.	εἶσθα	ἴῃς, ἴῃσθα	n/a	ἴθι
3 sg.	εἶσι	ἴῃ, ἴῃσι	ἰείη, ἴοι	ἴτω
2 du.	n/a	n/a	n/a	n/a
3 du.	n/a	n/a	n/a	n/a
1 pl.	ἴμεν	ἴομεν	n/a	none
2 pl.	n/a	n/a	n/a	ἴτε
3 pl.	ἴασι	ἴωσι	n/a	ἰόντων

Imperfect

	Singular	Dual	Plural
1st	ἤϊα	n/a	ἤομεν
2nd	ἤεισθα	n/a	ἦτε
3rd	ἤει, ἤϊε, ἦε, ἴε	ἴτην	ἴσαν, ἤϊσαν, ἤϊον

Suggested reading: Monro 1891; Chantraine 1953; 1958; Colvin 2007: 49–53, 197–205; Wachter 2015.

ODYSSEY

BOOK 1

Text and Apparatus

ἄνδρά μοι ἔννεπε, Μοῦσα, πολύτροπον, ὃς μάλα πολλὰ
πλάγχθη, ἐπεὶ Τροίης ἱερὸν πτολίεθρον ἔπερσεν·
πολλῶν δ' ἀνθρώπων ἴδεν ἄστεα καὶ νόον ἔγνω,
πολλὰ δ' ὅ γ' ἐν πόντῳ πάθεν ἄλγεα ὃν κατὰ θυμόν,
ἀρνύμενος ἥν τε ψυχὴν καὶ νόστον ἑταίρων.   5
ἀλλ' οὐδ' ὣς ἑτάρους ἐρρύσατο, ἱέμενός περ·
αὐτῶν γὰρ σφετέρῃσιν ἀτασθαλίῃσιν ὄλοντο,
νήπιοι, οἳ κατὰ βοῦς Ὑπερίονος Ἠελίοιο
ἤσθιον· αὐτὰρ ὃ τοῖσιν ἀφείλετο νόστιμον ἦμαρ.
τῶν ἁμόθεν γε, θεὰ θύγατερ Διός, εἰπὲ καὶ ἡμῖν.   10
ἔνθ' ἄλλοι μὲν πάντες, ὅσοι φύγον αἰπὺν ὄλεθρον,
οἴκοι ἔσαν, πόλεμόν τε πεφευγότες ἠδὲ θάλασσαν·
τὸν δ' οἶον, νόστου κεχρήμενον ἠδὲ γυναικός,
νύμφη πότνι' ἔρυκε Καλυψὼ δῖα θεάων,
ἐν σπέεσι γλαφυροῖσι, λιλαιομένη πόσιν εἶναι.   15
ἀλλ' ὅτε δὴ ἔτος ἦλθε περιπλομένων ἐνιαυτῶν,
τῷ οἱ ἐπεκλώσαντο θεοὶ οἶκόνδε νέεσθαι
εἰς Ἰθάκην, οὐδ' ἔνθα πεφυγμένος ἦεν ἀέθλων,
καὶ μετὰ οἷσι φίλοισι. θεοὶ δ' ἐλέαιρον ἅπαντες
νόσφι Ποσειδάωνος· ὃ δ' ἀσπερχὲς μενέαινεν   20
ἀντιθέῳ Ὀδυσῆϊ πάρος ἣν γαῖαν ἱκέσθαι.
ἀλλ' ὃ μὲν Αἰθίοπας μετεκίαθε τηλόθ' ἐόντας,
Αἰθίοπας, τοὶ διχθὰ δεδαίαται, ἔσχατοι ἀνδρῶν,
οἳ μὲν δυσομένου Ὑπερίονος, οἳ δ' ἀνιόντος,
ἀντιόων ταύρων τε καὶ ἀρνειῶν ἑκατόμβης.   25
ἔνθ' ὅ γε τέρπετο δαιτὶ παρήμενος· οἱ δὲ δὴ ἄλλοι
Ζηνὸς ἐνὶ μεγάροισιν Ὀλυμπίου ἀθρόοι ἦσαν.
τοῖσι δὲ μύθων ἦρχε πατὴρ ἀνδρῶν τε θεῶν τε·
μνήσατο γὰρ κατὰ θυμὸν ἀμύμονος Αἰγίσθοιο,
τόν ῥ' Ἀγαμεμνονίδης τηλεκλυτὸς ἔκταν' Ὀρέστης·   30
τοῦ ὅ γ' ἐπιμνησθεὶς ἔπε' ἀθανάτοισι μετηύδα·

---

1 ἄνδρά a] ἄνδρα MSS* | πολύτροπον MSS] πολύκροτον T | πόλλα MSS*]
πάντων a   3 νόον MSS] νόμον T   6 ὣς a] ὡς MSS* T
7 αὐτῶν MSS*] αὐτοὶ a   10 ἁμόθεν a] ἀμόθεν b   12 ἔσαν a] ἴσαν b
15 σπέεσι a] σπέσσι b T, σπέσι MSS*   19 οἷσι φίλοισι MSS*] οἷς ἑτάροισι a
21 ἱκέσθαι MSS*] ἰδέσθαι a   23 Αἰθίοπας MSS] Αἰθίοπες T
24 οἳ μὲν...οἳ δ' MSS] ἠμὲν...ἠδ'T   27 ἀθρόοι a] ἀθρόοι b, T
30 om. a   31 ἔπε' ἀθανάτοισι μετηύδα MSS*] ἔπεα πτερόεντα προσηύδα
a, ἔπεα πτερόεντ' ἀγόρευεν b

Translation

The man—tell me, Muse, [of him] of many turns, who was very
 widely
Made to wander, after he had sacked the sacred citadel of Troy.
Many were the people whose cities he saw, and got to know their
 dispositions;
Many were the pains that on the sea he suffered in his spirit,
Fighting for his own life and the safe return of his comrades.   5
But not even so did he save them, eager though he was;
For they perished because of their own wickedness,
Fools—who consumed the oxen of Hyperion the Sun god.
So he robbed them of their day of safe return.
From some point or other, goddess daughter of Zeus, tell us also
 of those things.   10
Now all the others, so many as had escaped sheer destruction,
Were at home, having [safely] escaped the war and the sea;
But that one man—longing for a safe return and for his wife—
The lady nymph Calypso, illustrious among goddesses, was
 detaining
In her hollow caves, desiring that he should be her husband.   15
But when, as the years rolled by, there came the twelvemonth
In which the gods had spun it as his destiny to return home,
To Ithaca—not even then was he safely free from his trials,
And among his friends. All the gods had pity on him,
Except for Poseidon; he was furiously angry   20
With godlike Odysseus, before he reached his own land.
But he [i.e. Poseidon] had gone to visit the far-off Ethiopians—
The Ethiopians who are divided into two groups, the farthest
 of men,
Some [dwelling] where Hyperion sets, others at his rising—
To partake of their sacrifice of bulls and rams.   25
So he was taking his pleasure there sitting at the banquet; but
 the others
Were assembled together in the house of Olympian Zeus,
And the father of men and gods began to speak to them,
For he recalled in his spirit the extraordinary Aegisthus,
Whom far-renowned Orestes, son of Agamemnon, had slain.   30
Remembering him, he began to address these words to the
 immortals:

"ὢ πόποι, οἷον δή νυ θεοὺς βροτοὶ αἰτιόωνται.
ἐξ ἡμέων γάρ φασι κάκ' ἔμμεναι· οἱ δὲ καὶ αὐτοὶ
σφῇσιν ἀτασθαλίῃσιν ὑπὲρ μόρον ἄλγε' ἔχουσιν,
ὡς καὶ νῦν Αἴγισθος ὑπὲρ μόρον Ἀτρεΐδαο   35
γῆμ' ἄλοχον μνηστήν, τὸν δ' ἔκτανε νοστήσαντα,
εἰδὼς αἰπὺν ὄλεθρον, ἐπεὶ πρό οἱ εἴπομεν ἡμεῖς,
Ἑρμειάν πέμψαντες, ἐΰσκοπον Ἀργειφόντην,
μήτ' αὐτὸν κτείνειν μήτε μνάασθαι ἄκοιτιν·
«ἐκ γὰρ Ὀρέσταο τίσις ἔσσεται Ἀτρεΐδαο,   40
ὁππότ' ἂν ἡβήσῃ τε καὶ ἧς ἱμείρεται αἴης.»
ὣς ἔφαθ' Ἑρμείας, ἀλλ' οὐ φρένας Αἰγίσθοιο
πεῖθ' ἀγαθὰ φρονέων· νῦν δ' ἀθρόα πάντ' ἀπέτεισεν."
τὸν δ' ἠμείβετ' ἔπειτα θεὰ γλαυκῶπις Ἀθήνη·
"ὦ πάτερ ἡμέτερε Κρονίδη, ὕπατε κρειόντων·   45
καὶ λίην κεῖνός γε ἐοικότι κεῖται ὀλέθρῳ,
ὡς ἀπόλοιτο καὶ ἄλλος ὅτις τοιαῦτά γε ῥέζοι.
ἀλλά μοι ἀμφ' Ὀδυσῆϊ δαΐφρονι δαίεται ἦτορ,
δυσμόρῳ, ὃς δὴ δηθὰ φίλων ἄπο πήματα πάσχει
νήσῳ ἐν ἀμφιρύτῃ, ὅθι ὀμφαλός ἐστι θαλάσσης·   50
νῆσος δενδρήεσσα, θεὰ δ' ἐν δώματα ναίει,
Ἄτλαντος θυγάτηρ ὀλοόφρονος, ὅς τε θαλάσσης
πάσης βένθεα οἶδεν, ἔχει δέ τε κίονας αὐτός
μακράς, αἳ γαῖάν τε καὶ οὐρανὸν ἀμφὶς ἔχουσιν·
τοῦ θυγάτηρ δύστηνον ὀδυρόμενον κατερύκει   55
αἰεὶ δὲ μαλακοῖσι καὶ αἱμυλίοισι λόγοισιν
θέλγει, ὅπως Ἰθάκης ἐπιλήσεται· αὐτὰρ Ὀδυσσεύς,
ἱέμενος καὶ καπνὸν ἀποθρῴσκοντα νοῆσαι
ἧς γαίης, θανέειν ἱμείρεται. οὐδέ νυ σοί περ
ἐντρέπεται φίλον ἦτορ, Ὀλύμπιε; οὔ νύ τ' Ὀδυσσεύς   60
Ἀργείων παρὰ νηυσὶ χαρίζετο ἱερὰ ῥέζων
Τροίῃ ἐν εὐρείῃ; τί νύ οἱ τόσον ὠδύσαο, Ζεῦ;"
τὴν δ' ἀπαμειβόμενος προσέφη νεφεληγερέτα Ζεύς·
"τέκνον ἐμόν, ποῖόν σε ἔπος φύγεν ἕρκος ὀδόντων;

---

35 Αἴγισθος ὑπέρ] Αἴγισθος· ὑπέρ Van Thiel   38 πέμψαντες ἐΰσκοπον
MSS] πέμψαντε διάκτορον p T | πέμψαντες κτλ. MSS] πέμψαντες Μαίης
ἐρικυδέος ἀγλαὸν υἱόν T   39 κτείνειν a T] κτεῖναι b   40 ἔσσεται
MSS T] ἔρχεται T   41 ἡβήσῃι MSS] ἡβήσει T   43 ἀπέτεισεν]
ἀπέτεισε p, ἀπέτισ(σ)ε(ν) MSS   49 πήματα πάσχει MSS] τῆλ' ἀλάληται T
50 ἀμφιρύτῃ MSS] ὠγυγίῃ T   51 δώματα MSS*] δώμασι a | νῆσος κτλ.]
om. a   52 ὀλοόφρονος MSS] ὀλοόφρονος T   56 δὲ a] δ' ἐν b
60 οὔ νύ τ' a] οὔ νύ κ' b, οὔνεκ' c

'Outrageous! Just look how mortals blame the gods!
For they say that evil things come from us. But they themselves also
Because of their wickedness suffer pains beyond what was
    appointed—
Even as now Aegisthus, beyond what was appointed, took to wife   35
The lawfully wedded spouse of the son of Atreus,
    and killed him when he had got safely home,
Knowing [that this meant] sheer destruction, since we had
    already told him—
Having sent Hermes, the keen-sighted slayer of guard dogs—
Neither to kill him nor to woo his wife.
"For from Orestes there shall come vengeance for the son of
    Atreus,   40
When he reaches manhood and starts to long for his own
    country."
So spoke Hermes, but he did not persuade the mind
Of Aegisthus, well-meaning as he [i.e. Hermes] was.
But now he [i.e. Aegisthus] has paid for it all together.'
Then the owl-eyed goddess Athena began her reply to him:
'Our father, son of Cronus, highest among rulers,   45
Yes indeed, that man at least is laid low in a fitting death;
Let anyone else who does such things also perish!
But my heart is in shreds over shrewd Odysseus,
The ill-starred one, who for a long time far from friends has been
    suffering sorrows
On a sea-girt island—at the place where the navel of the sea is: 50
The island is wooded—and a goddess has her home there,
The daughter of baleful Atlas, who knows
The depths of the whole sea, and himself holds the pillars,
The lofty ones that keep the earth and heaven apart.
His daughter is detaining the wretched man [i.e. Odysseus] as he
    mourns,   55
And with soft and wheedling words she continually
Beguiles him, so that he might forget Ithaca. But Odysseus,
Eager to see even just the smoke springing up from
His native land, longs to die. Now then, does not your
Dear heart have any regard [i.e. for him], Olympian one? Now
    did not Odysseus   60
Use to oblige you by making sacrifices by the ships of the Argives
In wide Troy? Now why are you so odious towards him, Zeus?'
In reply to her spoke Zeus, the gather of clouds:
'My child, what sort of word has escaped the barrier of your teeth?

πῶς ἂν ἔπειτ' Ὀδυσῆος ἐγὼ θείοιο λαθοίμην,   65
ὃς περὶ μὲν νόον ἐστὶ βροτῶν, περὶ δ' ἱρὰ θεοῖσιν
ἀθανάτοισιν ἔδωκε, τοὶ οὐρανὸν εὐρὺν ἔχουσιν;
ἀλλὰ Ποσειδάων γαιήοχος ἀσκελὲς αἰέν
Κύκλωπος κεχόλωται, ὃν ὀφθαλμοῦ ἀλάωσεν,
ἀντίθεον Πολύφημον, ὅου κράτος ἐστὶ μέγιστον   70
πᾶσιν Κυκλώπεσσι· Θόωσα δέ μιν τέκε νύμφη,
Φόρκυνος θυγάτηρ, ἁλὸς ἀτρυγέτοιο μέδοντος,
ἐν σπέεσι γλαφυροῖσι Ποσειδάωνι μιγεῖσα.
ἐκ τοῦ δὴ Ὀδυσῆα Ποσειδάων ἐνοσίχθων
οὔ τι κατακτείνει, πλάζει δ' ἀπὸ πατρίδος αἴης.   75
ἀλλ' ἄγεθ' ἡμεῖς οἵδε περιφραζώμεθα πάντες
νόστον, ὅπως ἔλθησι. Ποσειδάων δὲ μεθήσει
ὃν χόλον· οὐ μὲν γάρ τι δυνήσεται ἀντία πάντων
ἀθανάτων ἀέκητι θεῶν ἐριδαινέμεν οἶος."
τὸν δ' ἠμείβετ' ἔπειτα θεὰ γλαυκῶπις Ἀθήνη·   80
"ὦ πάτερ ἡμέτερε Κρονίδη, ὕπατε κρειόντων,
εἰ μὲν δὴ νῦν τοῦτο φίλον μακάρεσσι θεοῖσιν,
νοστῆσαι Ὀδυσῆα πολύφρονα ὅνδε δόμονδε,
Ἑρμείαν μὲν ἔπειτα, διάκτορον Ἀργειφόντην,
νῆσον ἐς Ὠγυγίην ὀτρύνομεν, ὄφρα τάχιστα   85
νύμφῃ ἐϋπλοκάμῳ εἴπῃ νημερτέα βουλήν,
νόστον Ὀδυσσῆος ταλασίφρονος, ὥς κε νέηται.
αὐτὰρ ἐγὼν Ἰθάκηνδ' ἐσελεύσομαι, ὄφρα οἱ υἱόν
μᾶλλον ἐποτρύνω καί οἱ μένος ἐν φρεσὶ θείω,
εἰς ἀγορὴν καλέσαντα κάρη κομόωντας Ἀχαιούς   90
πᾶσι μνηστήρεσσιν ἀπειπέμεν, οἵ τέ οἱ αἰεί
μῆλ' ἁδινὰ σφάζουσι καὶ εἰλίποδας ἕλικας βοῦς.
πέμψω δ' ἐς Σπάρτην τε καὶ ἐς Πύλον ἠμαθόεντα
νόστον πευσόμενον πατρὸς φίλου, ἤν που ἀκούσῃ,
ἠδ' ἵνα μιν κλέος ἐσθλὸν ἐν ἀνθρώποισιν ἔχῃσιν."   95
ὣς εἰποῦσ' ὑπὸ ποσσὶν ἐδήσατο καλὰ πέδιλα,
ἀμβρόσια χρύσεια, τά μιν φέρον ἠμὲν ἐφ' ὑγρήν
ἠδ' ἐπ' ἀπείρονα γαῖαν ἅμα πνοιῇς ἀνέμοιο.

---

70 ἐστὶ MSS*] ἔσκε a | ὅου MSS*] ὅο a   71 νύμφη MSS*] μήτηρ a T
72 om. a   73 σπέεσι a] σπέα(σ)ι MSS*   83 πολύφρονα MSS*]
δαΐφρονα a   85 Ὠγυγίην MSS] ὠγυλίην T   88 Ἰθάκηνδ' MSS* p]
Ἰθάκην a | ἐσελεύσομαι MSS*] ἐλεύσομαι a T   93 Σπάρτην MSS T] Κρήτην
T | ἠμαθόεντα MSS*] ἠμαθόεσσαν a   93ab κεῖθεν δ' ἐς Κρήτην τε παρ'
Ἰδομενῆα ἄνακτα / ὃς γὰρ δεύτατος ἦλθεν Ἀχαιῶν χαλκοχιτώνων add. a
95 ἔχῃσιν MSS*] ἔλησιν a, λάβῃσιν b   97–8 MSS] om. T, ath. Aristarchus

How could I in such a case forget godlike Odysseus,   65
Who exceeds all mortals in mind and has given exceeding many
   sacrifices
To the immortal ones, who possess the wide heaven?
But Poseidon, who rides the earth, is perpetually stubborn
In his anger over the Cyclops, whom he [i.e. Odysseus] robbed
   of the sight of his eye,
Godlike Polyphemus, whose might is greatest   70
Among all the Cyclopes. The nymph Thoösa gave birth to him,
Daughter of Phorcys, ruler of the sea that cannot be dried up,
Having had sex with Poseidon in hollow caves.
Since then Poseidon, shaker of the earth, has not actually been
   trying to kill
Odysseus, but makes him wander away from his fatherland.   75
But come, let us here all take thought for
His safe return, about how he might come back. And Poseidon
   shall put aside
His anger; for he will not be able, against all [of us],
To carry on the quarrel by himself contrary to the will of the
   immortal gods.'
Then the owl-eyed goddess Athena answered him: 80
'Our father, son of Cronus, highest among rulers,
If this is indeed what the blessed gods want,
That ingenious Odysseus should return safely to his house,
Then let us urge on Hermes, the messenger, and slayer of
   guard-dogs,
To the island of Ogygia, so that with all speed   85
He may declare to the beautiful-haired nymph our unfailing will:
For the safe return of stout-hearted Odysseus, that he might get
   safely back.
But I shall go to Ithaca, so that I might even more
Urge on his son and put passion in his mind:
To call the long-haired Achaeans to the assembly   90
And make a declaration before all the suitors, who continually
Slaughter his sheep in abundance together with shambling black oxen.
And I shall send him to Sparta and to sandy Pylos,
To inquire about the safe return of his dear father,
   if he might hear of it somewhere,
And be the object of good renown amongst people.'   95
Having spoken thus she fastened beneath her feet her beautiful
   sandals,
Immortal and golden, which carried her both over the water
And over the boundless earth as fast as the gusting wind.

εἵλετο δ' ἄλκιμον ἔγχος, ἀκαχμένον ὀξέϊ χαλκῷ
βριθὺ μέγα στιβαρόν, τῷ δάμνησι στίχας ἀνδρῶν 100
ἡρώων, τοῖσίν τε κοτέσσεται Ὀβριμοπάτρη.
βῆ δὲ κατ' Οὐλύμποιο καρήνων ἀΐξασα·
στῆ δ' Ἰθάκης ἐνὶ δήμῳ ἐπὶ προθύροις Ὀδυσῆος,
οὐδοῦ ἔπ' αὐλείου· παλάμῃ δ' ἔχε χάλκεον ἔγκος,
εἰδομένη ξείνῳ, Ταφίων ἡγήτορι Μέντῃ. 105
εὗρε δ' ἄρα μνηστῆρας ἀγήνορας· οἳ μὲν ἔπειτα
πεσσοῖσι προπάροιθε θυράων θυμὸν ἔτερπον,
ἥμενοι ἐν ῥινοῖσι βοῶν, οὓς ἔκτανον αὐτοί.
κήρυκες δ' αὐτοῖσι καὶ ὀτρηροὶ θεράποντες
οἳ μὲν ἄρ' οἶνον ἔμισγον ἐνὶ κρητῆρσι καὶ ὕδωρ, 110
οἳ δ' αὖτε σπόγγοισι πολυτρήτοισι τραπέζας
νίζον καὶ προτίθεν, τοὶ δὲ κρέα πολλὰ δατέοντο.
τὴν δὲ πολὺ πρῶτος ἴδε Τηλέμαχος θεοειδής·
ἧστο γὰρ ἐν μνηστῆρσι, φίλον τετιημένος ἦτορ,
ὀσσόμενος πατέρ' ἐσθλὸν ἐνὶ φρεσίν, εἴ ποθεν ἐλθών 115
μνηστήρων τῶν μὲν σκέδασιν κατὰ δώματα θείη,
τιμὴν δ' αὐτὸς ἔχοι καὶ κτήμασιν οἷσιν ἀνάσσοι.
τὰ φρονέων, μνηστῆρσι μεθήμενος, εἴσιδ' Ἀθήνην.
βῆ δ' ἰθὺς προθύροιο, νεμεσσήθη δ' ἐνὶ θυμῷ
ξεῖνον δηθὰ θύρῃσιν ἐφεστάμεν· ἐγγύθι δὲ στάς 120
χεῖρ' ἕλε δεξιτερὴν καὶ ἐδέξατο χάλκεον ἔγχος,
καί μιν φωνήσας ἔπεα πτερόεντα προσαύδα·
"χαῖρε, ξεῖνε, παρ' ἄμμι φιλήσεαι· αὐτὰρ ἔπειτα
δείπνου πασσάμενος μυθήσεαι ὅττεό σε χρή."
ὣς εἰπὼν ἡγεῖθ', ἡ δ' ἕσπετο Παλλὰς Ἀθήνη. 125
οἳ δ' ὅτε δή ῥ' ἔντοσθεν ἔσαν δόμου ὑψηλοῖο,
ἔγχος μέν ῥ' ἔστησε φέρων πρὸς κίονα μακρήν
δουροδόκης ἔντοσθεν ἐϋξόου, ἔνθά περ ἄλλα
ἔγχε' Ὀδυσῆος ταλασίφρονος ἵστατο πολλά·
αὐτὴν δ' ἐς θρόνον εἷσεν ἄγων, ὑπὸ λῖτα πέτασσας, 130

99–100 MSS] ath. Aristarchus   110 ἄρ'] ἆρ Van Thiel, del. Bentley
112 πρότιθεν, τοί δὲ T] προτίθεντο ἰδὲ MSS | δάτεοντο Knight, West] δατεῦντο
MSS   117 κτήμασι a] δώμασι b | ἀνάσσοι a] ἀνάσσει b
124 πασσάμενος MSS*] παυσάμενος a

And she took up her strong spear, tipped with sharp bronze,
Heavy, large, and stout, with which she subdues the ranks of men— 100
Of champions, whenever She-of-the-mighty-father is angry with
    them.
And she went darting down from the peaks of Olympus.
She came to rest in the land of Ithaca at the doorway of Odysseus,
On the threshold of the courtyard, and in her hand she held her
    bronze spear,
In the guise of a guest-friend, Mentes, leader of the Taphians. 105
And she came upon the arrogant suitors. Now they were
Delighting their spirits at a board game in front of the doorway,
Sitting on hides of oxen which they themselves had killed.
For their benefit the heralds and the busy servants were
Some of them mixing wine and water in mixing bowls, 110
Others cleaning the tables with honeycomb sea-sponges
And setting them out, whilst others were distributing large
    amounts of meat.
By far the first to see her was godlike Telemachus,
For he was sitting among the suitors, sorrowing in his dear heart,
Imagining his father in his mind's eye, if perhaps he might arrive
    from somewhere 115
And scatter the suitors throughout the house,
Whilst himself getting honour and being master of his own property.
Thinking on that, and sitting among the suitors, he looked upon
    Athena.
He went straight through the doorway and felt indignation in
    his spirit
That a stranger should stand for a long time at the doors.
    Then standing nearby 120
He grasped her right hand and took from her the bronze spear.
He spoke up and began to address winged words to her:
'Greetings, stranger. In our house, you shall be treated kindly,
    then later
When you have had a meal, you shall tell what it is you need.'
Having spoken thus he led the way, and she, Pallas Athena,
    followed. 125
Now when they were inside the high house,
Taking the spear he stood it up against a tall pillar,
Inside a well-polished spear-stand, where in addition
There stood many spears belonging to stout-hearted Odysseus.
Then he led her and seated her on a chair
    —spreading out linen cloths beneath her— 130

καλὸν δαιδάλεον· ὑπὸ δὲ θρῆνυς ποσὶν ἦεν.
πὰρ δ' αὐτὸς κλισμὸν θέτο ποικίλον ἔκτοθεν ἄλλων,
μνηστήρων μὴ ξεῖνος ἀνιηθεὶς ὀρυμαγδῷ
δείπνῳ ἀδήσειεν, ὑπερφιάλοισι μετελθών,
ἠδ' ἵνα μιν περὶ πατρὸς ἀποιχομένοιο ἔροιτο.   135
χέρνιβα δ' ἀμφίπολος προχόῳ ἐπέχευε φέρουσα
καλῇ χρυσείῃ, ὑπὲρ ἀργυρέοιο λέβητος,
νίψασθαι· παρὰ δὲ ξεστὴν ἐτάνυσσε τράπεζαν.
σῖτον δ' αἰδοίη ταμίη παρέθηκε φέρουσα,
εἴδατα πόλλ' ἐπιθεῖσα, χαριζομένη παρεόντων·   140
δαιτρὸς δὲ κρειῶν πίνακας παρέθηκεν ἀείρας
παντοίων, παρὰ δέ σφι τίθει χρύσεια κύπελλα·
κῆρυξ δ' αὐτοῖσιν θάμ' ἐπῴχετο οἰνοχοεύων.
ἐς δ' ἦλθον μνηστῆρες ἀγήνορες. οἳ μὲν ἔπειτα
ἑξείης ἕζοντο κατὰ κλισμούς τε θρόνους τε.   145
τοῖσι δὲ κήρυκες μὲν ὕδωρ ἐπὶ χεῖρας ἔχευαν,
σῖτον δὲ δμῳαὶ παρενήνεον ἐν κανέοισιν,
κοῦροι δὲ κρητῆρας ἐπεστέψαντο ποτοῖο.
οἳ δ' ἐπ' ὀνείαθ' ἑτοῖμα προκείμενα χεῖρας ἴαλλον.
αὐτὰρ ἐπεὶ πόσιος καὶ ἐδητύος ἐξ ἔρον ἕντο   150
μνητσῆρες, τοῖσιν μὲν ἐνὶ φρεσὶν ἄλλα μεμήλει,
μολπή τ' ὀρχηστύς τε· τὰ γάρ τ' ἀναθήματα δαιτός.
κῆρυξ δ' ἐν χερσὶν κίθαριν περικαλλέα θῆκεν
Φημίῳ, ὅς ῥ' ἤειδε παρὰ μνηστῆρσιν ἀνάγκῃ.
ἤτοι ὃ φορμίζων ἀνεβάλλετο καλὸν ἀείδειν,   155
αὐτὰρ Τηλέμαχος προσέφη γλαυκῶπιν Ἀθήνην,
ἄγχι σχὼν κεφαλήν, ἵνα μὴ πευθοίαθ' οἱ ἄλλοι·
"ξεῖνε φίλ', εἰ καί μοι νεμεσήσεαι ὅττι κεν εἴπω·
τούτοισιν μὲν ταῦτα μέλει, κίθαρις καὶ ἀοιδή,
ῥεῖ', ἐπεὶ ἀλλότριον βίοτον νήποινον ἔδουσιν,   160
ἀνέρος, οὗ δή που λεύκ' ὀστέα πύθεται ὄμβρῳ

132 αὐτὸς MSS*] αὐτὴν a, αὐτῃ b   134 δείπνῳ MSS*] δεῖπνον a | ἀδήσειεν
a] ἀηδήσειεν b, ἀδήσειεν c   139 om. a   146 ἔχευαν MSS*] ἔχευον a
147 παρενήνεον MSS] παρενήεον Bekker   148 om. a
148a νώμησαν δ' ἄρα πᾶσιν ἐπαρξάμενοι δεπάεσσιν add. a   157 πευθοίαθ'
οἱ ἄλλοι MSS T] πευθοίατο ἄλλοι T   158 εἰ MSS* T] ἦ a, ἦ b
159 τούτοισιν MSS] ἄλλοισιν T

A beautiful and embellished [chair], and there was a footstool
   beneath her feet.
And beside her he himself set an intricate couch, apart from those
   others,
Lest the guest be distressed by the suitors' din
And be sated with the meal, having come among arrogant persons;
And also so that he could ask him about his [i.e. Telemachus']
   absent father.   135
A maidservant brought the water for washing their hands
   and poured it out from a jug,
A beautiful one made of gold, above a silver basin,
For them to wash. And she set up beside [them] a long smooth table.
Then the worthy stewardess brought bread and set it before them,
Putting out [on the table] many foods, giving generously of
   what there was.   140
Then the carver lifted up and set before them platters of meats
Of all kinds, and beside them he set goblets made of gold.
And a herald went about repeatedly among them pouring out wine.
Then there came in the haughty suitors. Now they
Took their seats in order on couches and chairs.   145
And for their benefit the heralds poured water over their hands,
And the female slaves piled up bread in baskets,
And the male servants filled the mixing bowls to the brim with
   drink.
They [i.e. the suitors] then thrust forth their hands to the foods
   that lay ready before them.
But once they had put off their desire for food and drink,   150
The suitors' minds were occupied with other things,
Song and dancing, for those are the adornments of a banquet.
Then a herald placed a very beautiful lyre into the hands of
Phemius, who sang amid the company of the suitors by compulsion.
He then, playing on the lyre, began to sing beautifully.   155
But Telemachus addressed owl-eyed Athena,
Holding his head close, so that those others might not hear.
'Dear guest—and at the risk of your taking offence at what I might
   go on to say—
These men are occupied with these things, the lyre-playing and
   bardic song,
At ease, since they are consuming someone else's livelihood
   without making compensation,   160
[The livelihood] of a man whose white bones are, I suppose,
   decaying in the rain

κείμεν' ἐπ' ἠπείρου, ἤ' εἰν ἁλὶ κῦμα κυλίνδει.
εἰ κεῖνόν γ' Ἰθάκηνδε ἰδοίατο νοστήσαντα,
πάντες κ' ἀρησαίατ' ἐλαφρότεροι πόδας εἶναι
ἤ' ἀφνειότεροι χρυσοῖό τε ἐσθῆτός τε.   165
νῦν δ' ὃ μὲν ὣς ἀπόλωλε κακὸν μόρον, οὐδέ τις ἥμιν
θαλπωρή, εἴ πέρ τις ἐπιχθονίων ἀνθρώπων
φῆσιν ἐλεύσεσθαι· τοῦ δ' ὤλετο νόστιμον ἦμαρ.
ἀλλ' ἄγε μοι τόδε εἰπὲ καὶ ἀτρεκέως κατάλεξον·
τίς πόθεν εἰς ἀνδρῶν; πόθι τοι πόλις ἠδὲ τοκῆες;   170
ὁπποίης δ' ἐπὶ νηὸς ἀφίκεο; πῶς δέ σε ναῦται
ἤγαγον εἰς Ἰθάκην; τίνες ἔμμεναι εὐχετόωντο;
οὐ μὲν γάρ τί σε πεζὸν ὀΐομαι ἐνθάδ' ἱκέσθαι.
καί μοι τοῦτ' ἀγόρευσον ἐτήτυμον, ὄφρ' ἐΰ εἰδῶ,
ἠὲ νέον μεθέπεις, ἦ καὶ πατρώϊός ἐσσι   175
ξεῖνος, ἐπεὶ πολλοὶ ἴσαν ἀνέρες ἡμέτερον δῶ
ἄλλοι, ἐπεὶ καὶ κεῖνος ἐπίστροφος ἦν ἀνθρώπων."
τὸν δ' αὖτε προσέειπε θεὰ γλαυκῶπις Ἀθήνη·
"τοίγαρ ἐγώ τοι ταῦτα μάλ' ἀτρεκέως ἀγορεύσω.
Μέντης Ἀγχιάλοιο δαΐφρονος εὔχομαι εἶναι   180
υἱός, ἀτὰρ Ταφίοισι φιληρέτμοισιν ἀνάσσω.
νῦν δ' ὧδε ξὺν νηὶ κατήλυθον ἠδ' ἑτάροισιν,
πλέων ἐπὶ οἴνοπα πόντον ἐπ' ἀλλοθρόους ἀνθρώπους,
ἐς Τεμέσην μετὰ χαλκόν, ἄγω δ' αἴθωνα σίδηρον.
νηῦς δέ μοι ἥδ' ἕστηκεν ἐπ' ἀγροῦ νόσφι πόληος,   185
ἐν λιμένι Ῥείθρῳ, ὑπὸ Νηΐῳ ὑληέντι.
ξεῖνοι δ' ἀλλήλων πατρώϊοι εὐχόμεθ' εἶναι
ἐξ ἀρχῆς, εἴ πέρ τε γέροντ' εἴρηαι ἐπελθὼν
Λαέρτην ἥρωα, τὸν οὐκέτι φασὶ πόλινδε
ἔρχεσθ', ἀλλ' ἀπάνευθεν ἐπ' ἀγροῦ πήματα πάσχειν   190
γρηῒ σὺν ἀμφιπόλῳ, ἥ οἱ βρῶσίν τε πόσιν τε
παρτίθει, εὖτ' ἄν μιν κάματος κατὰ γυῖα λάβῃσιν
ἑρπύζοντ' ἀνὰ γουνὸν ἀλῳῆς οἰνοπέδοιο.
νῦν δ' ἦλθον· δὴ γάρ μιν ἔφαντ' ἐπιδήμιον εἶναι,
σὸν πατέρ'· ἀλλά νυ τόν γε θεοὶ βλάπτουσι κελεύθου.   195
οὐ γάρ πω τέθνηκεν ἐπὶ χθονὶ δῖος Ὀδυσσεύς,

167 θαλπωρή MSS*] ἐλπωρή a T   171–3 om. a T   171 δ' MSS] τ' T
172 εὐχετόωντο MSS*] εὐχετόωνται a   174 ἐΰ West] ἐΰ MSS
175 μεθέπεις MSS*] μεθέπῃ a   177 καὶ κεῖνος MSS* T] κἀκεῖνος a
183 ἐπ' MSS*] ἐς a   186 ὑπὸ Νηΐῳ MSS*] ὑπονηΐῳ a T   188 τε MSS
T] τι T   192 παρτίθει T] παρτιθεῖ Allen, Von der Muehll, Van Thiel, West
195 om. a   196 πω MSS] που T

As they lie on the dry land, or else a wave is rolling them about
    in the sea.
If they were to see that man safely returned to Ithaca,
They would all pray to be lighter on their feet,
Rather than to be richer in gold and raiment.   165
But as things are, he has died a wretched death, nor is there for
    us any
Comfort, even if someone among earthly men
Says that he is coming back. The day of that man's safe return is lost.
But come now, tell me this, and recount it truly,
Who and whose are you? Where are your city and parents?   170
On what kind of ship did you arrive here, and how did the sailors
Bring you to Ithaca? Who did they declare that they were?
For I really do not think that you arrived here on foot.
And tell me this truly, so that I may know well,
If you are a new visitor here, or are you a family   175
Friend, since there used to come to our house many
Different sorts of men, when that man too used to go about
    among the living.'
Owl-eyed Athena addressed him in turn:
'Well then I shall tell you these things most truly:
I declare that I am Mentes, of shrewd Anchialus   180
The son, and I rule over the Taphians, who love the oar.
Now I have come down here with my ship and my companions
Sailing over the wine-dark sea to men who speak other tongues,
To Temesa to acquire copper, and I bring iron of dark hue.
This ship of mine is moored in the country, away from the city,   185
In the harbour of Reithrum, beneath wooded Neium.
So we can claim to be family friends of each other
From the outset, [as you will discover] if you go and ask old
Laertes the champion, who they say no longer comes to
The city, but far away in the country suffers sorrows   190
With his old maidservant, who sets before him food
And drink, whenever weariness overtakes his limbs
As he creeps about the high ground of his vineyard.
And now I have come. For indeed they told me that he was in
    residence—
Your father [I mean]; but now the gods are hindering him from
    his path.   195
For godlike Odysseus has not yet perished from the earth,

ἀλλ' ἔτι που ζωὸς κατερύκεται εὐρέι πόντῳ,
νήσῳ ἐν ἀμφιρύτῃ, χαλεποὶ δέ μιν ἄνδρες ἔχουσιν,
ἄγριοι, οἵ που κεῖνον ἐρυκανόωσ' ἀέκοντα.

αὐτὰρ νῦν τοι ἐγὼ μαντεύσομαι, ὡς ἐνὶ θυμῷ   200
ἀθάνατοι βάλλουσι καὶ ὡς τελέεσθαι ὀίω,
οὔτε τι μάντις ἐὼν οὔτ' οἰωνῶν σάφα εἰδώς·
οὔ τοι ἔτι δηρόν γε φίλης ἀπὸ πατρίδος αἴης
ἔσσεται, οὐδ' εἴ περ τε σιδήρεα δέσματ' ἔχησιν·
φράσσεται ὥς κε νέηται, ἐπεὶ πολυμήχανός ἐστιν.   205
ἀλλ' ἄγε μοι τόδε εἰπὲ καὶ ἀτρεκέως κατάλεξον,
εἰ δὴ ἐξ αὐτοῖο τόσος πάϊς εἰς Ὀδυσῆος.

αἰνῶς γὰρ κεφαλήν τε καὶ ὄμματα καλὰ ἔοικας
κείνῳ, ἐπεὶ θαμὰ τοῖον ἐμισγόμεθ' ἀλλήλοισιν,
πρίν γε τὸν ἐς Τροίην ἀναβήμεναι, ἔνθα περ ἄλλοι   210
Ἀργείων οἱ ἄριστοι ἔβαν κοίλης ἐνὶ νηυσίν·
ἐκ τοῦ δ' οὔτ' Ὀδυσῆα ἐγὼν ἴδον οὔτ' ἐμὲ κεῖνος."
τὴν δ' αὖ Τηλέμαχος πεπνυμένος ἀντίον ηὔδα·
"τοιγὰρ ἐγώ τοι, ξεῖνε, μάλ' ἀτρεκέως ἀγορεύσω.
μήτηρ μέν τέ μέ φησι τοῦ ἔμμεναι, αὐτὰρ ἐγώ γε   215
οὐκ οἶδ'· οὐ γάρ πώ τις ἑὸν γόνον αὐτὸς ἀνέγνω.
ὡς δὴ ἐγώ γ' ὄφελον μάκαρός νύ τε' ἔμμεναι υἱός
ἀνέρος, ὃν κτεάτεσσιν ἑοῖς ἔπι γῆρας ἔτετμεν.
νῦν δ' ὃς ἀποτμότατος γένετο θνητῶν ἀνθρώπων,
τοῦ μ' ἔκ φασι γενέσθαι, ἐπεὶ σύ με τοῦτ' ἐρεείνεις."   220
τὸν δ' αὖτε προσέειπε θεὰ γλαυκῶπις Ἀθήνη·
"οὐ μέν τοι γενεήν γε θεοὶ νώνυμνον ὀπίσσω
θῆκαν, ἐπεὶ σέ γε τοῖον ἐγείνατο Πηνελόπεια.
ἀλλ' ἄγε μοι τόδε εἰπὲ καὶ ἀτρεκέως κατάλεξον·
τίς δαίς, τίς δὲ ὅμιλος ὅδ' ἔπλετο; τίπτε δέ σε χρεώ;   225
εἰλαπίνη ἦε γάμος; ἐπεὶ οὐκ ἔρανος τάδε γ' ἐστίν,
ὥς τέ μοι ὑβρίζοντες ὑπερφιάλως δοκέουσιν
δαίνυσθαι κατὰ δῶμα. νεμεσσήσαιτό κεν ἀνήρ
αἴσχεα πόλλ' ὁρόων, ὅς τις πινυτός γε μετέλθοι."
τὴν δ' αὖ Τηλέμαχος πεπνυμένος ἀντίον ηὔδα·   230
"ξεῖν', ἐπεὶ ἄρ δὴ ταῦτά μ' ἀνείρεαι ἠδὲ μεταλλᾷς,

---

201 τελέεσθαι MSS*] τετελέσθαι a, τελέσεσθαι b   204 οὐδ' MSS] ἀλλ' T
|τε MSS, T] (ϝ)έ Cobet   206 κατάλεξον MSS*] ἀγόρευσον a   208 γὰρ
MSS, T] μὲν T   211 ἐνὶ MSS*] ἐπὶ a   214 ἀγορεύσω MSS*]
καταλέξω a   222 νώνυμνον Wolf, ?p] νώνυμον MSS   225 δὲ a T] δαὶ
b T, δ' c

But he is still alive and being detained somewhere upon the
    broad sea,
On a sea-girt island, and harsh men are holding him,
Savages, who I surmise are keeping that man back against his will.
But now I shall make you a prediction, just as the immortal gods   200
Put it into my spirit, and as I think it shall come about,
Although I am no seer, nor clearly versed in the lore of birds:
From his dear fatherland he shall not for long
Be absent, even though he be held fast by bonds of iron.
He will contrive a way to return, since he is resourceful.   205
But come now, tell me this, and recount it truly,
Whether you are indeed the grown-up child of Odysseus himself.
For in your head and your beautiful eyes you look fearfully like
Him—[I say this] because we so often spent time with each other
Before he went on board ship for Troy; when indeed others also,   210
The very best of the Argives, went away in their hollow ships.
Since that time, I have not seen Odysseus, nor he me.'
Then in reply to her prudent Telemachus began to speak:
'Well then, friend, I shall speak to you most truly.
My mother says that I am his, but I   215
Do not know. For nobody ever yet knew his own descent.
Would that I were the son of some wealthy
Man, whom old age finds in possession of his own property.
But as things are, he who is the most ill-starred of mortal men,
That is whose son they say I am—since you ask me this.'   220
Owl-eyed Athena addressed him in turn:
'I tell you the gods have not made your lineage without renown
For the future, since Penelope brought forth such a one as you.
But come now, tell me this, and recount it truly,
What meal, what throng is this? Why ever do you need it?   225
Is it a feast or a wedding? Since at any rate this is not a potluck
    meal—
So arrogantly exuberant do they seem to me as they
Feast throughout the house. It would be a cause of indignation
To a man of good sense, should he come along and see [so] many
    disgraceful deeds.'
Then in reply to her prudent Telemachus began to speak: 230
'Friend, since you ask me and enquire about these things,

μέλλεν μέν ποτε οἶκος ὅδ' ἀφνειὸς καὶ ἀμύμων
ἔμμεναι, ὄφρ' ἔτι κεῖνος ἀνὴρ ἐπιδήμιος ἦεν·
νῦν δ' ἑτέρως ἐβόλοντο θεοὶ κακὰ μητιόωντες,
οἳ κεῖνον μὲν ἄϊστον ἐποίησαν περὶ πάντων   235
ἀνθρώπων, ἐπεὶ οὔ κε θανόντι περ ὧδ' ἀκαχοίμην,
εἰ μετὰ οἷς ἑτάροισι δάμη Τρώων ἐνὶ δήμῳ,
ἠὲ φίλων ἐν χερσίν, ἐπεὶ πόλεμον τολύπευσεν.
τῷ κέν οἱ τύμβον μὲν ἐποίησαν Παναχαιοί,
ἠδέ κε καὶ ᾧ παιδὶ μέγα κλέος ἦρετ' ὀπίσσω.   240
νῦν δέ μιν ἀκλειῶς Ἅρέπυιαι ἀνηρέψαντο·
οἴχετ' ἄϊστος ἄπυστος, ἐμοὶ δ' ὀδύνας τε γόους τε
κάλλιπεν· οὐδέ τι κεῖνον ὀδυρόμενος στοναχίζω
οἶον, ἐπεί νύ μοι ἄλλα θεοὶ κακὰ κήδε' ἔτευξαν.
ὅσσοι γὰρ νήσοισιν ἐπικρατέουσιν ἄριστοι   245
Δουλιχίῳ τε Σάμῃ τε καὶ ὑλήεντι Ζακύνθῳ,
ἠδ' ὅσσοι κραναὴν Ἰθάκην κάτα κοιρανέουσιν,
τόσσοι μητέρ' ἐμὴν μνῶνται, τρύχουσι δὲ οἶκον.
ἣ δ' οὔτ' ἀρνεῖται στυγερὸν γάμον οὔτε τελευτὴν
ποιῆσαι δύναται· τοὶ δὲ φθινύθουσιν ἔδοντες   250
οἶκον ἐμόν· τάχα δή με διαρραίσουσι καὶ αὐτόν."
τὸν δ' ἐπαλαστήσασα προσηύδα Παλλὰς Ἀθήνη·
"ὦ πόποι, ἦ δὴ πολλὸν ἀποιχομένου Ὀδυσῆος
δεύε', ὅ κε μνηστῆρσιν ἀναιδέσι χεῖρας ἐφείη.
εἰ γὰρ νῦν ἐλθὼν δόμου ἐν πρώτῃσι θύρῃσιν   255
σταίη, ἔχων πήληκα καὶ ἀσπίδα καὶ δύο δοῦρε,
τοῖος ἐὼν οἷόν μιν ἐγὼ τὰ πρῶτ' ἐνόησα
οἴκῳ ἐν ἡμετέρῳ πίνοντά τε τερπόμενόν τε,
ἐξ Ἐφύρης ἀνιόντα παρ' Ἴλου Μερμερίδαο·
οἴχετο γὰρ καὶ κεῖσε θοῆς ἐπὶ νηὸς Ὀδυσσεύς   260
φάρμακον ἀνδροφόνον διζήμενος, ὄφρα οἱ εἴη
ἰοὺς χρίεσθαι χαλκήρεας· ἀλλ' ὃ μὲν οὔ οἱ

---

234 ἐβόλοντο a T] ἐβούλοντο MSS*, ἐβάλοντο b T, βούλοντο c   238 del.
Hennings   240 ἦρετ' p, Cobet, Brandreth] ἦρατ' MSS
241 Ἅρέπυιαι Fick] Ἅρπυιαι MSS | ἀνηρέψαντο Döderlein] ἀνηρείψαντο MSS
242 ἄπυστος MSS*] ἄφαντος T, ἄπιστος a   243 στοναχίζω West (1998a,
xxxv)] στεναχίζω MSS   246 Σάμῃ] Σάμῳ T   247 κάτα
κοιρανέουσι T] κατακοιρανέουσι MSS T   252 δ' ἐπαλαστήσασα MSS T]
δὲ παλαστήσασα T   254 δεύε' Knight, Van Leeuwen] δεύῃ MSS*, δεύει a
259 Ἴλου MSS T] Ἴρου T   260 καὶ κεῖσε a] κἀκεῖσε MSS* p
261 ὄφρα οἱ εἴη MSS*] ὄφρα δαείη T ?p, ἤν που ἐφεύροι a

This house had a chance of being rich and extraordinary
So long as that man was in residence.
But as things are the gods have determined otherwise, devising evil
    things:
They have made that man lost to sight beyond all   235
Persons. For I should not be so aggrieved were he actually dead,
If he had died among his companions in the land of the Trojans,
Or in the arms of his friends, having seen the war through to
    the end.
Then all the Achaeans would have made a burial mound for him,
And indeed he would have won great renown for his son in
    the future.   240
As things are, Harpies have snatched him away so that he is
    without renown.
He is gone, lost to sight and to hearing, and for me pain and
    weeping
Are what he has left behind. And as I mourn I do not groan for
    that man
Alone—for now the gods have prepared many other evil woes
    for me.
For as many as are noblest and rule over the islands,   245
Dulichium and Same and wooded Zacynthus,
And as many as are lords throughout rocky Ithaca,
All these are wooing my mother and consuming the household.
She neither refuses hateful marriage, nor is she able to bring it to
Completion; and they with their eating are wasting   250
My household. Soon indeed they will destroy even myself.'
Then in lively indignation Pallas Athena began to address him:
'Outrageous! For absent Odysseus great indeed is your
Need—to lay hands upon the shameless suitors.
Would that he were now to come and, at the front gates of the
    house,   255
Take his stand, with his helmet and shield and two spears,
Being such as he was when first I saw him
In our house, drinking and enjoying himself,
On his way back from Ephyra from [seeing] Ilus, son of Mermerus.
For Odysseus had gone there on board a swift ship,   260
Seeking a murderous poison so that he might
Smear it on his bronze-tipped arrows. But he [i.e. Ilus] did not

δῶκεν, ἐπεί ῥα θεοὺς νεμεσίζετο αἰὲν ἐόντας,
ἀλλὰ πατήρ οἱ δῶκεν ἐμός· φιλέεσκε γὰρ αἰνῶς.
τοῖος ἐὼν μνηστῆρσιν ὁμιλήσειεν Ὀδυσσεύς·   265
πάντες κ' ὠκύμοροί τε γενοίατο πικρόγαμοί τε.
ἀλλ' ἤτοι μὲν ταῦτα θεῶν ἐν γούνασι κεῖται,
ἤ κεν νοστήσας ἀποτείσεται, ἦε καὶ οὐκί,
οἷσιν ἐνὶ μεγάροισι· σὲ δὲ φράζεσθαι ἄνωγα
ὅππως κε μνηστῆρας ἀπώσεαι ἐκ μεγάροιο.   270
εἰ δ' ἄγε νῦν ξυνίει καὶ ἐμῶν ἐμπάζεο μυθῶν·
αὔριον εἰς ἀγορὴν καλέσας ἥρωας Ἀχαιούς
μῦθον πέφραδε πᾶσι, θεοὶ δ' ἐπὶ μάρτυροι ἔστων.
μνηστῆρας μὲν ἐπὶ σφέτερα σκίδνασθαι ἄνωχθι,
μητέρα δ', εἴ οἱ θυμὸς ἐφορμᾶται γαμέεσθαι,   275
ἄψ ἴτω ἐς μέγαρον πατρὸς μέγα δυναμένοιο·
οἳ δὲ γάμον τεύξουσι καὶ ἀρτυνέουσιν ἔεδνα
πολλὰ μάλ', ὅσσα ἔοικε φίλης ἐπὶ παιδὸς ἕπεσθαι.
σοὶ δ' αὐτῷ πυκινῶς ὑποθήσομαι, αἴ κε πίθηαι·
νῆ' ἄρσας ἐρέτῃσιν ἐείκοσιν, ἥ τις ἀρίστη,   280
ἔρχεο πευσόμενος πατρὸς δὴν οἰχομένοιο,
ἤν τίς τοι εἴπῃσι βροτῶν, ἢ ὄσσαν ἀκούσῃς
ἐκ Διός, ἥ τε μάλιστα φέρει κλέος ἀνθρώποισιν.
πρῶτα μὲν ἐς Πύλον ἐλθὲ καὶ εἴρεο Νέστορα δῖον,
κεῖθεν δὲ Σπάρτηνδε παρὰ ξανθὸν Μενέλαον·   285
ὃς γὰρ δεύτατος ἦλθεν Ἀχαιῶν χαλκοχιτώνων.
εἰ μέν κεν πατρὸς βίοτον καὶ νόστον ἀκούσῃς,
ἦ τ' ἂν τρυχόμενός περ ἔτι τλαίης ἐνιαυτόν·
εἰ δέ κε τεθνηῶτος ἀκούσῃς μηδ' ἔτ' ἐόντος,
νοστήσας δὴ ἔπειτα φίλην ἐς πατρίδα γαῖαν   290
σῆμά τέ οἱ χεῦαι καὶ ἐπὶ κτέρεα κτερεΐξαι
πολλὰ μάλ', ὅσσα ἔοικε, καὶ ἀνέρι μητέρα δοῦναι.
αὐτὰρ ἐπὴν δὴ ταῦτα τελευτήσῃς τε καὶ ἔρξῃς,
φράζεσθαι δὴ ἔπειτα κατὰ φρένα καὶ κατὰ θυμόν,

---

268 ἀποτείσεται Fick] ἀποτίσ(σ)εται MSS T   270 κε MSS*] κεν a p
273 ἐπὶ μάρτυροι (/ἐπιμ-) MSS] ἐπιμάρτυρες T   275 μητέρα MSS*]
μητήρ a T   276 ἴτω MSS] ἴμεν Bentley   278 om. a | ἔπεσθαι MSS*]
ἔσεσθαι a   282 ἤ' West (1998, xxxi)] ἦ MSS   285 δὲ Σπάρτηνδε a]
δ' ἐς Σπάρτηνδε b, δὲ Σπάρτην τε c T, δ' ἐσπάρτην τε d, δ' ἐς Σπάρτην τε e, δ'
ἐς Κρήτην τε T (δὲ Κρήτηνδε Buttmann) | παρὰ ξανθὸν Μενέλαον MSS* T]
παρ' Ἰδομενῆα ἄνακτα aT cf. 93   289 τεθνηῶτος a T] τεθνειῶτος b
290 δὴ ἔπειτα Wolf] δ' ἤπειτα MSS*, δ' ἔπειτα a, δήπειτα West   291 χεῦαι
a] χεῦσαι MSS* T, χεῦσον b   292 del. Hermann   294 δήπειτα cf. 290

Give it him, for he was in awe of the indignation of the everlasting
    gods.
But my father gave it to him; for he loved him fearfully.
Would that, being like that, Odysseus might join battle with
    the suitors.   265
Then they would all die early, having attained a bitter kind of
    marriage.
But indeed these things lie in the lap of the gods,
Whether he returns home safely and takes vengeance or not,
In his house. But I urge you to ponder
How you will drive the suitors out of the house.   270
But come now, listen and take heed of my words.
Tomorrow call the Achaean champions to an assembly,
And make a clear speech to them all—and let the gods be
    witnesses.
Bid the suitors to disperse to their own property,
And bid your mother—if her spirit is eager to marry,   275
Let her go back to the house of her mighty father.
They will furnish a wedding and prepare a dowry,
A very large one, such as it is fitting should accompany a dear
    daughter.
But to you I shall give shrewd advice, if you will heed it:
Fit out a ship with twenty oarsmen—the best [ship] you have—   280
And go to enquire after your father, who has been absent a
    long time,
If some mortal man should tell you of him, or you hear from Zeus
Some rumour—which is the chief bringer of news to people.
First go to Pylos and ask illustrious Nestor,
And from there to Sparta to see fair-haired Menelaus,   285
For he was the last of the bronze-clad Achaeans to return.
If you hear that your father is alive and safely on his way home,
Then indeed you could endure for yet another year, in spite of
    being worn out.
But if you hear that he has died and is no longer,
Then come safely home to the land of your fathers   290
And heap up a mound for him and celebrate his funeral with
    grave goods—
Very great in number, as many as is fitting, and then give your
    mother to a husband.
But when you have finished doing these things,
Then ponder in your mind and in your spirit,

ὅππως κε μνηστῆρας ἐνὶ μεγάροισι τεοῖσιν   295
κτείνῃς ἠὲ δόλῳ ἢ ἀμφαδόν. οὐδέ τί σε χρὴ
νηπιάας ὀχέειν, ἐπεὶ οὐκέτι τηλίκος ἐσσί.
ἦ οὐκ ἀΐεις οἷον κλέος ἔλλαβε δῖος Ὀρέστης
πάντας ἐπ' ἀνθρώπους, ἐπεὶ ἔκτανε πατροφονῆα,
Αἴγισθον δολόμητιν, ὅ οἱ πατέρα κλυτὸν ἔκτα;   300
καὶ σύ, φίλος, μάλα γάρ σ' ὁρόω καλόν τε μέγαν τε,
ἄλκιμος ἔσσ', ἵνα τίς σε καὶ ὀψιγόνων ἔϋ εἴπῃ.
αὐτὰρ ἐγὼν ἐπὶ νῆα θοὴν κατελεύσομαι ἤδη
ἠδ' ἑτάρους, οἵ πού με μάλ' ἀσχαλόωσι μένοντες·
σοὶ δ' αὐτῷ μελέτω, καὶ ἐμῶν ἐμπάζεο μύθων."   305
τὴν δ' αὖ Τηλέμαχος πεπνυμένος ἀντίον ηὔδα·
"ξεῖν', ἤτοι μὲν ταῦτα φίλα φρονέων ἀγορεύεις,
ὥς τε πατὴρ ᾧ παιδί, καὶ οὔ ποτε λήσομαι αὐτῶν.
ἀλλ' ἄγε νῦν ἐπίμεινον, ἐπειγόμενός περ ὁδοῖο,
ὄφρα λοεσσάμενός τε τεταρπόμενός τε φίλον κῆρ   310
δῶρον ἔχων ἐπὶ νῆα κίῃς, χαίρων ἐνὶ θυμῷ,
τιμῆεν, μάλα καλόν, ὅ τοι κειμήλιον ἔσται
ἐξ ἐμε', οἷα φίλοι ξεῖνοι ξείνοισι διδοῦσιν."
τὸν δ' ἠμείβετ' ἔπειτα θεὰ γλαυκῶπις Ἀθήνη·
"μή μ' ἔτι νῦν κατέρυκε, λιλαιόμενόν περ ὁδοῖο.   315
δῶρον δ' ὅττι κέ μοι δοῦναι φίλον ἦτορ ἀνώγῃ,
αὖτις ἀνερχομένῳ δόμεναι οἶκόνδε φέρεσθαι,
καὶ μάλα καλὸν ἑλών· σοὶ δ' ἄξιον ἔσται ἀμοιβῆς."
ἣ μὲν ἄρ' ὣς εἰποῦσ' ἀπέβη γλαυκῶπις Ἀθήνη,
ὄρνις δ' ὣς ἀνόπαια διέπτατο· τῷ δ' ἐνὶ θυμῷ   320
θῆκε μένος καὶ θάρσος, ὑπέμνησέν τέ ἑ πατρός
μᾶλλον ἔτ' ἢ τὸ πάροιθεν. ὃ δὲ φρεσὶν ᾗσι νοήσας
θάμβησεν κατὰ θυμόν· ὀΐσατο γὰρ θεὸν εἶναι.
αὐτίκα δὲ μνηστῆρας ἐπῴχετο ἰσόθεος φώς.
τοῖσι δ' ἀοιδὸς ἄειδε περικλυτός, οἳ δὲ σιωπῇ   325
εἴατ' ἀκούοντες· ὃ δ' Ἀχαιῶν νόστον ἄειδεν
λυγρόν, ὃν ἐκ Τροίης ἐπετείλατο Παλλὰς Ἀθήνη.

---

295 κε a] δὴ b   297 νηπιάας MSS T] νηπιίας, νηπῖας (Wackernagel)
298 ἦ Barnes] ἦ a, om. b   300 ὅ a T] ὅς MSS* T   305 αὐτῷ
MSS*] αὐτῶν a   313 ἐμέ' Van Leeuwen] ἐμεῦ MSS   314 ἠμείβετ'
ἔπειτα θεὰ MSS*] αὖτε προσέειπε θεὰ a, ἀπαμειβομένη προσέφη b
315 μή μ' ἔτι MSS*] μήκετι a   316 ἀνώγῃ a] ἀνώγει MSS*
318 ἔσται a T] ἔσσετ' b, ἔστω c   320 ἀνόπαια MSS* T] ἀνοπαῖα T, ἀν'
ὄπαια a T, ἀν' ὀπαῖα T

How you might kill the suitors   295
In your house, either by some trick or else openly. And you must not
Hold on to childish ways, since you are no longer of such an age.
Have you not heard what renown illustrious Orestes won
Among all people, when he killed the slayer of his father,
Wily Aegisthus, because he had killed his [i.e. Orestes'] renowned
      father?   300
And you, friend—for I see that you are very handsome and tall—
Be strong, so that someone born in later days may speak well of you.
But I shall go down at once to the swift ship,
And to my comrades, who I suppose are very irritated at waiting
      for me.
But you yourself must take thought [for what I say] and pay
      heed to my words.'   305
Then in reply to her prudent Telemachus began to speak:
'Friend, indeed you say these things with kindly intent,
Like a father to his son, and I shall never forget them.
But come now, stay, eager as you are to be on your way,
So that having taken a bath and delighted your dear heart,   310
You might go to your ship with a gift, rejoicing in your spirit—
A valuable, most beautiful [gift], that will be an heirloom for you
From me, such as dear friends give to one another.'
Then the owl-eyed goddess Athena began her reply to him:
'Do not detain me any longer now, desirous as I am to be on my way.   315
But as for whatever gift your dear heart might urge you to give me,
Give it to me when I come back again for me to take back home
      with me—
And choose one that is very beautiful: it will be worth some return to
      you [in future].'
When she had thus spoken, owl-eyed Athena departed,
And like a bird she flew through the smoke-vent in the roof.
      And into his spirit   320
She put power and courage, and reminded him of his father
More than before. And he, seeing it in his mind,
Was astonished in his spirit. For he reckoned that it was a god.
Immediately then the godlike warrior [i.e. Telemachus] started to
      approach the suitors.
The celebrated bard was singing for them, and they in silence   325
Sat listening. He was singing of the Achaeans' return home,
A baneful one from Troy, which Pallas Athena had imposed.

τοῦ δ᾽ ὑπερωϊόθεν φρεσὶ σύνθετο θέσπιν ἀοιδήν
κούρη Ἰκαρίοιο, περίφρων Πηνελόπεια·
κλίμακα δ᾽ ὑψηλὴν κατεβήσετο οἷο δόμοιο   330
οὐκ οἴη, ἅμα τῇ γε καὶ ἀμφίπολοι δύ᾽ ἕποντο.
ἣ δ᾽ ὅτε δὴ μνηστῆρας ἀφίκετο δῖα γυναικῶν,
στῆ ῥα παρὰ σταθμὸν τέγεος πύκα ποιητοῖο,
ἄντα παρειάων σχομένη λιπαρὰ κρήδεμνα·
ἀμφίπολος δ᾽ ἄρα οἱ κεδνὴ ἑκάτερθε παρέστη.   335
δακρύσασα δ᾽ ἔπειτα προσηύδα θεῖον ἀοιδόν·
"Φήμιε, πολλὰ γὰρ ἄλλα βροτῶν θελκτήρια οἶδας
ἔργ᾽ ἀνδρῶν τε θεῶν τε, τά τε κλείουσιν ἀοιδοί·
τῶν ἕν γέ σφιν ἄειδε παρήμενος, οἱ δὲ σιωπῇ
οἶνον πινόντων· ταύτης δ᾽ ἀποπαύε᾽ ἀοιδῆς   340
λυγρῆς, ἥ τέ μοι αἰεὶ ἐνὶ στήθεσσι φίλον κῆρ
τείρει, ἐπεί με μάλιστα καθίκετο πένθος ἄλαστον.
τοίην γὰρ κεφαλὴν ποθέω μεμνημένη αἰεί
ἀνδρός, τοῦ κλέος εὐρὺ καθ᾽ Ἑλλάδα καὶ μέσον Ἄργος."
τὴν δ᾽ αὖ Τηλέμαχος πεπνυμένος ἀντίον ηὔδα·   345
"μῆτερ ἐμή, τί τ᾽ ἄρ᾽ αὖ φθονέεις ἐρίηρον ἀοιδόν
τέρπειν ὅππῃ οἱ νόος ὄρνυται; οὔ νύ τ᾽ ἀοιδοί
αἴτιοι, ἀλλά ποθι Ζεὺς αἴτιος, ὅς τε δίδωσιν
ἀνδράσιν ἀλφηστῇσιν ὅπως ἐθέλῃσιν ἑκάστῳ.
τούτῳ δ᾽ οὐ νέμεσις Δαναῶν κακὸν οἶτον ἀείδειν·   350
τὴν γὰρ ἀοιδὴν μᾶλλον ἐπικλείουσ᾽ ἄνθρωποι,
ἥ τις ἀκουόντεσσι νεωτάτη ἀμφιπέληται.
σοὶ δ᾽ ἐπιτολμάτω κραδίη καὶ θυμὸς ἀκούειν·
οὐ γὰρ Ὀδυσσεὺς οἶος ἀπώλεσε νόστιμον ἦμαρ
ἐν Τροίῃ, πολλοὶ δὲ καὶ ἄλλοι φῶτες ὄλοντο.   355
ἀλλ᾽ εἰς οἶκον ἰοῦσα τὰ σ᾽ αὐτῆς ἔργα κόμιζε,
ἱστόν τ᾽ ἠλακάτην τε, καὶ ἀμφιπόλοισι κέλευε
ἔργον ἐποίχεσθαι· μῦθος δ᾽ ἄνδρεσσι μελήσει
πᾶσι, μάλιστα δ᾽ ἐμοί· τοῦ γὰρ κράτος ἔστ᾽ ἐνὶ οἴκῳ."
ἣ μὲν θαμβήσασα πάλιν οἰκόνδε βεβήκει·   360
παιδὸς γὰρ μῦθον πεπνυμένον ἔνθετο θυμῷ.
ἐς δ᾽ ὑπερῷ᾽ ἀναβᾶσα σὺν ἀμφιπόλοισι γυναιξίν
κλαῖεν ἔπειτ᾽ Ὀδυσῆα, φίλον πόσιν, ὄφρα οἱ ὕπνον

---

330 κατεβήσετο a] κατεβήσατο MSS* T   336 θεῖον MSS*] δῖον a
337 οἶδας MSS] ᾔδεις T   344 ath. Aristarchus   346 ταρ αὖ West]
τ᾽ ἄρ αὖ MSS*, τ᾽ ἄρα a, Wolf   351 ἐπικλείουσ᾽ MSS T] ἐπιφρονέουσ᾽ T
352 ἀκουόντεσσι MSS T] ἀειδόντεσσι T, ἀϊόντεσσι T   353 ἀκούειν MSS
p] ἀΐειν p   356-9 ath. Aristarchus

From the upper storey, she heeded his inspired song in her
   mind, did
The daughter of Icarius, most prudent Penelope.
And she came down the high stair from her quarters,   330
Not on her own—two handmaids followed together with her.
But when she, illustrious among women, came to the suitors,
She stood by the pillar that held up the solidly made roof,
Holding before her cheeks her brilliant white mantilla—
And a trusty maidservant stood on each side of her—   335
Then in tears she began to address the godlike bard:
'Phemius, since you know many other things to charm mortals,
Deeds of men and gods, which the bards make famous,
Then sing one of those as you sit here, and let them in silence
Drink wine; but leave off from this singing,   340
Baneful as it is, which always distresses my dear heart in my
Breast, since I in particular am touched by an unforgettable grief.
For such a person do I miss, remembering always my
Husband, whose fame is wide throughout Hellas and the central
   Peloponnese.'
Then in reply to her prudent Telemachus began to speak: 345
'Mother mine, why ever do you begrudge that the faithful bard
   should
Give pleasure in whatever way his mind stirs itself to do so?
   I tell you the bards are not
To blame, but Zeus is probably to blame, who makes his
   dispensation
To grain-eating men, just as he chooses for each one.
It is no cause for indignation that this man sings of the evil fate
   of the Danaans,
For people celebrate all the more whatever song   350
Is newest as it does the rounds among its hearers.
But let your heart and spirit endure to listen;
For Odysseus was not the only one to lose his day of safe return
At Troy, for many other warriors perished too.   355
But go into the house and attend to your own work,
The loom and distaff, and bid the maidservants
To set about their work. Speaking will be taken care of by men—
All of them, and especially me: for I am the one with power in
   the house.'
Astonished, she was gone back into the house;   360
For she had taken to her spirit the prudent speech of her son.
She went up to the upper storey with her women attendants,
And started then to weep for Odysseus, until

ἡδὺν ἐπὶ βλεφάροισι βάλε γλαυκῶπις Ἀθήνη.
μνηστῆρες δ' ὁμάδησαν ἀνὰ μέγαρα σκιόεντα·   365
πάντες δ' ἠρήσαντο παραὶ λεχέεσσι κλιθῆναι.
τοῖσι δὲ Τηλέμαχος πεπνυμένος ἤρχετο μύθων·
"μητρὸς ἐμῆς μνηστῆρες, ὑπέρβιον ὕβριν ἔχοντες,
νῦν μὲν δαινύμενοι τερπώμεθα, μηδὲ βοητύς
ἔστω, ἐπεὶ τό γε καλὸν ἀκουέμεν ἐστὶν ἀοιδοῦ   370
τοιοῦδ' οἷος ὅδ' ἐστί, θεοῖς ἐναλίγκιος αὐδήν.
ἠῶθεν δ' ἀγορήνδε καθεζώμεσθα κιόντες
πάντες, ἵν' ὕμιν μῦθον ἀπηλεγέως ἀποείπω,
ἐξιέναι μεγάρων· ἄλλας δ' ἀλεγύνετε δαῖτας,
ὑμὰ κτήματ' ἔδοντες, ἀμειβόμενοι κατὰ οἴκους.   375
εἰ δ' ὕμιν δοκέει τόδε λώϊτερον καὶ ἄμεινον
ἔμμεναι, ἀνδρὸς ἑνὸς βίοτον νήποινον ὀλέσθαι,
κείρετ'· ἐγὼ δὲ θεοὺς ἐπιβώσομαι αἰὲν ἐόντας,
αἴ κέ ποθι Ζεὺς δῶσι παλίντιτα ἔργα γενέσθαι.
νήποινοί κεν ἔπειτα δόμων ἔντοσθεν ὄλοισθε."   380
ὣς ἔφαθ'· οἳ δ' ἄρα πάντες ὀδὰξ ἐν χείλεσι φύντες
Τηλέμαχον θαύμαζον, ὃ θαρσαλέως ἀγόρευεν.
τὸν δ' αὖτ' Ἀντίνοος προσέφη, Εὐπείθεος υἱός·
"Τηλέμαχ', ἦ μάλα δή σε διδάσκουσιν θεοὶ αὐτοί
ὑψαγόρην τ' ἔμεναι καὶ θαρσαλέως ἀγορεύειν.   385
μή σέ γ' ἐν ἀμφιάλῳ Ἰθάκῃ βασιλῆα Κρονίων
ποιήσειεν, ὅ τοι γενεῇ πατρώϊόν ἐστιν."
τὸν δ' αὖ Τηλέμαχος πεπνυμένος ἀντίον ηὔδα·
"Ἀντίνο', εἴ πέρ μοι καὶ ἀγάσσεαι ὅττι κεν εἴπω,
καί κεν τοῦτ' ἐθέλοιμι Διός γε διδόντος ἀρέσθαι.   390
ἦ φὴς τοῦτο κάκιστον ἐν ἀνθρώποισι τετύχθαι;
οὐ μὲν γάρ τι κακὸν βασιλευέμεν· αἶψά τε οἱ δῶ
ἀφνειὸν πέλεται καὶ τιμηέστερος αὐτός.
ἀλλ' ἤτοι βασιλῆες Ἀχαιῶν εἰσὶ καὶ ἄλλοι
πολλοὶ ἐν ἀμφιάλῳ Ἰθάκῃ, νέοι ἠδὲ παλαιοί,   395
τῶν κέν τις τόδ' ἔχῃσιν, ἐπεὶ θάνε δῖος Ὀδυσσεύς·
αὐτὰρ ἐγὼν οἴκοιο ἄναξ ἔσομ' ἡμετέροιο
καὶ δμώων, οὕς μοι ληΐσσατο δῖος Ὀδυσσεύς."

367 ἤρχετο μύθων MSS*] ἀντίον ηὔδα a   370 τό γε MSS* T] τόδε a T
371 θεοῖς MSS*] θεῷ a   373 ὕμιν a T] ὑμῖν b, ὕμμιν c   376 ὕμιν a T]
ὑμῖν b, ὕμμιν c, ὕμμιν d   377 ὀλέσθαι MSS*] ὀλέσ(σ)αι a   379 αἴ
MSS] εἴ T | ποθι MSS*] ποτε a   388 ἀντίον ηὔδα MSS*] ἦρχ' ἀγορεύειν a
389 εἴ πέρ μοι καὶ ἀγάσσεαι MSS* T] (καὶ om. a), εἰ καί μοι νεμεσήσεαι (cf. 158)
T, ἦ καί μοι νεμεσήσεαι Wolf

The owl-eyed goddess Athena let sweet sleep fall over her eyelids.
But the suitors made a din throughout the shadowy house;   365
And they all prayed to lie beside [her] in bed.
And to these the prudent Telemachus began to speak:
'Suitors of my mother, with your overweening exuberance,
Let us now enjoy ourselves in feasting, and let there be no
Shouting, for this is a fine thing—to listen to a bard   370
Such as this one, who in voice is like the gods.
But as soon as it is dawn, let us make our way to the place of
     assembly and sit down,
All of us, so that I may make a blunt declaration to you:
To leave this house. Occupy yourselves with other feasts,
Consuming your own property, moving from one house to
     the next.   375
But if this seems to you to be better and
More profitable, that the livelihood of one man should perish
     without vengeance,
Carry on devouring: but I shall call out to the everlasting gods,
In the hope that Zeus will grant me deeds of requital.
In that case you would die inside the house without vengeance.'   380
So he spoke, and they all bit their lips
In wonder at Telemachus, because he spoke boldly.
In turn Antinous, son of Eupeithes, addressed him:
'Telemachus, indeed the gods themselves are teaching you
To be a boaster and to speak boldly.   385
Let the son of Cronus not make you chieftain in sea-girt
Ithaca—a thing that runs hereditarily to you in your family.'
Then in reply to him prudent Telemachus began to speak:
'Antinous, even if you should feel angry at what I say,
Even so should I want to gain this (*sc.* chiefdom) if Zeus were
     to give it.   390
Do you reckon that this is the meanest thing in people's eyes?
It is in no way a mean thing to be a chieftain. His house
     immediately
Becomes wealthy and he himself more esteemed.
But there are many other chieftains of the Achaeans
In sea-girt Ithaca, both young and old,   395
Of whom one might get this, since illustrious Odysseus is dead.
But I shall be lord over our house
And slaves, whom illustrious Odysseus carried off as booty for me.'

τὸν δ᾽ αὖτ᾽ Εὐρύμαχος, Πολύβου πάϊς, ἀντίον ηὖδα
"Τηλέμαχ᾽, ἤτοι ταῦτα θεῶν ἐν γούνασι κεῖται,　　　　400
ὅς τις ἐν ἀμφιάλῳ Ἰθάκῃ βασιλεύσει Ἀχαιῶν·
κτήματα δ᾽ αὐτὸς ἔχοις καὶ δώμασιν οἷσιν ἀνάσσοις,
μὴ γὰρ ὅ γ᾽ ἔλθοι ἀνήρ, ὅς τίς σ᾽ ἀέκοντα βίηφιν
κτήματ᾽ ἀπορραίσει᾽, Ἰθάκης ἔτι ναιεταώσης.
ἀλλ᾽ ἐθέλω σε, φέριστε, περὶ ξείνοιο ἔρεσθαι,　　　　405
ὁππόθεν οὗτος ἀνήρ· ποίης δ᾽ ἐξ εὔχεται εἶναι
γαίης; ποῦ δέ νύ οἱ γενεὴ καὶ πατρὶς ἄρουρα;
ἠέ τιν᾽ ἀγγελίην πατρὸς φέρει ἐρχομένοιο,
ἦ᾽ ἐὸν αὐτοῦ χρεῖος ἐελδόμενος τόδ᾽ ἱκάνει;
οἷον ἀναΐξας ἄφαρ οἴχεται, οὐδ᾽ ὑπέμεινεν　　　　410
γνώμεναι· οὐ μὲν γάρ τι κακῷ εἰς ὦπα ἐῴκει."
τὸν δ᾽ αὖ Τηλέμαχος πεπνυμένος ἀντίον ηὖδα·
"Εὐρύμαχ᾽, ἤτοι νόστος ἀπώλετο πατρὸς ἐμοῖο·
οὔτ᾽ οὖν ἀγγελίῃ ἔτι πείθομαι, εἴ ποθεν ἔλθοι,
οὔτε θεοπροπίης ἐμπάζομαι, ἥν τινα μήτηρ　　　　415
ἐς μέγαρον καλέσασα θεοπρόπον ἐξερέηται.
ξεῖνος δ᾽ οὗτος ἐμὸς πατρώϊος ἐκ Ταφοῦ ἐστίν·
Μέντης Ἀγχιάλοιο δαΐφρονος εὔχεται εἶναι
υἱός, ἀτὰρ Ταφίοισι φιληρέτμοισιν ἀνάσσει."
ὣς φάτο Τηλέμαχος, φρεσὶ δ᾽ ἀθανάτην θεὸν ἔγνω.　　　　420
οἱ δ᾽ εἰς ὀρχηστύν τε καὶ ἱμερόεσσαν ἀοιδήν
τρεψάμενοι τέρποντο, μένον δ᾽ ἐπὶ ἕσπερον ἐλθεῖν.
τοῖσι δὲ τερπομένοισι μέλας ἐπὶ ἕσπερος ἦλθεν·
δὴ τότε κακκείοντες ἔβαν οἰκόνδε ἕκαστος.
Τηλέμαχος δ᾽, ὅθι οἱ θάλαμος περικαλλέος αὐλῆς　　　　425
ὑψηλὸς δέδμητο, περισκέπτῳ ἐνὶ χώρῳ,
ἔνθ᾽ ἔβη εἰς εὐνὴν πολλὰ φρεσὶ μερμηρίζων.
τῷ δ᾽ ἄρ᾽ ἅμ᾽ αἰθομένας δαΐδας φέρε κεδν᾽ εἰδυῖα
Εὐρύκλει᾽, Ὦπος θυγάτηρ Πεισηνορίδαο,
τήν ποτε Λαέρτης πρίατο κτεάτεσσιν ἑοῖσιν,　　　　430
πρωθήβην ἔτ᾽ ἐοῦσαν, ἐεικοσάβοια δ᾽ ἔδωκεν,
ἶσα δέ μιν κεδνῇ ἀλόχῳ τίεν ἐν μεγάροισιν,

---

402 δώμασιν οἷσιν MSS*] δώμασι σοῖσιν a, West　　404 ἀπορραισει᾽
Bentley] ἀπορραίσει MSS ∣ Ἰθάκης MSS*] Ἰθάκης γ᾽ a ∣ ναιεταώσης MSS]
ναιετοώσης T　　408 ἐρχομένοιο MSS* T] οἰχομένοιο a T
414 ἀγγελίῃ a] ἀγγελίης MSS*, ἀγγελίην b ∣ ἔτι πείθομαι MSS* T] ἐπιπείθομαι a
415 ἥν τινα MSS* T] ἤν τινα a T　　419 om. a　　424 δή τότε κτλ.
MSS T] δή τότε κοιμήσαντο καὶ ὕπνου δῶρο ἔλοντο T　　428 τῳ δ᾽ ἄρ᾽
ἅμ᾽] τῳ δ᾽ ἄμα a ∣ εἰδυῖα MSS] ἰδυῖα Bentley

In reply to him then Eurymachus, son of Polybus, began to speak:
'Telemachus, indeed this question lies in the lap of the gods,   400
Who shall be chieftain over the Achaeans in sea-girt Ithaca.
But you can keep your property yourself and rule over your house;
Nay, let there not come any man who, by force and against your will,
Should deprive you of your property, so long as Ithaca is still
    inhabited.
But I should like, my very brave fellow, to ask you about the stranger,   405
Where this man comes from. And from what kind of land does
    he claim to
Come? Where now is his family and ancestral soil?
Does he bring some message of your father's coming?
Or does he come here desiring (*sc.* to deal with) some business
    of his own?
How suddenly he sprang up and is gone, nor did he wait behind   410
For us to get to know him: for in face he looked in no way like an
    ill-born man.'
Then in reply to him prudent Telemachus began to speak:
'Eurymachus, my father's safe return is indeed lost.
So I am no longer believing any message—were one to come from
    some quarter—
Nor do I give heed to any prophecy, that my mother   415
Having summoned a prophet into the house, should ask about.
But this man is a family friend of mine from Taphos.
He declares that he is Mentes, of shrewd Anchialus
The son, and he rules over the Taphians, who love the oar.'
So spoke Telemachus, but in his mind he recognized the immortal
    goddess.   420
And so it was to dancing and lovely song
That they turned and took delight, and waited for evening to
    come on.
And as they were taking their delight, dark evening did come on.
Then indeed they went away to lie down, each one to his house.
As for Telemachus, where in the very beautiful courtyard his high   425
Bedchamber was built, in a conspicuous spot,
Thither he went to his bed, planning many things in his mind.
Together with him she carried the blazing torches—did the
    well-disposed
Eurycleia, daughter of Ops the son of Peisenor:
Laertes once bought her in exchange for goods of his,   430
When she was still in the prime of youth, and he gave
    the value of twenty oxen for her,
And he honoured her as much as his trusty wife at home,

εὐνῇ δ᾽ οὔ ποτ᾽ ἔμικτο, χόλον δ᾽ ἀλέεινε γυναικός·
ἥ οἱ ἅμ᾽ αἰθομένας δαΐδας φέρε, καί ἑ μάλιστα
δμῳάων φιλέεσκε, καὶ ἔτρεφε τυτθὸν ἐόντα. 435
ὤϊξεν δὲ θύρας θαλάμου πύκα ποιήτοιο,
ἕζετο δ᾽ ἐν λέκτρῳ μαλακὸν δ᾽ ἔκδυνε χιτῶνα·
καὶ τὸν μὲν γραίης πυκιμηδέος ἔμβαλε χερσίν.
ἡ μὲν τὸν πτύξασα καὶ ἀσκήσασα χιτῶνα,
πασσάλῳ ἀγκρεμάσασα παρὰ τρητοῖσι λέχεσσιν, 440
βῆ ῥ᾽ ἴμεν ἐκ θαλάμοιο, θύρην δ᾽ ἐπέρυσσε κορώνῃ
ἀργυρέῃ, ἐπὶ δε κληῖδ᾽ ἐτάνυσσεν ἱμάντι.
ἔνθ᾽ ὅ γε παννύχιος, κεκαλυμμένος οἰὸς ἀώτῳ,
βούλευε φρεσὶν ᾗσιν ὁδὸν τὴν πέφραδ᾽ Ἀθήνη.

436 ὤϊξε(ν) MSS T] ὤειξεν Fick, cf. West 1998a, xxxiii.   438 γραίης
MSS*] γρηὸς a, γραὸς b   442 ἱμάντι MSS* p T] ἱμάντα a

And he never went to bed with her, and avoided the anger of
   his wife.
She (i.e. Eurycleia) carried the blazing torches together with him,
   and she especially
Among the female slaves loved him, and reared him when he
   was little.   435
And he opened the doors of the solidly made bedchamber
And sat on the bed and took off his soft tunic,
And put it into the hands of the shrewd old woman.
She folded that tunic and smoothed it
And hung it on a peg beside the bedstead bored with holes,   440
And took a step to go out from the bedchamber, and pulled the
   door to by the handle
Which was made of silver, and she pulled the bolt into place using
   the strap.
There it was that he, all night long and covered in the wool of
   a sheep,
Deliberated in his mind over the journey of which Athena had
   told him.

Commentary

1–10 The proem. The poet states the subject of the epic in a passage dense with programmatic references. It looks forward to the themes and action of the poem as a whole, but also back to the *Iliad*. The opening of the *Odyssey* plainly echoes that of the *Iliad*: there is the invocation of divine aid, the request for recitation, and the statement of the subject matter. Given (as we saw in the Introduction, pp. 1–2, 37–8) that the *Odyssey* is later in date than the *Iliad*, it is reasonable to suppose that any apparent contrast with the earlier poem is deliberate (see below).

1 ἄνδρά The first word of the *Iliad* is μῆνιν, normally used to describe the wrath of the gods (Muellner 1996; Pulleyn 2000: 116–17). The *Odyssey* begins not with a rare word for an uncommon thing but with an ordinary word for a man. He is not actually named until l. 21. This is one instance of a pervasive narrative device: Odysseus repeatedly conceals his name (most memorably from the Cyclops: *Od.* 9.366–7). This is connected by some with ideas of magic and taboo concerning names (Austin 1972; Olson 1992). But it is surely more a matter of art: Odysseus is a master of stratagem and lies, an attribute that saves his life. It takes on a rather less creditable colour at the very end of the poem when he conceals his identity from his aged and grieving father (*Od.* 24.232–79). It seems that all instances of verse-initial ἄνδρα in the *Odyssey* refer more or less directly to Odysseus (Kahane 1992). Its marked deployment as first word of the poem sets the pattern for these later allusive uses. This sort of concealed referentiality is echoed in the use of deictic pronouns later in this book (see 163 n.).

In his Teubner edition, M. L. West (2017: 1) prints here ἄνδρά with two acute accents. This is contrary to the supposed 'rule' that a paroxytone word with a trochaic ending when followed by an enclitic takes no accent on its final syllable. But Herodian knew of accentuations such as ἄλλός τις and ἔνθά ποτε (Probert 2003: 148) and such writings are found in MSS (M. L. West 1998a: xviii). It seems that a sequence of vowel plus nasal (μ, ν) or liquid (λ, ρ) was equivalent to a diphthong. In the surviving musical notation of the Delphic Paeans, we find that such sequences are given two notes, just like long vowels (Vendryes 1904: 85–6). ἄνδρα could thus in principle be treated like other words of trochaic shape and take two accents before an enclitic. The first accent when written in the MSS is acute rather than the expected circumflex; but the pronunciation of ἄλλός τις, ἔνθά ποτε, etc. would have been equivalent to that of (e.g.) οἶκός τις (Probert 2003: 149). Aristarchus knew the accentuation ἄνδρά μοι but refused to allow it into his text on the basis that it would create 'cacophony' in the opening word (Chandler 1881: 279). If the rule was of general application, it is not to be disapplied here simply because Aristarchus did not like the result. All but one of the MSS that have accents transmit ἄνδρα not ἄνδρά, but that could well be the result of Aristarchan influence.

μοι The poet unusually interposes his own personality here, in a way that he does not in the proem of the *Iliad*. He seems to make himself the mouthpiece of the Muse. But he later uses the pl. ἡμῖν (10 n.).

ἔννεπε In the *Iliad* a goddess is asked to *sing*; here the Muse is asked to *tell*. We might see in all this no more than an elegant variation (Μοῦσα ~ θεά; ἔννεπε ~ ἄειδε). But speaking and singing are not the same thing. Σ finds ἄειδε appropriate to the opening of the *Iliad* since the poet wanted to add the pleasure of song to an otherwise difficult subject; here, by contrast, Σ remarks that ἔννεπε makes Homer seem more like an orator than a bard. Words of the family ἀειδ-/ἀοιδ- are specific to bardic song, given to mortal singers by the Muses (*Od.* 8.43, 64, 73; cf. 1.155 n.). But it is commoner for the Muse to be asked to 'tell' than to 'sing' (*Il.* 2.484; 11.218; 14.508; 16.112).

The verb ἐνέπω is said to be archaic and to impart solemnity (S. R. West 1988: 69). Its archaism may perhaps be surmised from its wide attestation in related languages (Frisk 1954–70: 1.521)—although not in the Indo-Iranian branch, whose evidence is often of high antiquity. As for solemnity, it is often used to refer to the speech of gods—mostly in the *Iliad* (*Il.* 2.761; 7.447; 8.412; 11.186), but also in the *Odyssey* (*Od.* 5.98). We might assume that this was the original sphere of use (Strunk 1957: 23), especially as it is also used in the *Iliad* to refer to the telling by humans of oracles and dreams, which are often divine in origin (*Il.* 2.80; 5.438). It is commonly associated with νημερτές ('inerrantly': e.g. *Il.* 13.470). It seems that this verb is used 'almost always of things which are of more than ordinary importance to the speaker' (*LfgrE*, s.v.). Peculiar to the *Odyssey* is the use of ἐνέπω—sometimes with νημερτές (*Od.* 3.93, 327; 4.323) but sometimes not (*Od.* 3.101, 247; 4.331; 17.529)—when news is being sought of the fate of Odysseus.

Although *Σ* glosses the verb as εἰπέ, there is no etymological connexion between the two. ἐνέπω (< *sek^w-) belongs with Lat. *insequelinsece* (Andr. *poet.* 1), Germ. *sagen*, and Eng. *say* (Fournier 1946: 47–8). The usual form has only one –ν–; the –νν– is Aeolic, the regular outcome in that dialect of *en–hek^{w}e* < *en–$_s$ek^{w}e* (De Decker 2015: 121, *pace* Wyatt 1969: 94–6).

Μοῦσα The θεά ('goddess') invoked in the first line of the *Iliad* must be a Muse; here, she is explicitly so called. Hesiod tells us that they are nine in number and gives us their individual names (*Th.* 76–9); Homer invokes them generically either as a group (*Il.* 2.484) or an individual (as here; also *Il.* 2.761).

It has been suggested that Μοῦσα meant 'lady of the mountain', adding the suffix –ya– to the root seen in Lat *mons, montis* (Wackernagel 1957: 2.1204, with a glance at the sort of nymphs who taught Theocritus (*Id.* 7.92)). This founders on the problem that this root is found nowhere else in Greek (*DELG* 716). It is more likely formed from PIE *men– which, in an extended form *mneH$_2$–, gives Gk. μέμνημαι ('remember') and μνημοσύνη ('memory') (Rix 2001: 435, 447). Scholars differ over the details (Watkins 1995: 110; Assaël 2000: 11–53; Janda 2010: 277–94) but the overall conclusion is persuasive. This has important consequences for our understanding of epic poetry: it is about memory. Hesiod tells us (*Th.* 54) that the Muses are the daughters of Μνημοσύνη. When the bards in the Homeric hymns use μνήσομαι (*h. Cer.* 495; *h. Ap.* 546; *h. Merc.* 580; cf. Richardson 2010: 82) to describe their next feat of poetic composition, they are tapping the spring of the Muses who know everything (*Il.* 2.485). This connexion between poetry and memory looks back to an age when poetry was not fixed in writing but confined to oral recitation (Metcalf 2015: 148–9). It would seem that the Muses are a distinctly Greek creation, with no counterpart in the cultures of the ancient Near East (M. L. West 1997a: 170). Poets in those cultures usually began simply 'I will sing' or 'let me sing' (Metcalf 2015: 25, 60, 101). The invocation of the gods in Greek epic would thus seem to be a curious mixture of diffidence (we are mortals and cannot know everything) and self-aggrandizement (this poem is guaranteed by the gods). It might also be said that this kind of address marks out a turning away from the ordinary world to that of storytelling (De Jong 2001: 5).

πολύτροπον The word is plainly derived from πολυ– ('much') and τρέπω ('turn') but its meaning is nevertheless ambiguous in Greek: does it refer to Odysseus' many travels or to his versatility of mind and his cunning? The word recurs only once (*Od.* 10.330) in a context no more helpful as to meaning. There is no reason to suppose that πολύτροπον is glossed by πλάγχθη in the following line and so must only refer to wanderings:

Odysseus did not embark on these travels out of curiosity and the epithet might more fittingly be supposed to describe a quality that is essential to the man rather than accidental (S. R. West 1988: 69). *Σ* says that the word refers to mental dexterity. Porphyry records that the critic Antisthenes thought this a term of blame, contrasting Odysseus with the simple nobility of Achilles and Ajax (cf. *Il.* 9.313). Cunning intelligence is a primary characteristic of his and one might place beside this compound others in πολυ– which are used of him and describe the same qualities: πολύμητις, πολύφρων, πολυμήχανος. The overall ambiguity may be preserved in English by translating 'of many turns'. A variant reading πολύκροτον ('cunning') is found in *Σ* to Ar. *Nu.* 260. The same epithet is applied to Odysseus in the Hesiodic *Catalogue* (fr. 198.3 MW). Whether it is what Homer composed is doubtful. *Σ* says simply τινὲς λέγουσι γράφεσθαι ('some say that there is written'), which suggests that this was a minority reading. It is not found in any of the papyri or MSS.

ὅς There are in Greek two forms that look the same: (i) a rel. pron. ὅς, ἥ, ὅ ('who, which') and (ii) a reflexive possessive adj. '(ϝ)ός, '(ϝ)ή, '(ϝ)όν (see 4 n. on ὅν). Here we are dealing with the rel. pron. It derives from PIE *yos (cf. Vedic *yás*), which was originally a demonstrative ('that') but lost that force in Greek and Indo-Iranian (Gonda 1954; Sihler 1995: 400).

μάλα πολλά The first word is meant to emphasize the second, which is neut. pl. and used adverbially—tr. 'very much' (*Σ* glosses as λίαν, πάνυ). The alliteration of *l* is noteworthy here. We need not suppose that the alliteration of an individual sound has a precise meaning (e.g. '*l* is a soothing liquid, whereas *s* is a threatening hiss'); it is enough to note it is a poetic device that lends force and colour to a phrase or line. A minority of MSS read πάντων rather than πόλλα. This spoils the alliteration and the run of words in πολ– (3 n.). It is also syntactically wrong, since μάλα does not elsewhere govern a gen. in this way, whereas it is frequently found in combination with parts of πολύς (Nordheider 2004: 1422–3).

2 πλάγχθη 3 sg. aor. ind. pass. < πλάζω ('to cause to wander'). The passive is important. Although LSJ glosses the form as 'rove, wander', Odysseus is not simply taking a gap-year to tour the world. These wanderings were visited upon him; as the poem unfolds, we will learn by whom and for what reason (cf. *Od.* 1.75). This is another example of suspense in the proem—the name of the hero and the reason for his wanderings are not immediately revealed to the audience.

The verb here lacks the augment that would normally be expected with such a form in later Greek. In Homer, the augment is sometimes present and sometimes not, a state of affairs also found in Vedic and Avestan. In Mycenaean Greek, by contrast, it is generally absent (with one or two

possible exceptions). It is hard to explain this distribution. It is reasonable
to assume that, given its regular appearance in Sanskrit and later Greek,
the feature was originally Proto-Indo-European (Szemerényi 1999:
296–9). It is not clear what, if anything, determines its use or omission in
Homer; it might be present and absent in one and the same line (e.g. *Od.*
1.39). In part, this might be a matter of metrical convenience. But the so-
called gnomic aorist (e.g. *Il.* 1.218) usually has the augment, so that there
might sometimes be a semantic motivation (cf. 216 n.).

The word itself is enjambed: the thought which began in the previous
line is not co-extensive with that line—but runs over into this one
before coming to an abrupt halt before a sense break (see Introduction,
pp. 19–20) with a new idea being introduced by ἐπεί. This combination of
run-over and sudden stop lends emphasis to πλάγχθη.

Τροίης This is where the action of the *Iliad* unfolded. Although that
poem dealt with what happened in the course of only just a few days, the
overall campaign at Troy lasted for ten years (*Od.* 5.107). We learn later
that Odysseus' wanderings had lasted for a further ten years (*Od.* 16.206).
This reference to Troy is meant to anchor us in the world of the *Iliad*, to
show that we are taking up the thread from there.

ἱερόν In later Greek, this may practically always be translated as 'holy'
or 'sacred' and refers to that which is set apart for the gods, by contrast
with what is ὅσιος and so safe for humans to touch (Burkert 1985: 269–70).
But a city, whilst home to temples and so to gods, can scarcely be thought
of as off limits; it is necessarily open to all who dwell there. Plainly Homer
does not use the word in the same way as later Greeks, applying it to
threshing floors (*Il.* 5.499), sentries (*Il.* 10.56), barley (*Il.* 11.631), a fish (*Il.*
16.407), a chariot (*Il.* 17.464), gatekeepers (*Il.* 24.681), and a troop of spearmen (*Od.* 24.81). Explanations that involve positing several Greek homonyms derived from different sources (Schulze 1892: 207–16) or one Greek
word derived from various PIE roots (García-Ramón 1992: 203) are not
without difficulty (Clarke 1995: 303 n. 30). A starting point is offered by the
well-known etymological correspondence between Gk. ἱερός and Vedic
iṣirá– (Duchesne-Guillemin 1937; Pagliaro 1961: 93–124). Since iṣirá–
means 'powerful', the uses of ἱερός to describe daylight (*Il.* 9.56) and darkness (*Od.* 11.194) might well be explained in terms of the power of the sun
(cf. μένος ἠελίοιο, *Il.* 23.190) and the speed with which night falls (*Il.* 12.463).
The other examples may likewise be explained in terms of vital energy
(Hooker 1980: 19–27): the fish darts in the water; the chariot moves rapidly; barley and threshing floors are connected with the bestowing of
nourishment and thus of life; sentries, spearmen, and even gatekeepers
are, or might need to be, energetic. Humans who are described as having
a ἱερὸν μένος (*Od.* 7.167; 18.34) might likewise embody vital force in their

very person. We may explain the application of ἱερός to more obviously sacred things such as altars (*Od.* 2.305) by noting that 'religious activity... draws and concentrates the abundant life and power of the gods into the channels that man has marked off for the purpose' (Clarke 1995: 306–8, 315). Returning to the ἱερὸν πτολίεθρον, we may note that cities are strikingly personified in Homer: they bow their heads when conquered (*Il.* 2.373) and have their headdress loosed when sacked (*Il.* 16.100). This is partly poetic artifice; but it also depends on the conception of a city as an organic unity where human life flourishes and is concentrated (Clarke 1995: 313–14).

πτολίεθρον Homer has a form πτόλις beside the more usual Ionic form πόλις. It was convenient for bards as the initial consonant cluster rendered a preceding light syllable metrically heavy. πτολίεθρον might be imagined as serving the same purpose, but there is in epic no corresponding form *πολίεθρον. Had it existed, it could have been used in the many formulae where the preceding word ends in a short vowel followed by a consonant (e.g. *Il.* 1.164; *Od.* 3.4). These forms in –ππ– are not bardic inventions; they are found in Linear B, Thessalian, and Arcado-Cypriot, so that some writers speak of 'Achaean' words that have found their way into the poetic language (Ruijgh 1957: 77–8; Palmer 1980: 67–9, 89). The precise motivation for these forms is obscure (Colvin 2007: 88–9).

ἔπερσεν It seems grandiloquent to say this, as though Odysseus sacked Troy all by himself. But Athena says later to Odysseus σῇ δ' ἥλω βούλῃ Πριάμου πόλις εὐρυάγυια ('it was by your counsel that Priam's city of the wide streets was taken; *Od.* 22.230). The allusion is presumably to the Trojan horse. Σ says that it was by Odysseus' οἰκεία φρόνησις ('innate prudence') that Troy was taken.

3 πολλῶν picks up πολλά in ll. 1 and 4. The repetition of this stem in ll. 1, 3, and 4 emphasizes the length of Odysseus' wanderings, the breadth of his knowledge, and the depth of his sufferings. Just as he is πολύτροπος, so in other respects parts of the word πολύς are applicable to him. We might also note that this effect is cemented by noticeable alliteration of the sound p: πολύτροπον and πολλά (l. 1), πλάγχθη, πτολίεθρον, and ἔπερσε (l. 2), πολλῶν and ἀνθρώπων (l. 3), πολλά, πόντῳ, and πάθεν (l. 4). It is not to be supposed that such alliteration is innately suggestive of pathos or anything else; nevertheless, it plainly lends emphasis to these lines. There might also be a glance at the *Iliad*, whose opening announces the loss of πολλὰς... ἰφθίμους ψυχάς (*Il.* 1.3).

ἀνθρώπων Unlike ἀνήρ (l. 1), this word denotes mankind in general. Odysseus mixes with all kinds of people, and that includes women such as Nausicaa and Arete. The proem does not prepare us for the fact that most of the people Odysseus meets are not human, e.g. Calypso, Circe, the Cyclopes, the Cicones, Scylla.

ἴδεν The stress on what Odysseus has seen is part of the general theme of his knowledge and experience. The verb is especially common in the first person when Odysseus is listing the spirits that he saw in Hades (e.g. *Od.* 11.235, 260, 266, 271, 281, 298, 306, 321, 326, 329).

ἄστεα Σ glosses this as πόλεις, πολίσματα. Whilst it is said (e.g. *DELG* 129–30) that ἄστυ denotes the city as a material place of dwelling whereas πόλις denotes a political reality, Homeric usage (at least) does not bear this out: πόλις sometimes denotes the city as a fortified entity (e.g. *Il.* 21.608). Whatever a city is, Odysseus does not visit many: Calypso and Circe live alone on their respective islands, the Cyclopes live in caves like hermits, the Lotus Eaters are too stoned to run a polity. Some critics conclude that the proem was composed for a different version of the story (Reece 1994: 160 n. 2). But a proem is not a table of contents; its purpose is to lay out the broad themes (Bassett 1923: 347).

Although ἄστεα conceals a digamma—cf. the Boeotian gen. ϝάστιος (*IG* VII 3170) and possibly also Mycenaean *wa-tu*—this has clearly been ignored in this instance (as in many others; see Introduction, pp. 47–8).

νόον This noun is derived from a verbal root, cf. λόγος < λέγω and τόμος < τέμνω (Stefanelli 2009: 219). The root is *nes- (see 5 n.), whose basic meaning is 'to save'; the connexion with mental activity perhaps arises from the notion of the mind surveying a cognitive landscape (cf. *Il.* 15.80–2), rather as τηρέω can refer to watching a thing as well as guarding it (Ruijgh 1967a: 371–2). νόος has also been connected with *neu-, which denotes moving the head (Heubeck 1987a: 236–8). The two roots might be related to each other (so, cautiously, Rix 2001: 411 n. 4). Here, if the text is sound, the noun refers to the mental disposition of the peoples whom Odysseus encountered (cf. *Od.* 4.267). Σ reports that Zenodotus preferred the reading νόμον which we might take as 'custom'; and Horace's renderings of this phrase (*Ars* 142; *Ep.* 1.2, 20) both refer to *mores hominum*. But νόος can refers to one's habitual disposition (*Od.* 6.121 = 9.176), an outer manifestation of inner thought (Clarke 1999: 122). *mores* is an apt rendering of that in Latin and does not tell against the received text.

ἔγνω Σ helpfully remarks that stupid persons might visit many cities and countries but come away with no γνῶσις. Perhaps travel does not unfailingly broaden the mind.

4 πολλά Cf. πολλῶν, 3 n.

ὅ γ' The forms ὁ, ἡ, τό in later Greek are used as the definite article. In Homer, the articular usage is not well developed and these forms have their original function as demonstrative pronouns (see 9, 157, 439 nn.).

The particle γε here has a resumptive force, the subject of this line being the same as that of the preceding one (Chantraine 1953: 159).

πόντῳ Cognate with Vedic *pátha-*, Avestan *paθa-*, πόντος refers to the sea as a path or highway (*DELG* 927–8), cf. ὑγρὰ κέλευθα (*Od.* 3.71). It probably originally meant 'way' and only came to mean 'sea' when used together with the name of a particular sea: thus at *Il.* 2.144–5 θάλασσα is used to describe the sea in general but is immediately followed by a reference to πόντου Ἰκαρίοιο (Moorhouse 1940; 1941; 1948; *contra* W. S. Allen 1947; 1948). Homer has many words for 'sea': θάλασσα, πέλαγος, πόντος, and ἅλς. At *Il.* 4.422–6, a scene is imagined from the shore with the sea described as θάλασσα, said by Lesky (1947: 13) to connote the noise of the waves close to land; out to sea, a wave forms a crest, πόντος fitly denoting the path which the wave will take; when it hits the shore and spews up foam, ἅλς (Lat. *sal*) hints at the salt tang of the breakers.

πάθεν ἄλγεα According to Aristotle (*Po.* 1459b14), whereas the *Iliad* is παθητικόν (about suffering), the *Odyssey* is ἠθικόν (about manners). But the *Odyssey* does not concentrate on manners and morals to the exclusion of suffering and death. The latter theme is stated prominently here and surely with a glance at μυρί'...ἄλγε' from the proem to the *Iliad* (1.2). There is a contrast, though: Achilles is an active dispenser of suffering (ἔθηκε) whereas Odysseus is a passive recipient (πάθεν).

ὅν This is a reflexive possessive adj. ('own') from the series ʼ(ϝ)ός, ʼ(ϝ)ή, ʼ(ϝ)όν (Chantraine 1983: 272–3). The inherited root was *swos-, cf. Lat. *suus* (Sihler 1995: 383). Some forms look like those of the rel. pron. ὅς, but that derives from *yos (1 n.).

κατά The positioning of the preposition after the first and before the second of the words that it governs is a poetic licence common in epic.

θυμόν Although sometimes translated as 'heart', this word does not denote the pumping organ situated in the thorax. It is cognate with Lat. *fumus* and refers to the breath drawn into the lungs (Clarke 1999: 61–83). It is thus semantically closer to Eng. 'spirit', but without the religious overtones of that word. Σ is exercised over whether this phrase goes with πάθεν (describing where he suffered) or with ἀρνύμενος (emphasizing the manner of his exertion). Since ἄλγεα are so often connected with the θυμός elsewhere in the poem (*Od.* 12.427; 13.263; 14.310; 15.487; 17.13), most modern editors punctuate with a comma after θύμον.

5 ἦν Cf. 4 n.

ψυχήν Etymologically this word denotes something like breath (*DELG* 1295). It is often, and unhelpfully, translated as 'soul'. We must not import later Greek ideas about metaphysics into archaic poetry. ψυχή is not the seat of mental life and consciousness; it describes the 'life' of a person at moments when it has been, or is at risk of being, lost (Clarke 1999: 53–60). Odysseus is struggling to keep the breath of life for himself and his comrades.

νόστον This is a key theme of the poem. The noun is formed from **nes-*, which has to do with getting people to safety (Kretschmer 1913: 308–9). If we compare the agential proper noun Νέστωρ with others such as Ἕκτωρ ('he who holds'), Μέντωρ ('he who counsels'), and Ἄκτωρ ('he who leads'), we can see that it probably means 'he who saves' (Tsitsibakou-Vasalos 1999: 122; cf. Myc. *ne-e-ra-wo = *Νεσέλαϝος*). The o-grade form νόστος refers to the result of the action: it is the act of having got to safety (cf. λόγος beside λέγω). If νόστος and νόος both derive from **nes-* (see 3 n.), perhaps the traditional language is hinting that the companions of Odysseus lost their νόστος because of their lack of νόος (Frame 1978: 33). Synchronically within Homer, νόστος refers primarily to getting safely home from Troy (Bonifazi 2009: 481). There was also a poem called Νόστοι in the Epic Cycle, that collection of archaic Greek epics other than the *Iliad* and *Odyssey* that 'provided a more or less continuous account of mythical history from the beginning of the world to the end of the Heroic Age' (M. L. West 2013: 1). It is likely that Greeks knew of other, non-Greek poems about sailors suffering hard returns (S. Morris 1997: 614) such as the *Tale of the Shipwrecked Sailor* (Parkinson 1997: 89–101).

ἑταίρων Σ remarks that it is good that Homer does not refer to Odysseus' men as 'citizens' or 'allies' but 'companions' as this shows τὸ δημοτικὸν τοῦ ἀνδρός ('the man's populist side'). This is an interesting but mistaken thought, unless all Homeric warriors were democrats. The word is used dozens of times in the *Iliad* to describe those who fought together at Troy (e.g. *Il.* 23.5; M. L. West 1978: 200 on Hes. *Op.* 183). On friendship between Odysseus and his men, see 19 n.

6 ὡς Greek has a demonstrative adv. of manner ὥς ('thus'), a rel. adv. of manner ὡς ('as'), a temporal ὡς ('when'), and a conjunction used in various ways ('that', 'in order that', 'since'). The sense here is plainly the first of these; but after οὐδέ and καί some ancient grammarians preferred to write the demonstrative adv. ὡς rather than ὥς (Probert 2003: 123). This does not affect other kinds of ὡς as they have no accent of their own.

περ Much has been written about this little word. Denniston (1954: 481–90) spoke of there being a basically 'intensive' force: it serves to emphasize the preceding word (*Od.* 8.187; *Il.* 24.504). Bakker (1988) has argued at considerable length that the word is to be understood in terms of scalarity, as marking oppositions between points on a scale such as men and gods (e.g. *Il.* 20.65). Chadwick (1996: 241–7) provides an elegant condensation: 'the particle generally serves to qualify an element in the sentence as one which might have been expected to invalidate it.' In this context it means 'even though': Odysseus tried very hard but failed.

7 αὐτῶν...σφετέρῃσιν Either of these possessives would suffice by itself. The line is probably modelled on *Il.* 4.409, the change from κεῖνοι to αὐτῶν creating a deliberately emphatic pleonasm. Porphyry (*ad Od.* 5.9) and Eusebius (*PE* 6.8.3) plainly had texts that read αὐτοί. That is an easier reading, but looks like a scribal correction; it is hard to see how the majority of MSS came by αὐτῶν.

ἀτασθαλίῃσιν This word carries strong disapproval, being used to describe Aegisthus (*Od.* 1.34) and repeatedly of the suitors (15×). There is no convincing etymology (Leumann 1950: 215). It denotes culpable and reckless conduct against which one has been specifically warned (*Od.* 1.38–9; 12.137–41 ~ 299–301) and for which one deserves to be punished. This is important as it introduces the theme of the apparently just retribution that is ultimately visited upon the suitors. But there is a difference between the suitors, who act of their own free will, and the companions of Odysseus, who are driven by hunger to slay the oxen of the Sun (12.327–32). See also 34 n.

ὄλοντο By no means did all die because of eating the oxen of the sun. Many were killed by the Cicones, Scylla, and the Cyclops. Cf. 34 n.

8 νήπιοι This word is of uncertain derivation. Some (e.g. Stanford 1959: 208) have seen in it a negative prefix νη- followed by the root in ἔπος, the resultant compound meaning 'not speaking', 'infantile'. But the PIE negative prefix was *n̥ – and its expected reflex in Greek is ἀ- or ἀν-. The long vowel in words like νήγρετος is regular where the root of the following word begins with a laryngeal (*n̥-H₁gr-); but νήπιος cannot be explained in that way (Sihler 1995: 106). Whatever its origin, νήπιος is frequently pejorative (*Il.* 15.104; 17.497), likening the addressee to a child (*Il.* 24.726). Telemachus however uses it of himself in a more neutral way that seems merely to indicate that he was too young to punish the suitors as they deserved (*Od.* 2.313). It is uncommon for the poet to intervene in his own voice to pass judgement on his characters. That said, νήπιος (whilst found in the mouths of characters in the epics (*Il.* 5.406; 20.296; *Od.* 9.44)), does often accompany the poet's own comments about a character who is culpably ignorant of what is going to happen to him (*Il.* 2.38, 873; 13.113; 16.46; 20.264; 22.445; *Od.* 22.370). It might be said that, to this extent, the word introduces an element of pathos (cf. Griffin 1976: 165): people suffer because of their ignorance of the larger picture. We might contrast Hesiod, who uses the term to accompany the wagging of his judgemental finger in the direction of his brother Perses (Hes. *Op.* 286).

κατά is a preverb that belongs with ἤσθιον in the next line. In later Greek we would expect κατήσθιον. On this so-called *tmesis*, see Introduction, pp. 57–8.

'Υπερίονος It is tempting to see in this name an old comparative in -ίων (e.g. κακίων *Od.* 14.56) formed to the root seen in ὑπέρ, the product being comparable with Lat. *super-ior*, 'the one that is above.' But this is ruled out by the fact that the *iota* in 'Υπερίονος is long whereas in old comparatives it was originally short (Sihler 1995: 361–2). We are probably dealing here with a suffix *-ī-won-* used to mark personal names (Ruijgh 1968: 140–6). Sometimes Hyperion is synonymous with the Sun (*Od.* 1.24); elsewhere, the Sun is called 'Υπεριονίδης (*Od.* 12.176) which, at first blush, might be thought to mean 'son of Hyperion' (cf. Hes. *Th.* 134, 371–4; *h. Cer.* 26 with Richardson 1973: 158). But the suffix in -ίδης is not necessarily a patronymic (Usener 1896: 20–5); Hyperionides might just be an epithet of the Sun, meaning the same as Hyperion.

'Ηέλιοο Outside the epic, we would expect 'Ηλίου. This word exhibits three features of the epic dialect at the same time: lack of aspiration (Chantraine 1958: 184–5); a gen. in -οιο as well as -ου (Sihler 1995: 259–60); and lack of contraction (Chantraine 1958: 32). The process did not stop at this stage as fully contracted 'Ηλιος is found at *Od.* 8.271. We may reconstruct 'Ηέλιος < *ἀ̄ϝέλιος < *ἀ̄σέλιος. The word is cognate with Lat. *sol* (*DELG* 410–11). That the sun should be a god is not surprising; but in Homer he is not a very important one. When Odysseus' men eat his cattle, it is to Zeus that he must go for a remedy (*Od.* 12.374–88).

9 ἤσθιον The verb completes the sense of the previous line by run-over and is given emphasis by being placed before a sense break (cf. πλάγχθη, l. 2; οὐλομένην *Il.* 1.2).

αὐτάρ This word is sometimes quite strongly adversative (*Il.* 1.118); here that sense is less strongly felt—they ate his oxen and he robbed them of their return. Although αὐτάρ and ἀτάρ differ in origin and use, Homer seems to use them interchangeably to suit the needs of the metre (Denniston 1954: 51, 55).

ὁ τοῖσιν Both of these words are demonstrative pronouns (cf. 4, 157, 439 nn.). The parts with a rough breathing are accented, unlike the articular use of the same forms (Probert 2003: 136–7). The dat. τοῖσιν is of disadvantage (Chantraine 1953: 73).

νόστιμον ἦμαρ The notion of νόστος has already been discussed (5 n.). The -ιμος suffix is remarkably productive in Homer: it grew in the soil of archaic Caland formations such as κύδιμος beside κυδρός and φαίδιμος beside φαιδρός. It then spread to words where there was no original alternation between /r/ and /i/: ἀοίδιμος, κάλλιμος, φύξιμος, νόστιμος, and many others. νόστιμος is confined to the *Odyssey* and reflects its central theme. It can be used of a person to mean that he is able or likely to return home (*Od.* 4.806; 19.85; 20.333; more often (12×) it is joined with ἦμαρ (itself also a purely epic feature beside Ionic ἡμέρη: Ruijgh 1957: 120–1). This produces a solemn, almost biblical turn of phrase. Other such expressions are δούλιον ἦμαρ, αἴσιμον ἦμαρ, μόρσιμον ἦμαρ; these refer to something bad whereas the νόστιμον ἦμαρ is basically something good even if capable of being lost (cf. 168 n.). The connotation of ἦμαρ in these cases is not so much of an objective day in the calendar lived by everyone but of a significant moment experienced by an individual or group (Onians 1951: 414–15).

10 τῶν This gen. is governed by the following εἰπέ ('tell us of these things'); cf. *Od.* 11.174.

ἁμόθεν γε 'from some point or other'. This seems remarkably casual, as though the poet does not care where he begins; but there is nothing artless about the arrangement of the narrative. In the *Iliad* (1.6), the Muse is asked to start from the precise point when the quarrel started; the primary narrative goes back to the beginning and the quarrel and its consequences unfold in real time. In the *Odyssey* the Muse, given a free choice, starts with a council of the gods at a point when Odysseus has already been wandering for a decade. The events leading up to this are told in flashback by Nestor, Menelaus, and Odysseus. This embedding of narratives is just one of the features that make the *Odyssey* a more complex tale than the *Iliad*. For a human singer picking up a tale from a particular point, cf. ἔνθεν ἑλών (*Od.* 8.500).

ἁμόθεν is a *hapax* in Homer but probably belonged to common Attic–Ionic (Shipp 1972: 314 n. 2). The form ἀμόθεν, with no aspiration, is found in some MSS but is not likely to reflect the oldest state of affairs (Chantraine 1958: 281).

εἰπὲ καὶ ἡμῖν This could mean 'Share with us what you already know': cf. *Il.* 2.483–5 on the contrast between human ignorance and the omniscience of the Muses; also *Od.* 9.16–17 for καί and the sharing of knowledge, this time by Odysseus as secondary narrator. It might alternatively mean 'Tell us as you have already told others' (cf. Ar. *Nu.* 357). Σ mentions both possibilities; but the former seems more likely here. By using ἡμῖν the poet now includes himself as part of the audience, unlike in l. 1. The whole proem is an example of ring-composition, beginning and ending with requests for a narrative.

11–21 Transition to Olympus. The poet now moves rapidly on to a position where Odysseus has been with Calypso (for seven years, as it will turn out: *Od.* 7.259). The narrative requires him to return to Ithaca and this comes about by decision of a council on Olympus. These lines explain what has been happening to Odysseus and his companions and make it clear that Odysseus is destined to return home. Far from spoiling the story, this simply means that we are treated to a different kind of narrative with much flashback.

11 αἰπὺν ὄλεθρον It has been suggested that ὄλεθρος and the cognate verb ὄλλυμι derive from a root meaning 'deep' or 'high' and look back to a widespread practice of inflicting death by flinging somebody from a precipice (Koch 1976). This would explain its affinity for αἰπύς (11× *Od.*; 14× *Il.*), with whose meaning it would then overlap. But there is no sense that the death that might have been suffered by Odysseus' men at Troy wold have been of this kind. The tradition probably does sometimes recall this allegedly original sense of ὄλεθρος, most poignantly at *Il.* 24.734–5; most often it does not.

12 οἴκοι Telemachus will go to visit Nestor and Menelaus at their homes in Books 3 and 4.

ἔσαν The MS variant ἴσαν does not yield the correct sense. ἔσαν here lacks the augment but ἦσαν is also very common in Homer.

πεφευγότες If we compare this perf. ptcp. with the aor. φύγον in the preceding line, we can appreciate the stative force of the perf.: they were in a continuing state of survivorship.

13 οἶον 'alone'—cognate with Lat. *unus*.

κεχρημένον perf. ptcp. < χράομαι in the sense of 'long for'.

γυναικός Σ remarks that it is proper for Homer to say this to show how Odysseus despises the erotic affections of the goddess Calypso. We might indeed be touched by this longing for his middle-aged wife over the delights of an ever-youthful goddess. But we are told that Odysseus has sex with Calypso (*Od.* 5.227) and Circe (*Od.* 10.347) so, whatever else might be true, we ought not to import ideas of chaste fidelity into Odysseus' longing for Penelope. See Introduction, p. 29.

14 νύμφη Nymphs are so common in European art and poetry that we risk misunderstanding them in early Greece. It can describe not only ill-defined female nature spirits who have sanctuaries in bosky groves near fountains (*Od.* 17.204–11) but also an ordinary woman such as Penelope (*Od.* 4.743). Here it denotes a goddess. Its etymology has never been satisfactorily settled: some scholars connect it with Lat. *nubo* ('marry'), but are at a loss to explain the origin of the internal nasal (Kretschmer 1909b, 1916). A more ingenious etymology connects it, through Proto-Ger. *wambo-* ('womb'), with PIE *wᵉ/ₒmbha-* which in the zero-grade yields *umbha-* and together with a prefix *(e)ni-* ('in') comes to mean 'pregnant woman' (Windekens 1982/3). If correct, this goes some way semantically towards explaining why νύμφαι are so often connected with motherhood: *Il.* 5.21–2; 14.444; 20.384. The anonymity in the last two cases is suggestive— as though there is a generic group of females who become involved in liaisons that give rise to unusual people and the poet is not always interested in their names. On the shield of Achilles, a group of brides are called νύμφαι (*Il.* 18.492). Iris calls Helen νύμφη φίλη (*Il.* 3.130); Penelope is referred to in this way both as a young bride (*Od.* 11.447) but also nineteen years later by Eurycleia (*Od.* 4.743). The nymph Calypso wants marriage with Odysseus (*Od.* 1.15). Circe, described as νύμφη at *Od.* 10.543, wants sex with Odysseus and gets it (*Od.* 10.333–5, 347). Whatever the etymology of νύμφη, its sphere of reference appears primarily to denote female reproductive potential.

πότνι᾽ This is an archaic word, as can be seen from its cognates in Skt. *pátni-* and Avestan *paθni-*, both meaning 'mistress', and Lat. *potis*, which denotes power. Within Greek it appears formally to belong beside πόσις ('husband'). It is far commoner in the *Iliad* (49×) than the *Odyssey* (23×). In the *Iliad*, it is frequently used of Hera (24×; *Od.* only 1×); the vast majority of its other appearances are with μήτηρ (21×), applied both to divine (*Il.* 1.357) and mortal (*Il.* 6.471) mothers. In the *Odyssey*, it is likewise used most often with μήτηρ (13×). It is also applied to Circe (*Od.* 10.394; 4×). There is an extensive literature concerning the Mycenaean parallel *po-ti-ni-ja* (Trümpy 2001: 413 n. 19) and much speculation is possible concerning the Mother Goddess (Godart 2001). It is sufficient here to note that the word chiefly refers to wives and mothers. But its application to virgin goddesses such as Athena (*Il.* 6.305; *Od.* 13.391) and Artemis (*Od.* 20.61) suggests that it had by a later (but still archaic) date broken free from this original sense and could mean simply 'lady'. The *Odyssey* uses the phrase νύμφη πότνια (as here) and πότνια νύμφη (*Od.* 5.149) when talking of Calypso. The collocation seems natural since both words can connote female fertility.

Καλυψώ This appears to be a speaking name (cf. 383 n.), somehow related to the root seen in καλύπτω so as to mean 'the concealer' (a common divine function: cf. *Il.* 5.23; 11.751). The etymology is obscure: agential nouns are not formed by adding –σώ to the root and the accent and the semantics are wrong for a verb in the future tense. The name fits since part of Calypso's function is to keep Odysseus concealed on her island and prevent his return. It stretches belief to argue that Καλυψώ might mean 'the veiled one' and that, because she lives in the middle of the sea, she is to be connected with the ale-wife Siduri in the Epic of Gilgamesh, who wears a veil and lives by the sea (*pace* M. L. West 1997a: 410–12).

That Calypso would like to make Odysseus ageless and deathless (*Od.* 5.135–6) perhaps reminds us of the immortality given to some heroes (*PMG* 291, 558; Pi. *N.* 10.7; Procl. *Chrest.* p. 109 Allen; Crane 1988: 15). But καλύπτω is also found in the context of death (*Il.* 4.503; 16.855) and burial (*Il.* 6.464).

In any event, Calypso is not simply a plot device to explain delay, but offers physical delights the resistance to which on the part of Odysseus seems laudable (Rutherford 1986: 146 with n. 6). In this respect she is very similar to Circe: both are described as δεινὴ θεὸς αὐδήεσσα ('an awesome goddess who uses human speech': *Od.* 12.449 ~ *Od.* 10.136; 11.8; 12.150—this last epithet being probably a relic from an era when gods were not thought to speak to humans (Dirlmeier 1970: 80–1)); both are said to be δολόεσσα ('tricky': *Od.* 7.245 ~ *Od.* 9.32); both are called νύμφη (*Od.* 1.14 ~ *Od.* 5.230; 10.543); and both are said to want Odysseus for a husband (*Od.* 1.15; 9.50 ~ *Od.* 9.52). But Circe is a figure from folk-tale, the type of the fearsome witch; Calypso is more subtly and attractively drawn so that Odysseus' departure involves much tact both on his part and that of the gods (Griffin 1980: 58–61).

δῖα θεάων δῖος < PIE *dyw-, cf. Skt. *divyá-*, Lat. *divus*. The name of the sky-god Ζεύς, Διός is likely derived from the same root (Sihler 1995: 337–9, *pace* Ruijgh 1967a: 133 n. 168). The original sense of δῖος was probably 'bright', but within Greek it could also mean simply 'of Zeus (*sc.* the Bright One)' (*Il.* 9.538). Over time, it was applied not only to things that are bright such as the sky (*Il.* 16.365), dawn (*Il.* 9.240), and the sea (*Od.* 3.153), but also to a horse (*Il.* 8.185), the Achaeans (*Il.* 5.451), Lacedaemon (*Od.* 3.326), Elis (*Od.* 13.275), a swineherd (*Od.* 22.162), Orestes (*Od.* 1.298), Helen (*Od.* 3.305), Charybdis (*Od.* 12.235), Penelope (*Od.* 23.302), Circe (*Od.* 13.155). This broader sense probably matches Eng. 'illustrious'. The gen. θεάων is partitive—'among goddesses'.

Schwyzer (1950: 116) believed that δῖα θεάων was modelled on the formula δῖα γυναικῶν; but it was more likely the other way about. At *Il.* 5.381 we find Διώνη, δῖα θεάων. It probably means 'Mrs Zeus, wife of Zeus among the goddesses' (Pulleyn 2006: 59–60; cf. Ruijgh 1967a: 133). δῖα θεάων is also used of Calypso, Circe, Eidothea, Aurora, and Athena—who are goddesses, but not married to Zeus. δῖα γυναικῶν is used only of Penelope and Helen, both mortal. It seems most likely that the phrase was coined for Dione, whose name contains the same root, was extended to five other goddesses and then used, less productively because later in the tradition, for two mortal women.

15 ἐν σπέεσι γλαφυροῖσι Caves are a common location for liaisons between gods and mortals: *Od.* 1.71–3; *h. Ven.* 262–3; *h. Merc.* 1–9; *h. Hom.*

18.1–9. A Freudian sense for the cave is not far to seek. Whilst nymphs' grottoes are places of prophecy (Ustinova 2009: 58), that is not a significant function of Calypso within the poem as we have it.

Most MSS read σπέσι, which is unmetrical. The correction σπέσσι appears in some witnesses but is morphologically anomalous: the correct dat. pl. of a noun of this kind would be σπέεσι (Chantraine 1958: 7; Sihler 1995: 307). That is printed here, but with hesitation—it being possible that the bards had already forgotten the correct inflexion and so formed σπέσσι by analogy with βέλεσσι (*Il.* 1.42).

λιλαιομένη πόσιν εἶναι This phrase is also used of Circe (*Od.* 9.32). The verb, pleasantly lilting in sound and perhaps even onomatopoeic (Tichy 1983: 230–1), is striking in meaning: deriving from PIE *las-, cf. Lat. *lascivus*, it denotes strong desire (*DELG* 640–1). Hesychius has a form λάσται which he glosses as πόρναι ('prostitutes') and which probably contains the same root. Although πόσις basically means 'lord' (cf. 14 n.), one cannot help feeling that Odysseus would have been more consort than lord in Calypso's cave.

16 ἔτος … περιπλομένων ἐνιαυτῶν Whilst ἔτος and ἐνιαυτός appear to be used more or less interchangeably (S. R. West 1988: 74; Emlyn-Jones 1967), one can draw inferences about the original sense of each word. Beekes (1969a) concludes that ἐνιαυτός refers originally to the anniversary of an event as the years go round (hence its use in the old formulae τελεσφόρον εἰς ἐνιαυτόν and περιπλομένων ἐνιαυτῶν, both of which involve the PIE root *kʷelH₁-, 'to go round', Rix 2001: 386–8) whereas ἔτος perhaps originally referred to a period of time, what English speakers might once have called 'a twelvemonth'. If ἔτος ever had that sense, it is not apparent in this line.

17 ἐπεκλώσαντο The image of spinning is connected with destiny in a number of Indo-European mythologies (M. L. West 2007: 380–5). At *Od.* 7.197, we hear of Κλῶθες ('spinners') who spin out the threads of destiny; elsewhere, the spinning is done by Αἶσα (*Il.* 20.127–8) or Μοῖρα (*Il.* 24.209–10). Both of these words are often translated as 'fate' but originally denote just a portion (34 n.). Perhaps some Greeks thought of personal Fates separate from the Olympian gods (cf. Hes. *Th.* 904–6); but in the world of the epics it is clear that fate is firmly under the control of Zeus (Pulleyn 2000: 32–3).

By telling us that the return of Odysseus is fated, Homer has removed any doubt about this element of the story. But this is just another example of his careful handling of narrative. The question is not whether Odysseus will get home but how he will accomplish it and what will stand in his way.

18 οὐδ᾽ ἔνθα The adv. is most naturally taken as temporal rather than spatial here and picks up on ἀλλ᾽ ὅτε δή (16). When the gods finally decided to set in motion the wheels of his return, not even then was Odysseus safe from toil and back among his own people. If ἔνθα is taken spatially to refer to Ithaca, it is a peculiarly intrusive and parenthetic reference to future events after Odysseus' homecoming.

19 οἷσι φίλοισι A number of MSS have οἷς ἑτάροισι. But is is not clear that the reference here is to Odysseus' lack of safety even among his companions (although he does refer to them as φίλοι (*Od.* 10.174, 12.153–4)). It seems more likely that the reference is to his being safe from danger and back with his own people on Ithaca.

ἐλέαιρον There are two families of words in Homer denoting pity: those built to the root ἐλ- (74×) and those built to οἰκτ- (18×). Of the former class, pity felt by gods accounts for twenty-three instances, the remaining fifty-one relating to mortal pity; of the latter group, there is no example of specifically divine pity. Poseidon does not pity Odysseus because he has blinded Polyphemus (*Od.* 1.69; Schenk 2008: 160), but he does pity the Achaeans when worsted in battle (*Il.* 13.15; 15.44). Athena pities Penelope (*Od.* 4.828), presumably as a result of her partisanship for Odysseus. Nestor appears to tell Agamemnon that Zeus pities him (*Il.* 2.27), although this is in the context of a deceptive dream. Whereas it is one of the defining characteristics of the Abrahamic God that He pities humans and has mercy on them, this is no part of the Homeric vision where humans are kinder than gods. The pity of the immortals is unpredictable and depends on their personal affections and dislikes.

20 Ποσειδάωνος Poseidon, Zeus, and Hades are brothers to each other and children of Cronus. The world was divided between them: Zeus got the heavens, Hades the underworld, and Poseidon the oceans with earth and Olympus being common to all (*Il.* 15.187–93). On the name, see 68 n.

ἀσπερχές This neut. sg. acc. adj. functions as an adverb. The prefixed alpha is intensive (or 'copulative'), being added to the root σπερχ- which denotes furious motion (e.g. of storm winds: *Il.* 13.334).

μένεαινεν The verb appears to be derived from the noun μένος ('force'), perhaps on the analogy of βλεμεαίνω. It denotes strong feeling and is ultimately derived from the root *men-, which has to do with the activation of the mind and also gives us μῆνις (Muellner 1996: 186–94) and Μοῦσα (*Od.* 1.1 n).

21 ἀντιθέῳ Morally speaking, there is often little to choose between humans and gods (Xenoph. B 11 D–K). The latter differ from the former chiefly in being more powerful and immune to age and death. Thus

human beings are most like gods when their deeds of valour are sufficiently exceptional. There is pathos in this (Griffin 1980: 82): the hero
whose mighty exploits earn him fleeting comparison with a god is nevertheless not saved thereby from being driven through storm and shipwreck,
nakedness, and the loss of his companions.

’Οδυσῆϊ The first naming of the hero of the poem. As pointed out
already (*Od.* 1.1 n.), not only is his name postponed until l. 21, his appearance is postponed to Book 5.

Inscriptions from the seventh century BC have the spelling ’Ολισευς.
The form of the name with *l* is common throughout mainland Greece and
reflected in Lat. *Ulixes.* The form with *d* is peculiar to the Greek epic tradition
(M. L. West 2014: 6–7). The name is probably pre-Greek in origin and of
obscure meaning; this offers the poet some scope for word-play (62 n.).

πάρος Functions like πρίν with the inf. in classical Greek. The subject
of the inf. is not Poseidon but Odysseus: it is expected to be in the acc.
(Chantraine 1953: 315–16) and is to be supplied from the dat. ’Οδυσῆϊ.

ἰκέσθαι A minority of MSS here read ἰδέσθαι (which would be metrical
assuming disregard of inherited initial digamma). A similar hesitation is
found at *Od.* 5.408, but there the majority MSS have ἰδέσθαι. Arriving at
one's homeland and seeing it are pretty much synonymous in this context;
but perhaps the mention of wanderings favours a verb of motion here.

22–95 The council on Olympus. As Poseidon has gone to see the
Ethiopians there is the opportunity for a council in his absence. This
important scene in some ways mirrors the council in the first book of the
Iliad. But there are differences. Although all the other Olympian gods are
present (26), only two take any active part: Zeus and Athena. Further, in
the *Iliad* Zeus had been entreated by special pleading from Thetis to sway
the course of events on earth so as to honour Achilles. Here by contrast we
see Zeus in a less partial light, concerned more generally with cosmic
justice. This does not mean that Poseidon and the other gods are any less
biased or capricious; but we might detect a slight shift in Zeus' relationship to justice between the *Iliad* and *Odyssey* (Lloyd-Jones 1983: 28–33;
M. L. West 2014: 48–50).

22 Αἰθίοπας This difficult word probably means 'with burnt faces'
(Pulleyn 2000: 229–31; S. R. West 1988: 75). In *Iliad* 1, Zeus and all the other
gods went to the Ethiopians for a feast. Whatever their other qualities
(Introduction, p. 32), they are also a convenient narrative device in both
epics to explain absence from Olympus.

μετεκίαθε We see here an extended form of the root seen in the pres.
stem κίω. Whilst formally this could be an imperf., it is more likely an aor.

as an accomplished action is indicated here (Chantraine 1958: 328; cf. *Il.* 11.714; 18.532).

τήλοθ' ἐόντας We glimpse here an ethnographic interest in those who dwell in faraway places (cf. ἔσχατοι ἀνδρῶν, 'farthest of men', 24). This recalls the Abii who live apart from other men and are also the most just (*Il.* 13.4, 6). Perhaps a similar moral excellence makes the Ethiopians the hosts of choice for the gods (Snowden 1970: 144–7); but this depends in part on arguing that ἀμύμων (*Il.* 1.423) means 'blameless', which is doubtful (*Od.* 1.29 n.; Pulleyn 2000: 149–50). The ability of their land to furnish a rich banquet that lasts twelve days (*Il.* 1.423–5) is far more likely to be what attracts the Olympians (Romm 1992: 50–2).

23 *Αἰθίοπας* This repetition, where classical Greek would use a rel. pronoun, is known as epanalepsis (Fehling 1969: 184–5). It is used to introduce supplementary information, especially in the Catalogue of Ships (*Il.* 2.671–3, 837–8, 849–50, 870–1). This is the only example of it in the *Odyssey* (Nünlist 2011: 142). It is a common feature of the paratactic style of later Ionic prose such as Herodotus (Denniston 1952: 92–5). This is not surprising: the majority of the Homeric language is Ionic and one might expect to find Herodotus not only sounding like Homer but following some of his stylistic turns (Boedeker 2002: 100). The figure may be an inherited PIE poetic device (M. L. West 2007: 106–7).

τοι This is a demonstrative pron. used as a rel. Classical Attic–Ionic has οἵ. Retention of the original PIE *toi* (Sihler 1995: 388–9) is found in West Greek (Colvin 2007: 47) as well as in Homer.

διχθά This division into two groups at the extremities of the earth is puzzling, given that Homer also has Ethiopians in Africa (Nadeau 1970: 339). We might be dealing with 'opposite coasts of a dimly perceived African continent' (Romm 1992: 49–50), but only if Africa was imagined as straddling the planet from East to West. For Herodotus (7.69–70; cf. 3.94) both Indians and Africans are Ethiopians (Schneider 2004: 15). Maybe the idea of two groups was taken over from Akkadian references to a land called *Melucha*, which seems to denote both the Sudan and a more distant country much farther East (Goukowski 1974: 111–17). The five references to Ethiopians in Homer fall into two groups. The majority have a mythical quality, referring to a people who live far away by Ocean, are visited by gods, and provide hecatombs (*Il.* 1.423; 23.205; *Od.* 1.22; 5.282). But when Menelaus is describing his wanderings (*Od.* 4.84–5) he locates them very precisely among other named nations in Africa in a way that suggests a real place visited by and known to real travellers (Lesky 1959: 33–5). If the ethonym does indeed refer to skin colour (22 n.), one might suspect that early Ionian speculation had concluded that any people who were close enough to the sun to be burned by it must dwell both where it rises and where it sets since this is where it is closest to Earth (Engels 1977: 16).

δεδαίαται 3 pl. perf. ind. pass. These forms in -αται are common in Homer and show a vocalic treatment of the inherited *n in the 3 pl. perf. pass., thus -αται instead of -νται (Sihler 1995: 479–80). Classical Greek uses -νται in vowel stems and the periphrastic perf. ptcp. in consonantal ones (Smyth 1956: 183; cf. 132, 155).

ἔσχατοι ἀνδρῶν See on τηλόθ᾽ ἐόντας (22 n.).

24 δυσομένου ... ἀνιόντος Local genitives describe where something happens (cf. *Il.* 9.219; *Od.* 3.251; 21.108–9; Chantraine 1953: 58).

δυσομένου The symmetry with ἀνιόντος, together with the general sense, requires this word to have a pres. sense (cf. Hes. *Op.* 384). But formally it appears to be a sigmatic fut. med. ptcp. If we look at the common expression δύσετό τ᾽ ἠέλιος σκιόωντό τε πᾶσαι ἀγυιαί (*Od.* 2.388 and passim), we find an imperf. (σκιόωντο) following what looks like an imperf. (or strong aor.) med. displaying an unexpected sigmatic infix. Since the sense here, at least (but see Pulleyn 2000: 232), ought plainly to be imperf., it has been suggested that δύσετο means 'was going to set'. If the sun was seen as either up or down, one would not say δύεται (for 'it is setting') or δύετο (for 'it was setting') but rather *δύσεται ('it is going to set') and δύσετο ('it was going to set')—the sigmatic element yielding a kind of 'future in the past' when coupled with the imperf. ending. If this is correct, δυσομένου means 'when it is going to set' (Roth 1974: 5–6).

25 ἀντιόων Σ glosses this pres. ptcp. with the fut. μεταληψόμενος ('in order to partake of'). This suggests that ἀντιόων was understood as purposive. For the most part the gods are seen as having nectar and ambrosia, which are food and drink for immortals and whose very names denote immortality (ἀμβροσίη < *n̥-mr-to-s cf. Lat. *im-mort-alis*; νέκταρ < *nek-terH₂ (cf. Lat. *nex, necis* + a suffix denoting 'to overcome', see Pulleyn 2006: 61–74). But Homer is inconsistent over this and the gods are sometimes said actually to dine on sacrificial meat—as here and at *Il.* 9.535. We may suppose that this represented a more primitive stage before the tradition decided that bloodless gods with ἰχώρ in their veins (*Il.* 5.339–42) could not depend on anything so base as meat and wine. For all that, they still accept sacrifice as γέρας ('prize'; *Il.* 4.49), an expression of the τιμή ('honour, worth') due to them (Pulleyn 2000: 34, 143–4). On the phenomenon of diectasis here, see Introduction, p. 52.

ἑκατόμβης It is generally supposed, by many modern scholars as by Σ, that this word originally denoted the sacrifice of a hundred oxen (ἑκατὸν βοῦς). But it refers to bulls and sheep, and elsewhere to bulls and goats

(*Il.* 1.315–16). This lack of specificity as to species is paralleled by numerical divergence: it is elsewhere used of fifty animals (*Il.* 23.146–8) or even just twelve (*Il.* 6.93, 115). One might conclude that this was just a linguistic slippage over time. But it is hard to imagine an actual, as opposed to imagined, sacrifice of one hundred oxen (Parker 2011: 167–9 deals with the same problem in later Greece). These animals were extremely expensive and the actual sacrifice of so many would be ruinous. Nor will it do to suppose that the word was confined to the epic imagination because it is not used consistently even there. On the basis of parallels in Indic sources, it has been argued that the word denoted a sacrifice that was intended to win the favour of the gods to so as to *bring in* a hundred oxen (Thieme 1952; Puhvel 1964).

26 τέρπετο It has often been said (e.g. Burkert 1983: 16) that sacrifice was for the Greeks bound up with feelings of guilt about killing. However this might be, here is an example of a sacrifice being viewed as a pleasurable meal. One might say that this is because the person rejoicing was immortal and had different standards. But Herodotus (8.99) also equates sacrifice with pleasure for the mortal participants. It is unlikely that so complex and central a feature of Greek religion could involve only one of two polar opposites (Parker 2011: 127–32 surveys the history and gives a careful account of the later evidence).

παρήμενος This word could mean no more than that Poseidon is seated and in attendance at the banquet. But it is also used of sitting by in idle detachment (*Il.* 1.488) or of taking one's ease (*Od.* 19.589–90). There are probably overtones of that here.

ἄλλοι In *Iliad* Book 1 the assembled gods on Olympus have a banquet which contrasts with the more wretched state of strife among the mortals on earth (*Il.* 1.575–604). Here however most of the gods are assembled for a serious discussion; only one of their number is enjoying a banquet and he is absent at a great distance.

27 Ζηνὸς...'Ολυμπίου The figure of Zeus in Homer plainly owes a good deal to the Indo-European sky-god *Dyews*, reflected in the Indic Dyāús. For example, he is said to live in the bright αἰθήρ (*Il.* 2.412; 4.166). But he is also a god of storms responsible for lightning (*Il* 1.580; 12.275), clouds (*Il.* 1.560; 4.30), and thunder (*Il.* 1.354; 14.54). These attributes suggest Near Eastern influence, as does the image of the gods all living together on Olympus to such an extent that Zeus can be identified with it as 'the Olympian one' (Pulleyn 2006: 48–53).

ἐνί The final syllable of this word, although phonetically short, is metrically heavy. This is not because it is followed by two consonants, but because of the phenomenon where a phonetically short vowel may be treated as metrically heavy if followed by a continuant such a λ, μ, ν, ρ (M. L. West 1982a: 15, 38).

μεγάροισι Some archaeologists (e.g. K. Werner 1993) use this word to refer to the principal hall in a Mycenaean palace, perhaps 'analogous to the great hall of a medieval English manor house or the dining hall of an Oxford or Cambridge college' (Wace 1962: 494). The sg. may be used in this way in Homer (*Od.* 17.604); the pl. may signify the entire dwelling of a god or mortal of any rank (Knox 1970). There is considerable overlap in this semantic field: the home of Laertes is described as οἶκος (*Od.* 24.358, 365), δώματα (*Od.* 24.361), δόμοι (*Od.* 24.362), μέγαρα (*Od.* 15.534; 24.412). Zeus had a δῶμα on Olympus (*Il.* 1.533), built for him by Hephaestus who had done the same for the other gods (*Il.* 1.606–8). These δω- houses seem to be the same as the μέγαρα that each god is later said to have (*Il.* 11.76).

ἀθρόοι The idea of gods who live on a mountain in the North and meet in an assembly is not part of the inherited Indo-European mythology, to judge from its absence in Indo-Iranian and related sources. It strongly suggests influence from the cultures of the Near East, several of which possess these story patterns (M. L. West 1997a: 177–9; Pulleyn 2006: 53–7).

Some MSS read ἀθρόοι. The prefix would appear to be PIE *sm-, cf. Gk. ἅμα, εἷς, Lat. *semel*; the root appears to be the same as in Skt. *sa-dhri-añc-* ('united'). The expected form would have the smooth breathing, the aspiration being lost by dissimilation before the aspirate -θ- (Grassmann's Law; cf. Schwyzer 1939: 257, 261; Risch 1974: 177). These forms with loss of aspiration spread by analogy to words such as ἄκοιτις, ἀολλής (*DELG* 2).

28–31 There is some subtlety in the arrangement of words in these lines so that l. 31 is a chiastic reflection of the elements of ll. 28–9: μύθων ἦρχε (A)...μνήσατο (B)...Αἰγίσθοιο (C)... : : τοῦ (C)...ἐπιμνησθείς (B)...ἔπε(α)...μετηύδα (A). In part this is a paratactic feature typical of epic diction; but it also shows that composition using this kind of traditional poetic language does not preclude conscious and elaborate verbal effects.

28 μύθων ἦρχε Zeus not only starts to speak, he tells the other gods a story and so becomes a secondary narrator within the primary narrative of the poet. This embedding is one of the many marks of sophistication in the poem. μῦθος has been defined as 'a speech-act indicating authority, usually performed at length, usually in public with a focus on full attention to every detail' whereas ἔπος is 'an utterance, ideally short, accompanying a physical act, and focusing on the message, as perceived by the addressee, rather than on performance as enacted by the speaker' (Martin 1989: 12). But watertight distinctions are not possible: these same

words of Zeus are described here as μῦθοι but only a few lines later as ἔπεα
(l. 31). Whilst there is plainly some overlap, it is probably correct to say
that ἔπος refers to words in a simple and unmarked way whereas μῦθος
denotes concerted speech and hence a plan or story (Fournier 1946:
211–16). Thus μῦθος is a natural (*Od.* 2.83, 137, 159), but not obligatory (*Od.*
1.31; 2.189), term for a speech made to an assembly. On other words for
speech-acts, see 56 n.

πατὴρ ἀνδρῶν τε θεῶν τε The sequence Ζεὺς πατήρ is cognate with Lat.
Jupiter < *Diespiter* and Vedic *dyáuḥ pitá* (Sihler 1995: 339). The fatherhood
of Zeus is plainly an inherited Indo-European idea. It is extended to gods
and men in this formula, which is without Indic parallel (M. L. West 2007:
186–91). Zeus is not father to all the gods as Hades and Hera and Poseidon
are his siblings, nor to all men, as the poems liberally attest. Nevertheless
the fiction of his universal fatherhood fits here with his concern for
universal justice.

29 ἀμύμονος This world is often translated as 'blameless', but that cannot
be correct in the light of the blame heaped upon Aegisthus in this passage.
It has been argued that the word in fact denotes bodily beauty and strength
and has no necessary connexion with morality (Anne Parry 1973: esp.
156). This finding is strengthened by the conjecture that the word derives
from a PIE root *H_2meu- meaning something like 'surpass' (Heubeck
1987b; Pulleyn 2000: 149–50).

Αἰγίσθοιο The Mycenaean family saga later known as the *Oresteia*
plays an important role in this book (Olson 1990). The poet refers to it in
his own voice here, although with no reference to Clytemnestra. Zeus will
tell the story to the gods (35–9), referring to Clytemnestra but not by
name. Athena then picks up the theme of just punishment and uses it
to contrast it with the fate of Odysseus (46–62). She will later use the
example of Orestes and Aegisthus to spur on Telemachus to action
(298 n.). These are not incidental references but important parts of the
thematic architecture.

30 τὸν…Ὀρέστης This line is omitted in two tenth-century MSS in the
Laurentian Library, the scribes perhaps not seeing that it is parenthetical
so that τοῦ ὅ γε in l. 31 picks up with no difficulty the reference to Aegisthus
at the end of l. 39.

Ἀγαμεμνονίδης Patronymics are extremely common in the *Iliad*:
being somebody's son is a matter of pedigree and marks out the bearer as
special (Kahane 2005: 39). They are much less common in the *Odyssey*,
where they serve the same function and are perhaps the more striking for
their comparative rarity: thus Phemius is called Τερπιάδης (*Od.* 22.330).
They take several different morphological forms (Stanford 1959: 330);

parallels across other PIE languages suggest high antiquity (Fortson 2009: 121). It is striking that Telemachus has no patronymic.

τηλεκλυτός This adj. is used only here and of the immortal horses at *Il.* 19.400. It is plainly an unusual and striking word. Its first element recalls the name of Telemachus (cf. 261–2 n.); but it also recalls Odysseus as he too has a fame that reaches far (*Od.* 9.20). Since Orestes is the archetypal figure of the avenger, there might be a hint here that Telemachus will assist Odysseus in his revenge (De Jong 2001: 13–14).

31 ἐμπιμνησθείς This word is from the same root as Μοῦσα (cf. 1 n.). Memory and recitation are intimately related and somehow divine (cf. *Od.* 4.17; 9.4).

ἔπε' See 28 n. The variants ἔπεα πτερόεντα προσηύδα and ἔπεα πτερόεντ' ἀγόρευεν are found in a small number of comparatively late MSS. They probably arose because ἔπε' ἀθανάτοισι μετηύδα is unique in Homer and it seemed better to replace it with a more familiar formula.

μετηύδα This imperf. tense indicates perhaps that Zeus was beginning to speak; at any rate, it focuses on the unfolding of his speech over time rather than presenting it as a discrete, point-like intervention (Chantraine 1953: 192–3).

32 πόποι Various later writers (Euph. 136; Lycoph., *Alex.* 943) thought, or purported to think, that this word meant 'gods'. Plutarch thought it a relic from the language of the immemorially ancient Dryopians (*Mor.* 22CD). It was also ascribed to the Scythians in the same sense (*EM* 823, 24). All of this looks like hopeless antiquarian conjecture; it is surely an onomato-poeic expression of annoyance or disgust (Kretschmer 1909a: 15–16). This being so, the correct accentuation of the preceding word is ὤ rather than ὦ—for an exclamation rather than an address.

νυ This enclitic (cf. νυν, νῦν) is found only in Epic, Boeotian, and Cypriot. It has a lively conversational force, 'now then'; cf. Fr. *alors*.

θεοὺς βροτοί Some MSS read βροτοὶ θεούς. This would require the cluster βρ- to be treated as syllable-releasing (i.e. νυ–βρο- rather than νυβ–ρο-) in order to preserve the syllable in νυ as metrically light (see Introduction, p. 48). Whilst this is not impossible, the phenomenon of a mute followed by a liquid being treated in this way is relatively uncom-mon with voiced plosives such as β (M. L. West 1982: 16–17).

αἰτιόωνται Mortals regularly blame gods for human ills in the *Iliad*. Achilles has a memorably pessimistic image of Zeus having two jars, one of good things and one of bad, from which he metes out to mortals either unmitigated evil or a mixture of good and bad but never pure good (*Il.* 24.527–33 with Macleod 1982: 133). Agamemnon blames his own mistreat-ment of Chryses and Achilles on Zeus and Fate and the Fury that goes about in the air (*Il.* 19.87). We might think it has more to do with his character. The poet refers to a mysterious Διὸς βουλή (*Il.* 1.5; 'plan of Zeus'), but there is no indication that this has anything to do with objective right and wrong. It would appear that, whilst the other gods of the *Odyssey*, especially Athena and Poseidon, are as biased and partial as in the *Iliad*, Zeus has nevertheless become sensitive to the sort of criticisms outlined above and this speech is meant to be an exculpation (Rutherford 1986: 146–8). Zeus plainly cares about justice, yet Odysseus still suffers; that paradox is not unique to Greek paganism. Cf. 234, 244, 348–9 nn.

33 καὶ αὐτοί Σ remarks that Aristarchus thought the καί was superfluous after δέ and reports an alternative reading οἵδε; but δέ here is adversative and καί emphasizes the pron. so that their appearing together is perfectly idiomatic.

34 σφῇσιν ἀτασθαλίῃσιν This word has already been used to explain why Odysseus' companions perished on their way home (7 n.). That explanation of their fate was not altogether satisfactory. Here the word has some programmatic force: the suitors exhibit the same kind of wicked behaviour as Aegisthus (*Od.* 22.416; P. V. Jones 1991: 104–5); Odysseus, heedful of the advice of the gods, will prevail over them (Dodds 1951: 32–3).

ὑπὲρ μόρον Of the various Greek words conventionally rendered into English as 'fate', μόρος and μοῖρα both denote a portion; αἶσα in an early Cypriot inscription refers to a measure of wine (*Inscr. Cret.* 148); πεπρωμένον comes from *πόρω ('provide'). These terms are more or less synonymous, denoting what has been meted out. ὑπὲρ αἶσαν and κατ' αἶσαν (*Il.* 3.59; 6.333) and κατὰ μοῖραν (*Il.* 1.286) are used to denote what is 'right'. Sometimes things do actually occur ὑπὲρ αἶσαν (*Il.* 16.780) or ὑπὲρ Διὸς αἶσαν (*Il.* 17.321; cf. *Od.* 1.17 n.); at others, characters merely fear that something will be ὑπὲρ μόρον (*Il.* 20.30; cf. 21.517). The sense here is that mortals, because of their own folly, suffer beyond what would otherwise be their natural lot. The ultimate dispenser is Zeus (*Il.* 24.527–33); there is no indication that he is subservient to any higher forces of destiny (*Il.* 16.433–49; Pulleyn 2000: 31–3).

Ἀτρείδαο A gen. in –αο– created by analogy with (unattested but inferred) masc. stems in –οο (–οιο > –οο > –ου). This is an Aeolic form; the Ionic form is Ἀτρείδεο (*Il.* 2.185 etc.; Chantraine 1958: 69, 200–1). Cf. 40 n.

36 ἄλοχον μνήστην Agamemnon in the *Iliad* referred to his wife as κουριδίη ἄλοχος (*Il.* 1.114). ἄλοχος describes someone who shares the same bed (λέχος). μνήστη comes from μνάομαι, taken by Osthoff (1883) for a desiderative built to PIE *gʷenā (cf. γυνή, 'woman', 'wife'). There are strong formal objections to this and a connexion with μέμνημαι *and* PIE

*men– ('to engage the mind'; cf. 1 n.) seems more likely (Benveniste 1954; *DELG* 702). Its use here finds an echo in μνάασθαι (*Od.* 1.39) and might recall the very name Κλυταιμ(ν)ήστρη (*Il.* 1.113) if there truly was a –ν– in it. Most MSS of Homer transmit the spelling Κλυταιμνήστρη; some have Κλυταιμήστρη. The former would mean 'famously wooed', the latter 'famous schemer' (< μήδομαι).

τόν Agamemnon.

νοστήσαντα This word normally denotes a safe return home from Troy by sea (5 n.). Agamemnon got his return but was robbed of the expected fruits of it. The pathos is not unlike that evoked by Priam who says that, whereas a bloody death is somehow glamorous for the young warrior, it is a pitiful thing for one who has safely reached old age (*Il.* 22.71–6). One might also contrast Menelaus, who has returned safely home to Sparta and is living quietly with Helen.

37 εἰδώς What is meant is that Aegisthus knew that this course of action would spell death for himself. It does not mean that he had murder in his heart: expressions with εἰδώς can denote disposition (335, 428 nn.), but only when followed by a neut. pl. adj. At *Od.* 4.534 Agamemnon is described as knowing his own imminent death.

αἰπὺν ὄλεθρον See 11 n.

πρό οἱ εἴπομεν Is πρό here a temporal adv. ('before') or a preverb in tmesis ('announce')? The former seems most likely (Chantraine 1953: 130) as no verb προειπεῖν is otherwise found in Homer.

38 The Massiliote text omits the line as printed in this edition and has instead πέμψαντες Μαίης ἐρικυδέος ἀγλαὸν υἱόν. The formula ἀγλαὸν υἱόν with its inflected variants is common enough in Homer, but is never used elsewhere of Hermes. Nor is the gen. Μαίης found in Homer with or without the epithet ἐρικυδέος. Μαιάδος is found, but only at *Od.* 14.435 (a line that has itself been thought suspect: Shipp 1972: 340). The Massiliote reading is surely a later fabrication. The variant Ἑρμείαν πέμψαντε διάκτορον ἀργειφόντην was widely current in antiquity (Zenodotus, Aristophanes, Oxy. 1087). The dual is not itself fatal to its authenticity since it might be that just Zeus and Athena are meant. But διάκτορον is far commoner than εὔσκοπον and might represent the easier variant, written by mistake and requiring πέμψαντε so as to provide the requisite light syllable in this position (S. R. West 1988: 80).

Ἑρμείαν Hermes is an odd figure in the epic pantheon. He is plainly better established on Olympus than, for example, Thetis or Iris; but he plays a subordinate role as messenger and 'fixer' to Zeus and Athena. He appears to be at least as old as the Linear B tablets (Heubeck 1970: 812 against Gérard-Rousseau 1968: 85–8). His epithet δῶτορ ἐάων ('giver of good things': *Od.* 8.335) is likewise of high antiquity, being cognate with Skt. *dátā vásūnām* (Durante 1962). His epithet ἐριούνιος is obscure in meaning but might be an old Cypriot term denoting speed (Bowra 1934: 68). His very name is controversial (Hainsworth 1988: 259), but is connected by most scholars with ἕρμα meaning a prop or stay (M. L. West 1997a: 34). Later sources tell how the gods tried to stone Hermes for killing Argus but ended up merely throwing their stones at his feet where they formed a cairn (Anticl. *FGrH* 140 F 19; Xanth. *FGrH* 765 F 29). It cannot be a coincidence that the stone pillars outside many Athenian homes were called Herms (Goldmann 1942: esp. 58 n. 2). Hermes was a god concerned not only with boundaries (Burkert 1985: 156) but also with their transgression. Thus he meets Priam by a boundary stone (*Il.* 24.349) and conducts him unseen to Achilles (*Il.* 24.337). He meets Odysseus on the boundary of Circe's domain (*Od.* 10.275–6) and is likewise uniquely suited to cross the boundaries of the kingdom of Hades (*Od.* 24.1–14). An extension of this is his role in arranging thefts (*Il.* 5.388–91; cf. *Il.* 24.109). It is as a trickster that he appears in the *Homeric Hymn to Hermes*, the first lengthy narrative that survives concerning him (Richardson 2010: 155–6).

ἐΰσκοπον The epithet probably means 'keen-sighted'. It is not easy to explain its relevance. Perhaps it derives from the slaying by Hermes of the keen-sighted Argus of the hundred eyes (Apollod. 2.1.2–3; Vernant 1991: 145–6; D. Steiner 1995: 193). That myth is not directly alluded to in Homer (ΣbT on *Il.* 2.103) and it is not usual for a divine epithet to refer to a single exploit of a god (M. L. West 1978: 368).

Ἀργειφόντην The commonest understanding of this epithet in antiquity was 'slayer of Argus' (thus Σ). As already discussed (foreg. n.), this is problematic because divine epithets refer to a standing characteristic not a one-off exploit. M. L. West (1978: 368–9) revived the hypotheses of Chittenden (1948) and Rhys Carpenter (1950) that the word means 'dog slayer'. This would fit with Hermes' connexion with theft and his epithet κύναγκα ('dog strangler'; Hippon. fr. 3a *IEG*). The word ἀργός < *ἀργρός ('swift') is applied to dogs (*Il.* 1.50), and (with a change in accentuation) is the name of Odysseus' dog (*Od.* 17.292). It might have been a virtual synonym for the animal. In narrative terms, it makes sense to send the dog-slayer to kill Argus whose function, if not his form (*pace* Tzetzes, *Exeg. in Il.* p. 153.13), is that of a guard dog. At a formal level, it is hard to see why an o-stem thematic noun like Ἀργός should form a compound in –ει– rather than –o– (Hainsworth 1988: 258–9). It has been suggested that it is an example of metrical lengthening (Kretschmer 1919: 45–9). If the original adj. was *ἀργρός, one might rather expect a stem with a Caland –*i* (Watkins 1995: 383–4). But that would yield *Ἀργιφόντης. Whatever the shape of the original stem, it seems likely that we are looking at an instance of metrical remodelling (Pulleyn 2000: 139).

39 μήτ' ...μήτε These infinitives depend on εἴπομεν (37) and are thus prohibitions. Zeus is giving the content of part of Hermes' message in indirect speech.

αὐτόν Agamemnon, readily supplied from τόν (36).

κτείνειν Some MSS have κτεῖναι. Killing is readily thought of as a single act which fits with the punctual nature of the aor.; the pres. inf. μνάασθαι seems, by contrast, to accord well with the durative nature of wooing. But to say that is to stultify the choice of the speaker in presenting the action how she will: a verb like 'swallow' is inherently perfective (punctual) in meaning, but that does not preclude its deployment in an imperfective sense, e.g. 'He became aware that his throat was sore as he was swallowing his food.' The speaker's free choice of viewpoint is readily apparent in a case such as: οὐ γὰρ ἐπ' ἀνὴρ, | οἷος Ὀδύσσεύς ἔσκεν, ἀρὴν ἀπὸ οἴκου ἀμῦναι. | ἡμεῖς δ' οὔ νύ τι τοῖοι ἀμυνέμεν ('There is no man like Odysseus was to ward off ruin from the house. But we are not such as to ward it off', *Od.* 2.58–60). One might suppose that warding off ruin is always a process; but the poet presents it punctually in the first of these two infinitives and as durative in the second. The freedom of a speaker over choice of aspect is not necessarily fettered by the inherent lexical semantics of a given verb.

μνάασθαι See on μνήστην (36 n.). The suitors are foreshadowed.

40 γάρ There is an abrupt change to direct speech (cf. ἔφαθ', 42). It is as though we are suddenly let in on the scene between Hermes and Aegisthus.

Ὀρέσταο Cf. Ἀτρείδαο (35 n.).

τίσις Lit. 'a paying back', from the same root as τίνω. Although there is a superficial similarity with τίω and τιμή ('value', 'honour'), there are formal problems with supposing that all these words come from the same root (*DELG* 1123).

ἔσσεται The MS variant ἔρχεται is either an inept gloss or an error in copying. Plainly this is a threat of future punishment if Aegisthus does not obey. If vengeance were already on its way, the threat would lose its point.

Ἀτρείδαο This does not agree with Ὀρέσταο: it is not usual to refer to a person by his grandfather's name (except for Achilles: *Il.* 2.860 and passim). The sense is that vengeance will come from Orestes *in respect of* the son of Atreus, i.e. Agamemnon. On the form, cf. 35 n.

41 ἡβήσῃ The noun ἥβη does not mean 'youth' in the sense of not being grown up; it refers to the vigour of entering upon adulthood (*DELG* 405). Thus *Il.* 13.484: καὶ δ' ἔχει ἥβης ἄνθος ὅ τε κράτος ἐστὶ μέγιστον ('[sc.

Aeneas] possesses the flower of ἥβη, which is the greatest power'). The suitors later express the hope that Zeus will destroy Telemachus before he comes to the ἥβης μέτρον (*Od.* 4.668). Eustathius apparently read ἡβήσει here. Whilst the fut. ind. is not uncommon after ἄν and κε(ν) in Homer (Chantraine 1953: 225–6), it is questionable in an indefinite temporal clause such as this. An apparent parallel at *Il.* 20.335, συμβλήσεαι, might well be a mistake for the subj. συμβλήεαι.

ἱμείρεται The related noun ἵμερος has definite erotic overtones (*Il.* 3.446; 14.198, 328). The longing that Orestes feels to rule over his land echoes the longing that Odysseus feels for death because he cannot return to his (59 n.).

Although the verb looks identical to a 3 sg. pres. ind. med., that is impossible here since a subj. is required after ὁππότ' ἄν (as the preceding verb demonstrates). ἱμείρεται is an aor. subj. med. (Chantraine 1958: 454–5). It is a 'short-vowel subjunctive', preserved in Homeric Greek and some other archaic texts (Introduction, p. 58). We have here a sigmatic aor. *ἱμερ-σ-ε-ται > ἱμείρεται with loss of sigma and compensatory lengthening of the root vowel (Chantraine 1958: 413 with 173; Sihler 1995: 216). The etymology is disputed but is probably *siH_2-mr-y^e/o- (Weiss 1998: 47–56), comprising a root meaning 'to bind' (cf. ἱμάς) and the affix seen in τέκμαρ. The morphologically more transparent 3 sg. pres. ind. med. appears a few lines later in a similar context (59 n.).

αἴης can mean 'earth' (e.g. *Il.* 3.243) but here more specifically denotes one's own 'land'—cf. the common formulaic phrase ἀπὸ πατρίδος αἴης (*Od.* 1.203 and passim). Later Greek has a word αἶα that means 'mother'. Although it has been argued (Brugmann 1903–4: 94–7; 1911–12: 206–8) that γαῖα is the result of a contamination between γῆ and αἶα, this poses more questions than it answers. It is more likely that an original γᾶ (PIE *(s)t(e)g-eH_2) was remodelled to γαῖα by analogy with the hypocoristic μᾶ (cf. Dor. μάτηρ) which had already been enlarged to μαῖα (Willi 2007: 169–70).

43 πεῖθ' The imperf. is conative, implying effort (Kühner and Gerth 1898: 140–2). Cf. 75 n.

ἀγαθὰ φρονέων Refers to how one is minded towards others, not to the rightness of one's reasoning, as one may deduce from the expressions φίλα φρονέων (*Od.* 1.307) and ὀλοὰ φρονέων (*Il.* 16.701).

ἀθρόα πάντ' ἀπέτεισεν Achilles says to Hector (*Il.* 22.271) ἀθρόα πάντ' ἀποτίσεις. These are the only two occurrences in Homer of this formula. It is reasonable to import the bitter and abusive tone of Achilles' words into this speech. There is a marked element of satisfaction in both places. The correct writing of the aor. of ἀποτίνω is ἀπέτεισε (Chantraine 1958: 13,

412). ἀπέτι(σ)σε is found in the MSS and looks like the aor. of ἀποτίω, with which it was easily confused; one papyrus has ἀπετεισε.

44 ἠμείβετ' Ingressive imperf. (Chantraine 1953: 192).

γλαυκῶπις Both elements of this compound have been the subject of controversy. Does -ωπ- refer to eyes or face? Does γλαυκ- mean 'owl' or is it a colour term denoting blueness? We may dismiss the possibility that Athena had a blue face. We may also discount the notion of her having the face of an owl. There is no sound archaeological evidence that she was ever conceived as the sort of human–animal hybrid we find in ancient Egypt and the poems certainly suggest nothing of the kind. We are left with a choice between blue eyes and the eyes of an owl. Both are possible but the parallelism with the epithet βοῶπις ('ox-eyed') commonly used of Hera is too striking to ignore. The eyes of Athena are uncannily bright, watchful, and piercing like those of an owl; those of Hera are large and brown like those of a cow (Pulleyn 2000, 183–4).

45 πάτερ ἡμέτερε The Greeks had neither at this period nor later any myth of creation by a Father Zeus that would make this phrase the Homeric equivalent of the Christian *Pater noster*. This line appears three times in the *Odyssey* (cf. *Od.* 1.81; 24.473) and once in the *Iliad* (*Il.* 8.31) and always in the mouth of Athena. Zeus is conventionally called πατὴρ ἀνδρῶν τε θεῶν τε (cf. 28 n.) even though several gods and most mortals are not in fact his children. But the addition of ἡμέτερε is not conventional but specific. It makes particular sense in the mouth of Athena who is his child, in common with most of the other gods present in the assembly. She uses a rather less homely formula to express shock at Zeus' intention to save Hector from death: ὦ πάτερ ἀργικέραυνε, κελαινέφες, οἷον ἔειπες (*Il.* 22.178). That these 'O father' speeches come from this particular daughter perhaps shows that she feels the bond of filiation more strongly than the other children of Zeus.

Κρονίδη This patronymic is found in Homer (*Il.* 36×, *Od.* 7×) beside the older form Κρονίων (*Il.* 47×, *Od.* 23×). That both are less frequent in the *Odyssey* reflects the less prominent role of the gods in that poem. But in both alike Κρονίων outnumbers Κρονίδης, an indication that the older form was better established in the tradition and came more readily to the mind of the bards.

ὕπατε This adj. is applied to Zeus 6× overall in Homer. Half of these involve oaths or exclamations with the formula ὕπατος καὶ ἄριστος (*Il.* 19.258; 23.43; *Od.* 19.303). Twice it is found in the context of Zeus as ὕπατον μήστωρα (*Il.* 8.22; 17.339). At *Il.* 5.756, we have the single use of the phrase Ζῆν' ὕπατον Κρονίδην. It is hard to judge the absolute age of these formulae; but one might assume that ὕπατος καὶ ἄριστος is old since it is found in oaths that might be part of a conservative religious language. It is tempting to connect this with Jupiter Optimus Maximus at Rome; but this only works at the semantic—rather than the etymological—level as the Lat. cognate for ὕπατος is *summus* rather than *maximus* and ἄριστος has none.

κρειόντων The gods are not in Homer referred to as κρείοντες except in this formula, which appears only 4× overall. κρείων is commonly used of mortal rulers (e.g. *Od.* 3.248 εὐρὺ κρείων Ἀγαμέμνων). It seems likely that Zeus is being described as the highest not among the gods but among all rulers.

46 καὶ λίην Σ glosses πάνυ μὲν οὖν ('quite so'): this is an interjection and not an adv. qualifying ἐοικότι ('altogether fitting').

γε 'At any rate': what is true of Aegisthus need not be true of Odysseus.

κεῖται The verb is regularly used of warriors and other persons brought down by death (e.g. *Il.* 16.776).

47 ὡς With no accent, normally means 'as'; but it is also used as here in an independent clause to introduce a wish (cf. *Il.* 18.107).

ἀπόλοιτο Etymologically (cf. 11 n.) and alliteratively this picks up ὀλέθρῳ at the end of the previous line.

ὅτις Has the same meaning as the commoner ὅστις ('who'). Its origin is uncertain (Chantraine 1958: 280; Sihler 1995: 400–1) but we see its constituent elements at *Od.* 16.257 ὅ κέν τις ... ἀμύνοι, where ὅ appears to be a rel. In any event, neither ὅστις nor ὅτις by itself means 'whoever'; the indefinite force comes from the overall syntax of the clause.

ῥέζοι The verb in this rel. clause is in the opt. because it depends on a principal clause that is itself in the opt. because it expresses a desire (cf. *Il.* 3.299; Chantraine 1953: 248).

48 δαΐφρονι In the *Iliad*, the word describes warriors (*Il.* 13.286; 14.387; 24.739) as though the first element might be δαΐ ('battle'). In the *Odyssey* its broader application, e.g. to a craftsman (*Od.* 8.373), suggests a connexion with δαήμων ('skilled'; Chantraine 1999, 248, 278). Either is possible here, but the *Odyssey* tends to stress Odysseus' cunning over his bellicosity. Maybe a word meaning 'thinking warlike thoughts' was later taken to mean 'clever' under the influence of δαήμων; more likely, a word meaning 'skilled' was extended to warriors as well as craftsmen (Snell 1978: 60–3).

δαίεται There are two homonymous verbs δαίω: the sense here must be 'is torn' rather than 'is set on fire'. The latter would be improbably erotic for a goddess like Athena. There is some deliberate verbal play in putting δαΐφρονι next to δαίεται (Vergados 2012: 19). There is also striking alliteration of *d* in this line that carries over into the next.

49 δηθά ('For a long time'). From a root **dwā-* (Chantraine 1999: 275), this word is related to δήν and, in a zero-grade, to Lat. *dūdum*.

φίλων ἄπο The noun is governed by the following preposition whose accent is thus thrown back (Probert 2003: 127–8).

πήματα πάσχει The formula πήματα πασχ- is unique to the *Odyssey* and, apart from a single significant occurrence at *Od.* 1.190 (*n.*), is confined to describing Odysseus (*Od.* 5.33; 7.152; 8.411; 17.444, 524). The pres. tense here indicates a process that has begun in the past and is continuing, as is made plain by the adv. δηθά (Chantraine 1953: 191); cf. *Od.* 1.75.

50 ἀμφιρύτῃ Strabo (1.2.18) preserves ὠγυγίη, a variant found in no MSS. The formulaic νήσῳ ἐν ἀμφιρύτῃ is found at *Od.* 1.198; 12.283.

ὀμφαλός . . . θαλάσσης This unique expression is without parallel in Greek literature. ὀμφαλός basically means 'navel' (cf. Lat. *umbilicus*). In historical times, a stone called the ὀμφαλός was shown at Delphi; it was taken to mark the mid-point of the earth. In the *Iliad*, ὀμφαλός may refer to the boss at the centre of a shield (*Il.* 13.192). Whilst all islands are surrounded with water, the image here is of a tiny spot in a vast ocean and so emphasizes Odysseus' isolation. Some ancients identified Calypso's island with Gozo (cf. 85 n.).

51 νῆσος The word has already appeared in the previous line. Some scholars prefer a comma at the end of 50, taking νῆσος here in apposition to ὀμφαλός. With the colon printed in this text, it is necessary to supply ἐστι here (Stanford 1959: 213). There is nothing especially harsh in this. For the repetition of a word in successive lines, cf. 23 n.

ἐν Is in tmesis with the following verb which governs the noun in the acc.

52 Ἄτλαντος Atlas is mentioned again only at *Od.* 7.245. Hesiod (*Th.* 517–19) describes him as a Titan who holds up the sky while standing on the earth. It might be thought that his name means 'sustainer', with copulative ἀ + τλάω (cf. Lat. *tollo*). But τλάω is used of supporting emotional, not physical, loads. It might be that the κρατέρη ἀνάγκη referred to by Hesiod (*Th.* 517) is enough to explain this: he is a man who must bear a mysteriously unexplained but indubitably unpleasant dispensation from Zeus (ταύτην . . . μοῖραν: *Th.* 520).

ὀλοόφρονος From expressions such as ὀλοιῇσι φρεσὶ θύει (*Il.* 1.342) and ὀλοὰ φρονέων (*Il.* 16.701), we may conclude that this compound means 'of evil intent'. It is used in the *Iliad* only to refer to animals: a water-snake (*Il.* 2.723), a lion (*Il.* 15.630), and a wild boar (*Il.* 17.21). In the *Odyssey*, it refers to Atlas, Minos (*Od.* 11.322), and Aietes (*Od.* 10.137). In each case, a female person is said to be related to a male who has this epithet: Calypso is daughter of Atlas, Ariadne is daughter of Minos, Circe is sister of Aietes.

Minos' behaviour towards Theseus and Aietes' towards the Argonauts is perhaps sufficient to explain the epithet in their case. It is unclear why it should particularly suit Atlas. It cannot really be a synonym of κρατερόφρων (Hes. *Th.* 509); that just means that he was tough-minded. Nor is it likely that it refers to him taking part in the revolt of the Titans against Zeus (*pace* Matthews 1978); Hesiod does not describe him as doing so (M. L. West 1966: 308). Already in antiquity it was speculated that the correct reading was ὀλοόφρονος ('he who thinks about everything') with a rough breathing (Tièche 1945: 69). But whilst one can explain the sequence -οο- in ὀλοός (*ὀλ-ο-ϝός < *ὀλ-ε-ϝός < *H₃el-H₁-wos), it has no place in ὀλός (<*sol-wos). We cannot be certain why ὀλοόφρων was chosen, but it creates an air of menace around Atlas and, more importantly, his daughter. That the uncanny figures of Calypso and Circe should have malevolent male relatives is unsurprising; it is harder to see how Ariadne belongs in their company.

ὅς τε The particle τε often follows the rel., but not in such a way that a single simple meaning may be attributed to such cases (Chantraine 1953: 239–40). Here it describes a characteristic attribute or function (cf. *Od.* 1.283, 348); it may also connote a habit or generalization (*Od.* 1.91, 338, 341) or a mere contingency (*Od.* 1.101).

53 πάσης βένθεα οἶδεν Quite why Atlas should have submarine associations is unclear since in Hesiod (*Th.* 517–19) he stands on the earth and holds up the heavens with his hands. Lesky (1950: 151) detected the influence of the Hittite Song of Ullikummi, which preserves an old Hurrian myth in which Kumarbi, former king in heaven, begat a stone-child Ullikummi as a means of revenge against the new king, Tesub. He ordered Ullikummi to be grafted into the shoulder of the Atlas-like giant Upelluri, who stands in the sea, whence Ullikummi grew swiftly and reached from the ocean up to heaven (Güterbock 1951: 138, 157–9). Upelluri has every reason to feel aggrieved at this treatment; if Atlas has been conflated with him, this might explain his epithet ὀλοόφρων.

κίονας The image of pillars supporting the heavens is not at home in Greek myth. It is perhaps Near Eastern in origin (M. L. West 1997a: 149 n. 205).

54 ἀμφίς Although this expression can mean 'surround' (cf. ἀμφὶς ἔχοιεν, *Od.* 8.340), the sense here has to be 'keep apart' (cf. ἀμφὶς ἐέργει, *Il.* 13.706) since the pillars do not surround anything.

55 ὀδυρόμενον See on ὠδύσαο (62 n.).

56 δέ In spite of its short vowel, the syllable is treated as heavy by virtue of the following continuant (Introduction, pp. 48–9). The reading δ' ἐν in some

sources is a (rather unidiomatic) correction by a scribe who overlooked this prosodic licence.

αἰμυλίοισι This hapax of unknown etymology is taken from this and other contexts (Hes. *Op.* 374; *h. Merc.* 317–18) to mean 'wheedling'.

λόγοισιν This is one of only two appearances of λόγος (or its parts) in Homer. The other is at *Il.* 15.393. In our context, the words are wheedling and soft, intended to delight Odysseus; in the *Iliad*, the words are used by Patroclus to delight the injured Eurypylus in his hut. But it would be a mistake, on this slender showing, to suppose that words of soft delight must be λόγοι: we find μαλακοῖς ἐπέεσσιν (*Il.* 6.337) and ἀγανοῖς ἐπέεσσιν (*Il.* 2.164). λόγος had not caught on as a word for speech in Homer; its related verb λέγω appears only 102× and often has its basic meaning of collecting. εἰπεῖν appears 837× and φημί 1092×. Nouns like φήμη and φάτις never simply mean 'word' and so it is not surprising that ἔπος predominates in this sense. On μῦθος, see 28 n.

57 θέλγει frequently has connotations of supernatural power. It refers to a change in the mental state of a person that may be brought about by the wand of Circe (*Od.* 10.213), a trick played by Apollo (*Il.* 21.604), the magic staff of Hermes (*Il.* 24.343), or the song of the Sirens (*Od.* 12.40, 44). There might here be an extended sense here of 'allure' since it is not clear that Calypso is using any magic.

The songs of Phemius occupy an intermediate position: they are not like the spells of Circe but are referred to as θελκτήρια (*Od.* 1.337); cf. 14.387; 17.514 for the charm of a well-told story. When Odysseus spins his tales on Scheria, the audience is gripped by an enchantment called κηληθμός (see 337 n.).

ὅπως...ἐπιλήσεται A unique example of ὅπως taking the ind. in a purpose clause (Chantraine 1953: 273).

58 καπνόν The smoke is presumably that of the hearth and this is synonymous with home.

ἀποθρῴσκοντα The only other appearances of this rare word are in the *Iliad*, where it twice comes second word (after νηός) and refers to a person disembarking energetically from a ship (*Il.* 2.702; 16.748). Its use here of smoke (in a different metrical position) is an unexpected and arresting innovation.

59 θανέειν ἱμείρεται Just as Orestes will long to rule over his ancestral land (41 n.), so Odysseus longs to die because of separation from his country. The erotic charge of the word (*Il.* 3.446; 14.198) is important in this context—whilst he did have a sexual relationship with Calypso (*Od.* 5.227), his visceral longing for Ithaca outweighs his physical attachment to her.

νυ This particle appears 3× in ll. 59–62, emphasizing Athena's indignant agitation.

60 φίλον ἦτορ Already in antiquity, scholars glossed φίλος as ἴδιος, feeling that the sense indicated possession rather than dearness. The possessive interpretation is supported by Kretschmer (1927), albeit with an etymology involving a possessive morpheme found otherwise only in Hittite and Lydian. Hooker (1987; cf. H. Fränkel (1975: 82–3)) argues that the basic sense always has to do with affective association. Robinson (1990) similarly finds that φίλος never has a merely possessive sense in Homer and refers to things that are dear or valued, especially when under threat. There plainly are places where φίλος must mean 'dear': Τεῦκρε φίλη κεφαλή (*Il.* 8.281) is an address by Agamemnon to Teucer. It can scarcely refer to Agamemnon's own head. If φίλος does mean 'own', then we have to assume pleonasm in expressions such as ὅν φίλον ἦτορ (*Il.* 15.182). It is also hard to rule out dearness in an expression such as ὅν φίλον υἱόν (*Il.* 19.4). Cf. 307 n.

61 χαρίζετο The noun χάρις refers to the delight (cf. χαίρω) that comes from giving and receiving (cf. 318 n.). It is common for mortals in prayer to remind the gods of their previous piety when seeking further favours (Pulleyn 1997: 16–38). For a related sense of this verb, see 140 n.

ἱερὰ ῥέζων 'doing holy things' is semantically (but not etymologically) equivalent to Lat. *sacra facere > sacrificere*. Sacrifice is one of the chief ways of garnering favour with the gods. There is probably here a glance back to τοιαῦτά γε ῥέζοι (47): Aegisthus does 'such (*sc.* wicked) things' whereas Odysseus does righteous things by sacrificing and yet is apparently to have no reward.

62 εὐρείη The image is of a large city spread over a wide area. The thought is probably not of Troy as a military target: the difficulty of taking Troy in the *Iliad* did not stem from its broadness. Rather we are to think of a sizeable centre of civil population. It is striking that the bardic repertoire has so many positive epithets to describe the well-built city of the enemy (Bowra 1960: 17–18). This particular epithet is not unique to Troy—it is also used for Cnossus (*Il.* 18.591) and Sparta (*Od.* 11.460).

ὠδύσαο It is hard not to think that there is a play between this word denoting hatred and the name Ὀδύ(σ)σεύς. Amid the mountainous bibliography on this (S. R. West 1988: 83), Stanford (1952) minutely discusses the difficulty of coming to a precise etymology. Starting from Odysseus' own connexion of his name (*Od.* 19.407–9) with the ptcp. ὀδυσσάμενος (cf. Lat. *odium*), he concludes that the active sense of 'man who deals out hate' is less likely than 'man doomed to be hated'. One might as well see a connexion with ὀδύνη, in which case ὀδυρόμενον (*Od.* 1.55) is also a play on words. Odysseus' name might well be pre-Greek in origin (*DELG* 775–6; M. L. West 2014: 7). In any event, the tradition feels free to make play with it in ways that do not oblige us to suppose that one specific meaning was always intended. See 21 n.

63 νεφεληγερέτα We have already seen (27 n.) that the function of Zeus as gatherer of the clouds is almost certainly a Near Eastern graft into his inherited function as god of the shining vault of the sky. It has been thought that this epithet started life as a vocative but was reinterpreted as a nominative by analogy with μητίετα (Chantraine 1958: 199). The objections to this are: (a) νεφεληγερέτα is never found with the voc. Ζεῦ; (b) μητίετα appears only once in the voc. (*Il.* 1.508) as against 18× in the nom.; (c) if this transference was conditioned by frequent use of the epithet in invocations, it is peculiar that Ζεῦ is found only 3× at the end of a line (*Il.* 1.508; 16.241; and *Od.* 1.62) whereas it is found 37× as first word. We must conclude (with Hooker 1967) that these were originally nominatives in *-ta* that commended themselves to the bards to avoid the 'overlength' that would result from the sequence -της Ζεύς (Drewitt 1908: 100–2; M. Parry 1928: 52 n. 1 = Adam Parry 1971: 41 n. 1).

64 σε A double acc.—the word has escaped you *and* the barrier of the teeth (Chantraine 1953: 42). The device is known as σχῆμα καθ' ὅλον καὶ μέρος ('figure of whole and part') and includes both the person who spoke the words and the place whence they came (Jacquinod 1989: 21).

ἕρκος ὀδόντων It seems quaint to refer to the teeth as a barrier that is passed by words when they exit the mouth. We cannot know whether this feeling was shared by the first audience of the *Odyssey*. Its function is to show that the speaker is about to correct his interlocutor; cf. Eng., 'Whatever can you mean?'

65 ἔπειτα This line is identical to *Il.* 10.243, where ἔπειτα emphasizes lexically the 'then' element of an 'if…then' conditional whose protasis is explicit in the previous line (cf. 290 n.). Here, by contrast, there is no protasis but the sense is the same, i.e. 'in such a case'.

66 περὶ μέν … περὶ δ' The first περί could be taken as a preposition governing the gen. and meaning 'beyond' (cf. *Il.* 4.375; *Od.* 7.108) or as a preverb in tmesis with the following ἐστί, the compound governing a gen. of separation (*Od.* 18.248). The sense is the same in either case. The acc. νόον indicates the respect in which Odysseus surpasses other mortals. The second περί is used adverbially as though it meant περισσῶς. The line sums up Odysseus' excellence in both human and divine terms.

68 Ποσειδάων Probably a voc. of πόσις (Kretschmer 1909a: 27–8; Kretschmer and Skutsch 1909: 382–3), followed by –δα– ('earth'; Willi 2007: 182–3), followed by a suffix in –ϝων (Ruijgh 1967b). The whole would mean 'lord of the earth'. By Hesiod's time, Earth is already seen as mating with Heaven (*Th.* 106). The idea of Poseidon as lord of the earth might be an influence from Sumerian EN.KI ('lord of the earth') which seems to have spread to neighbouring cultures (Palmer 1963: 255–6).

γαιήοχος The etymology 'he who holds the earth' (γαῖα + o-grade of ἔχω) is ruled out on formal grounds: Laconian Γαιάϝοχο (*IG* V i 213) shows that the second element is not ἔχω < *segʰ– but something beginning with *w, probably *wegʰ–, cf. Lat. *vehor* (Rix 2001: 661–2). If so, it might refer to Poseidon riding on the earth (Janko 1992: 48). It is hard to see how it could refer to his riding *under* it (*pace* Nilsson 1967: 448), even if the sea was conceived as a flood upon which the terrestrial disc floated (Hainsworth 1988: 368–9). It has been suggested that the original sense was probably lost to the poet and audience, who connected –οχος with ἔχω (S. R. West 1988: 83); but nothing in the text encourages this reading. What Poseidon specifically 'holds' is the sea (*Il.* 15.189–90). Alternatively the second element might be connected with Lat. *vexare* and refer to the causing of earthquakes (*DELG* 219).

ἀσκελές This is probably a compound of ἀ copulative + σκέλλω ('to dry, parch') meaning that his anger is tough and desiccated. The possibility that the alpha is privative and means anger that never dries up is attractive but unlikely beside the corresponding adj. meaning something like 'withered' (*Od.* 10.463). Poseidon's anger was characterized in dynamic terms earlier on (ἀσπερχές, 20 n.); this gives it a more static, material feel.

69 Κύκλωπος Homer nowhere says that the Cyclopes in general and Polyphemus in particular have only one eye. The word gives little away: it plainly points to *roundness*, but not singularity (*DELG* 598). The idea is obviously implicit in the story and the blinding would have been pointless had Polyphemus had a second seeing eye. But nothing explicit is said about it either in the detailed initial ethnographic description of the Cyclopes (*Od.* 9.105–39) or when Odysseus is explaining his stratagem (*Od.* 9.316–33). Hesiod makes the Cyclopes children of Heaven and Earth: there are three of them, they are named, none is called Polyphemus, and they fashion the thunder-weapon of Zeus (*Th.* 133, 139–41). Homer, by contrast, makes Polyphemus the son of Poseidon and a nymph (*Od.* 1.71–3); he is no cosmic armourer but the folk-tale type of the blinded ogre. It would seem that, for reasons that we cannot now discover, Homer has introduced him among the Cyclopes who were not otherwise imagined as ogres (*Od.* 6.5–6 remarkably has them as ἀνδρές) or as one-eyed (Mondi

1983: 22–3). Hesiod does say that the Cyclopes had one circular eye in their forehead (*Th.* 143–5); but this somewhat laboured passage could well be a Just So story influenced by the Polyphemus episode in the *Odyssey* (*pace* Page 1955: 14).

ὀφθαλμοῦ The gen. denotes deprivation, an extension of its common ablatival sense (Chantraine 1953: 64).

70 ἀντίθεον The word often denotes the superhuman prowess of human warriors (*Il.* 5.663; 10.112). It does not imply moral approbation, being applied also to the suitors (*Od.* 14.18). Zeus would scarcely describe in favourable terms the impious Polyphemus who proudly declared that he did not care one jot for him (*Od.* 9.273–8). The epithet draws attention simply to his physical might (cf. Hes. *Th.* 142).

Πολύφημον Nestor in the *Iliad* speaks of a Lapith of the same name who is also ἀντίθεος (*Il.* 1.264). Perhaps both name and epithet were lifted as a unit from that context. There is a Trojan with a similar name, Πολυφήτης, who is likewise ἀντίθεος (*Il.* 13.719). Lapith and Trojan are obscure characters who do not surface again in Homer; their names and epithet were thus available for the poet of the *Odyssey* to apply to his new and far more memorable creation, the one-eyed cannibal giant in the cave. He chose Πολύφημος, a descriptive compound name of a kind common enough at all periods, but differing from those of great heroes such as Atreus, Nestor, Ajax which are opaque in meaning and probably older within the tradition. πολύφημος is twice used as an adj.: once of a place of assembly (*Od.* 2.150) and once of the bard Demodocus (*Od.* 22.376). LSJ gloss the former as 'many-voiced, wordy' and the latter as 'abounding in songs and legends'. Polyphemus is neither a public speaker nor a bard; his name seems more likely to denote one who is spoken about rather than one who speaks (cf. πολύαινος: *Il.* 9.673; 10.544; 11.430; *Od.* 12.184). Given that Demodocus is called περικλυτός ('very famous', *Od.* 1.325 n.) as well as πολύφημος, we might conclude that both denote fame. Some have detected overtones of infamy in the name through an association with the negative word φῆμις (Kanavou 2015: 20); but see 154 n.

ὅου A gen. of the lexeme whose nom. is ὅς. The original gen. of stems such as this was in –οιο, which developed by loss of iota and contraction into –ου, both types being attested in the epics. There must have been an intermediate stage in –οο, which is latent in some parts of the transmitted text that will not scan as written: e.g. ἀνεψίου κταμένοιο at *Il.* 15.554 is unmetrical whereas ἀνεψίοο κταμένοιο is not (Chantraine 1958: 45). οἷο, ὄο, and οὗ would all be possible developments from the inherited PIE *yos (Sihler 1995: 400); ὅου is a synthetic form peculiar to the epic dialect, perhaps invented by a process similar to diectasis (cf. 25 n; Chantraine 1958: 82).

It is tempting but mistaken to print ὅο κράτος as a restoration of 'the original'. Homer must have had ὅου since only this could be the analogical model for ἑῆς (*Il.* 5.371; 16.208; *Od.* 8.524; 19.395; Janko 1992: 346).

κράτος ἐστὶ μέγιστον Physical attributes such as martial prowess (ἀλκή, *Il.* 9.39) and the flower of youth (ἥβης ἄνθος, *Il.* 13.484) are said to be κράτος μέγιστον. This raises the question of what κράτος is by itself; it may be a predicate of ἀλκή but that does not imply identity. κράτος seems to have a range of meanings from physical hardness (*Od.* 9.393) to kingly rule (*Od.* 11.353). Whatever its etymological associations, it appears in Homer to denote superiority (Breuil 1989; cf. 359 n.).

The other attestations of this formula run from a masculine caesura in the third foot and apply to Zeus (*Il.* 2.118; 9.25; *Od.* 5.4). This one runs from a feminine caesura in the same foot, and the use of the awkwardly stretched ὅου results from the attempt to weld an old established formulaic ending to a new beginning. This is one of those places where we see the monumental poet at work adapting inherited material to new contexts—in this case, the newly created Polyphemus is described with language normally used of Zeus. Whereas the latter's power is absolute (*Il.* 8.18–27), this instance must refer to Polyphemus' relative strength as 'greatest' among the other Cyclopes (πᾶσιν Κυκλώπεσσι, next n.).

71 πᾶσιν Κυκλώπεσσι Given the anarchic character of the society of the Cyclopes, this dat. after κράτος does not mean that Polyphemus exercises any kind of direct rule over them. The reference is rather to his sheer physical power (O'Sullivan 1990: 14–16) and the dat. is locatival ('among', Chantraine 1953: 80). We may contrast the benign political κράτος of Alcinous (*Od.* 11.353).

Θόωσα We do not otherwise hear of her in the epics. Hesiod mentions a daughter of Nereus called Θοή (*Th.* 245), a speaking name that evokes the swift rushing of the waves. The Phaeacians have similar names, made up to suit the nautical context (*Od.* 8.111–16; esp. Θόων at 113). Θόωσα was called into being by analogy with these other names of the same root. Hesiod makes the Cyclopes children of Uranus and Gaia (*Th.* 133, 139). This radically different parentage for Polyphemus is Homer's invention; it is not clear what antecedents he had in mind for the rest of the Cyclopes (cf. *Od.* 1.69 n.).

νύμφη The word can be used of any female, mortal or immortal (14 n.). Here it describes, as often, a sexually available person whose function is to provide a convenient if obscure mother for an exceptional character begotten by a well-known male deity.

72 Φόρκυνος Hesiod says that Phorcys is son of Gaia and Pontus (*Th.* 233–8). Others of his terrible progeny include the Graeae (*Th.* 270), the Gorgons (*Th.* 274), and an unnamed serpent that guards golden apples beneath the earth (*Th.* 333–5). The half-woman half-snake monster known as Echidna was another of his descendants (*Th.* 295–300). Hesiod does not make the Cyclopes part of this genealogy; Homer wants to provide his new creation Polyphemus with suitably monstrous relatives.

ἁλὸς...μέδοντος At *Od.* 13.96, 345 Phorcys is referred to as ἁλίοιο γέροντος ('the old man of the sea'). The same title is also given to Proteus (Od. 4.349) and Nereus (Hes. *Th.* 1003; cf. 233–4). Phorcys is plainly a figure of equal dignity, if not so well known (M. L. West 1966: 235, 232–3).

ἀτρυγέτοιο This common word is in all but one case (*Il.* 17.425: αἰθήρ) used of the sea. Σ glosses as τῆς ἀκαταπονήτου meaning 'inexhaustible' as though from ἀ- privative and τρύω ('wear out'). This leaves the –γετ– component unexplained. The common modern connexion with τρυγάω ('unharvested') does not account for the short ε (Chantraine 1999: 135). The analysis in terms of ἀ- copulative and τρύζω (<*τρυγ-ι̯ō) and the suffix seen in νιφετός (Leukart 1986) points, if correct, to the 'murmuring' of the sea. But it fits less well with αἰθήρ; the reference could scarcely be to thunder, since that does not murmur. The most attractive solution starts from the verbs τρύγει, ἐτρύγη glossed in ancient lexical lists as ξηραίνει, ἐξηράνθη (to do with drying out). With privative alpha, the sense would be 'which cannot be dried out' (Vine 1998: 62–4). This fits the sea very well (cf. Aesch. *Ag.* 958) and also the αἰθήρ, home of clouds and rain.

73 σπέεσσι For caves as places of sexual encounter, cf. 15 n.

74 ἐκ τοῦ Elsewhere this expression is temporal rather than causal (cf. *Il.* 8.296; 13.779; 15.69; *Od.* 1.212); there is no reason to take it otherwise here.

ἐνοσίχθων This epithet of transparent meaning finds a parallel in ἐννοσίγαιος (*Il.* 8.440, etc.). Poseidon is god of earthquakes as well as of the sea (Burkert 1985: 137–8).

75 οὔ τι κατακτείνει The verb is conative, indicating counterfactually what might be imagined as the aim of a vindictive divine parent in these circumstances (Chantraine 1953: 190). For the pres. describing an action begun in the past and continuing into the present, cf. 49 n.

πλάζει Cf. πλάγχθη (2 n.)

76 ἄγεθ'...περιφραζώμεθα It might seem peculiar to coordinate a 2 pl. impv. with a 1 pl. hortative subj. But ἄγετε is invariable and means 'come now' irrespective of whether the subsequent address is in the first or second person (cf. *Il.* 2.139). περιφραζώμεθα is not found elsewhere in Homer or again in Greek before Nicander (*Ther.* 541). Perhaps we are to admire the skilful incorporation of a six-syllable word spanning three feet with no metrical lengthening or other adaptation by the bard.

οἴδε i.e. 'we who are here.'

77 ὅπως ἔλθῃσι It is not easy to say whether this is an indirect question ('as to how he shall return') or a purpose clause ('so that he may return'). The two may be genuinely indistinguishable in some cases; the use of the subj. is not decisive (Chantraine 1953: 233, 294, 297).

μεθήσει It is striking to find a fut. ind. following on from an aor. subj. but there is a parallel for such a movement at *Il.* 1.587–8 (Chantraine 1953: 354). There is no warrant for amending the text to μεθήσῃ.

79 ἐριδαινέμεν Aeolic inf. (Introduction, p. 57).

82 μακάρεσσι This epithet has a strong affinity for the gods in the *Iliad* (where 16 of 18 appearances apply to them). It is used only slightly more freely to describe humans in the *Odyssey* (5.306; 6.154, 155, 158; 11.483). It is chiefly found in contexts referring to the eternal life of the gods (*Od.* 5.7), the idyllic ease of their existence (*Od.* 6.42–6), and their lack of dependence on mortal food and drink (*Il.* 5.339–42). It is reasonable to conclude that its application to humans is metaphorical and depends on its usual reference to divinity (cf. Heer 1969: 4–11).

πολύφρονα Some MSS read δαΐφρονα. The latter might be a contamination from l. 48 or it might be an original reading. πολύφρονα is attested in a papyrus (PTeb. 695) of the second century BC, but there is no guarantee that early witnesses must preserve the authentic reading. Far more telling is that this line recurs at *Od.* 14.424; 20.239; 23.204—and in all of these places πολύφρονα is found without δαΐφρονα appearing as a variant in the tradition.

ὅνδε δόμονδε It is often supposed that we have here a suffix –δε, indicating motion towards a place, added to ὅν δόμον. If so, the usage is of limited application: we do not find *ὅνδε . . . οἶκόνδε, for example. Perhaps the tradition viewed ὅνδε δόμονδε as the 'motion towards' case of the unit whose 'motion away from' case is οἶο δόμοιο (cf. *Od.* 1.330; 18.8; 21.5; Hoekstra 1989: 223).

84 διάκτορον Another somewhat opaque epithet of Hermes (cf. 38 n.). Hesychius derived it from διάγω, thinking of his role as messenger (Chittenden 1948: 29–30); we might also add guide to the living (*Il.* 24.337, 437, 447) and escort to the dead (*Od.* 24.5). But one would expect an athematic (3rd declen.) agential noun *διάκτορα < *διάκτωρ rather than this thematic (2nd declen.) διάκτορον. Janko (1978) argues plausibly that *διάκτωρ, attested in the much later Greek poet Bianor (first century AD) and lexicographer Hesychius (fourth century AD), already existed in

Homer's time and was remodelled into the thematic declension (e.g. Χάροψ *Il.* 11.426 beside Χαρόποιο *Il.* 2.672). Other etymologies proliferate; none convinces (*DELG* 277).

ἀργειφόντην See 38 n.

85 Ὠγυγίην As the word is always found with the noun νῆσος, there is no way to tell whether it is an adj. describing the island or a proper noun in apposition. MSS do not help since, at all material times, Greek writing made no distinction between lower and upper case. Hesiod (*Th.* 806) took the word as an adj., describing the waters of the Styx and apparently meaning 'primeval' (cf. Call. *Jov.* 1.40; Pollux 9.189). Apollonius of Rhodes (4.573–5) placed Ogygia in the Eastern Adriatic, on the Illyrian coast; Strabo (7.3.6.52–4) reports that Callimachus identified it with the Maltese island of Gozo. The fifth-century BC poet Antimachus appears to have read Ὠγυλίην, perhaps the island of Ogylus off the coast of the Peloponnese on the way to Crete (S. R. West 1988: 85–6).

86 ἐϋπλοκάμῳ This suggests a braided or plaited lock of hair, the styling perhaps being that adopted by Hera at *Il.* 14.175–7 (Hainsworth 1988: 261).

νημερτέα The adj. normally denotes precision (< *η̣- + ἁμαρτάνω: 'not' + 'miss the mark'). Here it describes something that will not fail to come to pass.

87 νόστον... νέηται The two words are based on the same root (*nes-). This might not have been obvious to a Greek in the eighth century BC, but the juxtaposition possibly belongs to a time when the connexion was still felt (cf. 3, 5 nn.).

ὥς κε νέηται See 77 n.

88 ἰθάκηνδ᾽ ἐσελεύσομαι. As between this and the MS variant ἰθάκην ἐσελεύσομαι, the form with -δε is to be preferred after ἐλεύσομαι (cf. *Od.* 17.52; *Il.* 6.365). ἰθάκηνδε ἐλεύσομαι is possible at the caesura (S. R. West 1988: 86) but has no MS attestation, being a conjecture of Ahrens.

89 μᾶλλον Telemachus is already eager but needs divine encouragement.

μένος... θείω Gods are often said to put qualities (*Od.* 1.321) or ideas (*Od.* 21.1) into people's φρένες or θυμός. μένος has been said to be a physical substance like a fluid or a gas, since 'at the stage of thought when these beliefs emerged, there was difficulty in conceiving anything except material entities' (Onians 1951: 51–2). This is not borne out by Homeric usage. The word is used not only of humans but of forces of nature such as wind and sun and fire; it refers not to some mysterious fluid but to vigorous, thrusting movement (Clarke 1999: 76 n. 33, 110–12).

90 κάρη κομόωντας It is hard to see why the epithet is used unless there are other persons who do not so wear their hair. Page (1966: 242–3) conjectured that the epithet was of high antiquity (perhaps coined at the time when Mycenaeans took over the wearing of long hair as a novelty from the Cretans) and was retained in the epic vocabulary long after the habit had been abandoned. But long hair was common at all periods from archaic to classical times (S. R. West 1988: 86).

Ἀχαιούς These are really just the inhabitants of Ithaca. Since the acc. pl. Ἰθακησίους is of the wrong shape to fit in a hexameter, the poet is obliged to choose another word.

91 μνηστήρεσσιν The suitors, so prominent a feature of the *Odyssey*, have not yet been mentioned. It is striking that their introduction should be made in this somewhat oblique fashion.

ἀπειπέμεν The inf. depends on μένος two lines earlier—Telemachus is to be given the strength to speak his mind to the suitors.

οἵ τε See 52 n.

οἱ The dat. is of disadvantage (Chantraine 1953: 73).

92 σφάζουσι The *vox propria* in Homer and later Greek to describe the bloody act of killing itself; see 108 n.

εἰλίποδας Probably 'shambling'. Hesychius glosses as διὰ τὸ ἑλίσσειν τοὺς πόδας ('because of rolling the feet') as though taken as from εἴλω. That verb comes from a root beginning with digamma (*ϝελ-νέ-ω, *DELG* 320). Although the versification consistently neglects the digamma, this might simply point to a late formation (Hainsworth 1988: 349).

ἕλικας This word, taken to mean 'twisted' (cf. ἑλίσσω), has been interpreted in context as an abbreviation for a compound meaning 'with twisted horns' (S. R. West 1988: 86). The absence of any word for horn is problematic; there are no parallels for such a startling brachylogy. Hesychius thought the word meant 'black'; cf. Call. fr. 299 (Pf.) beside *Il.* 2.825. The idea is a respectable one and not necessarily a desperate guess by a puzzled reader in a later generation. Instead of saying 'twisted cows' when he meant 'cows with twisted horns', Homer might simply have meant that the cows were *black*.

93 Σπάρτην According to Σ on *Od.* 3.313, Zenodotus read here Κρήτην (cf. 285 n.). But in the poem as we have it Telemachus goes not to Crete but to Sparta. Lines 93a–b (see apparatus) were added by a later hand in an unhappy attempt at harmonization (cf. 286 n.). Why would Zenodotus amend the text in a way that contradicts what comes later? One view is that he did not: he was working from a completely different version in which Telemachus did go to Crete (Reece 1994: 165–8). If such an atypical variant had existed, we would surely hear reports from other writers. Another explanation is that Homer originally planned to send Telemachus to Crete, changed his mind but forgot to amend his text (S. R. West 1981: 173–5; 1988: 43; M. L. West 2014: 108): Κρήτην is what Homer composed and the editor must print it (M. L. West 1998b: 100). But there is a less startling alternative. Odysseus' lying stories often involve him adopting the identity of a Cretan; Crete thus bulks large in the poem. Perhaps what Zenodotus had was a rhapsode's text marked up for delivery in Crete in the hope that this tantalizing reference (albeit unfulfilled) might please a Cretan audience. We are not obliged to attribute Κρήτην to the monumental composer.

ἠμαθόεντα The noun Πύλον is fem. (cf. *Od.* 2.308; 4.702). Is it then being treated as masc. here? It is arguable that adjectives in -ϝεντ- were sometimes treated in Homer as of two terminations, so that the masc. and fem. are the same (Witte 1911: 109–10). The MS correction ἠμαθόεσσαν is thus probably a later correction.

95 κλέος ἐσθλόν Fame is a central theme of epic, mediated to future generations through heroic song (cf. *Il.* 6.357–8). Achilles at one point usurps the role of the bard and sings of the κλέα ἀνδρῶν (*Il.* 9.189). κλέος is from the same root as κλύω ('to hear') and has direct etymological cognates in Skt., suggesting that it was part of the inherited PIE epic tradition (M. L. West 2007: 397–8; Pulleyn 2000: 12).

ἔχῃσιν It might seem odd to say that fame takes possession of the man rather than the other way about (e.g. *Il.* 5.3). MSS variants include ἕλῃσιν and λάβῃσιν, neither of which elsewhere has κλέος as subject. There is a good parallel for κλέος as subject of ἔχω at *Il.* 17.143.

96–143 Transition from Olympus and Athena's visit to Ithaca. This part of the book combines a number of traditional story types. The overall narrative is of a god, usually as here in disguise, meeting a mortal (De Jong 2001: 17 gives numerous parallels). The scene is also an example of the typical visitation scene which may contain some or all of the following: visitor arrives, finds the person sought, is received by the host, has a meal, converses, is given a bath and bed and gift. Within this framework, the theme of hospitality is central. It is not just an important part of Greek life: it is a central concern of the poem. Some hosts are good (Nestor, Menelaus, Telemachus) whereas others are bad (Polyphemus, suitors).

96–102 These lines are preceded by asterisks in MS Laurentianus 32.34 (tenth–eleventh century AD). Σ comments that Aristarchus marked 97–8 as spurious, belonging rather to Hermes (*Od.* 5.44–6). The Massiliote text omitted them; but they are in some papyri and all the medieval MSS.

Aristarchus also thought that 99–101 were interpolated from the *Iliad* (cf. *Il.* 5.746–7; 8.390–91). One might see in 97–8 signs of careless editing; on the other hand, Athena is behaving rather like Hermes. As for 99–101, there is no reason why the poet cannot lift lines from a martial passage of the *Iliad* and reintroduce them in a context where Mentor is going to spur on Telemachus to what will eventually be the bloody killing of the suitors.

97 ἀμβρόσια 'immortal', not to distinguish these sandals from others that suffer death, but to indicate that they belong to gods and are somehow infected by their charisma (Pulleyn 2006: 62 n. 72, 67).

χρύσεια It is hard to imagine golden sandals being particularly useful *qua* sandals. But gold is associated with prestige and divinity in the stylized world of the poem—to the extent that Aphrodite is herself 'golden' (*Il.* 3.64).

φέρον This unaugmented imperf. is most probably simply that—it describes what the sandals did. One might be tempted to see here a relic of the old PIE injunctive: a form unmarked for tense which took its temporal reference from the surrounding verbs (Clackson 2007: 131–2). M. L. West (1989) gives examples of pres. stems with secondary endings and no augment that take their temporal cue from adjacent and unambiguous pres. tense forms and are used describe the habitual attributes of divine persons. Such an interpretation of φέρον seems unlikely here since there are no neighbouring pres. forms to give the verb a present colouring.

ὑγρήν 'the wet'. This way of referring to the sea, already found in the *Iliad* (*Il.* 14.308; 24.341), might well be a kenning. M. L. West (1966: 287) compares γλαυκήν ('the grey', Hes. *Th.* 440). It is unclear what fem. noun is to be understood: θάλασσα seems crass. More likely is ὁδός; cf. ὑγρὰ κέλευθα (*Il.* 1.312).

98 πνοῆς Most dialects form the dat. pl. of these a-stem nouns in –αις. In epic, the more usual dat. pl. ends in –ῃσι; forms in –ῃς are much rarer (Chantraine 1958: 201–2). Before a vowel, of course, elision means that one could be dealing with either (Janko 1982: 56–7, 110–11). In the Hittite *Song of Ullikummi*, Kumarbi takes up his staff and binds the very winds themselves to his feet. It might be that the idea of sandals that carry a god as swiftly as the winds is a glance at this (M. L. West 1997a: 191).

99 εἵλετο … χαλκῷ This line is found in arming scenes in the *Iliad* (10.135; 14.12; 15.482). There is nothing objectionable in their presence here. It suggests that Athena is going into battle against the suitors—if not to fight them herself, then to encourage Telemachus to do so.

100 βριθὺ μέγα στιβαρόν Adjectives are accumulated into a striking asyndetic sequence. Although this formula is used of Athena's spear (*Il.* 5.746; 8.390), it is also used of mortals' weapons (*Il.* 16.141, 802; 19.388).

101 τοῖσίν τε κοτέσσεται The verb is a short-vowel aor. subj. (cf. 41 n.) from κοτέω with doubling of the *s* for metrical and/or expressive purposes (Chantraine 1958: 178–9). τοῖσίν τε introduces a rel. clause where the subj. indicates a contingency (cf. 52 n.). It is not necessary to have a modal particle such as κε/ἄν (e.g. *Il.* 9.117; *Od.* 14.85–6; Chantraine 1953: 245; Colvin 2016: 79).

Ὀβριμοπάτρη This appears to mean 'she of the mighty father'. ὄβριμος is not applied to Zeus himself in the poems; of living beings, it is used only for Ares (*Il.* 5.845) and Hector (*Il.* 8.473). Ὀβριμοπάτρη stands alone as a proper noun rather than an epithet. The first element of the compound is either a prosthetic ὀ- (Meillet 1926) or a dialectal variant of ἁ-copulative (Sommer 1934: 42 n. 3) plus the same root βρι- seen in βριαρός, βρίθω (*DELG* 196–7). We might sense a connexion between the βριθὺ ἔγχος in the preceding line (n.) and Ὀβριμοπάτρη who possesses it.

102 Οὐλύμποιο The opening vowel sound has been lengthened for the sake of the metre (Wyatt 1969: 90).

καρήνων Not only men (*Il.* 11.500) but also towns (*Il.* 2.117) and Olympus have 'heads'. In towns these are walls and battlements; on Olympus they must be peaks. The notion of mountains and hills having heads is a commonplace in the Hebrew Bible (Gen. 8:5; Exod. 19:20; 24:17; 34:2 and 34×) and Akkadian texts (Reiner and Roth 1999: 282). Whether this Greek image is a Semitic borrowing or an independent development we cannot tell.

103 δήμῳ The word may refer to the common people as opposed to the nobility (*Il.* 2.198; *Od.* 7.11) or, as here, to the actual land where the people live.

προθύροις The πρόθυρον (lit. 'fore-door') is sometimes the entrance to the μέγαρον (27 n.), sometimes, as here, to the αὐλή ('courtyard').

104 παλάμῃ … ἔγχος The bearing of weapons by visitors seems to have been normal, even on short journeys (S. R. West 1988: 88).

105 ξείνῳ The word covers what to us might seem like two separate ideas. It often means a 'stranger', a person whom the speaker does not recognize (cf. *Od.* 1.123). But it also describes someone who, although once a stranger, has become a known friend through the institution of ξενίη or 'guest-friendship'. In an archaic community, a person who moves outside his own social group has no longer any kin, any home, or any protection under the law (*Il.* 9.63). His only hope of being safe in another setting is if he is a guest-friend of the group he is visiting or if he becomes a suppliant. To this extent the guest-friend and the suppliant are uncomfortably alike (Gould 1973: 91 with n. 14a, 92–4); cf. 175–6 n. We cannot immediately tell which sense of the word is at play here. Telemachus soon asks whether Mentes is a complete stranger or a guest-friend (175–6) and learns that he is the latter (187). The appropriate English translation will differ from place to place in Book 1 depending on who is speaking and whether the status of the ξεῖνος has been fully ascertained.

Ταφίων We hear elsewhere that the Taphians are pirates (*Od.* 15.427; 16.426) and slave-traders (*Od.* 14.452; 15.427). They cannot readily be identified on a map. It has been fancifully suggested that the name is a pun and means 'people from the land set apart' since τάφος means 'grave' (Deroy 1946). But there was a Mt. Taphiassos in Locris on the north coast of the Gulf of Corinth (Str. 9.4.8; 10.2.4) and various nearby places beginning with Ταφ– (Str. 10.2.14, 20; D.S. 8.17.1). It was probably this area that the poet had in mind.

Μέντη This name inevitably invites comparison with the Μέντωρ, another persona adopted by Athena and one who plays a considerable part in Book 2. Given the existence of other character doublets in the narrative such as Calypso and Circe or Eurycleia and Eurynome (Fenik 1974: 172–207), it is not surprising that readers should have asked the same question about Mentes and Mentor. Wilamowitz-Moellendorff (1884: 6–7) thought that Mentes was a later invention, modelled on Mentor. Linguistic considerations tend to support this (Fraenkel 1910: 73). Agential nouns ending in –της are generally built to compound stems (κυνηγέτης, ἐπιβρεμέτης, παραιβάτης, etc.) whereas those built directly to the root (as here) generally end in –τηρ/–τωρ (Chantraine 1933: 314, 321–2). Μέντης must therefore be a later formation, albeit still within the period of the productive bardic tradition, produced at a date when the original compounding rules were no longer being observed. The fact that Mycenaean, which is early, had a form *e-qe-ta* (cf. Pindaric ἐπέτας) is not a disproof; the suffix in –ετης is a special case whose additional short vowel shows that it is a separate entity generalized from stems ending in a laryngeal (Ruijgh 1967a: 119 n. 100). None of this means that Mentes is to be dismissed as an insignificant echo of his philologically older counterpart. His function in this book is clearly pivotal. Whilst some detect here a fusion of the work of two different poets (Rüter 1969: 127), it is a mistake to see these episodes in such reductionist terms. They form part of an integrated narrative that makes sense in its own terms.

106 ἀγήνορας The word probably meant in origin 'leader of men' (ἄγω + ἀνήρ), and thus by extension 'brave' (*Il.* 12.300); but it would appear very soon to have been subject to reinterpretation (perhaps ἄγαν + ἀνήρ, *DELG* 10) as meaning 'arrogant' (*Il.* 9.699). This is surely the sense here. It is unusual to find such terms of moral evaluation in the mouth of the poet himself (cf. *Il.* 2.870–5). De Jong (2001: 19–20) plausibly sees this as 'embedded focalization': the narrator chooses a word to represent the situation as seen through the eyes of Mentes.

ἔπειτα Used very occasionally in the progressive sense of 'Now...' when setting a scene (cf. *Od.* 4.354).

107 πεσσοῖσι This is the sole occurrence in either epic of this word. Σ and Hesychius suggest that it refers to dice; but Soph. fr. 479.4 (*TrGF IV*) indicates that dice and πεσσοί are different things. Eur. *Supp.* 409 suggests that the latter are gaming pieces. It is difficult enough to reconstruct any classical board-games in detail (Laser 1987: 123–6) and impossible to know what Homer had in mind here (Kurke 1999). We may dismiss as playful antiquarianism Athenaeus' idea (16f–17b) that the suitors were playing something like marbles and taking aim at a large one called 'Penelope'.

θυμὸν ἔτερπον In later Greek, πεσσοί are described as an ἄλυπος διατριβή ('pain-free pastime', Gorgias fr. 82 B 11a (30) DK) and a τερπνὸν ἀργίας ἄκος ('pleasurable cure for idleness', Soph. fr. 479.4 (*TrGF IV*)). Things look less anodyne when the players are killing Odysseus' cattle, lounging on the skins, and ignoring a stranger in the doorway.

108 ἔκτανον αὐτοί It was very unusual for the meat of a species that was typically offered in sacrifice to be eaten without there in fact being a sacrifice (Parker 2011: 131–2). There is no mention of sacrifice here—but this might be an example of narrative compression: we cannot conclude that there was no sacrifice simply because none is mentioned. A similar question arises at *Od.* 8.180–2; whether this is an instance of compression or whether hunting was a special case we cannot tell (see 225 n.). At all events, the energy involved in slaughtering the cattle seems oddly contrary to the overall idleness of the suitors; but they are said to do the same at *Od.* 17.180–2. One might expect them to order servants to kill their food for them. Nevertheless, this way of putting the matter emphasizes their transgressive behaviour: in killing that to which they have no right, they are likened to Odysseus' companions who killed the oxen of the Sun (cf. 7–9 nn.).

109 κήρυκες At first blush, helping with dinner appears beneath the dignity of a herald. S. R. West points out (1988: 89–90) that their involvement in such matters (e.g. *Il.* 9.174; 18.558) might be an extension of their duties in sacrificial contexts (*Il.* 3.245 ff., 274 ff.). Whether this corresponds to any historical reality we cannot now tell.

θεράποντες These are clearly servants but not slaves. The same person may be both κῆρυξ and θεράπων (*Il.* 1.321) and there is no indication that the former are slaves (see 398 n). Patroclus was a θεράπων in the house of Peleus (*Il.* 23.90). Eteoneus, θεράπων of Menelaus, is referred to as κρείων; his function in greeting honoured guests is plainly not compatible with low status (*Od.* 4.22). θεράποντες perform a variety of tasks in the *Odyssey*: they help with ship's gear on setting sail (*Od.* 4.784) and coming into land (*Od.* 16.326, 360), they distribute food (*Od.* 16.253), and act as porters for valuable possessions (*Od.* 18.297, 300).

ὀτρηροί A standard epithet for θεράποντες; obviously connected with ὀτρύνω, it presumably denotes busily bustling about.

110 ἄρ' Bentley proposed to delete the particle altogether and allow the inherited digamma in ϝοῖνον to produce a heavy syllable in the preceding μέν; this is not the MS tradition, but the thought would be that a scribe ignorant of digamma felt that a short syllable was needed to regularize the metre. However, since the digamma is often ignored in Homer, there is no more reason to restore it here than elsewhere. Van Thiel prints ἄρ; but this is the worst of all worlds. The form ἄρ is mostly found in the MSS before consonants. If the digamma is observed, the first foot will be spondaic and we may dispense with the particle altogether; if it is not observed, the elided form is needed.

οἶνον…ὕδωρ Greeks always mixed their wine with water: a common ratio was three parts water to one part wine but several others are mentioned in the sources (H. Wilson 2003: 114–16). The antiquity of the practice is suggested by the attestation of *ka-ra-te-ra* (cf. κρητήρ) in the Linear B tablets (Griffin 1995: 100). The theme is one of importance in the story of the Cyclops, when Odysseus gave neat to the Cyclops a wine that normally needed twenty measures of water in order to be potable. Whatever the relationship in that passage between a δέπας and a μέτρον (*Od.* 9.209), the point remains that the wine needed very considerable dilution. The idea of mixing one's wine was so fundamental that even the gods are described as doing the same with their nectar (*Od.* 5.93).

111 τραπέζας It would seem from the fact that these tables are being 'put out' that they are not part of the permanent furniture of the room.

112 πρότιθεν, τοὶ δέ Thus Allen's OCT (1917–19), following Aristarchus; Van Thiel (1991) follows the MS tradition προτίθεντο ἰδέ. But the MSS reading represents the *lectio facilior* and is probably an attempt to dispose of the unusual imperf. ind. act. form πρότιθεν. In Attic–Ionic, the expected form with augment would be προὐτίθεσαν. The form adopted here is

archaic (Morpurgo Davies 1964: 147); it may be compared with μεθίεν (*Od.* 21.377) and ξυνίεν (*Il.* 1.273).

κρέα πολλά An uncommon phrase whose few occurrences are thematically significant. Its sole appearance in the *Iliad* (8.231) is in a context where Odysseus is criticizing the Achaeans for taking their fill of meat and wine when they ought not to be. The same pejorative tone is evident here and at *Od.* 17.331 where it again describes the suitors. In both cases, they are taking generous helpings of what is not theirs. It is significant that its only other occurrence (*Od.* 24.364) is after the suitors have been killed and Telemachus and faithful retainers are back in the house eating plentifully of what is properly their own.

δατέοντο The MSS all have δατεῦντο. Certainly the metre requires a single heavy syllable here. This can be had with δατέοντο, assuming synizesis of -εο-. This was surely the original writing; later interference with the text, not before the fourth century BC, resulted in widespread replacement of -εο- by -ευ- in cases where the metre calls for a monosyllable (Bolling 1923: 172; M. L. West 1998a: xxii).

113–43 This is one of many typical scenes involving the reception of a guest and the giving of hospitality. They may contain any of a number of standard elements: the guest arrives and waits at the door, is seen by the host, is approached by the host, relieved of his weapon, welcomed verbally, led inside, and given a meal (De Jong 2001: 20). Here there is an evident contrast between good and bad host: Telemachus is doing what the suitors ought to be doing instead of lounging on skins; cf. 96–324 n.

113 τὴν κτλ. This line recurs once only, with the first word replaced by τόν, at *Od.* 17.328 when Telemachus is the first to see Eumaeus coming into the house ahead of Odysseus. In both cases, the watchful attentiveness of Telemachus is stressed. On the gender of the pronoun, see 125 n.

Τηλέμαχος At l. 88, Athena had referred to Telemachus just as 'the son' (υἱόν). It is striking that his naming, like that of Odysseus (cf. 1, 30 nn.), is postponed to this point.

114 ἧστο…τετιημένος ἦτορ This line introduces a short ring composition, completed by μεθήμενος (118) picking up ἧστο here. The poet takes us briefly into the mind of the young man, showing his isolation amid a crowd, his private thoughts, and their contrast with the merriment surrounding him.

ὀσσόμενος This is not a common word and has to do with forming a mental image (cf. ὄσσε < PIE *H_3ek^w-). It occurs in the *Iliad* when Agamemnon harbours hostile intent (κάκ᾽ ὀσσόμενος) towards Calchas

(*Il.* 1.105) and where Iris declares she has none towards Priam (*Il.* 24.172). It is possible that this hostile sense was original (cf. *Il.* 14.17). If so, Telemachus is not so much engaged in wistful recollection as in resentful brooding. His animus is directed at the suitors and not at his father, who is described as ἐσθλόν in a way that suggests that this is how Telemachus sees him. (On such embedded focalization, cf. 108 n.)

116 μνηστήρων τῶν μέν The phrasing is peculiar: τῶν is redundant in any event. There has perhaps been some re-working of an existing formula (S. R. West 1988: 92; cf. 151).

σκέδασιν ... θείη An odd periphrasis, where a verb by itself might have been expected. A similarly unusual construction is found at *Od.* 24.485 (ἔκλησιν θέωμεν). In any event, there is some understatement or euphemism here. Odysseus does not merely scatter the suitors: he and Telemachus kill them all.

117 τιμήν On its face, the line means that Telemachus hopes that Odysseus will exercise rule in his own dominion and enjoy the honour that belongs to the king. There is perhaps also the sense that honour would accrue from scattering the suitors.

κτήμασιν The dat. with ἀνάσσω in Homer almost always refers to ruling over people rather than things. But the parallel κτεάτεσσιν ἀνάσσω (*Od.* 4.93) shows that there is nothing formally wrong with the syntax here (Chantraine 1953: 80). A minority of MSS have δώμασιν, perhaps an interpolation from *Od.* 1.402.

118 μεθήμενος An end to the short ring composition begun at 114 (ἧστο). This compound, of apparently transparent meaning, is unique in all of Greek. It is a surprising coinage, not least because it does not differ much in sense from the metrically equivalent παρήμενος (*Od.* 1.26, 339; 13.407).

119 νεμεσσήθη It is commonly said that νέμεσις is a sort of divine punishment for human ὕβρις (227 n.). But νέμεσις, with its related verbal forms, is more often in Homer predicated of humans than of gods. It has to do with indignation at the transgression of behavioural norms. To that extent, it gives the lie to the surprising idea that Homeric characters feel shame rather than guilt and that their moral standards come from outside rather than from within. That notion originated in anthropological discourse (Mead 1937: 493–5; Benedict 1947: 223) and has been adopted by some classicists (e.g. Dodds 1951: 17–18, 28–63). But there are plenty of places where Homer makes people say that they feel indignation at other people's conduct (*Od.* 6.286–8; 15.69–71) and so show that they have internal mechanisms of moral evaluation (Dickie 1978: 94; Cairns 1990).

120 ἐφεστάμεν One does not leave strangers without a reception (cf. *Od.* 7.160). Zeus himself is said to care for the treatment of visitors (*Od.* 9.269–71). The suitors, albeit squatters, are the *de facto* occupants of the place and so the duties of hospitality, and the penalties for its breaches, fall upon them. See 406–7 n.

121 χεῖρ’ ἕλε δεξιτερήν This is part of a ritualized series of actions for receiving a ξεῖνος (cf. *Od.* 3.35).

122 φωνήσας It is occasionally said (Rijksbaron 2002: 6, 122–3) that the aor. ptcp. indicates relative time, marking an action as anterior to the main verb, so that (e.g.) ὡς ἄρα φωνήσας ἡγήσατο must mean 'having spoken thus, he led the way' (*Od.* 2.413). But that is deceptive: the aor. ptcp. marks aspect, so as to exclude the idea of duration (Humbert 1954: 169–70, cf. Chantraine 1953: 188–9). In any event anteriorty is ruled out since the act of speaking consists in the very words that follow; a better translation is that Telemachus 'spoke up'. Cf. 336, 356 nn.

    ἔπεα πτερόεντα The conventional translation is 'winged words'. The epithet is never used of birds in Homer, which are always πετεηνοί (e.g. *Il.* 2.459); but it is applied to arrows (e.g. *Il.* 4.117). The thought is presumably of a feathered arrow reaching its mark (Pulleyn 2000: 180–1). The conventional rendering need not be abandoned: a feathered arrow may in some sense be thought of as winging its way. In the Vedic hymns, words are said to fly like birds (*RV* 1.25.4) and like arrows (*RV* 9.69.1).

123 χαῖρε This impv. is found with an instrumental dat. in a prayer (*Il.* 10.462), the sense being perhaps, 'take this with pleasure'. This is likely just a special case of a wider use between host and guest: food, drink, and gifts can be handed over with the wish that the recipient rejoice in them. In time, the dat. complement could be dropped and χαῖρε used by itself to point to the same relationship (Wachter 1998). This explains why the word is used upon meeting (*Il.* 9.197; *Od.* 13.229); its use upon taking leave, found in the *Odyssey* (*Od.* 5.205; 13.39, 59; 15.151) but not in the *Iliad*, is presumably a later development.

    ξεῖνε The sense here might be thought to be 'stranger'; but any stranger might easily turn out to be a 'guest-friend' with a claim on the household (cf. 176 n.).

    φιλήσεαι 2 sg. fut. ind. med. but pass. in meaning. This undifferentiated med./pass. seems to be old in Homer: it is only in one late passage (*Il.* 10.365) that a specific fut. pass. is found (Chantraine 1958: 447). On the ending, see 158 n.

124 δείπνου See 134 n.

πασσάμενος In the ritual of ξεινία the meal always precedes the asking and answering of questions (*Il.* 11.777–81; Gould 1973: 91 with n. 90). The same is true for suppliants (*Od.* 7.153–77; Gould 1973: 79). The single MS that reads παυσάμενος here shows the same vacillation at *Od.* 4.61; it is to be rejected as the *lectio facilior*.

125 ἢ δ' ἕσπετο κτλ. The poet never shares the illusion of the characters that Mentes is a male human being. The same fem. markers recur at 113, 130, 213, 230, 252, 306, 314, 319.

Παλλάς This is the first use of this name in the *Odyssey*. Its etymology is obscure and various folkloric connexions with παλλακή ('girl') or πάλλω ('shake'; cf. Zeus' aegis) are unconvincing. It might be a borrowing from Semitic *baʾalat* ('mistress'; cf. Baʾal: Lewy 1895: 251; Carruba 1968: 939–42).

128 δουροδόκης This word is unique in Homer, who is not otherwise concerned with such niceties (*Il.* 6.213). Eustathius thought that the pillars were fluted and that the spears rested in these flutes. Alternatively, we are to think of some free-standing receptacle, like an umbrella stand. Once the spear has been deposited, we hear no more of it; Athena at the end of this scene vanishes from sight (*Od.* 1.320; cf. Porph. *ad Il.* 1.449).

ἔνθά περ On the accentuation, see 1 n.

ἄλλα Not 'other' since this is a spear not of Odysseus but of Mentes; tr. 'as well' (cf. *Od.* 6.84; 9.367). This little scene of the stowing of the spear in the unique receptacle appears to have been called into being precisely in order to glance at the weapons of Odysseus and so create a frisson foreshadowing his return.

130 θρόνον An imposing type of chair with a high back and sometimes armrests (Richter 1966: 13; Laser 1968: 55). Already attested in the Linear B tablets (Chadwick and Baumbach 1963: 203), it seems to have been the most prestigious kind of chair in the Homeric poems. Zeus has one (*Il.* 1.536), as do Nestor (*Il.* 11.645) and Achilles (*Il.* 24.522). Menelaus offers one each to Telemachus and Pisistratus (*Od.* 4.51) as does Calypso to Hermes (*Od.* 5.86). Alcinous has several in his palace for himself (*Od.* 6.308) and his council (*Od.* 7.95–9). Athenaeus (192e–f) suggests a hierarchy with θρόνος at the top, followed by the κλισμός, and with the δίφρος as the humblest kind of seat. In later Greek θρόνος becomes a metonym for royalty (Soph. *Ant.* 166). That said, it is sometimes used interchangeably with κλισμός (*Il.* 11.623 vs. 645; 24.515 vs. 597; cf. 132 n. *infra*).

λῖτα Telemachus gives the guest something padded to sit on rather than just the hard chair. An adj. λίς describes a rock that is περίξεστος ('polished'; *Od.* 12.64, 79) and so appears to mean 'smooth'; cf. λεῖος

(Fraenkel 1910: 89–90). It is possible that this adj. does duty here for a noun, 'smooth (*sc.* stuff)'. More likely we are looking at the result of a linguistic confusion. A masc. noun (ϝ)ἑᾱνός denotes an article of clothing (e.g. *Il.* 3.385; 21.507; cf. ἕννυμι, Myc. *we-a₂-no-i*). A superficially similar adj. ἑᾱνός has no digamma and long alpha and describes cloth (*Il.* 5.734) and metal (*Il.* 18.613). The adj. is taken to mean 'fine' but lacks any clear etymology. If we look at the phrase ἑανῷ λιτί κάλυψαν (*Il.* 18.352; 23.254) and make allowance for (a) the common disregard for digamma, and (b) a not unknown hesitation over vowel length (Shipp 1961: 17 n. 29), one can appreciate how it might have begun life meaning, 'covered with a cloth (ἑ.) that was fine (λ.).' but was subsequently reinterpreted to mean 'covered with a fine (ἑ.) cloth (λ.).'—perhaps with popular etymology helping to connect λίς with λίνον (*DELG* 643). λῖτα, the form under discussion here, would thus have been analysed as a noun. It could be a 3rd-declen. masc. sg. or a 2nd-declen. neut. pl. Athenaeus (48c) takes it as the latter, cf. Linear B *ri-ta* (= λῖτα) beside the unambiguous pl. *pa-we-a* (φάρεα) (Chadwick and Baumbach 1963: 218). One might think the 3rd-declen. dat. sg. λιτί (*Il.* 18.352; 23.254) unlikely to have arisen from an original 2nd-declen. neut. pl. λῖτα—the traffic tends to be the other way; but the Mycenaean evidence is not easy to dismiss (*pace* Shipp 1961: 17). Athenaeus (*supra*) takes this kind of fabric to be undyed and lacking in embroidery, the sort of thing that goes underneath a more elaborate production (cf. *Od.* 10.352–3).

131 καλὸν...ἦεν This line is an ascending tricolon, made of three members each of which is longer than the preceding one. This figure is found already in the Vedic hymns, which is a marker of its high antiquity in the PIE poetic tradition (Gonda 1976: 225; M. L. West 2004). It is possible that it originated in hymns and prayers (Pulleyn 1997: 145–6).

καλὸν δαιδάλεον Refers to the θρόνον, not the λῖτα (cf. 130 n. for reasons).

θρῆνυς 'footstool'—is built to the same root as θρόνος, both words appearing to come from a root meaning 'support, carry'; cf. Skt. *da-dhara* (*DELG* 443). Drawings can be found in Laser 1968: 47, 51.

132 κλισμόν A chair with a sloping back, this was the characteristic form of Greek seat and appears to be without any oriental models (Richter 1966: 33 and corresponding plates). It was used by both gods (*Il.* 8.436) and mortals (Helen: *Od.* 4.136; contrast *Il.* 3.424). Athenaeus (192e–f) implies that in terms of prestige it fell between a θρόνος and δίφρος—the cheapest kind of seat (*Od.* 20.259).

ἄλλων This is generally taken with μνηστήρων at the beginning of the next line. Such usage is not unparalleled, but equally it is not common. If one puts a comma after ἄλλων then ὀρυμάγδῳ in the next line will depend on μνηστήρων (Jacobson 2000). The guest is seated apart from 'the others', who include the various attendants (109–12); but it is the din of the suitors that Telemachus worries about.

134 δείπνῳ This noun refers to the main meal taken during the day: this might be around midday (*Il.* 11.84–6) or earlier if necessary (*Il.* 2.381). δόρπον is always the evening meal. The distinction is apparent at *Od.* 20.390–4, where the poet remarks that the suitors had eaten their δεῖπνον but that the only δόρπον they would taste was death (Richardson 1973: 190). At *Od.* 4.61 there is an odd reference to a δεῖπνον being taken after nightfall (cf. *Od.* 3.497); but characters later refer to that same meal in terms of δόρπον (*Od.* 4.194, 213). It is likely that δεῖπνον is an error for δόρπον in the present case (S. R. West 1988: 196); how early this came about we cannot tell.

ἀδήσειεν MSS alternatives are ἀδήσειεν and ἀηδήσειεν. If we read ἀηδήσειεν < ἀηδέω ('take no pleasure in', 'be repelled by'), the sense is good and the metre avoids (by correption) the hiatus that is involved with either of the alternatives. The problem is that ἀηδέω is a hapax, otherwise unattested in Greek before Hesychius. ἀδήσειεν presumably takes its aspirate from a mistaken analogy with ἀνδάνω, whose opposite is wanted here. ἀδήσειεν has been connected with the perf. ptcp. ἀδηκότες (*Il.* 10.98; *Od.* 12.281) itself derived from either (a) ἄδην (cf. Lat. *satis*) so as to mean 'sated'/'having had enough of' or (b) privative ἀ + ἡδύς/ἀνδάνω (~ 'displeased'). In (b), it is hard to see how *ἀϝαδηκότες could yield ἀδηκότες when digamma was lost, especially when we have Attic ἀηδής (*DELG* 19–20). On balance the derivation from ἀδήν seems the least problematic.

ὑπερφιάλοισι This term is frequently, although not exclusively, applied to the suitors. It is generally taken to mean something like 'arrogant', 'overbearing'. This being so, it is striking that it is used of the suitors by their leader at *Od.* 21.289. But then it is used of the Cyclopes (*Od.* 9.106), whose leader Polyphemus is happy to describe himself and his fellows in terms of the utmost arrogance (*Od.* 9.275–8). Ancients fancifully connected it with ὑπὲρ φιάλην, with the idea of a cup running over (Ion Trag. 19 F 10 (*TrGF I*)). Moderns compare ὑπερφυής and Lat. *superbus* (*DELG* 1158).

135 μιν This pron. can be masc. or fem. Athena/Mentes was presented as female a few lines earlier (αὐτήν, 130); but the subject has since changed to the masc. ξεῖνος (133) with which two following participles agree. μιν must therefore be masc. here. There is some subtlety in the shifting way that the audience's perception of the visitor's sex are focalized: here we are seeing through Telemachus' eyes, whereas at l. 130 we enjoyed the perspective of the omniscient narrator.

136 χέρνιβα 'water for washing hands'. This practice before meals is common in the *Odyssey* (*Od.* 4.52; 7.172; 10.368; 15.135; 17.91). It was also normal at later Greek symposia (Pollux 6.92.1). Since at *Od.* 4.52 diners wash their hands even when they have come straight from being bathed by servants (*Od.* 4.49), it is reasonable to attribute sacral significance to the action. It is thus not clear why the characters of the *Iliad* are never shown washing their hands before eating. In that poem, the practice is mentioned only twice: before a sacrifice (*Il.* 1.449) and before a libation (*Il.* 24.304). Whilst not all of these type-scenes contain every possible element (cf. Kirk 1981: 64), this can scarcely explain the complete absence of the practice from the *Iliad*. One can only conclude that the poet did not feel it was as appropriate to the martial setting at Troy as it was to the settled domestic world of the *Odyssey*. Although Σ *ad Il.* 1.449 remarks that one did not wash one's hands *after* eating διὰ τὸ ἅψασθαι τῶν θυσιῶν ('because of having had contact with sacrificial offerings'), it appears to have been usual in later Greece to do so (Athenaeus 128e). This seems only natural in a society where people ate with their fingers. Porphyry probably came nearest to the truth when he says that Homer does not spell out every detail of a scene (*ad Il.* 1.449).

προχόῳ The dat. is instrumental, indicating that with which the water is poured over their hands (Chantraine 1953: 76–7).

137 ὑπὲρ...λέβητος This is the basin that catches the water. At *Il.* 24.304, the attendant has in her hands both a πρόχοον and χέρνιβον; the latter denotes a vessel like the λέβης rather than the water itself (Ginouvès 1962: 312; Richardson 1993: 304–5).

138 νίψασθαι The inf. indicates purpose—'for them to wash their hands' (Chantraine 1953: 300–1). It has been suggested, on the basis of the expression χέρνιβα τ' οὐλοχύτας τε κατήρχετο (*Od.* 3.445), that χέρνιψ was a libation in water comparable to those usually made in wine. But the lie is given to this here as the inf. makes the purpose of the water very plain (Ginouvès 1962: 311 n. 10). χέρνιβα κατήρχετο is thus zeugmatic and does not mean 'made a first-fruit offering of the lustral water' but rather 'began the rite with the lustral water'. Cf. *Il.* 1.449: χερνίψαντο δ' ἔπειτα καὶ οὐλοχύτας ἀνέλοντο.

ἐτάνυσσε Some commentators see here the opening out of a folding table. If such a thing existed, it is not found in the archaeological record (Laser 1968: 60–8). τανύσσω does not denote unfolding so much as stretching out a lengthy object (cf. *Od.* 15.283). It is instructive to look at *Il.* 9.213: ἀνθρακίην στορέσας ὀβέλους ἐφύπερθε τάνυσσεν ('when the coals had been spread out, the spits were laid out on top'). It is reasonable to think of a trestle table whose top was stretched over supports. In the *Iliad*, this formula does not appear at all. Tables are, in fact, only rarely mentioned in that poem, probably reflecting a difference in ethos and emphasis (cf. 136 n.). In both poems, tables are only brought out when needed (cf. *Il.* 24.476; cf. *Od.* 7.232).

139 σῖτον is sometimes food as opposed to drink (*Od.* 9.87) but here plainly refers to bread as opposed to meat. This was probably its original meaning. It has been conjectured that the Mycenaean sign *si* is a modification of an ideogram for grain and that the word is borrowed from a Minoan word of the same meaning (Ruijgh 1970).

140 εἴδατα πόλλ' ἐπιθεῖσα This line was criticized by Athenaeus (193b) who said that, if the ταμίη set εἴδατα before the guests, these must have been leftovers of meat so that there was no need to introduce a carver in the next line. But εἶδαρ just means 'food' (< ἔδω) and παρεόντων need mean no more than 'what was in the house'. Homeric meals are highly stylized and participants are not often shown eating food other than meat. In reality, the Greek diet was never heavily based on meat and these εἴδατα πολλά could well have been a glance at foods to be enjoyed in addition to the large slices of meat (cf. 142 n.).

χαριζομένη The servant is showing favour or generosity by distributing victuals (cf. 61, 318 nn.).

παρεόντων The partitive gen. indicates the whole from which the servant took the portions (Chantraine 1953: 51).

141 κρειῶν This form is somewhat unexpected beside the nom. κρέας (*Od.* 8.477). The expected κρεάων is found at *Hy. Merc.* 130. κρεῖων might have been a bardic substitute; if so, it is not clear why the tradition retained κεράων and τεράων (Chantraine 1958: 209–10; Meissner 2006: 122–3).

142 παντοίων Unless hyperbolic, this suggests that the εἴδατα, whatever they might have been, were not meat.

χρύσεια κύπελλα A κύπελλον is a larger sort of cup used by persons of rank (*Od.* 4.58) and gods (*Il.* 1.596). It is interchangeable, presumably for metrical reasons, with the δέπας (*Il.* 24.285 vs. 305). Greeks of the archaic period no doubt looked back with awe at an age when persons drank from golden goblets. The so-called Cup of Nestor, a modest pot found in Ischia and dated 750–700 BC, bears an inscription apparently declaring that it was the cup used by Nestor (*Il.* 11.631–7). This maybe indicates an ironic contrast between the heroic age and that in which the epics were finally composed (Meiggs and Lewis 1988: 1–2).

143 ἐπῴχετο See 324 n.

144–57 Before the important episode in which Mentes speaks to Telemachus, Homer focuses for a second time on the suitors. At 106–8 they were playing games and violating social and religious norms by ignoring the presence of a visitor. Here they come in for dinner and engage in song and dance. They are then consigned to the background whilst they listen to the song of Phemius. They will not come back into focus until 325 (n.).

144 ἐς δ' ἦλθον The suitors enter and take a separate meal. Although the same elements are present as for Mentes (entrance, sitting down, washing, serving of food, pouring of wine), this episode is described in a far more summary way. This points up Telemachus' attentiveness as a host and shows the proper way to receive guests (W. C. Scott 1971).

145 ἑξείης ἕζοντο κατὰ κλισμούς τε θρόνους τε This line recurs at *Od.* 3.389 and 24.385. The order is probably determined by rank (cf. from a much later age Luke 14:8–10). It has already been seen that a θρόνος indicates higher prestige than a κλισμός (130, 132 nn.).

146 ὕδωρ This formula presents the same kind of χέρνιψ described at 136 (n.).

    ἔχευαν Some MSS have ἔχευον, which is a later attempt to create an imperf. to match ἕζοντο (145) and παρενήνεον (147). The Homeric imperf. of χέω would have been the unmetrical ἔχεον (Poulengeris 2001: 39–40). There is nothing especially surprising about an aor. keeping company with an imperf. (Chantraine 1953: 192–4); it is a question of how the speaker wishes to present each action.

147 δμῳαί The delicate translation is 'maidservants'; the more accurate is 'female slaves'; see 398 n.

    παρένηνεον This is the commonest reading in the MSS (cf. *Od.* 16.51); some witnesses have παρένηεον. In later Greek, the basic verb is νέω ('to pile up'). This is unattested in Homer, although νητός (*Od.* 2.338) presupposes it. For the verb, the pres. stem must have been *νηέω (to judge from imperfects at *Il.* 23.139, 163, 169; 24.276). Since forms with the second ν are best attested, these were not later scribal errors but an early (if mistaken) creation of the bards, perhaps unfamiliar with imperfects in -ήεον (Hoekstra 1989: 268; cf. Schwyzer 1939: 648 n. 3).

148 κοῦροι … πότοιο This line is omitted by one papyrus and some medieval MSS as an interpolation, the wine having already been poured (143). But that first pouring was for Telemachus and Mentes before the entrance of the suitors (144), who will also have wanted their drink. ἐπιστέφομαι is a metaphor for filling cups to the brim (Pulleyn 2000: 240). We may suppose that the κοῦροι pouring wine were slaves just as much as their female counterparts (147 n.) who served the food.

149 ὀνείαθ' The pl. of ὄνειαρ whose termination in -αρ is parallel to that of other food words: εἶδαρ (140), ἄλειαρ (*Od.* 20.108). The derivation must be from the same root as ὀνίνημι, indicating that food does you good.

ἴαλλον This is an arrestingly dynamic term ('thrust') and indicates the zeal with which they set about their food.

150 This is a common formulaic line for ending a meal. The narrative has dwelt on some length on the service of two meals, one for Telemachus and Mentes and one for the suitors. But, as is generally the case, the meal is then dismissed in one line so that we may move on to the next scene. But cf. 369 n.

152 μολπή τ' ὀρχηστύς τε Aristarchus thought that μολπή never denoted singing but only dancing or play (Lehrs 1865: 138–41). But the phrasing here suggests that μολπή and dancing are two different things. It is hard to imagine the sightless Demodocus dancing, especially while singing and playing the lyre (*Od.* 13.27; cf. 4.17–18). But there are contexts where μολπή appears to denote a mixture of song and acrobatics (*Il.* 18.605–6) and others where it includes—and might even refer solely to—dance (*Il.* 1.472; 16.182–3). It is thus an elastic term (Pulleyn 2000: 241). Cf. 421 n.

ἀναθήματα δαιτός To call song an adornment of the feast underlines the prestige attached to bardic recitation, the poet giving us a glance at his own profession (154 n.). This expression recurs only once (*Od.* 21.430) when Odysseus, having shot the arrow through the axe heads, says that it is time for food and song. But no dinner follows. Instead the bloody events that immediately unfold are in sharp contrast to the easeful character of the present episode (Thomas 2014: 93).

153 ἐν χερσὶν . . . θῆκεν It does not follow from this that Phemius could not see and needed the instrument to be placed into his hands. The bard Demodocus is explicitly said to be blind (*Od.* 8.64). But Phemius is later described as wondering whether to leave the house and take refuge at the altar of Zeus; he abandons this idea in favour of falling at the knees of Odysseus as a suppliant (*Od.* 22.330–43). The former would not be easy for a man who could not see and he accomplishes the latter without anyone to guide him through the *mêlée* to Odysseus.

κίθαριν The Greek lyre at the time of composition would have been made of wood with a sound-box made of (or perhaps shaped like a) tortoise shell and probably at first only four strings, the number being increased to seven in the seventh century (M. L. West 1992: 50–6). *h. Merc.* 39–54 gives a mythical account of its invention, mentioning seven strings.

περικαλλέα On compounds of this shape, see 329 n.

154 *Φημίῳ* A 'speaking name', obviously derived from the same root as Gk. *φημί*, Lat. *fama*. There is debate as to whether the immediate derivation is from *φῆμις*, whose connotations are usually negative (Bakker 2002: 142) or from the more neutral *φήμη*. It is easy to see the *i*-stem *φῆμις* behind *Φήμ-ι-ος* (Bader 1974: 32); but if *τιμή* can give rise to *τίμιος*, then *φήμη* could presumably do likewise (Kamptz 1982: 115). The name is fitting since fame is one of the chief things that define heroic verse. Singers make famous the deeds of men (*κλείουσιν*, *Od.* 1.338); Demodocus sings the *κλέα ἀνδρῶν* in a song whose own *κλέος* reaches the heavens (*Od.* 8.73–4). In the figures of the bards Homer is also showing us himself. Odysseus says that his *κλέος* reaches the heaven (*Od.* 9.20), his prestige arising in part from his taking on the mantle of the story-teller (Macleod 1983: 3–4).

These bardic appearances are limited to the *Odyssey*, but that may be explained by the fact that the action of the *Iliad* unfolds on a battlefield where is little room for such diversions. But, even there, Achilles is found *singing* the *κλέα ἀνδρῶν* ('renowns of men', *Il.* 9.189). This tends to blur the line between warrior and bard: the man who kills Hector is self-aware and can see himself poetically as part of the wider picture of human suffering (cf. *Il.* 24.518–51). Helen knew this too and reminded Hector (*Il.* 6.357–8) that mortals are made to suffer precisely in order that they may become a subject of song for future generations (*ὡς καὶ ὀπίσσω | ἀνθρώποισι πελώμεθ' ἀοίδιμοι ἐσσομένοισι*). The idea of undying fame finds parallels in Indic and reaches into the deep past of the common PIE poetic tradition (M. L. West 2007: 406–10).

ἀνάγκη That Phemius does not serve the suitors freely will be important later when he pleads to Odysseus for his life and can stress that he acted unwillingly and under compulsion (*Od.* 22.344–53).

155 *φορμίζων* The use of this verb with *κίθαρις* (153 n.) suggests that the poet viewed the *φόρμιγξ* as interchangeable with it. Both nouns have no reliable PIE etymology and are probably borrowings into Greek. *φόρμιγξ* has the same suffix as *σῦριγξ* ('reed pipe') and *σάλπιγξ* ('trumpet'). It seems likely that this was peculiar to Greek; if there was another language that used this suffix for musical instruments, it has left no trace.

ἀνεβάλλετο Σ glosses as *ἀνεκρούετο, προοιμιάζετο, ἀρχὴν ἐποιεῖτο*. We may surmise that this denotes striking up on an instrument or beginning to sing. Here the latter must be meant in view of the following *ἀείδειν* ('to sing'). In contrast to *Od.* 8.266, we are not told the theme of the song. See 156 n.

ἀείδειν This is the *vox propria* (*Od.* 8.45, 73, 83) to describe the function of bards (ἀοιδοί); see 328, 337 nn.

156 αὐτάρ Having introduced Phemius and his theme, the poet leaves him to fade into the background whilst Mentes and Telemachus talk (Thomas 2014: 90). The narrative does not return to the song until l. 325.

157 ἄγχι σχὼν κεφαλήν κτλ. Likewise at *Od.* 4.70, Telemachus puts his head close to Pisistratus so that he might not be overheard admiring Menelaus' wealth—but is in fact heard (*Od.* 4.76). At *Od.* 17.592, Eumaeus adopts the same intimate posture to speak to Telemachus so that the suitors do not overhear.

πευθοίαθ' οἱ ἄλλοι Aristarchus read πευθοίατο ἄλλοι, against the majority of MSS, viewing the sharp hiatus as preferable to having οἱ as an almost fully fledged definite article. But it is from such collocations that the definite article eventually arose (cf. *Il.* 1.11, 33 with Pulleyn 2000: 124; Chantraine 1953: 162). See 4, 9, 439 nn.

158–77 Telemachus questions Mentes. Once a guest has eaten, but not before (124 n.), it is usual for there to be talk. Before asking the obvious questions about the identity and provenance of his guest, Telemachus begins with a remarkable outburst mourning the death of his father, whom he does not name but refers to only obliquely (see 163 n.), and bemoaning the current state of affairs in Ithaca.

158 εἰ καί is the reading of the overwhelming majority of medieval MSS. ἦ καί is a variant found as a correction in one (albeit generally reliable) medieval MS. This latter is undoubtedly an easier reading: its force is slightly ironic, 'Will you, I wonder, take offence…?' ἦ is an affirmative particle ('certainly'), but is often found in questions (Chantraine 1953: 10–11). εἰ καί is harder and involves an ellipsis: '*even if* you take offence (*sc.* I shall say this anyway)'. West and Van Thiel both cite *Od.* 1.389 as a place where the MSS agree on εἰ rather than ἦ. The parallel is striking, although in that case the apodosis of the condition is made explicit, unlike here.

νεμεσήσεαι The notion that Mentes might feel νέμεσις (119 n.) at what is about to be said shows that Telemachus is aware that he is beginning his speech somewhat unusually (cf. 389 n.). Formally the verb could be 2 sg. fut. ind. med. or 2 sg. aor. subj. med. < νεμεσάω. There being no conjunction (or other marker) calling for the subj., we may take this to be an ind. (cf. 123 n.). The ending –εαι is from an older *-εσαι; the sigma has dropped out but the ending has not yet contracted to the –η of classical Attic (Chantraine 1958: 474). The form –εαι, albeit relatively archaic, is nevertheless an innovation within Greek (Sihler 1995: 476).

159 κίθαρις καὶ ἀοιδή This must be the playing and song of Phemius, not the suitors, as is evident from the proximate mention of κίθαρις (153) and ἀείδειν (155). See 421 n.

160 ῥεῖ’ The ease with which the suitors live, consuming what is not theirs, is a recurrent theme and foreshadows their doom by association with the companions of Odysseus who ate the oxen of the Sun (see 7, 34 nn.).

νήποινον A neut. sg. adj. functioning as an adv. and qualifying ἔδουσιν: the suitors act with impunity, cf. 377, 380 nn.

161 ἀνέρος See 163, 377 nn.

161–2 λεύκ’ ὀστέα...κυλίνδει Eumaeus (*Od.* 14.133–6) and Laertes (*Od.* 24.290–2) likewise both conjure up scenes of Odysseus’ flesh as carrion for scavengers. This image of the corpse being abused and going without proper funeral rites is abhorrent to Homeric sentiment (*Il.* 16.545, 559, 671–5; 19.26, 30–3; 22.71–6); this is one reason why the mutilation of Hector’s corpse in the *Iliad* is so shocking (Segal 1971; Vernant 1991: 70–4). The syntax is somewhat harsh since ὀστέα is subject of πύθεται but object of κυλίνδει.

ἦ’ Most editors print ἦ but it is then hard to explain how this vowel does not suffer correption before the following εἰν. It is more likely that we are dealing with an elided ἦέ (M. L. West 1998a: xxxi).

163 κεῖνον Telemachus does not refer to his father by name, using instead deictics (Bonifazi 2012) such as κεῖνος (163, 235, 243), ὁ (166, 168, 215, 220, 239), μιν (241), or parts of ἀνήρ (161, 233). This is a sharp contrast with Athena-Mentes, who uses his name very often (196, 207, 212, 253, 260, 265). (S)he also calls him ‘your father’ (195, 281, 287). This relates to the theme of the suppression of Odysseus’ name (cf. 1 n.). That often has to do with prudent concealment of Odysseus’ true name from his enemies; but here it is more complex. As De Jong (2001: 18) has pointed out, Telemachus feels real uncertainty about his parentage and position and one of Athena-Mentes’ tasks is to allay these. (S)he succeeds, to judge from Telemachus’ language after their encounter (396, 398, 413). It is noteworthy that the suitors do not doubt Telemachus’ lineage (387).

εἰ...ἰδοίατο This opt. could indicate a freestanding wish, in which case we should place a full stop at the end of the line (cf. *Il.* 15.571). It is more likely to be the protasis to the following opt. ἀρησαίατ’: so not, ‘Would that they might see him return. Then they would wish...’ but, ‘If they were to see him return, they would wish.’ These ideas are quite hard to separate. The protasis might have begun life as a wish rather than a speculation (Chantraine 1953: 275–6). Cf. 255 n.

νοστήσαντα On this theme, see 5 n.

164–5 ἐλαφρότεροι...| ἢ' ἀφνειότεροι There is a grim humour here: a large stash of other people's property is no good if you are running for your life. The idea of being light on one's feet makes us think back to the reference to the suitors' dancing (152); the contrast foreshadows their lack of prowess in running away from Odysseus in Book 22 (Thomas 2014: 91–3).

τε ἐσθῆτός There is no hiatus since inherited digamma is observed at the beginning of the noun here (cf. Lat. *vestis*).

166 ἀπόλωλε κακὸν μόρον The internal acc. (Chantraine 1953: 41) qualifies the verb with words that echo its sense but are genetically unrelated (cf. *Il.* 3.417; *Od.* 13.384). This differs from *figura etymologica*, where the verb and the acc. noun are cognates (e.g. *Od.* 9.303).

167 θαλπωρή Some MSS have ἐλπωρή in the text or margin. Both readings were known to the Alexandrians. θαλπωρή, if genuine, occurs only here in the *Odyssey* whereas ἐλπωρή occurs in four other places. θαλπωρή, the less familiar word, was probably original and ἐλπωρή a later scribal gloss.

εἰ This use of εἰ before a subj. without any modal particle is unknown in Attic but found in Homer, more often in the *Iliad* than the *Odyssey*. This suggests that it was gradually falling out of use (Chantraine 1953: 279).

περ 'even if'; cf. 6 n.

φῆσιν 3 sg. pres. subj. act. The ind. would be φησίν. Elsewhere in the *Odyssey* (11.128; 23.275) we find φήη. The form ending in –σι is an innovation by analogy with the ind. (Chantraine 1958: 43, 462). Subjunctives in –σι are properly written without iota (subscript or adscript) before the sigmatic element (M. L. West 1998a: xxxi; Pulleyn 2000: 226).

168 ὤλετο νόστιμον ἦμαρ Of the eleven occurrences of νόστιμον ἦμαρ, five refer to its loss (*Od.* 1.9, 168, 354; 17.253; 19.369). This is part of a larger pattern: the word νόστος exhibits a close affinity for parts of the verb ὄλλυμαι (Bonifazi 2009: 493 with n. 39). Just as νόστος points etymologically to salvation and return (cf. 5, 9 nn.), so its juxtaposition with ὤλετο (cf. 11 n.) creates an especially pointed contrast.

169 εἰπὲ... κατάλεξον This sort of doublet is common in Homer. It is also a feature of Irish oral poetry (O'Nolan 1978). But this does not mean that we ought to attribute it to the stock of inherited PIE poetic figures. Such parallelism is also integral to Hebrew poetry such as the Psalms.

170–2 This rapid sequence of questions marks a turning from Telemachus' own thoughts to questions about the stranger. It is echoed in part by the questions of Eurymachus at 406–9 (n.).

τίς πόθεν εἰς ἀνδρῶν; This is often taken (e.g. ΣMᵃ) to mean 'Who are you and where do you come from?' But πόθεν can refer to parentage rather than geographical origin (*Od.* 17.373; 19.162). Mentes' answer (*Μέντης Ἀγχιάλοιο δαΐφρονος εὔχομαι εἶναι*, 172) suggests that this is how he understood the question. Both Old Avestan (*Yasna* 43.7) and Classical Skt. (*Mahabharata* 1.131.34) preserve questions in the form, 'Who are you and *whose* are you' (Geldner 1904: 52). This suggests that we are dealing with an old PIE expression (Wackernagel 1926: 299–300; Floyd 1992). The parallel is not entirely satisfying since Avestan *kahiiā* and Skt. *kásya*, whilst corresponding precisely with each other in phonetic terms, are etymologically cognate with Homeric *τέο* (Attic *τίνος*) rather than *πόθεν*.

πόθι...τοκῆες Now the questioning moves on to geography. It is not about *who* are his parents or *what* his city but about *where* they are.

171–3 These lines were suspected by Aristarchus. Σ remarks that the lines sit better in the mouth of Eumaeus who is surprised that the ragged figure before him could have secured passage on any ship (*Od.* 14.188–90). But are these questions really so surprising in the mouth of an islander meeting a stranger?

171 ὁπποίης Introduces an indirect question (presumably depending on the verbs of speaking in 169). It is an awkward intrusion when all the other questions are direct in form.

172 εὐχετόωντο The verb designates solemn or emphatic speech of various kinds and so may include a prayer, a boast, or a claim of ancestry (Pulleyn 1997: 59–64).

173 οὐ...ἰκέσθαι It is hard not to think that there is an element of humour in this formulation. Perhaps audiences were already used to this particular quip.

174 ἔΰ is to be preferred to ἐΰ in writing this adv., usually identified as the neut. of ἐΰς. The later Greek form εὖ could not result from the contraction of *ἐΰ: the usual rules would yield *εὔ. To account for εὖ, we must suppose that the accent was originally on the first syllable (M. L. West 1998a: xx–xxi). Such retraction in adverbs finds a parallel in τάχα beside ταχύς.

175–6 πατρώϊος...| ξεῖνος For the institution of ξεινίη, see 105, 120 nn. These rights are exercisable not only between the original parties but also between their successors—hence πατρώϊος.

175 ἠέ...ἦ The usual sequence in direct disjunctive questions is ἦ or ἦε in the first member followed by ἦ or ἦε in the second. The particles ἠέ and ἦε both appear to rest on ἦ 'indeed' + *ϝε 'or' (Lat. -ve). ἠέ exhibits a proclitic treatment of the first element ἠ- (Chantraine 1953: 293-4; Probert 2003: 123-4).

νέον In context, what is being asked is not whether Mentes has arrived *recently* but *for the first time*.

176 ἴσαν Could be 3 pl. unaugmented imperf. ind. act. of εἶμι (Chantraine 1958: 285) or the pluperf. of οἶδα (*Od.* 4.772; Chantraine 1958: 420). The former seems more likely (S. R. West 1988: 99), the syntax without a preposition after the verb of motion finding a parallel at *Od.* 18.194.

δῶ Σ takes this to be a short form of δῶμα, but that is to put the cart before the horse. δῶ appears 23× in Homer, always in the sg. and 22× in the acc. δῶμα appears 242× exhibiting both sg. and pl. forms of most cases (except for the dat. sg. and gen. pl.). Surely δῶ was the original form: being of limited scope, it was remodelled to δῶμα in order to assign it to a recognizable morphological type as and when other parts of the paradigm were needed. Cf. 392 n.

δῶ looks like a root noun formed to the root *$d^e/_om$- seen in δόμος. The loss of final *-*m* is surprising as one would expect *δων (Lejeune 1976: 80-1); but Greek ἀηδώ and εἰκώ beside ἀηδών and εἰκών offer parallels (Szemerényi 1979: 224). Final nasals disappeared early within PIE; their presence in Greek is not a case of retention but of later restoration by analogy with oblique cases (Georgiev 1960: 69). O-grade vocalism is unexpected in a monosyllabic neut. root noun (Dunkel 1982/3b: 191); but the cognate Armenian *town* ('house') has it too (Clackson 1994: 137). Some imagine an original directional marker –δω like –δε in ἡμέτερόνδε (*Od.* 15.513): so *ἡμετερόνδω meant 'to our (*sc.* place)' until –δω was detached and understood to mean 'house' (e.g. *Il.* 1.427). But why would that happen unless δῶμα already existed (Durante 1970: 52)? Moreover Linear B (e.g. TH Of 26) has a form *do-de* which in context must mean 'to the house'; if that is right, *do-* cannot mean 'to' (Spyropoulos and Chadwick 1975: 88-9).

177 ἄλλοι Probably this has the sense of ἄλλοιοι ('of all different kinds'), cf. *Il.* 21.22.

κεῖνος See 163 n.

ἐπίστροφος A *hapax* (unless it should be read instead of ἐπίσκοπος at *Od.* 8.163). Aeschylus (*Ag.* 397) uses this adj. to mean 'conversant with', which does not make sense here. The verb στρέφομαι can mean 'to go about' (Soph. *El.* 516; Solon 37.6 IEG), so perhaps ἐπίστροφος ἀνθρώπων means 'going about among men'. The gen. probably indicates contact (Chantraine 1953: 52) and is understandable after a word beginning with ἐπι- (*Il.* 13.613). The rare but related adv. ἐπιστροφάδην appears at *Od.*

22.308 when Odysseus is killing the suitors—a more sinister kind of going about among men.

178–212 Mentes answers Telemachus' question by posing as a trader in metals who knew Odysseus in the past. It is the beginning of a careful strategy to find a way into Telemachus' affection and so encourage him to action.

179 μάλ' ἀτρεκέως The irony is that much of what Mentes says is a lie, albeit conveying the essential truth that Odysseus is not dead. Lying is one of the central activities of the poem: Odysseus does so to practically everyone including his own servant Eumaeus (using these same words of Athena: *Od.* 14.192), to his son (through the mouth of Eumaeus: *Od.* 16.61), to his wife (*Od.* 19.165–202), and to his father (*Od.* 24.244–79). Much art goes into the elaboration of these lies. Athena supports Odysseus because she is shrewd and admires the same qualities in him. There is a very self-conscious scene later where the pair enjoy lying to each other (*Od.* 13.253–351) and Athena explicitly says that they are well matched in their mental qualities (*Od.* 13.291–302).

180 Μέντης See 105 n.

Ἀγχιάλοιο This is not a real name but an off-the-cuff invention to suit a sailor. It turns up again in the almost comic catalogue of such names possessed by Phaeacians (*Od.* 8.112). The gen. denotes origin (cf. *Il.* 20.241; Chantraine 1953: 57).

δαΐφρονος See 48 n.

εὔχομαι See 172 n.

181 ἀτάρ This particle is often quite strongly adversative in the sense of 'but' or 'however' (e.g. *Il.* 1.506; *Od.* 2.240); but sometimes, as here, it serves only to mark a transition to a related topic with no real sense of contrast (*Il.* 2.313; *Od.* 9.335).

Ταφίοισι See 105 n.

φιληρέτμοισι This is another term shared with the Phaeacians (*Od.* 11.349; cf. 180 n.).

182 ὧδε Aristarchus is reported to have held that ὧδε in Homer always means 'thus' and never 'hither' (which it plainly does in later Greek, e.g. Soph. *O.T.* 144). Nevertheless 'hither' seems certain at *Il.* 10.537 (Hainsworth 1993: 207). To take πρόμολ' ὧδε at *Il.* 18.392 to mean not 'come here' but 'come just as you are, without delay' (*Σ* ad loc.) is artificial in the extreme (Leaf 1888: 244).

183–4 Bronze is the metal most often mentioned in the poems, reflecting the influence of the Aegean Bronze Age on the poetic tradition. The contemporaneous use of bronze and iron in Homer is often said to show how the epic tradition has fused together elements from disparate periods. Bronze did not immediately fall out of use when iron became available (Kirk 1960: 191); Mentes' activities would fit any period after about 950 BC when imports from the wider Mediterranean world began again (Donlan 1997: 651–2). The Taphians are also described as pirates (*Od.* 15.427; 16.426); this is a relic from a state of affairs rather earlier than that of burgeoning trade between settled communities (Introduction, pp. 31–2).

183 πλέων Scanned as one syllable by synizesis.

οἴνοπα A compound whose first element is plainly οἶνος ('wine') and whose second probably corresponds with that of αἶθοπα and νώροπα. The root *H_3ek^w- gives both ὄσσε and ὦπα in Greek. Since neither wine nor sea has either eye or face, we are dealing with a metaphor: it makes sense to think of 'face', in the sense of 'aspect'. Wine is said to be ἐρυθρός ('red') in Homer (*Od.* 5.165; 9.208, etc.); some suggest that the epithet describes the redness of the sky reflected by the sea at sunrise and sunset (Buchholz 1871–85: 62). But epic language does not assign epithets based on something that is true only under some conditions (Kober 1932: 85–6). Unmixed wine is also said to be μέλας ('black': *Od.* 5.265; 9.196, 346); but the sea around Greece is no more black than it is elsewhere (*pace* Lesky 1947: 162–3). Opinions about what the sea looked like to Greeks are inevitably subjective. One might recall that Homeric Greeks did not drink from glasses and that wine seen in a cup made from metal or earthenware will look dark with perhaps some highlights of reflected light (Irwin 1974: 28, 202; Griffin 1987: 51). This seems a plausible point of comparison between wine and sea. The word is also used to describe ploughing oxen (*Il.* 13.703; *Od.* 13.32): perhaps this refers to their dark hides gleaming with the sweat of toil. The name *wo-no-qo-so* given to oxen in Linear B (KN Ch 897) might be an idiosyncratic attempt to write *woinok*^{w}*s* = ϝοῖνοψ (Melena 2014: 37, 114, *pace* Lejeune 1963: 6 n. 16).

πόντον The expected word when what is being described is the flat expanse of the open sea; cf. 4 n.

ἀλλοθρόους It has been argued that this means that Temese (184 n.) must have been in a place where Greek was a foreign language so that Cyprus is ruled out (T. W. Allen 1910: 303). But non-Greek languages were spoken in Cyprus at all times before and after the composition of the epics (Steele 2013).

184 Τεμέσην Strabo (6.1.5) identified this with Tempsa in Southern Italy; but it is more likely to have been Tamassos (modern Politiko) in Cyprus (Hill 1940: 9 n. 1), the island being a notable centre for the production of copper (Knapp and Kassianidou 2008) to the extent that it gave its name to the metal (Lat. *aes cuprum*).

χάλκον Whilst the word in Homer generally denotes the hardened alloy bronze used for weapons, it is probable that Mentes is acquiring raw materials from Cyprus (see foreg.) so that the sense 'copper' is better here.

αἴθωνα σίδηρον probably denotes mild steel (i.e. iron with a small admixture of carbon) rather than pure elemental iron (Gray 1954: 1 n. 4). The epithet has long been a puzzle. Σ says that it means either μέλας ('black') because the metal has not yet been worked or λαμπρός ('bright') because of the 'shining fire'. These diametrically opposite explanations reflect an understandable confusion: words of the root αἰθ- may have an act. ('burn' = 'bright') or pass. ('burnt' = 'dark') meaning (*DELG* 32–3; Pulleyn 2000: 229–30, 238). αἴθων is used of iron, cauldrons (*Il.* 9.123), tripods (*Il.* 24.233), an eagle (*Il.* 15.690), horses (*Il.* 2.839), oxen (*Il.* 18.372), a bull (*Il.* 16.488), a lion (*Il.* 11.547); αἴθοπα is used only of wine (*Od.* 2.57), bronze (*Od.* 21.434), smoke (*Od.* 10.152). Hector's horses are called Ξάνθος, Πόδαργος, Αἴθων, and Λάμπος (*Il.* 8.185): the first two refer to colour but the last must mean 'bright' which might suggest the same for the third (Leaf 1886: 84). The conjecture (Edgeworth 1983) that all things that are αἴθων are, or may be, 'brown' is ingenious but unconvincing: to explain Odysseus' choice of the pseudonym Αἴθων (*Od.* 19.183), appeal is made to the manliness of a brown complexion. The formulae αἴθωνι σιδήρῳ (*Il.* 4.485) and αἴθοπι χαλκῷ (*Il.* 4.495) used in close proximity not only suggest some interchangeability in epithets but also reflect some inconsistency on the part of the poet as between which of the two metals is commonly in use (Lorimer 1950: 119). Other epithets denoting the colour of iron in Homer are πολιός ('grey') and ἰόεις ('dark'). Whilst it is unsafe to assume that all three epithets must be synonymous, the precise meaning is lost to us and 'dark' is as good a conjecture as any.

185–6 These lines were thought spurious by Aristarchus. That l. 185 is the same as *Od.* 24.308 does not weigh heavily against either. The form Ῥείθρῳ is Attic and one would expect Ῥέεθρῳ in the predominantly Ionic context of the poem; but Atticisms are not automatic proof of spuriousness (M. L. West 1966: 79–82). Σ points to the similarity between the name Νήϊον and the mountain Νήριτος mentioned by Odysseus (*Od.* 9.22); but this does not decide anything. One might think that ὑπὸ Νηΐῳ looks like a false division of the obscure epithet ὑπονηΐος found at *Od.* 3.86; but it might be the other way round, with the compounded epithet resulting from a failure to recognize the toponym. It is not surprising if the tradition shows uncertainty about words not often used in areas whose geography was not well worked out.

185 νηῦς It seems to have been standard practice for a leader to leave his ship and companions (182) at the shore while going ahead in person or with a few chosen men to make contact with the locals (*Od.* 9.193–6). Plainly there is a narrative convenience in this too: Mentes cannot have sailed alone (cf. 171–2) but it would be a distraction to have his crew with him at Odysseus' house, stepping impatiently from foot to foot whilst he interviewed Telemachus. Cf. 304 n.

187 εὐχόμεθ' The sense is 'we can claim to be…' (cf. 172 n.). Mentes uses the pl. as he latches on to the invitation contained in ll. 175–6.

188 τε Aristarchus proposed τι ('if you ask him something'); but it makes less good sense here than the generalizing τε. Mentes omits the apodosis of this conditional: 'if you go and ask… [*sc.* you will find that he confirms this]'.
　εἴρηαι 2 sg. pres. subj. med. of εἴρομαι: εἴρ-η-αι < *εἴρ-η-σαι < *εἴρ-ε-εσαι (Sihler 1995: 476, 594).

189 Λαέρτην This is the first mention of Odysseus' absent father. The name is not transparent in meaning; it might be a compound of λαός and the root seen in the form ἔρετο which Hesychius glosses as ὡρμήθη ('rush'). If so, it might mean, 'he who makes the host set out' (*DELG* 612). It would thus have connotations of military prowess that contrast with his current sad state. That Mentes speaks knowingly of Laertes' condition is meant to bolster his claim to be a friend of the family.
　ἥρωα does not simply mean 'hero' in the sense of a person who surpasses others in bravery and derring-do. In the *Iliad*, it is used for warriors before Troy; the *Odyssey* extends it to non-combatants of lesser rank such as the bard Demodocus (*Od.* 8.483) and the herald Mulius (*Od.* 18.423). This apparent softening of terms of originally more martial colour has parallels elsewhere (324 n.). In later Greek, ἥρως is also applied to demigods such as Hercules. But the word existed before Homer, being found in a religious context in the Mycenaean Greek compound *ti-ri-se-ro-re* = *τρισ-ήρωι (Chadwick and Baumbach 1963: 201). Perhaps ἥρως, a word with no certain cognates, originally meant something like 'lord', making it suitable both for mortals and gods (*DELG* 417).
　φασί It suits Mentes to be deliberately vague about his source of information (cf. ἔφαντ', 194). The audience knows that Athena has this knowledge directly. It has been said that she is suppressing her divine omniscience to play the role of a mortal who must rely on hearsay (De Jong 2001: 26). But only Menelaus (*Od.* 4.379, 468) asserts that the gods in general know everything, whereas Poseidon is ignorant of developments on Olympus because he has gone to see the Ethiopians (*Od.* 5.286–7) and Hera is

famously able to deceive Zeus (*Il.* 14.352–60). The poet attributes omniscience to the Muses (*Il.* 2.485) but they are a special case. Athena has knowledge that Telemachus does not, but that is not the same as omniscience.

190 ἔρχεσθ'… πάσχειν The image evokes pathos. We will soon see the aged Nestor and the middle-aged Menelaus living quietly but regally at home. The idea of Laertes living like a peasant is contrary to ethos and expectation. It appears that he has chosen this life out of grief (*Od.* 16.138–45; cf. 11.187–94). We cannot assume that old men automatically abdicated their power as a matter of custom: Nestor, Menelaus, Idomeneus, Peleus, and Priam plainly did not do so. It is more likely that he has been removed for the benefit of the plot (Calhoun 1962: 436). The suitors' behaviour would scarcely be tolerated if the king were living in the palace.

πήματα πάσχειν This formula is otherwise unique to Odysseus and echoes an earlier reference to his sufferings (49 n.). Father and son are thus subtly linked.

191 γρηἳ σὺν ἀμφιπόλῳ The servant is not named; to do so here would take Laertes out of the spotlight. When we hear of her again, she is called Σικέλη γρηῢς (*Od.* 24.291). This most likely means 'old woman from Sicily' rather than 'an old woman, Sicele'. In later Greek, but not in epic (429 n.), slaves were given names that reflected their geographical origin (cf. Terence's *Andria*). The type of the faithful retainer is an important one in the poem: Eurycleia, Eumaeus, and Philoetius are contrasted with those servants who give their loyalty to the suitors.

βρῶσίν τε πόσιν τε This formula recurs several times in the *Odyssey*. It is a more generic version of σῖτόν τ' ἔφερεν καὶ οἶνον ἐρυθρόν (*Od.* 13.69, 72).

192 παρτίθει The preverb παρά has lost its second vowel by apocope, a common Aeolic feature (Thumb 1959: 2). Some editors accent this word παρτιθεῖ, the athematic τίθημι being treated as though it were a contracting verb *τιθέω. This was common in Ionic (Buck 1910: 115). But it is odd to find an Ionic feature at the end of a word whose initial member has been subject to apocope, virtually unknown in that dialect (Chantraine 1958: 88). Venetus A writes τίθει at *Il.* 13.732, the accent implying a non-contracted suffix. This in turn might point to an original Aeolic παρτίθη (Chantraine 1958: 299) which, in the Attic alphabet, would have been written as ΠΑΡΤΙΘΕ, where E represented ε, ει, or η. When the new Ionic alphabet was adopted after 403 BC, this might easily have been misinterpreted as ΠΑΡΤΙΘΕΙ (Schwyzer 1939: 145–8).

193 ἑρπύζοντ' An extended form of ἕρπω. This rare word is found otherwise only at *Il.* 23.225 (of Achilles mourning Patroclus by his pyre) and *Od.*

13.220 (of Odysseus grieving for Ithaca by the seashore unaware that he has arrived home). In both instances, it is correlated with ὀδύρετο ('he grieved') in the previous line and is followed by παρά. This suggests that its original application is to young men reduced to creeping about by their grief. Its use here of an old man without ὀδύρετο and with the preposition ἀνά following it suggests some adaptation of a traditional formula to create pathos in this comparatively late part of the poem. The language is calculated to arouse indignation and pity in Telemachus.

γουνόν An obscure word glossed by *Etymologicum Magnum* (239, 5) as ὑψηλὸς τόπος ('high place').

ἀλωῆς Sometimes refers to a threshing floor (e.g. *Il.* 5.499) and sometimes to prepared ground such as a garden, orchard, or vineyard (*Od.* 6.293). The context generally makes clear (as here) which sense applies (Richter 1968: 97–8).

194 μιν We might at first hearing take this to refer to Laertes, the last person mentioned. But its true referent, which is also that of the adj. ἐμπιδήμιον in agreement, is deliberately held over until the next line (see 195 n.).

ἔφαντ' On this deliberate vagueness as to informants, cf. 189 n.

ἐπιδήμιον This word will be picked up significantly by Telemachus (233 n.).

195 σὸν πατέρ' Mentes' speech is striking in that just over a third of the lines exhibit run-over (Introduction, pp. 19–20). Generally this produces a sense of energy in the delivery: the speaker's thought overruns the boundary of the verse where it originated. In this case there is a significant element of surprise: we did not know whom Mentes would name and these words acquire emphasis both from being enjambed at the start of the line and by coming before a break in sense.

θεοί The pl. is a misrepresentation: Poseidon is responsible.

βλάπτουσι κελεύθου The gen. is of separation—Odysseus is being kept from his path home (Chantraine 1953: 64). The verb in Homer generally has to do with physical entanglement (*Il.* 6.39) or interference (*Il.* 15.489).

196 οὐ γάρ πω τέθνηκεν This is a bombshell. Mentes is not saying that Odysseus was alive when last he saw him; he is saying that he is alive *now* and only absent because restrained by others. The audience knows the truth of the matter but Telemachus does not. In a world where news was scarce and reliable news even scarcer, there was always the question of whether to believe the messenger. Not much later on, Mentes himself contemplates the possibility that Odysseus might be dead (289 n.).

δῖος Ὀδυσσεύς On the epithet, see 14 n. This is the first actual use in this conversation of the name of Odysseus, which has been deliberately suspended for effect (cf. 163, 195 nn.). The name is used twice more in quick succession in this speech (207 n., 212). By the end of his third and final speech, Mentes will have spoken the name six times in all (*Od.* 1.196, 207, 212, 253, 260, 265). This encourages Telemachus to do the same; see 354 n.

197 κατερύκεται This echoes κατέρυκει (55). It is the first of several echoes of the description earlier by Athena of Calypso's detention of Odysseus. Athena in the guise of Mentes fashions elements of her earlier speech to Zeus into a story calculated to motivate Telemachus.

198 νήσῳ ἐν ἀμφιρύτῃ The first half of this line echoes Athena's description of Calypso's island (50 n.). The second half is a lie—Odysseus' situation seems more heroic in the eyes of his son if it is said that he is detained by men rather than by a sexually alluring woman.

199 ἄγριοι In case imprisonment by men is not impressive enough, Mentes adds in enjambment that these are savages. We think again of the enchanting desires of Calypso (15, 57 nn.); no savages are at work. Perhaps Athena herself would rather think of her favourite mortal man as not risking amorous entanglement with another goddess. In spite of her abjuration of the works of Aphrodite, she appears to feel a certain attraction to Odysseus (*Od.* 13.291–302).

200 μαντεύσομαι The use of this technical term is meant to convey the authority of inspired prophecy. The audience appreciates the irony that the speaker is divine and has no need of the arts of divination in order to tell the future. See 202 n.

200–1 ἐνὶ θυμῷ | ἀθάνατοι βάλλουσι As Σ remarks, Mentes means that the gods have put this thought *into* his mind. For ἐνί with the dat. used thus, cf. *Il.* 13.628–9; *Od.* 8.501. This formula appears in Homer only here and at *Od.* 15.173, where Helen declares that Odysseus will return and take revenge. For this sense of βάλλω, see 364, 438 nn.

τελέεσθαι Fut. inf. med. in pass. sense (Chantraine 1958: 450).

202 οὔτε τι μάντις ἐὼν κτλ. This apparently disarming modesty sits oddly beside the portentous use of μαντεύσομαι (cf. 200 n.). It is also ironic, since Mentes has no need of prophecy.

οἰωνῶν The partitive gen. is common with verbs of knowing to indicate practical knowledge of a thing, e.g. *Il.* 11.710; 12.229 (Chantraine 1953: 56).

203 ἔτι The second syllable is heavy since δῆρον conceals δϝ- (cf. Lat. *dudum*; *DELG* 274–5).

φίλης See 60 n.

204 εἴ πέρ τε...ἔχῃσιν On the spelling of the subj., see 167 n. A subj. without κε or ἄν is used to express general contingencies; the particle τε is common in such cases but not essential: cf. *Il.* 1.81 vs. *Od.* 7.204 (Chantraine 1953: 279). Who or what is the subject of the verb? There is no certain example in Homer of ἔχω being used to describe a person as possessing his bonds (contrast Hes. fr. 37.4 MW and *h. Merc.* 157). But there is a parallel for the use of ἔχω to describe bonds as holding a person (*Od.* 8.340); that passage also involves an ellipse of με that is arguably every bit as harsh as the absence of a stated object here. We may thus take δέσματα as subject without needing to adopt Cobet's ἕ instead of τε.

205 Odysseus is indeed πολυμήχανος but we have not yet been explicitly told that he is scheming to get home. We have heard only that he is grieving, hindered by Calypso, yearning for home, and longing to die (55, 58–9). Mentes injects a note of hope for Telemachus. But it will take the intervention of Hermes to change matters. If Odysseus' unaided wit could have compassed his escape, it would have done so by now.

206 ἀτρεκέως Mentes is a liar (cf. 179 n.), but he expects others to tell the truth. Telemachus will use the same adv. to reply with the unexpected—and perhaps artful—assertion that he is not sure who his father is (214).

207 τόσος Draws attention not to any greatness on Telemachus' part—he has not had time to achieve that (contrast *Il.* 9.546)—but to his being an adult now (cf. οὐκέτι τηλίκος at 297).
    πάϊς The word could scan here either as a disyllable, which it does 87×, or as a monosyllable, which it does 18×. It is hard to know in cases like this what difference it makes, or how to decide what Homer originally sang. The non-contracted forms were clearly earliest (Bechtel 1908: 225–7); but there are inconsistencies even within individual formulae (M. L. West 1998a: xxiii, xxv).
    Ὀδυσῆος The word is positioned emphatically at the end of the line. It stands in apposition to αὐτοῖο, which would by itself have been a sufficient, if oblique, identification (163 n.). But this explicit naming is part of Athena's deliberate plan to encourage in Telemachus an acknowledgement of his father (196 n.)

208 αἰνῶς It would be easy to conclude that this word has been weakened to mean little more than 'very'; cf. Eng. 'You look terribly like him'. But S. R. West (1988: 102) compares Nestor's reaction to the same phenomenon (*Od.* 3.123): he experiences σέβας, religious awe. This suggests that something genuinely uncanny was felt to attach to such resemblances.

ὄμματα καλά Athena's admiration of the eyes seems a peculiarly intimate detail. The epithet καλά is not otherwise applied to ὄμματα in the epics except when the spirit of Patroclus visits Achilles (*Il.* 23.66). Whether there is any erotic frisson in either passage must be for the reader to determine (cf. *Il.* 3.397 for the ὄμματα μαρμαίροντα of Aphrodite).

209 ἐπεί Rather like γάρ: 'I can say this because…'.

τοῖον An adv. qualifying θαμά (cf. *Od.* 20.302); it is more commonly used to qualify adjectives (*Il.* 23.246; *Od.* 15.451).

210 ἀναβήμεναι Aor. inf. act. in -μεναι (Chantraine 1958: 487), built to the root βη- < *g^weH_2. For the etymologically distinct βαίνω, see 211 n.

211 οἱ ἄριστοι See 157 n.

ἔβαν 3 pl. aor. ind. act. of βαίνω. The paradigm is subtly suppletive: βαίνω < *g^wem- ('come', cf. Vedic *gácchati*; Rix 2001: 209–10) whereas ἔβην < *g^weH_2- ('take a step', cf. Vedic *ágāt*; Rix 2001: 205). The existence of ἔβημεν with a long root vowel (*Od.* 13.241) beside ἔθεμεν (*Od.* 3.179) shows that the former is a later formation, the result of levelling within the paradigm. The secondary form *ἔ-βη-ντ will have been shortened to ἔβαν by the operation of Osthoff's Law (Sihler 1995: 483 with 58).

κοίλης It has been perceptively noted (Ward: forthcoming) that this epithet tends in Homer to be used where people have left home in search of glory or material gain *by those who are left behind*.

213–20 In answer to a fairly long speech from Mentes, Telemachus replies tersely. Asked about his parentage, he makes a cagey and ungallant response reflecting his own anguish and uncertainty: either as the son whose father's goods he ought to be protecting but cannot, or as the heir apparent whose inheritance is being stolen before his eyes.

213 πεπνυμένος This is generally taken to mean 'wise' or 'prudent'. There is debate as to whether and how the word may be connected with πνέω ('to breathe'). Clarke (1997/8) adduces good evidence for a link between breathing and thought on the semantic level. There remains room for doubt from a morphological perspective (e.g. Harðarson 1993: 194–5; Rix 2001: 489). This need not preclude Greek poets from treating them as though they were related. See also 216, 229 nn.

214 Telemachus uses almost the same formula that Mentes used (179 n., cf. 206). There is much emphasis on truth and falsehood in this exchange, in a way that is programmatic for the whole poem.

215 μήτηρ μέν…ἐγώ γε This raises for the first time the theme of Penelope's faithfulness which will recur at many points in the epic

(Gilchrist 1997: 114–15). When Antinous says that Penelope hopes to marry again (*Od.* 2.91), Telemachus does not deny this (*Od.* 2.130–1). He later says that she is torn between chastity and remarriage (*Od.* 16.73–7); but Penelope herself says as much to the disguised Odysseus (*Od.* 19.524–9), which suggests that no great shame can attach to the fact. When Odysseus proves his identity to Penelope by telling the secret of the construction of their marriage bed (*Od.* 23.184–204), she puts her faithfulness beyond doubt. Cf. 248–51, 299f. nn.

τοῦ An almost contemptuous reference to his father (cf. 163 n.). This questioning of his own identity by a young man is curiously outside the usual scope of epic concerns. Goethe said that epic portrays human beings working outside themselves, engaged in battles and journeys, whereas tragedy shows them turned in upon themselves. This astonishing outburst, almost modern in its sentiment, shows the epic genre outstepping its own bounds (Fränkel 1975: 92). This might not be unconnected with the Telemachy being a conception later not only than anything in the *Iliad* but also than the Wanderings which constitute the core of the *Odyssey* (M. L. West 2014: 98, 110–13).

216 οὐκ οἶδ' Specifically, Telemachus is saying that he cannot necessarily accept his mother's word; more generally, he is showing that he is no gullible youth. It is not accidental that the epithet πεπνυμένος makes its first appearance in a context where Telemachus is grappling with the question of who he is and is going to be: he will grow into his epithet (Heath 2001: 138).

ἑὸν γόνον The thought is commonplace (cf. Lat. *incertus pater, mater certa*).

ἔγνω The so-called gnomic aor. is used for the statement of a timeless truth. In ordinary epic narrative, aorists are unaugmented in 50–60 per cent of cases (Drewitt 1912: 45). Gnomic aorists by contrast almost always have the augment (Chantraine 1958: 484). Whatever is true of the general distribution of the augment, it was a practically obligatory marker for gnomic statements (Platt 1891: 217–21).

217 μάκαρος A term normally used of gods in the *Iliad* (cf. 82 n.); by extension, it refers to the easy life enjoyed by rich men (as the reference to possessions in the next line makes clear).

τε' MSS write τευ (= τινος). But, to judge from the inscriptions, ευ is a much later contracted writing of εο (Chantraine 1958: 58–9). We may suppose an original τεο in all cases (well attested in MSS at *Il.* 2.225; 24.128). This cannot have undergone correption as though it were a diphthong; τεο was more likely elided to τε' (M. L. West 1998a: xxii).

218 ἀνέρος The inherited form is ἀνδρός (*Il.* 3.62) and what we see here is a novelty (Sihler 1995: 292–3). Perhaps it was formed on analogy with the nom. pl. ἀνέρες, which is original and beside which ἀνδρές represents an innovation. The older forms are retained to the extent that they remain metrically useful.

κτεάτεσσι...γῆρας The martial society depicted in the epics is not one in which the principal characters expected to reach old age. The shortness of life gives rise to the heroic ethic, most memorably articulated by Sarpedon in the *Iliad*. He remarks that people would scarcely become warriors if they could live on free from old age and death; but, since death is all around, one might as well seek heroic glory (*Il.* 12.322–8). Death in battle is the sort of thing that will be remembered in song and passed down to future ages (*Il.* 6.358). The corollary of this outlook is that any warrior who has survived to old age ought to be left alone to enjoy his declining years in peace (*Il.* 22.71–6). The sort of prosperity that Telemachus has in mind here is exemplified by Menelaus (*Od.* 4.72–5).

ἔτετμεν This gnomic aor. (216 n.) is a reduplicated thematic type like ἔ–πε–φνε (*Il.* 5.69). The forms τέτμον and ἔτετμον are without a corresponding pres. in regular use. The hapax τέμει (*Il.* 13.707) probably represents a fleeting appearance of the pres. stem (Chantraine 1958: 309).

219–20 ὅς...| τοῦ In classical Attic prose, the rel. clause generally follows the main clause (or 'matrix'). Here the rel. precedes the matrix and is picked up by an anaphoric pron. (τοῦ) in the next line (cf. *Il.* 4.232–3). To judge from a similar state of affairs in Hittite, Vedic, and archaic Latin, this 'left detachment' was probably a feature of the PIE parent language (Chantraine 1953: 236; Clackson 2007: 174–5; Probert 2015: 44–5, 230 n. 52).

220 φασι This is not the vagueness that Mentes employs to conceal the identity of his non-existent human informants (189, 194 nn.). Telemachus is simply referring to people in general in Ithaca.

221–9 In response to this short and graceless speech from Telemachus, Mentes makes an equally short speech asking what is the occasion for all the feasting.

222 νώνυμνον The MSS have νώνυμον. This will not scan and was corrected by Wolf to the reading adopted here, which is also historically correct. The etymology is problematic but is probably $* n̥-H_3nomn-$ (Sihler 1995: 87). The epic tradition also knows a morphologically younger form ἀνώνυμος (*Od.* 8.552) which exhibits loss of the last nu by dissimilation. That is probably responsible for the reading of the MSS.

ὀπίσσω An adv. which means 'backwards' is regularly used in epic to denote the future since the future is unknown, unseen, and, in that sense, may be said to lie behind us (Palm 1969; Dunkel 1982/3a).

223 Πηνελόπεια This is the first mention of the name of Odysseus' wife, although she was mentioned as the object of his longing as early as l. 13. She will figure rather more towards the end of the book. Telemachus has said that he does not know who his father is. This clever reply diverts attention from the question of who his father is and stresses the renown that will be his because his legitimate mother, Penelope, has engendered such a son (τοῖον).

In antiquity, it was often said that Penelope was originally called Ἀρναία or Ἀρνακία but changed her name to Penelope to reflect her rescue by a flock of ducks of a kind known as πηνέλοψ (Σ Od. 4.797; Eust. Od. 1422.5; Σ Pi. O. 9.79d; Tzetzes *ad Lyc.* 792). This has all the appearance of an attempt to rationalize a name which needs no more explanation than when a person in a story is called Rose or Marigold (Gilchrist 1997: 58). The Hesiodic Catalogue provides parallels for women being named after birds: Ἀλκυόνη (fr. 10a. 96 MW), cf. ἀλκύων ('kingfisher'); Μερόπη (fr. 169.3 MW), cf. μέροψ ('bee-eater'); and Ὀρτυγίη (fr. 150.26 MW), cf. ὄρτυξ ('quail'). More speculative is the derivation (Kamptz 1982: 70) from πήνιον ('bobbin') and ὀλόπτω ('tear out'). Whilst this neatly links her name with the central motif of the unfinished web, it is difficult to explain such a compound in formal terms and the verb ὀλόπτω is not attested before Callimachus. Even if this is a mistaken popular etymology, it reflects the theme of Penelope's prudence in her scheming to defeat the suitors (see 329 n.). Later links between Penelope (in Doric Πανελόπα) and the god Pan are likewise fantasies arising after the time of the epics (Gilchrist 1997: 50–65 is judicious on the limits of what may reasonably be inferred).

224 Athena does not need to ask this; she knows. But, in narrative terms, Mentes' question allows Telemachus to expatiate on the conduct of the suitors and thereby engage further the sympathy of the audience.

225 δαίς Sometimes the sacrificial context of δαίς is explicit (*Il.* 24.69; *Od.* 8.61); at other times, it is just a synonym for a grand communal meal (*Il.* 4 259). See 108 n.

τίς δὲ ὅμιλος The alternate reading τίς δαὶ ὅμιλος was favoured by Aristarchus but must be wrong. δαί is a conversational particle that is common in Attic but alien to Ionic (Valk 1949: 172–3). It is only weakly attested in Homer. The instance at *Il.* 10.408 probably reflects δ' αἴ, emended by Aristarchus who objected to such apparent articular usages in Homer (Erbse 1972: 212–13; cf. 157 n.). At *Od.* 24.299 δαί has more support including one papyrus but still remains in the minority. In the present case, only two MS have δαί. Given that δέ is at home in Ionic and is attested by the vast majority of witnesses, it is to be preferred. It also involves a hiatus, which makes it the *lectio difficilior*; δαί was likely written under the influence of δαίς earlier in the line.

τίπτε A small number of MSS read τίς δέ σε χρείω; These presumably reflect some doubt over the authenticity of τίπτε, which is nevertheless widely attested in Homer. It is most likely a syncopated form of τί ποτε (Szemerényi 1964: 218–19). It functions as an adv. here, as almost everywhere in Homer (except *Od.* 11.474). It indicates an amazed question. The etymology (Schwyzer 1939: 266) that appeals to *k^wid-pe (cf. Lat. *quippe*) > *titpe > τίπτε (by metathesis) is unattractive because of the absence of any parallel for a particle *-pe elsewhere in Greek. The ingenious derivation from *k^wid-k^we- (Lillo 1992) relies on that sequence being attested in *τί τε (allegedly seen in τί τ' ἄρ(α)—e.g. *Il.* 12.409; 18.6; *Od.* 23.264); but τε is not truly present in those cases, only the first letter of the particle ταρ, whose origin is quite separate from that of τε (Watkins 1995: 150–1; West 1998a: xxix; Katz 2007). Cf. 346 n.

σε It is tempting to suppose an ellipse here of a verb such as ἱκάνει. More likely, the acc. is the result of the noun χρέω being felt to function like a verb (cf. *Il.* 11.606; Chantraine 1953: 40).

χρέω The word as printed is scanned as one syllable by synizesis. χρή was originally a noun, which with only one exception always governs a dependent inf. with an ellipse of ἐστι (Shipp 1972: 31). It appears that a fem. noun *χρηώ was generally written χρειώ (a feature of the old Attic alphabet; cf. 192 n.) and later shortened to χρεώ (R. W. Werner 1948: 63–4; Redard 1953: 65–6).

226 εἰλαπίνη ἦε The last syllable of the first word merges with the first of the next to form a single heavy syllable (synecphonesis). εἰλαπίνη must be at least a partial synonym for δαίς (225 n.). Some Σ say that this is a great feast (εὐωχία) where people sit in companies massed together, which seems a rather late and militaristic interpretation. Mentes means that this is a grand affair, comparable in scale to a marriage feast; it is not what he would expect in a private house under normal circumstances. ΣM^a says that an εἰλαπίνη is always sacrificial: see 108 n.

γάμος ἐπεί Contrary to the usual rules, the second syllable of γάμος is metrically heavy. A final ς is sometimes *not* transferred to the following word (*ga-mo-se-pei*) but is treated as closing the syllable; it belongs with the broader phenomenon of lengthening by resonant (Chantraine 1958: 179; M. L. West 1982: 15–16).

ἔρανος According to *Σ*, a meal to which each participant contributed, adding pointedly that the suitors would not devour their own food in this way. An ἔρανος is described, but without the word being used, at *Od.* 4.621–3. This is a meal in the palace of Menelaus who, in spite of his great wealth (*Od.* 4.73–5), was nevertheless content to adopt a style of eating less lavish than that of the suitors. It appears that εἰλαπίνη, γάμος, and ἔρανος conventionally belong together as types of meal in epic diction (*Od.* 11.415). The closest equivalent in English is probably a potluck meal.

227 ὥς τε Two constructions are possible: (i) ὥς specifically qualifies the ptcp. and means that the suitors seem to be eating *like* men ὑβρίζοντες, in which case there is a strong asyndeton between this clause and the preceding one (cf. *Od.* 8.491; 10.295; Chantraine 1953: 325) or (ii) without asyndeton, ὥς both qualifies the adv. ὑπερφιάλως and is tantamount to ὅτι (so *Σ*HQT) so that the sense is '(*sc.* I say this is not a potluck meal) *so arrogantly* do they seem to me to behave ὑβρίζοντες as they dine' (cf. *Od.* 3.246). We cannot tell for sure, but (ii) at least avoids a rather harsh asyndeton.

ὑβρίζοντες A word that 'every Greek scholar thinks he understands' (Chadwick 1996: 292). Detailed studies starting from later sources have argued either that ὕβρις denotes the 'committing of acts of intentional insult, of acts which deliberately inflict shame and dishonour on others' (Fisher 1992: 148) or 'having energy or power and misusing it self-indulgently' (MacDowell 1976: 21). Another view maintains that ὕβρις says more about individual disposition than actions performed; one can thus have victimless ὕβρις (Cairns 1996: 32). Of the few studies that have concentrated on Homer, one (Hooker 1975) concludes that ὕβρις is morally colourless, meaning no more nor less than 'exuberant physical strength'. This explains why it is practically always associated with another word describing the way in which the ὕβρις is manifested or the moral reaction that one might have to it: ὑπερφιάλως (here), ὑπέρβιος (*Od.* 1.368; 4.321), ἀτάσθαλος (*Il.* 11.695; *Od.* 3.207; 24.352), κακομήχανος (*Od.* 16.418). Found without qualification (*Od.* 4.627 = 17.169), it may have no more moral overtone than κύδεϊ γαίων (*Il.* 1.405). This fits very well with a recent and persuasive etymology (Nikolaev 2004) which takes ὕβρις to mean 'power' (*$H_x$ió/é(H_2)g^w-ri-), quite probably cognate with ἥβη and ἁβρός (*$H_x$iáH g^w-ro-). Given its frequent collocation with negative words in Homer, one can see how ὕβρις was on its way to becoming a freestanding term of disapproval in later sources.

ὑπερφιάλως See 134 n.

228 νεμεσσήσαιτο here refers to indignation felt by a human being; the word is more often used of humans than gods in Homer (119 n.). It is often thought that Greeks in general had a neatly articulated theology in which human ὕβρις led to divine νέμεσις; one looks in vain for evidence of this in Homer.

229 ὅστις…γε μετέλθοι The opt. follows on from νεμεσσήσαιτο quite naturally as the rel. clause describes the hypothetical person feeling this indignation.

πινυτός has been argued to be related to πεπνυμένος and, through it, to πνέω (Clarke 1997/8; cf. 213 n.). Its proximity to πεπνυμένος in the next line suggests that the tradition saw the words as connected.

231–51 In response to what might have been thought quite an encouraging announcement, Telemachus emphatically declares that Odysseus is dead and gone for good. This is a psychologically convincing portrait of a long-suffering person wary of being given the good news that he longs to hear lest it turn out to be false. This is echoed by Penelope (*Od.* 19.215–19; 23.35–6, 62–8). At the level of plot, Telemachus' stance also allows Mentes to deliver further information and instructions.

232 μέλλεν The force is 'had a chance of being', 'might have been' (cf. *Od.* 18.138; van Leeuwen 1894: 277–80). This usage is consciously picked up in the Ionic prose of Herodotus, where the imperf. of μέλλω is used to describe things that may be viewed in retrospect as having been somehow in (or out of) the script of history (Gould 1989: 76–7). This is not surprising if the verb is connected with the stem seen in ἔμολον ('I went') (Szemerényi 1951). In this instance the expectation is defeated: that is the force of νῦν δέ (234 n.).

ἀφνειός Related to ἄφενος ('wealth') albeit the link is obscured by loss of a vowel, perhaps by syncope (Szemerényi 1964: 144–7). The wealth of the house is a common enough preoccupation (cf. *Od.* 4.71–5), taken up strikingly in Aesch. *Ag.* 958–962.

ἀμύμων See 29 n.

233 κεῖνος See 163 n.

ἐπιδήμιος At 194, Mentes lyingly said that he had been told that Odysseus was 'in town'. Although his purported expectation of seeing his old friend was frustrated, the circumstance gave Mentes the opportunity to deliver the stunning news that Odysseus would be returning. Telemachus takes up Mentes' ἐπιδήμιος, perhaps rather wistfully. He has been told that 'the man' is his father but he is unsure (see 216 n.); he emphatically does not believe that 'that man' will return; all he does know is that the fortune of the house depended on his being ἐπιδήμιος.

234 ἐβόλοντο Looks like an inexplicable variant of ἐβούλοντο, which most MSS transmit but which is unmetrical. βούλοντο is not widely attested and is a transparent attempt to regularize the morphology. ἐβάλοντο is an old alternative, intended to mean that the gods 'considered' matters otherwise; but it would be odd for this verb to be used without the place of ratiocination being specified (cf. *Il.* 20.196; *Od.* 12.281; Buttmann 1836: 199). ἐβόλοντο cannot be dismissed as a simple invention of the bards to suit the metre: it is attested epigraphically in areas of Arcadian, Cypriot, and Ionic speech (Thumb 1959: 118, 134, 278) in contexts that are unlikely to be the result of epic influence. Formally, ἐβόλοντο might be a strong aor. (Szemerényi 1966: 49) or an imperf. We cannot (*pace* Platt 1899: 382) dismiss this latter on the ground that the sense requires a completed action which the imperf. is not apt to express. The imperf. can represent the starting point of a development still felt (Chantraine 1953: 192).

κακὰ μητιόωντες Whilst this expression does not recur, the *Odyssey* takes divine malevolence for granted (*Od.* 3.166; 14.243), as does the *Iliad* (*Il.* 4.21; 7.478). This has implications for the view that sees the theodicy of the *Odyssey* as more advanced and later than that of the *Iliad* (see Introduction, p. 35).

235 ἄϊστον... περὶ πάντων The adj. means literally 'not to be seen' (Sihler 1995: 623), from alpha privative plus *weid-*, cf. Gk. εἶδον < *ἐ-ϝιδ-ο-ν and Lat. *video, visi* (Rix 2001: 665–7). The idea of not seeing his father is obviously foremost in Telemachus' mind: this word recurs very quickly at 242 (n.).

236 ἀκαχοίμην reduplicated 1 sg. aor. opt. med. of ἄχομαι. The opt. for a past counterfactual is extremely unusual—one would expect the ind. This is probably an archaism (Colvin 2016: 80).

237 δάμη 3 sg. aor. ind. pass. of δάμνημι. It is easy to imagine that this verb means 'to tame' and that its extension to killing is a metaphor. But there are only two examples of its meaning 'tame' in Homer (*Il.* 23.655; *Od.* 4.637); otherwise it frequently means 'kill', including when applied to a wild animal (*Il.* 9.545). The sense of taming is found in the epithet ἱππόδαμος (*Il.* 2.23; 4.352). The slippage between meanings is the same as in Eng. 'subdue'.

238 τολύπευσεν The verb refers to the winding of carded wool into a ball ready for spinning (Maurice 1991: 161–3). Penelope plays on this sense when she refers to herself 'winding' (= 'accomplishing') deceits as she wove the web by day and unpicked it by night (*Od.* 19.137–50). Here the thought is of having endured war, seen it through to the end. The word is possibly borrowed into Greek from Hittite (or another Anatolian

language) where the form *tarup(p)-* refers to the winding of wool
(Joseph 1982).

239 τύμβον The word refers to a mound of earth heaped up (*Od.* 12.14)
over the burnt remains as a sign of the dignity (γέρας) due to the dead
person (*Il.* 16.457). It does not refer to the inhumation of a corpse in a
'tomb'. The verb θάπτω, although generally translated as 'bury', is associated in Homer with cremation (*Od.* 11.72–4; 12.12–13). Burning was the
normal method of disposing of the dead in the Homeric poems. In the real
world, inhumation was much commoner than cremation in the Mycenaean
period (Mylonas 1962: 486); during the sub-Mycenaean and geometric
periods they alternated in complex ways (I. Morris 1987: 18–21). The pref-
erence for cremation in Homer is primarily aesthetic: the corruptible flesh
is driven off and only white bones remain (Vernant 1991: 69–70; Redfield
1994: 179–80). This is the antithesis and surest avoidance of rotting and
corruption (cf. 161 n.)

Παναχαιοί This word is confined to this formula in the *Odyssey* (*Od.*
14.369 ~ *Od.* 24.32). It is slightly commoner in the *Iliad*, but almost always
in the phrase ἀριστῆες Παναχαιῶν (e.g. *Il.* 7.73). Achaea is a part of Greece,
not Greece itself; but even without the prefix, Ἀχαιοί is used—like
Δαναοί—to denote the entire Greek host (*Il.* 1.17, 42).

240 ᾧ παιδὶ μέγα κλέος The mound is the objective sign of the worth of
the dead man (cf. *Od.* 4.584). κλέος can spread like the rays of the sun at
dawn (*Il.* 7.451) and reach up to heaven (*Od.* 9.20); it is thus unsurprising
that it may accrue to relatives as well as to oneself (*Il.* 6.446).

ἤρετ᾽ All MSS transmit ἤρατ᾽, which is peculiar as the sense leads one
to expect part of ἄρνυμαι, whose aor. ought to be the strong form ἤρετο.
Such an error is unlikely to have originated with the bards themselves,
who knew the strong inflexion (ἀροίμην (*Il.* 18.121), ἀρέσθαι (*Il.* 7.203)).
More likely is the influence of Attic scribes thinking of the far commoner
weak aor. ἤρατο (< αἴρω, 'to lift'), which is not attested in Ionic
(Wackernagel 1916: 221). Eustathius knew the strong variant at *Il.* 14.510
and Brandreth, Cobet, and West would write it in all cases (Chantraine
1958: 387–8) instead of ἤρατο. Although what is printed here is contrary to
all the medieval MSS, one papyrus has the strong aor. and, for the reasons
given, this is likely to be what Homer sang.

241 Ἀρέπυιαι The MSS all transmit Ἅρπυιαι. But the spelling ΑΡΕΠΥΙΑ
(dual) is found on an Aeginetan vase dated to 620 BC (Furtwängler 1882;
Beazley 1956: 5 No. 4). The MSS reading is probably a later, syncopated
version of this (Szemerényi 1964: 210). The form printed here is more
likely to be original and was adopted by Fick. These are surely the same

female persons described by Hesiod (*Th.* 265–9) as children of Thaumas and Electra, who have beautiful hair and fly on swift wings alongside the birds and the winds. They are on this showing neither birds nor winds but winged women; thus at any rate they appear on the vase already mentioned. Hesiod makes their number two and their names Ἀελλώ and Ὠκυπέτη, both of which suggest a connexion with storm winds and flight. Homer has one called Ποδάργη, whose name likewise denotes swiftness (of foot), said to be the mother of one of the horses of Achilles (*Il.* 16.149–51).

Ἁρέπυια is probably a 'barely acclimatized loanword' that simply happens to look rather like ἁρπάζω ('to snatch'; Szemerényi 1964: 203–13). However the noun is written, it violates Hermann's Bridge according to which Homer does not allow a word break between the two light elements of a dactylic fourth foot. Breaches are rare, approximately one in every 550 lines (M. L. West 1982: 38 n. 18). See further next n.

ἀνηρέψαντο The sense is clearly 'snatched away' (cf. *Od.* 20.66, 77). The form is more problematic. What is printed is a correction by Döderlein. The MSS all have ἀνηρείψαντο, which might be 3 pl. aor. ind. of an unattested *ἀν-ερείπομαι. The act. ἐρείπω (*Il.* 15.361) means to throw or dash down; it is hard to get from this to 'snatch'. Döderlein's proposed ἀνηρέψαντο avoids this, fits the metre, and is supported by Pindar *Pae.* 6.136 (Maehler). Of what is ἀνηρέψαντο the aor.? There might have been a compound ἀν-ερέπτομαι. But ἐρέπτομαι means 'to feed on' (*Il.* 2.776; *Od.* 9.97); the semantic link between snatching and feeding is obscure, unless there is a parallel in Eng. *snack* beside *snatch* (Szemerényi 1964: 204). Alternatively there might have been a form *ἀνα-ρέπτομαι (cf. MS Laurentianus 32.16 at Hes. *Th.* 990). In that case, a connexion is likely with Lat. *rapio* < PIE *rep-* (Szemerényi 1964: 210). It need not follow that the noun Ἁρέπυιαι is from the same source—see foreg. n. It is nevertheless likely that the poet intended the verb to echo the noun: an example of *figura etymologica* based on folk etymology.

242 ἄϊστος ἄπυστος The device of juxtaposing (with or without a conjunction) two or more adjectives with the same prefix is common in Homer (*Il.* 2.201; 9.63, 158; 13.41) and later Greek (Aesch. *Ag.* 79; *Cho.* 55; Hdt. 1.32.6). That it is found likewise in the Vedas and the Avesta suggests that it was an inherited Indo-European stylistic figure of some antiquity (Durante 1976: 151–2). The first adj. echoes 235 (n.).

242–3 ὀδύνας … ὀδυρόμενος The use of two words from the same root, concerning pain, is emphatic enough by itself. In the context of a discussion about Odysseus, it is hard to not see another play on the meaning of his name—as earlier with ὠδύσαο, a word from a different semantic field (62 n.).

243 στοναχίζω Most texts read στεναχίζω. There is a verb στένω with e-grade vocalism and a noun στόνος that exhibits the o-grade. This is perfectly normal, cf. λέγω/λόγος. But we also find a noun στοναχή, that is plainly an expansion of στόνος. When a verb is formed by adding the suffix -ιζω to this enlarged noun, there is no justification for changing the vocalism of the stem to the e-grade. In the same way λογίζομαι was formed from λόγος and nobody would write *λεγίζομαι to agree with λέγω. The form στοναχίζω is commonly found in MSS (M. L. West 1998a: xxxv).

244 θεοὶ ... ἔτευξαν Coming so soon after a similarly pessimistic evaluation of divine justice (234 n.), these words underline the idea of the gods as not only not caring for humans but actually acting with malevolence towards them. Whatever Zeus might say to defend the gods from such charges (32 n.), his discourse does not seem to have filtered down to the human characters in the poem. They continue to take a dim view of divine conduct.

246–7 Δουλιχίῳ κτλ. The identification of these Homeric place-names has been a matter of much debate. The last century alone has seen at least twenty-three conjectures, albeit some overlap more or less with others (Bittlestone et al. 2005: 550–62). Most are now agreed that by Ζάκυνθος Homer means the Ionian island called by the same name in modern Greek. If the island known today as Ithaki is the same as Homer's Ἰθάκη, the picture will be as set out in Map 2a. But recent research, both geological and philological, suggests a highly plausible alternative. Σάμη (with a variant reading Σάμος, not to be confused with the Aegean island of the same name) is used by Homer to refer to modern Cephalonia, except for the westernmost part (nowadays called Paliki). That part was what Homer called Ἰθάκη. It is today joined to the eastern section of Cephalonia by a narrow isthmus which in antiquity was covered by the sea, making Homer's Ἰθάκη a separate island to the west. The entire area is much affected by earthquakes; tectonic plate movements after Homer's time made Cephalonia into one island by pushing up a land bridge above sea level (Bittlestone et al. 2005: 36, 412, 568). What Homer refers to as Δουλίχιον is the island known in modern Greek as Ithaki. Map 2b shows what this hypothesis looks like in practice. As long ago as Propertius (2.14.4), the homeland of Odysseus was referred to as Dulichium. This can only be because by this date Ἰθάκη was no longer an independent island but already formed part of modern Cephalonia. Ancient observers thus looked around for another island as a candidate for the home of Odysseus and settled on the one now called Ithaki but then known as Δουλίχιον (Diggle 2005: 515–16).

248–51 The way that Telemachus describes the conduct of the suitors towards his mother reveals the considerable tension between mother and son that will surface again later in the book (346–60). He views them chiefly as an economic threat and seems not to appreciate that his mother's delay is not a sign of weakness but part of a deliberate plan to avoid remarriage (*Od.* 2.93–110). This is all part of the theme of whether Penelope has been—or ought to be—faithful to Odysseus (cf. *Od.* 2.53–4 vs. *Od.* 23.149–51) who, for all anyone knows, is probably dead (*Od.* 1.161–2). Cf. 215 n.; 299f. n.

248 μητέρ᾽ ἐμὴν...οἶκον That Telemachus mentions the impoverishment of the house and the wooing of his mother in the same breath is revealing. One might suppose that it is part of his unsympathetic characterization, arising from his seeing loss of patrimony and potential loss of mother as the same kind of mischief. It is common in the epic for women to be described in economic terms: Laertes gave the value of twenty oxen for Eurycleia (*Od.* 1.430–1). She is a slave; but the same is true of wives, albeit they cost more: Iphidamas is said to have paid a hundred oxen for his wife, promising a further thousand animals—sheep and goats together (*Il.* 11.244–5).

249 στυγερόν As Σ says, this is the marriage seen through the eyes of Penelope, not Telemachus. Although he was as a child opposed to his mother's remarriage (*Od.* 19.530–1), he is now in favour of it (*Od.* 2.53–4). His reasons become plain from what he goes on to say (De Jong 2001: 29–31).

250–1 φθινύθουσιν ἔδοντες | οἶκον ἐμόν It appears to be unusual that the suitors have moved in for the long term and are living off the resources of the house. We have elsewhere a glimpse of an alternative and perhaps more normal wooing where Penelope goes to her father's house, a dowry is assembled, the suitors stay in their respective houses and compete for her hand through the generosity of their gifts (*Od.* 16.390–3). It is also striking that Telemachus describes the house as his. One might imagine that it belongs to Odysseus; but he is thought to be dead. When Telemachus discovers that his father is still alive, he no longer favours the idea of his mother's remarriage (*Od.* 16.33–5). The idea that the suitors are simply there to take advantage of free food and drink is one repeated by Penelope (*Od.* 21.68–72). But the poet tells us that they are beguiled by her looks (*Od.* 18.212–13) and Eurymachus himself speaks of her surpassing beauty

(*Od.* 18.245–9). They perhaps do not all have the same motives: Eurymachus says that Antinous really wanted the kingship (*Od.* 22.49–53). The mechanism for becoming king is not clear; cf. 386–402 n.

251 διαρραίσουσι The verb ('smash into pieces') is strikingly metaphorical used of a person. It is used more obviously of the house itself at *Od.* 2.48–9.

252–305 There is a marked change of tone. After Mentes' initial quite long speech of introduction (178–212), Telemachus' terse and cynical retort (213–20), Mentes' short gentle further speech of inquiry (221–9), and Telemachus' despairing reply (230–51), Mentes becomes much more direct. He begins by telling a suggestive and programmatic story about Odysseus' archery, suggests that Odysseus will probably be back within a year to kill the suitors himself, and ends with an explicit instruction to kill the suitors if Odysseus does not return.

252 ἐπαλαστήσασα This rare compound verb is unique in Homer and not found again in Greek until Apollonius of Rhodes; the simple form is found twice (*Il.* 12.163; 14.21). The noun ἀλάστωρ often refers to an avenging entity in later Greek (Aesch. *Ag.* 1501); but in Homer it can be a personal name (e.g. *Il.* 4.295). The adj. ἄλαστος is used to describe grief or pain (*Od.* 1.342; 4.108). Those who connect this verb with λαθεῖν (*DELG* 54–5) can point to a faultless formal correspondence and at least some semantic link: Athena feels an indignation that is akin to the vengeance that *does not forget*. Others appeal to a putative verb *λάω ('see') and a connexion with the evil eye (Muller 1929) and set ἄλαστος beside Lat. *in-vis-us* ('that which has been envied'). But Lat. *in-* corresponds not to Greek ἀ- but ἐν- (Sihler 1995: 439–40; Beekes 2010: 62); one alternative is to view the ἀ- as prothetic (Prévot 1935a: 249–50). Overall the connexion with λαθεῖν is easier. It is possible that the word commended itself here because of its consonance with Παλλάς later in the line (S. R. West 1988: 107). The variant reading δὲ παλαστήσασα is to be rejected—there is no parallel for this verb, the invention of unhelpful scribes. We may wonder whether the bards themselves or the audience could say what this verb meant beyond denoting strong disapproval.

254 δεύε' The MSS all have δεύῃ. We are dealing with 2 sg. pres. ind. med. < δεύομαι, whose original form was δεύ-ε-σαι: upon loss of intervocalic sigma, the first result was δεύεαι (cf. ἔδεαι, *Il.* 24.129). Before a vowel, one might have the contracted δεύῃ, whose final syllable is treated as light by correption, or the uncontracted δεύεαι, whose final syllable is lost by elision (cf. βούλομ' ἐγώ, *Il.* 1.117). The result is metrically the same in either case. Van Leeuwen (1886: 336–43; cf. M. L. West 1998a: xxii) preferred the latter approach, contraction not being a common feature of epic morphology. Since δεύε' lacks transparency, later scribes probably replaced it with δεύῃ. The variant δεύει is an Atticism (Sihler 1995: 476).

ὅ κε… ἐφείη The opt. with κε after a main clause in the ind. has here, in combination with the rel. pronoun, the force of a final (purpose) clause: 'you need Odysseus (*who might >*) *in order to* lay hands upon…' (Chantraine 1953: 249).

255–6 εἰ γὰρ…| σταίη 'Would that….' εἰ γάρ + opt. is often presented as a freestanding grammatical construction to express wishes. εἰ was not in origin a subordinating conjunction but probably meant something more like 'come now' (Chantraine 1953: 274–5; Dunkel 1985). At *Od.* 15.180 we find a wish expressed without εἰ followed by a statement of what will result if the wish comes true: οὕτω νῦν Ζεῦς θείη…| τῷ κέν τοι καὶ κεῖθι θεῷ ὣς εὐχετοώμην ('May Zeus make it so; in that case, I would pray to you there as a god'). One can appreciate how, in cases where εἰ ('come now') was added, it came to be reinterpreted as a conditional particle, e.g. *Il.* 7.28: ἀλλ' εἴ μοί τι πίθοιο, τό κεν πολὺ κέρδιον εἴη ('but *come*, may you do as I say; that would be much more advantageous' > '*if* you were to do as I say…'). Cf. 255 n.

256 πήληκα Homer has four words for helmet: κόρυς (46×), κυνέη (28×), τρυφάλεια (15×), πήληξ (10×). They are used more or less interchangeably. Metrical considerations might determine some choices—but not all (Stubbings 1962: 514). πήληξ is the least common term and so might refer to an unusual kind of helmet; the detail is now irrecoverable.

δύο δοῦρε It was common (*Il.* 3.18; 10.76; 11.43; 12.298; 13.241; 16.139; 21.145) but not invariable (*Il.* 10.31; 15.474) practice for Homeric warriors to fight with two spears. The terms δόρυ and ἔγχος both refer to spears; the latter appears to have been heavier than the former (Stubbings 1962: 517–18; cf. 100 n.).

257–66 τοῖος ἐὼν…|…πικρόγαμοί τε There is a close echo of this thought in the wish of Menelaus that Odysseus would re-appear with all the prowess he showed in days gone by and kill the suitors (*Od.* 4.341–6; cf. *Od.* 17.132–7). When the suitors have been killed, the same trope is used to great effect by Laertes who wishes that he could have been present at the events of the previous day with the same vigour he had when he conquered the town of Nericus (*Od.* 24.376–81). These wistful reflections on his vanished greatness echo Nestor's evocation of his palmy days of conquest (*Il.* 7.132–57; cf. 1.260–72).

258 πίνοντά τε τερπόμενόν τε There is a marked contrast between the licensed and approved pleasures of a guest-friend and the same conduct on the part of the suitors which is unlicensed and thus disgraceful. Contrast *Od.* 1.365–6 where Telemachus invites the suitors to eat.

259 Ἐφύρης There were a number of towns of this name in Greece. *Σ*, apparently relying on Apollodorus of Athens (*FGrH* 244 F 180), concludes that Thesprotian Ephyra is meant, in the west of Greece and well to the north of Ithaca. Ephyra is mentioned again as a source of poison at *Od.* 2.328–30. Egypt has a similar reputation for its φάρμακα (*Od.* 4.227–30). On the identity of the poison, see 261 n.

Ἴλου This is not the famous son of Dardanus after whom Troy was called Ilium. Nothing else is known of this son of Mermerus. The variant reading Ἴρου is attributed by *ΣHM* to Proxenus (*FGrH* 703 F 3) but has nothing to commend it.

Μερμερίδαο Mermerus was a son of Jason and Medea (Pausanias 2.3.6, 9). It is not surprising that a descendant of Medea should be connected with poisons given her infamous expertise in that field. Since μέρμερος means something like 'baneful' (*Il.* 10.48), this patronymic is an apposite speaking name (cf. 383 n.) meaning 'Son of Baneful' (Stanford 1959: 227).

260 θοῆς See Introduction, p. 13.

261–2 This mention of Odysseus wanting poison for his arrows is remarkable for two reasons. First, there is no reference to poison arrows anywhere else in Homer (unless very obliquely at *Il.* 4.217–18 where Machaon sucks the blood from Menelaus' arrow wound instead of just washing it—contrast *Il.* 11.829–32). Second, archery is somewhat denigrated in the *Iliad*. τοξότα ('archer') is one of the insults hurled by Diomede at Paris (*Il.* 11.385). Heroes of the first rank do not use the bow in the *Iliad*: Odysseus took no part in the archery competition at the funeral games for Patroclus (*Il.* 23.850–83). But the situation is nuanced. The name Telemachus suggests one who fights from afar (S. R. West 1988: 107); if archery was shameful, would Odysseus have given his son that name? Odysseus himself boasts at length to the Phaeacians of his prowess with the bow (*Od.* 8.214–33). The contest in Book 22 depends on the fact that Odysseus is the only man strong enough to string it. The bow is also vital to the elimination of the suitors: without such a weapon, it would be impossible to think of overcoming 108 suitors. Perhaps the disapproval that is felt for the bow in the *Iliad* derives from its ability to destroy with such mechanical efficiency. There is a difference in outlook in this respect between the two poems. At any rate, the use of poison arrows is plainly very unusual. Some analytical critics (Dirlmeier 1966) have seen here the inept integration of an earlier and incompatible kind of story about Odysseus; but perhaps the poet deliberately included this glance into

Odysseus' past in order to hint at another side to his character. What is foreign to the ethos of the *Iliad* is not automatically bad.

261 φάρμακον It has been conjectured that the poison in question was a plant, *Helleborus orientalis* L., which grows plentifully in Epirus and nowhere else in Greece (Schmiedeberg 1918: 23). *Od.* 4.229–30 suggests that φάρμακα are generally seen as plants that grow from the earth. They may be wholesome (*Il.* 4.218; 5.401) or, more often, baneful (*Il.* 22.94; *Od.* 2.329; 10.236, 394; cf. 10.213, 290, 317). It is noteworthy that the μῶλυ revealed by Hermes as a magical defence to φάρμακα likewise grows from the ground (*Od.* 10.302–3). φάρμακον might by its very etymology point to this origin in the earth if it means 'that which is borne' (*DELG* 1178–9): φέρω might yield a zero-grade noun *φάρμα with an extension to *φάρμαξ and so φάρμακον; cf. ἔμρα, ἔρμαξ. An alternative etymology from *bherH– ('cut'; cf. Lat. *forare*) also points to the earth and evokes the magical lore surrounding the cutting of roots for magical and medicinal purposes (Delatte 1936). But plants are not the only poisonous things. Heracles had arrows dipped in the deadly blood of the Hydra (Stesichorus fr. 19.35–6 DF); and snake venom was used in real life to make poison arrows (Arist. *Mir.* 845a1–9).

ὄφρα οἱ εἴη The simple verb is used like ἔξεστι in Attic prose ('so that it might be possible for him to…'). The textual variants do not commend themselves. δαείη is not elsewhere used with an infin. ἤν που ἐφεύροι is likewise never found with an inf. and an opt. calls for εἰ not ἤν.

ἀνδρόφονον This adj. is used 20× in the *Iliad*, almost always of Hector himself (e.g. *Il.* 1.242) but sometimes of others (*Il.* 4.441; 6.134), including the hands of Achilles (*Il.* 18.317 = 23.18; 24.479). In the *Odyssey* it appears uniquely here, of an inanimate thing and for a purpose unthinkable to the ethical outlook of the *Iliad*. So we see the epic tradition moving on in its use of a traditional epithet. See Introduction, pp. 14–15. Knowledge of poisonous plants must have gone back to the earliest times, but the *Iliad* prefers not to dwell on such matters. This entire episode hints at a darker world of magic (Artelt 1937: 44–5), which the *Odyssey* not only does not conceal but explores with quite some appetite in the story of Circe.

263 νεμεσίζετο The verb generally denotes feeling righteous indignation against somebody else and takes the dat. (*Il.* 5.757; 8.407; *Od.* 2.239). The use of the acc. here is unique and the sense is of standing in awe of another's indignation. Cf. 119 n.

αἰὲν ἐόντας A comparatively rare way of referring to the immortality of the gods, but not necessarily a late feature of epic language (cf. *Il.* 1.290, 494).

264 φιλέεσκε The ending in -σκω has many apparent functions in Homer: iterative, intensive, inchoative, and causative. Whether these can be reduced to a single underlying sense is a matter of dispute. In this instance, at least, we are dealing with such seamless iteration that it makes more sense to think of a stative (Zerdin 1999: 302).

αἰνῶς There is something uncanny about a friendship that causes one to risk divine wrath: see 208 n.

265 ὁμιλήσειεν Often used of simply keeping company (e.g. *Od.* 2.21), this verb can also denote thronging about (*Il.* 16.641) or joining battle (*Il.* 11.523). The context makes it plain that this last sense is intended here. The opt. resumes the syntax of the wish begun at 255–6 but interrupted by the excursus on the poisoned arrows.

266 This striking and pointed line recurs at *Od.* 4.346; 17.137. The hope for the early death of the suitors is often expressed, albeit in other terms (*Od.* 3.223–4; 15.523–4; 17.475–6; 20.116–17, 306–8). The working out of retributive justice is central to the overall narrative arc of the *Odyssey*.

πικρόγαμοι For the use of πικρός with a noun that would usually be positive or neutral, cf. Eur. *Bacch.* 357. The primary thought is that the suitors will, instead of the expected sweet marriage, meet only with bitter death. But there is a widespread thought in Greek myth that marriage is itself a kind of death (Barringer 1991: 662); one has only to consider the story of Persephone. The suitors will become bridegrooms of death.

267 θεῶν ἐν γούνασι κεῖται The lap of the gods is an English cliché but the underlying thought is hard to recover. The expression might refer to the practice of placing offerings on the knees of seated cult statues (*Il.* 6.90–2; cf. Leaf 1888: 207; Kirk 1990: 167–8) in such a way that the offering is taken out of human control and left to the gods to accept or reject. An alternative view is that the image is of threads passing over, or lying on, the lap of a seated spinner (Onians 1924; M. W. Edwards 1991: 112–13). The gods are often said to spin the fate of mortals (Hainsworth 1988: 333–4; Pulleyn 2000: 31–2).

268 ἀποτείσεται Cf. 43 n.

270 κε See 254 n.

271 εἰ δ' ἄγε On the force of εἰ, see 255–6 n.

272 ἀγορὴν ... ἥρωας The word ἀγορή signifies an assembly or gathering (< ἀγείρω). It may also denote the place where such a gathering takes place (*Il.* 7.382; *Od.* 6.266); but the sense of 'market place' is not found in Homer (M. I. Finley 1977: 78). At *Il.* 18.497 the assembly comprises the λαοί ('troops'); at *Od.* 3.214, in peacetime, the same word refers to the general citizenry of Ithaca. Likewise ἥρωας here potentially denotes all free men (cf. 189 n.). The heralds summon all the men in the group (*Od.* 2.6–7; cf. 3.137, 141; *Il.* 2.788–9), but how far down the social scale the summons goes we cannot tell. Thersites is a person of low station, but there is no suggestion that he is not a qualified participant (*Il.* 2.198, 214, 246). There plainly were procedural norms about how and when an assembly was to be called and run (Hölkeskamp 2002). Although the assembly sometimes voted on the distribution of booty (*Il.* 1.123, 126, 135), its function was not generally to make decisions but to enable matters of importance to be announced and discussed (Osborne 2004: 212).

Ἀχαιούς See 90 n.

273 μῦθον On distinction between ἔπος and μῦθος, cf. 28 n.

πέφραδε An unaugmented reduplicated 2 sg. aor. impv. act. of φράζω. The type is very common (Chantraine 1958: 395–8), but a sigmatic aor. φράσε is also found (*Od.* 11.22). Both forms are old. The root φραδ– probably represents a zero-grade of φρήν, with the δ being an extension (Chantraine 1933: 360; 1999: 1225, 1228); cf. 294 n. The basic meaning in Homer appears to be 'show' rather than 'tell'. The med. sense 'consider' (*Od.* 1.269) is really 'show to oneself'.

ἐπὶ μάρτυροι ἔστων The gods are invoked as witnesses and are sometimes said to police human conduct (*Il.* 3.280; 22.255). The human actors in the assembly will witness the events in the prosaic sense; the gods are mentioned because of a concern with justice (Introduction, pp. 17, 35). Zenodotus is said to have preferred a form ending –ες but, to judge from *Il.* 7.76, the form in –ος is to be preferred.

275 μητέρα δ' This is an extreme case of anacoluthon since the acc. is not a proper subject for ἴτω (Chantraine 1953: 16). Bentley emended ἴτω to ἴμεν, which makes for an attractive parallelism with μνηστῆρας... σκίδνασθαι in the preceding line. It regularizes the syntax but without explaining how the acc. got into the tradition: the nom. μήτηρ would scan perfectly here. Most likely the poet introduced this acc. after ἄνωχθι but then switched to ἴτω with its greater sense of immediacy.

θυμὸς ἐφορμᾶται γαμέεσθαι As Telemachus has just made it clear (*Od.* 1.249) that Penelope does not want to marry, it is baffling why Mentes should set up a scenario based on the assumption that she does. It is even odder given that one possible outcome of the mission that Mentes is proposing is that Telemachus will return with the news that Odysseus is alive, in which case a remarriage for Penelope makes no sense. Plainly the narrative requires Telemachus to go on a journey; it does not require these provisions concerning his mother's return to her father's house. Some

have supposed that *Od.* 1.275–8 have been interpolated from *Od.* 2.195–7,
where the remarks make more sense in the mouth of Antinous (Page 1955:
57–8). Alternatively, Mentes is deliberately ignoring what he knows and
exaggerating his advice in order to spur Telemachus into action.

276 δυναμένοιο The lengthening of the vowel first syllable is abnormal. It
perhaps came about by analogy with γεινάμενος beside γενόμενος, the
bards assuming that these participles in –άμενος had to have a long first
vowel (Wyatt 1969: 119–20).

277 οἱ δὲ The members of the household of her father Icarius. This is confirmed by παιδός (278 n.); Penelope is the daughter of the house. See next n.
　　ἀρτυνέουσιν ἔεδνα In later Greek, ἔδνον (of which ἐέδνον is an epic
form) means 'dowry'. That meaning would fit the current context perfectly
(Reden 1995: 50 n. 24). But in Homer ἐέδνον normally denotes a gift given
by a suitor to the bride's father, i.e. 'bride-price' (S. R. West 1988: 110–11). It
has been suggested that gifts passed in both directions at a marriage, from
bride's family to suitor and *vice versa*, so that there is no inconsistency in
the Homeric picture (M. I. Finley 1955; Lacey 1966). But it is difficult to
point to any one marriage in the text that is unambiguously described as
involving that sort of two-way exchange (Snodgrass 1974: 116–17). It has
been asserted with some boldness that ἐέδνα never really denotes dowry
but always bride-price (Perysinakis 1991). This fits with the fact that bride-
price was probably the earliest meaning of this root, to judge from cognates in other languages (*DELG* 312). But there are three unarguable
instances where a father gives or offers to give gifts to a groom to accompany marriage to his daughter: *Il.* 6.192–5; 9.146–8; *Od.* 7.314 (Reden 1995:
50 with n. 23). It also involves taking ἀρτύνω as equivalent to 'amass',
which cannot be right; the verb denotes preparation, getting things in
order (cf. *Od.* 14.469; 24.153). We are left with the conclusion that Homer
uses the word in two different ways, the tradition conflating marriage
practices from different periods (Snodgrass 1974: 118).

278 ἐπί This preposition with the gen. most usually means 'on'. Σ glosses
as μετά; this gives good sense but there is no convincing parallel for it. To
say that the construction implies a 'goal' is a step further into the dark
(*pace* Chantraine 1953: 107–8). If ἐπί is not a preposition governing the
gen. but a preverb in tmesis with ἕπεσθαι, then the gen. must be one of
price ('as great as ought to follow, as the price of a wife'). But this is strained
with ἕπεσθαι. The feebly attested MS variant ἔσεσθαι yields no better sense.
　　παιδός This might seem an odd term to use of a middle-aged mother.
But παῖς does not have to indicate infancy; it may denote filiation with no
connotation of tender years. Thus the word is applied to the warrior

Agapenor (*Il.* 2.609), the prophet Helenus (*Il.* 7.44), Hector (*Il.* 3.314; 24.749), and an unnamed son who returns to his father after ten years' absence (*Od.* 16.18). Penelope is the daughter of her father's house, irrespective of her age.

280 νῆ'... ἐρέτῃσιν ἐείκοσιν Crews of twenty oarsmen are nothing out of the ordinary (*Od.* 1.280; 2.212 = 4.669; 4.778; 9.322); the same number went on the mission to Chryse (*Il.* 1.309). But ships are also described as having a crew of fifty (*Il.* 2.719-20; 16.169-70). Odysseus divides his crew into two and sends Eurylochus and twenty-two others to reconnoitre the house of Circe (*Od.* 10.203-5); given that he had lost six men to the Cyclops (*Od.* 9.289, 311, 344), there must have been fifty-two at the outset. The usual eighth-century Greek oared vessel had fifty oarsmen and two officers (Morrison and Williams 1968: 46-50). There were fifty-two oarsmen on the ship that took Odysseus from Scheria (*Od.* 8.34-6). We may conclude that twenty was a conventional number for smaller missions and for trade.

ἄρσας Epic sigmatic aor. ptcp. act. < ἀραρίσκω; Attic uses the strong aor. ἀραρών.

282 ὄσσαν This derives from **wek^w* + *ia/iH₂* and is connected with ὄπα, ἔπος, and Lat. *vox* (*DELG* 845). Whilst in Hesiod it can denote the voice of the Muses (*Th.* 10, 43, 65, 67), in Homer it is confined to rumour—which is described as the Διὸς ἄγγελος ('messenger of Zeus') at *Il.* 2.93.

283 ἥ τε See 52 n.

κλέος In this context, the word cannot denote heroic fame (e.g. *Il.* 4.197; 22.514; cf. 194 n.) so much as mere 'news' (*Il.* 11.227; *Od.* 16.461). The former probably arose as a specialized sense of the latter. We see the primitive sense here: just as ὄσσα is that which is spoken (282 n.), κλέος is that which is heard (cf. 95 n.).

285 It appears that Zenodotus knew a text which contemplated here (but did not go on to narrate) a journey by Telemachus to Idomeneus in Crete rather than to Menelaus in Sparta. His text read δ'ἐς Κρήτην παρ' Ἰδομενῆα ἄνακτα. His l. 285 together with the next are also found in some MSS as supplements after l. 93 (see apparatus there and 93 n.).

286 ὅς As is clear from the sentence structure, ὅς here is not a rel. pron. but a demonstrative meaning 'he' (cf. *Il.* 21.198; 23.9).

δεύτατος Although the comparative δεύτερος means 'second', the superlative means 'last'. Both words are built to the root seen in δεύομαι, itself extracted from δέω, and denoting inferiority or lack (*DELG* 267). The epithet is not obviously apt for Idomeneus (93, 285 nn.) since Nestor reports that he got safely back to Crete without losing any men (*Od.*

3.191–2). But when Telemachus asks Nestor how Agamemnon came to be killed by Aegisthus and where Menelaus was at the time (*Od.* 3.248–52), Nestor explains that Menelaus was driven off course and was thus wandering for seven years (*Od.* 3.279–311). δεύτατος is thus much more appropriate for Menelaus and neatly deals with the question of where he was when his brother died.

χαλκοχιτώνων This common epithet of the Achaeans (24×) appears to indicate the wearing of a brazen tunic. But there is no evidence for this in the historical record and it would appear that a corselet worn over the tunic is meant (Page 1966: 245–7). Whether this subtlety was appreciated by the audience may be doubted: the overall image was probably of a soldier wearing brazen armour.

287 βίοτον Here not 'sustenance' (cf. 160), but 'life' itself (cf. *Od.* 5.394).

288 ἐνιαυτόν The thought is that Telemachus could endure the behaviour of the suitors at home even for another year if he knew that his father was returning. There is no suggestion that the mission itself ought to last for a year.

289 τεθνηῶτος The gen. is common after a verb of perception to indicate a person about whom one learns something, just as the acc. is regular for a noun describing what is heard at ll. 282, 287 (Chantraine 1953: 54–5). The variant reading τεθνειῶτος is not original (R. W. Werner 1948: 51–6; Sihler 1995: 621; Rix 2001: 144–5). It is surprising for Mentes to put forward the possibility that Odysseus might be dead when he has recently and emphatically declared that he is still alive (196 n.). The thought is presumably that he might have met his death in the interim since Mentes last had news. Although the overall aim of Mentes is to encourage Telemachus, the possibility of Odysseus' death give more purpose to the news-gathering mission to Pylos and Sparta.

290 νοστήσας κτλ. It is hoped that Odysseus will come safely back to the land of his fathers; if that is not possible, then Telemachus must do so in his stead. But this cannot be taken for granted in any event and, in fact, the suitors plan to murder Telemachus (*Od.* 4.822–3, 842–7).

δὴ ἔπειτα MSS almost all read δ' ἤπειτα—which is nonsense. The minority δ' ἔπειτα is unmetrical. Wolf's emendation to δὴ ἔπειτα calls for correption of a monophthong, which is unusual but not unknown (*Il.* 11.138, 386; 20.220; *Od.* 1.26; 9.311; 10.281; 12.330, 399; 15.477; 22.165). M. L. West's emendation to δἤπειτα substitutes one prosodic rarity for another; and Aristarchus avoided crasis (Chantraine 1958: 85). ἔπειτα here emphasizes the 'then' element in the apodosis of an 'if…then' conditional clause (cf. *Il.* 10.243; see 65 n.)

291 χεῦαι This is an imperatival inf. of χέω. The same syntax applies to κτερεΐξαι later in the line, δοῦναι (292), and φράζεσθαι (294). Within the Homeric poems, the imperatival inf. is used 193× as against some 1300 imperatives. This distribution calls for comment; it may be said that the inf. is 'marked', i.e. doing something different from the unvarnished imperative with which it alternates. It has been suggested (Allan 2010) that the inf. so used indicates a set of instructions aimed at solving a problem when aspects of the solution have already been outlined using imperatives (Chantraine 1953: 316) or commends a course of action ('script') that is appropriate in a given social situation.

κτέρεα κτερεΐξαι The κτέρεα are material goods given to mark the status of the deceased. The construction is a cognate acc. where the roots of the noun and verb echo each other.

292 πόλλα μάλ᾽, ὅσσα ἔοικε Is a direct echo of the description of the bridal gifts at 278 (n.). Hermann deleted this line, perhaps because it seemed to him to fit less well here than in the earlier context. But thinking that one can see into the poet's decision-making process is dangerous and can lead to the delusion that one knows better than the poet what he ought to have said. In fact, there is nothing inept or unfortunate in the repetition. These words have a marked pathos coming so soon after 278: there it was a matter of gifts for Penelope's second marriage, here it is a question of grave goods for her first husband.

294 φράζεσθαι... κατὰ φρένα καὶ κατὰ θυμόν It is fitting to find φράζεσθαι connected with φρήν in this way given the likely etymological connexion between the two words (273 n.). The appearance of θυμός might seem less expected, since that is often associated more with passion than calculation (Caswell 1990: 28); but there are no examples of conflict between θυμός and φρήν (Clarke 1999: 65).

296 κτείνῃς It is a further indication of the exaggerated nature of the advice that Mentes gives that simply driving the suitors away is not offered as an alternative. Maybe the thought is that they could return, possibly with reinforcements, and take Penelope by force. This formulation obviously foreshadows the killing of the suitors at the end of the poem. It sets up an expectation that this is what Odysseus' return will chiefly be about.

ἠὲ δόλῳ ἢ᾽ ἀμφαδόν The contrast is between a killing made easier by the use of trickery and an open fight with the suitors. Polyphemus complains that Οὖτις is trying to kill him δόλῳ οὐδὲ βίηφιν ('by trickery and not by force', *Od.* 9.408). Odysseus had made the Cyclops drunk, which was δόλος; but the blinding with a red-hot sharpened tree-trunk surely was βίη, just not of a kind that he had seen coming. Perhaps Mentes envisages making the suitors more drunk than usual or drugging them as an aid to killing them. δόλος is often a term of opprobrium (*Od.* 3.235; 4.92); but Odysseus boasts of his own trickery (*Od.* 9.19–20) and the scheme of Penelope (*Od.* 2.106) is surely supposed to be admired (300 n.). The idea of a killing done ἀμφαδόν is expanded at *Od.* 11.120 to include 'with sharp bronze'.

297 νηπιάας An abstract noun corresponding to the adj. νήπιος. The expected nom. is *νηπίη or *νηπιίη (Wackernagel 1916: 227–9; Chantraine 1958: 83). But the dat. νηπιέῃ (*Il.* 9.491) and νηπιέῃσι (e.g. *Il.* 15.363) point to a nom. *νηπιέη. Perhaps this is analogical beside ἠνορέη (Leumann 1950: 110 n. 72). The double vowel in –ααs is an example of diectasis (cf. 25 n.), just as the forms ending in –εῃ/–εῃσι exhibit a preceding short vowel of the same colour.

ὀχέειν A frequentative from ἔχω: 'hold on to', 'keep on with'.

298 ἦ οὐκ Will not scan unless the first word is run into one long vowel with the following diphthong. This precise kind of synecphonesis involving a single long vowel before a diphthong is rare, which is presumably why one MS omits it. But there are parallels (Chantraine 1958: 84).

κλέος...δῖος Ὀρέστης This episode was introduced early on by the poet (29 n.) and referred to by Zeus (32–43) in a lesson about retributive justice; here it is again on the lips of a goddess in disguise who wants to persuade Telemachus to kill the suitors. It produces some odd resonances (Gilchrist 1997: 114–15): Orestes' mother was the notoriously unfaithful and murderous Clytemnestra (*Od.* 11.422–3; 24.199–201) and Orestes was known even at this date to have killed her (*Od.* 3.310). Whilst Athena goes to a good deal of trouble to promote the image of Odysseus in the mind of Telemachus, she is not so concerned to dispel his coolness towards his mother (215 n.).

ἔλλαβε We learn ἔλαβε as the 'normal' aor. form, so that ἔλλαβε might at first blush look like an artificial and secondary creation of the bards to suit the metre. But the original root was *sleH₂gʷ- (cf. Aeginetan hλαβων, Thumb 1932: 117). This will regularly have yielded ἔλλαβε as the earliest Greek form (Sihler 1995: 171). Doubtless its simplification to ἔλαβε occurred quite soon. So the bardic tradition retained an old form ἔλλαβε that was still useful rather than inventing it by doubling the λ in ἔλαβε.

299 πατροφονῆα This epithet appears only three times in Homer, always in this form, always referring to Aegisthus (*Od.* 3.197, 307). But Aegisthus did not kill his own father; he is only a parricide when viewed through the avenging eyes of Orestes, whose father he had indeed slain. There is no reference to killing one's own father in Homer, unless in some lines of disputed authenticity (*Il.* 9.458–61; Griffin 1995: 130) where Phoenix alarmingly describes how he wanted to kill his father because of a love affair but some god prevented him from becoming πατροφόνος (adj. rather than noun in -ευς). In any event, Mentes' comparison is exaggerated since the suitors have not, in fact, killed Odysseus.

300 δολόμητιν The epithet δολομῆτα, formed slightly differently, is applied once to Zeus by Hera (*Il.* 1.540). But δολόμητις is used chiefly for Aegisthus (*Od.* 3.198, 250, 308; 4.525) and once for Clytemnestra with whom he is closely associated (*Od.* 11.422). It is never used of Odysseus, in spite of the fact that it might be thought to recall in form and meaning his common epithet πολύμητις (e.g. *Od.* 9.1) and that he himself boasts of his trickiness (*Od.* 9.19–20). Cf. 296 n.

ὅ οἱ Most MSS have ὅς οἱ, which Aristarchus rightly corrected to ὅ ('because'). The pron. οἱ originally began with digamma, cf. Delphic ϝοι < PIE *swoi (Sihler 1995: 377). Replacing it with ὅς would create an unmetrical heavy syllable. There is ample evidence that the bards still felt the initial digamma in such cases: apparent hiatus before οἱ is found c.600× in Homer (Chantraine 1958: 146–7).

πατέρα κλυτὸν ἔκτα Mentes is spelling out for emphasis what he has already said with πατροφονῆα (299 n.). Such amplification is typical of epic diction. But there is also the elaboration that the father was κλυτός— in fact, the supreme commander of the Greek contingent in the *Iliad*. Cf. 30 n.

301 φίλος A nom. form for a voc. sense is uncommon but not unknown (e.g. *Il.* 3.276). Some examples may continue inherited PIE patterns; others might just be metrically convenient (Chantraine 1953: 36).

302 ἔσσ' An elision of ἔσσο: impv. of εἰμί with a med. ending (Chantraine 1958: 287). The form is rare instead of the usual ἴσθι (itself morphologically complex, Sihler 1995: 553).

ὀψιγόνων The notion of how those in the future might speak of one was central to epic sensibility (*Il.* 3.353; 7.87; 16.31; *Od.* 3.200), being linked with the idea of one's κλέος being mediated to later generations by song (*Il.* 6.358; 9.189; cf. *Od.* 1.154, 325 nn.).

303–4 νῆα ... | ... ἑτάρους The companions were mentioned at 182 and the ship at 185. Mentes is ending where he began. His companions and ship, like Phemius and his song, had been allowed to fade into the background. It is Phemius whom the poet will choose to revisit shortly.

304 με Object of μένοντες and not of ἀσχαλόωσι, which takes a gen. for its object rather than an acc. (*Od.* 2.193; 19.159).

305 καὶ ἐμῶν ἐμπάζεο μύθων This phrase occurred at l. 272 when Mentes emphatically began to give his advice: εἰ δ' ἄγε νῦν ξυνίει κτλ. The repetition of the second half of the line here is an example of ring composition: the advice ends where it began. It is thus also marked off as a discrete unit from the rest of the speech.

306–24 There follows a passage in which Telemachus is shown once more as a conscientious host who respects the conventions of guest-friendship. He offers Mentes the sorts of gifts that are usually exchanged on such occasions. Mentes replies that the gifts can wait for another time as he is in a hurry. Telemachus gets the sense that his visitor was perhaps a god.

307 φίλα φρονέων This must mean that Mentes is thinking kindly thoughts, rather than merely his own ones; this gives the lie to the notion that Homeric φίλος is only a possessive adj. (cf. 60 n.).

308 ὥς τε πατὴρ ᾧ παιδί Growing up without his father, Telemachus casts others in the role. That he does not question Mentes' advice is perhaps an indication of his relative youth and inexperience. Described as πεπνυμένος (307), he is nevertheless not yet grown to the shrewdness of his father (216 n.). When Telemachus comes to the hut of Eumaeus, the scene is described in terms of a father affectionately welcoming home a long-absent son (*Od.* 13.406; cf. 16.17). But that comparison is made by the poet in the voice of the narrator: we are not seeing Eumaeus through the eyes of Telemachus. The latter is mature enough to use this language of fatherhood ironically later in the poem when talking to Antinous (*Od.* 17.397).

309 ἐπειγόμενος The gen. is one of goal (Chantraine 1953: 53–4). This expression is picked up in more unusual language at 315 (n.).

310 λοεσσάμενος The provision of a bath is a normal part of hospitality scenes (*Od.* 3.464–6; 4.48–9; 8.426–7).

    τεταρπόμενος The reduplicated aor. (here in the med. voice) is an archaic type, albeit still quite common in epic (Chantraine 1958: 395–6). The delight to which the verb refers must be some entertainment that Telemachus would lay on if Mentes wished it (Reece 1992: 28–9). This might be song and dance (*Od.* 8.246–65), sport and games (*Od.* 4.18–19), or listening to bardic song (*Od.* 1.152–5).

311 δῶρον Like a bath, gifts are also a standard part of the Homeric hospitality scene (*Od.* 4.128–32, 589–619; 8.389–95; 13.135–8; 15.83–5; 21.13–14; 24.273–9; *Il.* 6.218–20; 10.269). Such gifts are never given in a vacuum with no expectation of reward; the whole point of ξεινίη is that it creates a web of mutual obligations (175–6 n.; M. I. Finley 1977: 64–6; Pulleyn 1997: 28–9). See also 316 n.

312 τιμῆεν κτλ. An ascending tricolon (cf. 131 n., Introduction, p. 20).

κειμήλιον The context shows that this unusual noun (4× Hom.) is plainly a kind of gift. It occurs as a pair with the *hapax* πρόβασις (*Od.* 2.75). Since the latter must refer elliptically to cattle as 'something that moves' (< πρό + βαίνω; cf. πρόβατα), the inference is that a κειμήλιον is something static, as one might suppose from its being built to the same root seen in the verb κεῖμαι ('lie') (cf. *Od.* 4.613; Frisk 1940: 42; 1943: 52). This reflects an ancient Indo-European distinction between property that moves and that which does not (Benveniste 1969: 1.43–5; M. L. West 2007: 101; Janda 2014: 479–512). κειμήλια are generally metals (*Il.* 6.48; 11.133; 23.616–18; *Od.* 10.40, 45; 15.101–2, 113–15); but they are not so heavy that a strong man cannot carry them (*Il.* 9.331). A woman's dress may also be a κειμήλιον (*Od.* 15.101, 105, 124–5). So whilst these items might be portable, and thus are not the sort of 'immoveable property' known to modern lawyers, their name implies and the poem shows that their purpose is to be kept in store.

313 ἐμέ' This is an elided form of ἐμέο and is to be preferred on grounds of antiquity to the later contracted ἐμεῦ with correption (van Leeuwen 1885: 215).

ξεῖνοι ξείνοισι This is an example of polyptoton, where a noun or adj. in one case is juxtaposed with the same noun or adj. in a different case. It is plainly a rhetorical device. In this case, it stresses the matching status and reciprocal relationship of the parties. It finds parallels in numerous other old Indo-European sources (M. L. West 2007: 113–16), so that we may take it to have been a feature of the inherited poetic tradition.

315 κατέρυκε, λιλαιόμενόν περ ὁδοῖο The idea that Mentes is eager to be back on his way was introduced at 309 (n.). It is repeated here with the unusual word λιλαιόμενον. This was last used of Calypso's sexual desire for Odysseus (15 n.). κατέρυκε here likewise recalls ἔρυκε applied to Calypso in the same context (14 n.). The language is so striking that this cannot be dismissed as an accident, or just what anyone would say who is keen to resume his travels. Mentes desires to be on his way as strongly as Odysseus wants to be on his (58–9). Telemachus ought also to be on his own way to find news of his father so that the plot can be released from the bind in which it has become stuck.

316 δῶρον Mentes has no time for such things. At the level of plot, the visit has achieved its purpose so that the poet does not need to linger over details. It has been suggested that Athena cannot accept a bath or gift because that would put her, as a goddess, under an unwonted obligation (Reece 1992: 56–7). But Mentes' refusal is really more a matter of narrative form than theological substance. Gods do not need warm baths; nor do they keep and display presents that they have received from humans. But there is still considerable give-and-take between gods and humans: gods accept sacrifice from humans and humans expect gods to remember their former offerings. When addressing gods, humans use formulae connected with ξεινίη (Pulleyn 1997: 16–38). If Mentes declines the gift, it is not because gods and humans are separated by some existential gulf that prohibits reciprocal relations.

φίλον ἦτορ ἀνώγῃ Mental activities are variously described in Homer as originating in the θυμός, φρένες, πραπίδες, κῆρ, κραδίη, and ἦτορ. Whilst some of these might have a specific location—thus φρένες are probably lungs and κῆρ/κραδίη denote the heart—it is hard to say anything with more precision (Clarke 1999: 54, 77, 79). Some of these terms, whilst not strictly synonymous, are used more or less interchangeably to describe the mental apparatus as a whole (Jahn 1987). But this does not imply that Homer or his contemporaries lacked a sense of the unity of the individual or of the mind (Pulleyn 2000: 37). It is rare for ἦτορ to be said to be a motivating factor in action; the commoner term is θυμός (Caswell 1990: 47, 49–50).

317 δόμεναι imperatival inf. (cf. 291 n.).

οἶκόνδε The accentuation here is the regular result of the addition of an enclitic suffix (-δε) to a word of trochaic shape (M. L. West 1998: xxviii; Probert 2003: 154).

φέρεσθαι Epexegetic inf. explaining what is to be done with the gift. Such inf. complements are commonly used and with great freedom (Chantraine 1953: 301).

318 καὶ μάλα καλὸν ἑλών To refuse a gift outright would have caused deep offence, so the strategy for Mentes' quick departure involves postponing the gift instead. But this is unusual and must have been felt as awkward. Such unabashed frankness about what one expects in a gift is surprising. Whilst expressed with less petulance, it is redolent of Agamemnon's concern that any substitute for Chryseis should be of the same value (ὅπως ἀντάξιον ἔσται, *Il.* 1.136).

ἄξιον…ἀμοιβῆς The thought is presumably that, if Telemachus visits Mentes' house in the future, he will receive a fitting gift in return. Athena will soon use the word again when, disguised as Mentor (*sic*), she prays to Poseidon for a χαρίεσσαν ἀμοιβήν | ἑκατόμβης ('pleasing return for the hecatomb', *Od.* 3.58–9). χαρίεσσα belongs etymologically with χαίρω and denotes the feelings of mutual favour that are created by gifts whether as between mortals or as between mortals and gods (*CEG* 326; *IG* I³ 791). Cf. 61 n.

320 ὄρνις δ' ὥς In other contexts ὥς (accented when following its noun) indicates likeness (*Il.* 3.2) but not identity. The use of ὥς does not of itself oblige us to conclude that Athena has turned into a bird. Gods are also likened to birds using a ptcp. of ἔοικα (*Il.* 7.59; 19.350; *Od.* 5.51, 337); but this by no means always indicates identity in appearance (*Il.* 3.449; 5.782; 16.582; *Od.* 9.190). The same is true of ἐναλίγκιος (*Il.* 14.290 vs. *Il.* 13.242). The sole example involving εἴκελος does make it plain that the goddess actually looks like a bird, but that is only because the word ἄντην is added (*Od.* 22.240); otherwise εἴκελος need not indicate identity (*Od.* 10.304). The most revealing scene is where Athena departs φήνη εἰδομένη ('look-ing like a lammergeier', *Od.* 3.371–3). First, εἰδομένη always denotes visual resemblance. Second, the astonishment of the Achaeans in general and of Nestor at what he ἴδεν ὀφθαλμοῖσι ('saw with his eyes') only makes sense if Athena had actually been seen to turn into a bird. The verb used there is ἀπέβη ('went away') rather than διέπτατο ('flew away') here: the mere fact of her departure is not enough to explain the amazement it caused. If it is correct that ἀνόπαια (see below) refers to the roof, then we must assume here that Athena has also become a bird. It is absurd to suppose that Mentes floated up in the air in human form only to squeeze through a small hole in the roof (S. R. West 1988: 116). Whilst it has been claimed that Homer never shows gods turning into birds (Dirlmeier 1967), the considerations already set out (taken together with others) make it plain that he sometimes does (Bannert 1978; Erbse 1980). To say that a god might assume the form of a bird or other animal is not to say that the gods were essentially theriomorphic. The epics make it clear that their bodies are like those of humans (*Il.* 1.46, 500, 528–30, 591), albeit heavier (*Il.* 5.837–9), bloodless, and not usually dependent on ordinary food (*Il.* 5.339–42; but cf. *Il.* 9.531).

ἀνόπαια This unique word was already opaque in antiquity. Σ says that Aristarchus thought it was an eagle; but this has the appearance of a guess and lacks corroboration. A Semitic origin has been suggested (Thompson 1936: 52–3), appealing to Heb. *'ᵃnāfāh* (Lev 11:19; Deut 14:18), cf. Akk. *anpatu*. But it is unlikely that a Semitic word of this shape would produce ἀνόπαια if borrowed into Greek (Prof. Geoffrey Khan, private communi-cation). In the strongly parallel scene at *Od.* 22.239, Athena flies up to the roof like a swallow. Maybe this is the form that she adopts here; but we are not thereby obliged to suppose that ἀνόπαια is a synonym for χελιδών, or even that it denotes a bird at all (Boraston 1911: 244–5; Arnott 2007: 14). Herodian (*Gr.* 2.133) glossed the word as 'invisible'; that is an unconvincing popular etymology (ἀν– + ὀπ– ('not + see')). Eustathius thought it meant 'upwards'. The same idea underlies the probably correct interpretation by a commentator (*Gramm. in An. Ox.* 1.83) who suggests that the word is a univerbated adj. from ἀνά ὀπήν where the latter element denotes the smoke vent in a roof. ὀπή meaning 'hole' is certainly attested in Aristophanes (*Pl.* 715; cf. Hipp. *Mul.* 2.114). Semantically, ὀπή must derive from the root *H_3ek^w- ('eye'); cf. Gk. ὄσσε, Lat. *oculus*: to be inoculated is to have a small hole made in one. An original stem in –*a*– would give rise to the suffix –*αιος* by the addition of the common morpheme –*ιος*: *H_2n–H_3ek^w–eH_2–*ios* > ἀν-οπ-α-ῖος with ὀπαῖος standing to ὀπή as βολαῖος to βολή. The short final vowel in ἀνόπαια suggests a neut. pl. adj. used as an adv.; the fem. sg. ought to end in –*αιή* (cf. *Il.* 5.360). An Attic Greek inscription (*IG* I³ 476.112–22: 408/7 BC) has the word ὀπαῖον that might denote a structure on the roof of a temple (cf. Plut. *Per.* 13.7). This interpretation gains support from the fact that Empedocles apparently uses ἀνόπαια to refer to the upwards motion of fire (31 B 51 DK) and that the steep path leading up above Thermopylae was called Ἀνόπαια (Hdt. 7.216). The accentuation of such words was already disputed in antiquity (Chandler 1881: 70–1, 117, 153); but this does not materially affect the discussion. Whether we read one word or two (ἀν' ὄπαια) is an unanswerable question; but the univerbated place-name in Herodotus weighs slightly in favour of the former.

διέπτατο Flight is sometimes metaphorical (cf. *Il.* 15.83, 172). But given that Mentes exits through a hole in the roof (see foreg. nn.), we may take it as literal (cf. *Il.* 5.99).

320–1 τῷ ... | μένος καὶ θάρσος Whilst Gk. μένος and Vedic *mánas* ('mind') are cognates, it does not follow that they mean the same thing. Heroes breathe μένος (*Il.* 3.8; 24.364), but it is also breathed into them by gods (*Il.* 10.482; 15.60). But it is unlikely simply to denote breath as it is applied not only to wind (*Il.* 5.524) but also to a river (*Il.* 21.383), the sun (*Od.* 10.160), fire (*Il.* 6.182), and a spear (*Il.* 13.444). It is maybe not a concrete thing at all so much as a process: vigorous, self-propelled, thrusting movement (Clarke 1999: 110–11). When it is used periphrastically to describe a hero, e.g. ἱερὸν μένος Ἀλκινόοιο (*Od.* 13.24), it denotes not simply strength but the dynamism of the character. ἱερός has similar connotations (2 n.) and so is apt to qualify μένος. These lines show Athena fulfilling the mission she proposed at l. 90. Such divine injection of μένος is common in the world of the epic (*Il.* 5.2, 470); but it is also possible for humans to rouse the existing μένος of others (*Il.* 6.72; 11.291; 15.514).

321 ὑπέμνησέν τε ἑ πατρός In the *Iliad*, when Priam comes boldly to the hut of Achilles to ransom his dead son, his first words are μνῆσαι πατρὸς σοῖο ('remember your father'; *Il.* 24.486). Priam is a father whose beloved son is dead; he begs Achilles to imagine how Peleus would feel in the same position. That is one of the most affecting scenes in the *Iliad*. Here, the situation is rather different. Telemachus is alive and well and is bidden to remember his father as part of a spur to action that will assist in a train of events culminating in the death of the suitors. But, especially against the background of the *Iliad*, the appeal to remember one's father is loaded with emotional power.

322 φρεσὶν ᾗσι νοήσας When Nestor sees Athena fly off in the form of a bird, the language is more straightforwardly of sight: ἴδεν ὀφθαλμοῖσι ('he saw with his eyes'; *Od.* 3.373). Telemachus apprehends the same thing in his φρένες, which are one of several seats of mental activity (Clarke 1999: 54, 79). But this does not mean that the experience is any less visual. The verb νοέω is connected etymologically with the PIE *nes-*, whose fundamental connotation is keeping things or people safe (cf. 3, 5 nn.). But νοέω can denote sight (e.g. *Il.* 9.223), the semantic field perhaps being similar to that of τηρέω in later Greek: 'keep under guard' > 'watch over' > 'observe' (cf. Lat. *tueri*). The choice of νοέω and φρένες focuses on Telemachus' interpretation of the experience (see on ὀΐσατο 323 n.).

323 θάμβησεν The verb denotes astonishment, sometimes said to be specifically divine in origin (Motte 1986: 170–2). Words from this root appear 22× in Homer. Of these, twelve do indeed relate to some divine epiphany (*Il.* 1.199; 3.398; 4.79; 8.77; *Od.* 1.320; 2.155; 3.372) or otherwise uncanny event (*Il.* 23.881; 24.482–4 (3×); *Od.* 24.101). But the other ten refer to purely human sources of astonishment such as the look of warriors (*Il.* 3.342; 23.728, 815), the authoritative speech of Telemachus (*Od.* 1.360 n.; 21.354), his voyage to Pylos (*Od.* 4.638), or the sight of Odysseus in the halls of Aeolus (*Od.* 10.16), or the hut of Eumaeus (*Od.* 16.178), or in his own house either in disguise (*Od.* 17.367) or in his own person (*Od.* 24.394). On this showing, there is no reason to privilege religious awe as the fundamental meaning. What is more revealing is that almost all of these instances involve characters seeing something. In well over half the cases, there is an explicit reference to visual perception (*Il.* 1.198; 3.342, 396; 4.79; 8.76; 23.728, 881; 24.482, 483; *Od.* 1.320; 2.155; 3.372; 16.179; 24.101, 391). In others, we can tell from the context that the source of astonishment is visual (*Il.* 232.815; *Od.* 10.63; 17.367). Only in three cases is astonishment a response primarily to words (*Od.* 1.360; 4.638; 21.354). Although θάμβος is not uniquely a response to something seen, it is overwhelmingly so. The verb is almost certainly the same seen in the perf. τέθηπα and the aor. ptcp. ταφών; but the visual element is rarely explicit in such cases (*Od.* 6.166), sometimes implicit (*Il.* 9.193; 11.777; *Od.* 16.12), sometimes absent altogether (*Od.* 23.105). The semantically related verb θαυμάζω exhibits a similar affinity for the visual. It is possible that θαυμάζω is etymologically linked with θηέομαι, the Ionic form of θέαομαι ('to look at'; Mette 1960). A bold attempt has been made to show a common root for θαμβέω and θαυμάζω (Szemerényi 1954: 262); but that is freighted with difficulty (*DELG* 422; Barton 1993: 2 n. 3). See also 360, 382 nn.

ὀίσατο Telemachus 'thought' or 'reckoned' that he had seen a god. By l. 420 (n.), this notion will have hardened into definite knowledge.

324 ἐπῴχετο Of the nine occurrences of ἐπῴχετο in Homer, six are in the *Iliad*. Five of these refer to an attack (*Il.* 1.50, 383; 5.330; 10.487; 15.676); one instance refers to moving among the troops in the heat of battle giving orders (*Il.* 17.356). Here, it might be tempting to think that Telemachus adopts a martial posture reminiscent of a hero embarking upon his *aristeia* at Troy. But other instances of ἐπῴχετο in the *Odyssey* do not support this: at *Od.* 1.143, the steward goes between Telemachus and Mentes pouring wine; at *Od.* 4.451, Proteus goes among his seals to count them. If we look at the participial forms ἐποιχόμενος etc. in the *Iliad* we find that, while many carry this warlike overtone, quite a few do not (e.g. *Il.* 1.31; 5.720). It would seem that the *Odyssey* continues this more everyday sense. See 358 n.

ἰσόθεος φώς The enigmatic word φώς (usually translated 'warrior') looks as though it might be connected with φῶς 'light'. A semantic link between the two is far from obvious (*DELG* 1170, 1238). Of the fourteen instances of this formula in Homer, twelve are in the *Iliad* and refer to warriors; two are in the *Odyssey* and refer to Telemachus. It has been suggested that what is alluded to is the brilliant splendour of these warriors, their shining glory (Peters *apud* Lamberterie 1997: 177–8). One can perhaps go further. Of the fourteen examples of the formula, eleven refer to a character who is, or has just been (e.g. *Il.* 11.644), in motion. The others refer to speaking (*Il.* 23.569), lighting a fire (*Il.* 9.211), or loading a wagon with animals (*Il.* 3.310). We know from other words that there is a connexion in Indo-European between swift movement and brightness (Pulleyn 2000: 139). Perhaps this word denoted originally not the glory of the warrior standing still in full panoply but his bright dash when in motion. Telemachus is not fighting before Troy. But, just as great warriors are called ἰσόθεος (or otherwise likened to a god) when setting out to do some great deed, so Telemachus is aptly so described here when he turns to deal with the suitors (cf. *Od.* 2.5; W. C. Scott 1974: 68–70). It is perhaps the beginning of his own *aristeia*.

When φώς appears on its own without ἰσόθεος, it can be more or less equivalent in meaning to ἀνήρ (*Il.* 17.377–8; *Od.* 8.159; 20.227). These are probably later uses (relatively speaking) where the original force of the word is no longer felt. Once again, the *Odyssey* seems to adapt to peacetime use words that seem more at home in the martial repertoire of the *Iliad*; cf. ἥρως (198 n.) and ἐποίχομαι (foreg. n.)

325–64 Now that Mentes has gone, the emphasis changes. In a relatively short but striking tableau, we have the first appearance of Penelope and Telemachus' spirited defence of poetic freedom. The song of Phemius, begun at 155 (n.), had been artfully allowed to fade into the background so that Telemachus and Mentes could conduct their interview in private whilst the attention of the suitors was focused on Phemius. Now the bard comes squarely back into the frame. This is one of several opportunities that are taken in the *Odyssey* to describe a bard at work; there is a 'meta-poetic' element here in that Homer is self-consciously showing us some-one like himself. The third element in this scene is that we see Telemachus defending Phemius and rebuking his mother—in which he appears first in a favourable, and then in a rather unfavourable, light. Similar rebukes of Penelope recur at *Od.* 17.46.56, 23.97–103 (Lord 1960: 171–3).

325 ἀοιδός This noun appears only once in the *Iliad* (24.720), in the pl. and denoting a group of professional singers at the funeral of Hector. Although Achilles is presented as singing to himself and Patroclus of the great deeds of men of old (*Il.* 9.189), his is a very unusual kind of performance. In the *Odyssey*, by contrast, ἀοιδός appears 36×. Maslov (2009: 9) talks of a bardic 'takeover of the epic tradition'. This might be going a little far, but the songs of Phemius and Demodocus are the focus of much self-aware attention in the *Odyssey*.

περικλυτός Some bards were itinerant, competing in prestigious com-petitions and winning prizes and fame (*Od.* 17.382–6). But, so far as we can see, Phemius lives in the palace of Odysseus and is a sort of superior ser-vant. One thinks of the ambiguous status and unhappy fate of the unnamed ἀοιδὸς ἀνήρ who lived in the house of Agamemnon, was instructed by the king on his departure to look after Clytemnestra, and was unceremoniously carried off by Aegisthus to die on a deserted island (*Od.* 3.267–8, 270–1). The notion of wide fame attaching to a bard whose life was spent in the house of one man must be wishful thinking on Homer's part. But it is part of a concerted presentation in the *Odyssey* of the bard as a man of consequence. On compounds in περι-, see 329 n.

σιωπῇ The suitors were dancing at 151–2. That they are now seated quietly listening to Phemius might say something about the power of epic song to charm its listeners (cf. 337 n.). *Σ* here says that the suitors are silent because they are paying attention, hoping to learn of the death of Odysseus. The poet is deliberately vague as to whether the song of Phemius tells of this (unreal) death or not (see 340 n.).

326 εἶατ' This is the form consistently given in the MSS. OCT ἦατ' must be a correction, based on the feeling that these forms ought to follow the vocalism of ἧμαι. Etymologically the vowel is long (*$H_1eH_1(s)$-nto > hēato, Rix 2001: 232), the aspiration perhaps the result of analogy with ἕζομαι (*DELG* 411–12). But there is more than one kind of ē in Greek. The spelling with -ει- in Ionic represents a long close vowel like Fr. *blé*; that with -η- represents a long open vowel like Fr. *mère* (Monro 1891: 385; W. S. Allen 1987: 70). The spelling with -ει- probably reflects the realization of the vowel in Ionic (Wyatt 1969: 147–8). This spelling would appear to be early, at least within the history of the epic tradition, and so ought to be retained.

ἀκούοντες Whereas κλύω has a very transparent PIE pedigree (Rix 2001: 334–5), ἀκούω is harder to place in the PIE tradition. It might be cognate with Gothic *hausjan* (*DELG* 50–1) and Lat. *caveo* (Prévot 1935b: 75). To judge from the prominence of its cognates in Vedic and Avestan, κλύω was originally the preferred term in poetry. But already by the time of Homer parts of ἀκούω (186×) considerably outnumber those of κλύω (107×). Some specialism remains apparent in the distribution. The impv. κλῦθι is confined to prayers (*Il.* 1.34 and 12×), ἄκουσον being found only once (*Od.* 6.325). Both verbs are used for the action of a god hearing a prayer (*Il.* 1.43 vs. 381). κλέος is also a term of prestige denoting the fame conferred by heroic poetry (338 n.).

νόστον Sometimes it was the audience that requested the topic for song (*Od.* 8.492–5); at other times, the singer chose the subject himself—which we may infer to have been the case here (347 n.). See also 5 n.

327 λυγρόν The word gains emphasis from being in runover from the previous line and coming first in the next one. One thinks of οὐλομένην ('accursed'; *Il.* 1.2), similarly placed and of similar meaning.

ἐπετείλατο...Ἀθήνη Nothing is said of the cause of her wrath, although Nestor (*Od.* 3.135) and Menelaus (*Od.* 4.502) both seem to take the story for granted. Alcaeus is our earliest explicit source to explain that Locrian Ajax had raped Cassandra in the temple of Athena (Merkelbach 1967).

328 ὑπερωϊόθεν The suffix -θεν is plainly still very productive at this period, being freely added to such nouns as the bards pleased in order to produce an ablative (Chantraine 1958: 242). In later Greek, it tends to be restricted to adverbs (πόθεν, ἐντεῦθεν, ἔνθεν, etc.). The ὑπερῴον was an upper storey (*DELG* 1158–9). It was reached by a staircase (cf. 330 n.). Eustathius (1921, 53) reports that οἱ παλαιοί ('the ancients'), by whom he presumably meant Hellenistic scholars, had busied themselves trying to draw plans of the palace of Odysseus to illustrate the action of the poem.

It seems unlikely that the ὑπερῷον was a second storey coextensive with the μέγαρον below (Knox 1973: 16–17). Numerous conjectures have been made as to its precise location: the most plausible is that which places it near the front corner of the μέγαρον (Bassett 1919: 293–301, 308–9). In any event, it is clearly unusual for Penelope to live this secluded life in the upper rooms. Whatever the position in later centuries, aristocratic women in the *Odyssey* such as Helen and Arete mixed freely with the men in the μέγαρον (*Od.* 4.120–2, 137, 184, 219; 7.53–5, 133–52). Penelope's seclusion is presumably the result of the arrival of the suitors. When she descends here from the upper floor, there probably comes to the suitors (and to the audience, for whom this is her first appearance) a certain erotic frisson (cf. 330 n.). She is beautiful as well as clever (cf. *Od.* 18.245–9).

σύνθετο This verb usually indicates an act of the mind in taking heed of something (*Il.* 1.76; 7.44). Sometimes it appears to mean little more than 'perceive' (*Od.* 20.92). But we must assume, given the overall pattern of use, that even these latter instances also connote an element of becoming aware of the content or meaning of something. In this case, she is perhaps not just hearing the song but drawing conclusions from it about her own situation (Halliwell 2009: 7). See 343 n.

θέσπιν ἀοιδήν The adj. is found only in this formula. It is generally taken to be a shortened form of θεσπέσιος ('divinely uttered')—probably a compound of the roots seen in θεός and ἐν(ν)έπω (cf. 1 n.). We see again the high status given to poetry in Homer, especially in the *Odyssey*. Both poems begin with a divine invocation: it is the gods who inspire, putting the bard on the path of poetic song (*Od.* 8.74–5; Durante 1976: 176–7). It has been conjectured that the formula came about through bardic reanalysis of an earlier term *θεσπιαοιδός denoting one who sings the words of the gods (Koller 1965). That is speculative, to put it no higher. The same applies to the analysis of ἀοιδός as a back-formation from ἐπαοιδή ('incantation'; *Od.* 19.457), although there is some attraction in seeing a connexion between bardic song and magical incantation—just as Lat. *carmen* and Irish *canaid* cover both ideas (Maslov 2009: 27). Cf. 336 n.

329 Penelope's description is made to fill an entire line, which has the effect of emphasizing her dignity and drawing attention to her entrance on the scene. This contrasts markedly with the almost throwaway fashion in which she is first mentioned by Mentes at 223. There, the stress was on Telemachus, not his mother. Here the focus is entirely on Penelope and so the language is correspondingly augmented. It is characteristic of epic style to dilate upon people and things of importance. Cf. 429 n.

κούρη Ἰκαρίοιο The variant Ἰκαρίου κούρη (*Od.* 19.546) is a later formation since the gen. ending in -οιο preceded that in -ου. The origin of the name Icarius is obscure. Homer refers to the Ἰκάριος πόντος (*Il.* 2.145) and Strabo knows of a Cycladic island Ἴκαρος or Ἰκαρία (14.635, 637). These place names are probably of pre-Greek origin from Asia Minor (Kamptz 1982: 292; Kerényi 1976: 152–3).

περίφρων The element περι- in these adjectival compounds appears originally to have meant 'all around' but to have taken on the connotation of 'to a high degree': thus περιμήκης ('very tall'; *Il.* 14.287), περικαλλής ('very beautiful'; *Il.* 1.603). It is possible that the starting point for this process was a word such as περικλυτός (*Od.* 1.325 above): it is a short step from saying that the bard is famous 'all around' to saying that he is simply 'very famous'. This adj. is almost always used of Penelope, who is a byword for prudence, even cunning (*Od.* 2.121–2). It is also used of Arete (*Od.* 11.345), the maid Eurycleia (*Od.* 19.357), and Adrastina (*Il.* 5.412). Although used by Hesiod of Hephaestus (*Sc.* 297, 313), the word is confined in Homer to women. This suggests that we are being told what it is that Homeric men purported to value in their spouses; whether the average man would truly have wanted a spouse as clever as Penelope—and likely thus cleverer than he—is open to doubt.

Πηνελόπεια If the name really does involve a pun on her ruse with the loom (223 n.), its collocation with περίφρων (see foreg.) would underline her aptitude at plotting (Felson-Rubin 1987: 64, 77).

330 κλίμακα Although this word is conventionally translated 'ladder', it is more likely that we are dealing here with stairs. We know that some Mycenaean houses had stairs (Wace 1951: 209) and this is surely what is meant here. It is hard to imagine a queen like Penelope having to negotiate a ladder. This is not to deny that, in later centuries, women in well-off households made use of ladders to get up and down from their quarters (Lysias 1.9; C. M. Edwards 1984: 64). It has been argued that the κλῖμαξ carried erotic connotations because that is how one got to the λέχος (Watkins 2007: 311–15), which was synonymous in Homer not so much with sleep but with sexual intimacy (*Il.* 1.31; *Od.* 8.269). But this does not apply so well to a context where the bedroom of Odysseus and Penelope was not upstairs but in a θάλαμος in the courtyard (*Od.* 23.190, 192; cf. 1.425 n.).

κατεβήσετο In view of the correlation with κλίμακα this can mean nothing other than that Penelope went downstairs. In his first edition of the *Iliad*, Leaf (1886: 216 on *Il.* 6.288) took this common-sense view; by the time of the second edition, he had come to think that there was no upper floor and that verb κατεβήσετο could refer to horizontal penetration into the depths of a house (Leaf 1900: 279). This makes no sense in the present context (see above on ὑπερῳόθεν, 328 n.). Furthermore, no verb compounded with ἀνά or κατά is ever unambiguously used to denote traversing a house or room (Gray 1955: 4–6). The present verb is surely the opposite of εἰσαναβαίνω, which denotes going upstairs (*Il.* 2.514) and to bed (*Il.* 8.291). On the form, see 24 n.

οἷο δόμοιο It is odd to find the upper rooms described as though they were an entire house. A similarly odd use of the whole to denote the part is found with οἶκος (356, 360; S. R. West 1988: 120).

331 οἴη This adj. is rare in later Greek, having been replaced almost entirely by μόνος. It is built with a suffix -ϝο- to the root *οἰ- seen in Lat. ū-nus, Skt. é-ka, Gk. οἴ-νη ('ace').

τῇ Could in theory be governed by the preceding ἅμα or the following ἕποντο, in which case ἅμα would be purely adverbial. The word order favours the former construction.

ἀμφίπολοι These are conventionally translated as 'maidservants'. It is hard to tell whether they were free (like θεράποντες; 109 n.) or a subset of the larger group of household slaves (398 n.). The etymology suggests simply 'go about' or 'attend to' (*DELG* 877–8) and has no necessary bearing on status (*pace* Gschnitzer 1976: 24–45). That Penelope is accompanied by them is a marker of her status but might also reflect a sense that it was not proper for her to go alone into places where she might meet men (cf. *Od.* 18.184).

332 δῖα γυναικῶν See 14 n.

333 σταθμόν This word has many meanings in Homer but they divide into two chief groups: an active sense of something that stands and a passive one of a place where standing takes place. This dichotomy is already apparent in Mycenaean (Baumbach 1971b: 393–4). The noun can thus indicate anything from a door-post (*Il.* 14.167; *Od.* 6.19) to a sheep-pen (*Il.* 2.470). It is unlikely here to refer to a door-post since τέγος usually means 'roof' and the collocation would make no sense unless the door-post also supports the roof (Knox 1973: 6 n. 1). If τέγος could refer by extension to the entire room or building, we would have good sense but a usage not otherwise found before Pindar (*P.* 5.41). The alternative is to take σταθμός as equivalent to 'pillar'. Whilst this precise sense in not always straightforwardly apparent in Homer, it is well in keeping with the other 'active' uses of σταθμός (Chadwick 1996: 257).

πύκα The basic meaning of this adv. is 'thickly' or 'solidly'. The associated adjectives πυκνός and πυκινός carry the same sense, but also sometimes connote shrewd intelligence (*Il.* 3.208; 14.294, etc.). One might see a connexion with ἐχεπευκές ('sharp'; *Il.* 1.51), cf. Lat. *pungo*. But it is hard to see how that meaning could be original since an evolution from 'sharp' to 'dense' is scarcely credible. It is perhaps more likely that we are dealing with two homonyms—one that covers the field from 'sharp' to 'shrewd' (cf. Eng. acute) and another that simply means 'dense' or 'thick' (Szemerényi 1964: 83–4). The idea of the roof being 'densely made' is presumably to say no more than that it is solid.

334 ἄντα παρειάων Penelope is holding her headdress in front of her cheeks, presumably to obscure her face. Perhaps she is trying to hide her tears; at the same time, she is putting a symbolic distance between herself and the suitors. Although it has been suggested on the basis of later iconographic evidence that Penelope is actually holding the garment away from her face (Haakh 1959), this does not fit with the usual sense of ἄντα which means 'in front of'. At *Od.* 4.115, Telemachus holds his cloak before his eyes (ἄντ᾽ ὀφθαλμοῖιν) to conceal his tears. It is bold (Russo 1992: 63) to connect this covering of the face with an alleged (Amory 1966: 55–6) tendency of Penelope to look only intermittently at things to which she ought to pay more attention.

λιπαρά The sheen of cloth is meant, cf. εἵματα σιγαλόεντα (*Il.* 22.154–5). This might simply be the result of vigorous washing (*Od.* 6.90–5); but perhaps the cloth was treated with oil (Shelmerdine 1995).

κρήδεμνα This garment was a longish piece of fine cloth, like a mantilla, placed on top of the head and falling down either side of the face (Kardara 1960: 352–3; Marinatos 1967: 13, 46, Taf. B IVd). The pl. for sg., as here, is not unusual in Homer (Chantraine 1953: 30–2). It has been suggested that the κρήδεμνον was a sort of close-fitting bag made of yarn or cloth and designed to keep the hair in place; but this will not fit with *Od.* 6.100, where Nausicaa and companions remove it before playing their ball game. One would scarcely remove something that would be so useful in keeping the hair away from the face during sport (Lorimer 1950: 385–6).

335 κεδνή This word, of wide application, lacks a convincing etymology (*DELG* 508–9). Σ T on *Il.* 17.28 connects it with κήδομαι ('to take care')—probably a popular etymology. ΣA on *Il.* 9.586 glosses κεδνότατοι as σωφρονέστατοι ('most prudent'). The common formula κέδν᾽ εἰδυῖα (*Od.* 1.428 n.) is explained by Σ as προσφιλῆ, συνετὰ φρονοῦσα ('thinking well-disposed, sagacious thoughts'). These examples point to a character's active disposition. Sometimes κεδνός seems to describe persons as the passive recipients of the love and worth attached to them by others: thus a spouse (*Il.* 24.730), a mother (*Od.* 10.8), parents (*Il.* 17.28), companions (*Il.* 9.586), servants (*Od.* 18.211), or even a ruler (*Od.* 14.170). But in none of these cases can the active sense quite be ruled out (Hoffmann 1914: 22). All these persons might be being presented in terms of the decency and kindness they show to others (cf. ἤπια εἰδώς; *Od.* 15.557).

336 δακρύσασα The aor. ptcp. does not mark temporal anteriority with respect to the main verb (122, 369 nn). Penelope is scarcely to be imagined as weeping, ceasing to weep, and then speaking; rather she is 'in tears' (cf. εὐξάμενος 'in prayer', *Il.* 19.257). The aor. indicates that the duration of the action is not at issue (Chantraine 1953: 188–9; Humbert 1954: 169–70). Penelope is particularly prone to tears in the *Odyssey*; there are more than forty references to her weeping or grieving for her husband (Monsacré 1984: 233 n. 19). This is partly a mark of her affection and fidelity. But weeping is not a uniquely feminine trait in the epic. Odysseus weeps (e.g. *Od.* 5.82–4, 151–3, 156–8; 8.521–2); on one occasion, he covers his face out of αἰδώς ('shame') so that the Phaeacians should not see him (*Od.* 8.83–9). But it is not clear that there was any shame in a man weeping (Föllinger 2009: 19). Achilles weeps in the *Iliad* (1.349), on which Σ cites the proverb ἀεὶ δ' ἀριδάκρυες ἀνέρες ἐσθλοί ('good men are always prone to tears').

θεῖον The bard is chiefly godlike because his singing is excellent (see 371 n.). But he is also a singer of divinely inspired songs (*Od.* 8.73, 498; 17.518–19); cf. 1.328 n.

337–55 The episode dealing with the song of Phemius is remarkable as an early example of meta-poetics, i.e. a poet self-consciously depicting poetry being created. There is the deliberate vagueness concerning the content of the song and thus what it might have meant for Telemachus, Penelope, the suitors, and the original audience.

337 ἄλλα Grk. ἄλλος can mean 'other' in the sense that the other things are of the same kind as what has already been mentioned (e.g. *Il.* 6.476). In this case, Penelope would be acknowledging that Phemius' song, whilst painful to her (341 n.), is nevertheless beguiling to others. But ἄλλος can also mean 'besides' or 'as well', with no sense that the thing described as ἄλλος is like what went before (e.g. *Od.* 6.84). In that case, Penelope need not be saying that this particular song is a θελκτήριον. The ambiguity is perhaps deliberate.

θελκτήρια This rare word appears 3× in Homer. At *Il.* 14.215, it refers to the erotic charms of the girdle of Aphrodite; at *Od.* 8.509, it refers to the possibility of leaving the Trojan horse as an offering to charm the gods. The related verb θέλγω is rather commoner (16×; see *Od.* 1.57 n.). Here the reference is to the beguiling charm of heroic song. When Odysseus tells the Phaeacians the story of his visit to the gloomy realm of Hades, he becomes a sort of embedded bard, comparable to Demodocus. When he finishes, the audience is silent (σιωπῇ), held in the spell (κηληθμῷ) of his words (*Od.* 11.334; 13.2). The rare word κηληθμός appears to be a synonym for θέλξις (Hdn. *Schem. Hom.* 113.1; Kraus 1955: 69). Eumaeus later speaks of Odysseus' words as being like those of a bard with divine power and explicitly uses the verb θέλγω to describe their effect (*Od.* 17.518–21). The Sirens lure men to their death with the charm of their song (θέλγουσιν ἀοιδῇ; *Od.* 12.44). There is a connexion between their song and that of the bards. They address Odysseus as πολύαιν᾽ Ὀδυσεῦ, μέγα κῦδος Ἀχαιῶν ('much-praised Odysseus, great strength of the Achaeans', *Od.* 12.184). The epithet πολύαινος is used only of Odysseus and (apart from here) only in the *Iliad* (9.673; 10.544; 11.430). Their use of it here shows that they can identify him as the great warrior from the *Iliad*. Furthermore, μέγα κῦδος Ἀχαιῶν is an epic label given to mighty heroes (*Il.* 9.673; 10.87, 544; 11.511; *Od.* 3.79). Their knowledge and use of language tends to bracket the Sirens with the Muses who know everything and can pass on their knowledge to bards (Pucci 1979: 122, 126–7). Indeed, Apollonius of Rhodes (4.892–6) makes the Sirens daughters of the Muse Terpsichore. One of the Sirens is said to have been called Θελξινόη (Σ to A.R. 4.892) or Θελξιέπεια (Eustathius 1709.45). Epic song is thus a particularly magical and compelling performance (Segal 1974: 142–4); but it is not necessarily a happy one. It has been conjectured (Maslov 2009: 27) that the very word ἀοιδός was a back formation from ἐπαοιδή ('incantation'; *Il.* 19.457); if that is true, magical charm is at the very root of epic song. See 57, 328 nn.

οἶδας The more usual form of the verb, even in Homer, is οἶσθα (Meillet 1953: 91; Sihler 1995: 571). οἶδας is a later Ionian replacement (Chantraine 1958: 469). One could correct οἶδας to οἶσθα without disturbing the metre; but no ancient witness has this reading. Zenodotus is reported to have written ᾔδεις here. That is peculiar as the normal pluperf. is ᾔδησθα (*Od.* 19.93) or ἠείδης (*Il.* 22.280). But to say that Phemius *knew* other poems makes poor sense in context. Schwartz proposed amending to ἀείδεις which gives good sense but is, in a sense, too easy and leaves unanswered the question of how οἶδας arose.

338 ἔργ᾽ ἀνδρῶν τε θεῶν τε The polar expression 'men and gods' is of a type common in the Indo-European poetic tradition (M. L. West 2007: 100); but the combination with ἔργα is unique in Homer. Similar phrases elsewhere refer not to heroic deeds but to land under the plough: ἀνδρῶν πίονα ἔργα (*Il.* 12.283) and ἔργ᾽ ἀνθρώπων (*Il.* 16.392; *Od.* 6.259) or βροτῶν (*Od.* 10.147). ἔργα can stand by itself for fields (*Od.* 16.140). This is one of sixteen occurrences of the phrase ἀνδρῶν τε θεῶν τε: in the other fifteen, it is always preceded by πατήρ and refers to Zeus. Perhaps we see here in this rather late part of the *Odyssey* a re-working of inherited material: the fusion of ἔργ᾽ ἀνθρώπων/βρότων/ἀνδρῶν with ἀνδρῶν τε θεῶν τε.

τά τε See 52 n.

κλείουσιν ἀοιδοί The verb is from the same root as the noun κλέος ('fame'), which is ultimately about something *heard*. The bard sings and the audience listens—and is ultimately the means by which renown spreads (351 n.). Achilles is depicted singing the κλέα ἀνδρῶν (*Il.* 9.189) in a way that makes κλέος practically a synonym for heroic song.

339 τῶν ἕν γέ σφιν ἄειδε If the Muses put the bard on the path of song (*Od.* 8.73–4), one might suppose that there was little scope for the audience to dictate the topic. He will sing as his heart bids (*Od.* 8.45; cf. 1.347 n.). But Odysseus asks Demodocus to change track to the tale of the Trojan Horse (μετάβηθι; *Od.* 8.492). This must reflect the realities of performance. However much the bards stressed their divine inspiration, it is hard not to imagine any pressure to give audiences what they wanted to hear.

παρήμενος See 26 n.

οἱ δὲ σιώπῃ These very words were used only a little earlier to describe the suitors sitting in silence listening to Phemius (325 n.). Quiet attentiveness was seemingly part of the etiquette for a bardic performance. This expectation is sarcastically defeated in the next breath: if the suitors cannot be quiet for the bard, they might at least drink in silence. They soon become utterly incapable even of this (365 n.).

340 πινόντων 3 pl. pres. impv. act.

ἀποπαύε' For ἀποπαύεο, 2 sg. pres. impv. med. In a similar way, Alcinous halts the song of Demodocus after perceiving that it is making Odysseus weep (*Od.* 8.97–103).

ταύτης...ἀοιδῆς Penelope says that this ἀοιδή *always* (αἰεί, 341) causes her suffering. This suggests that she has heard it before; but Telemachus says that it is something very new (see 352 n.). The apparent paradox can be resolved if we think about the nature of epic performance. Bards working in a purely oral tradition (like Homer before the moment of monumental composition) do not produce the same fixed song for performance time and again (Lord 1960: 99–123): so ταύτης ἀοιδῆς does not mean 'this known composition' since none such exists. What is meant rather is 'cease from this act of singing (*sc.* upon which you are now engaged).' ἀοιδή can have this sense in early Greek (D'Angour 1997: 340) and most likely denotes here a broad general theme, like the οἴμη or 'path of song' (*Od.* 8.74) upon which Demodocus was engaged (Pagliaro 1961: 39; Thornton 1984: 148–9). Just as Demodocus sang of the siege of Troy, Phemius sang of the νόστος of the Achaeans. What is new is not the theme but the precise manner of its treatment. Penelope does not want to hear anything, old or new, from this repertoire because it raises anxiety about the fate of Odysseus. Σ conjectures that Penelope intervened lest Phemius sing of the death of Odysseus and so excite the suitors' hopes (cf. 325 n.). But the language used in this episode is deliberately ambiguous as to whether

Penelope or the suitors might actually believe Odysseus dead (see 342, 343 nn.).

341 λυγρῆς The adj. is related to λευγαλέος ('grievous', 'baneful'). Whilst the connexion with Lat. *lugeo, luctus* is apparent, λυγρός need not denote mourning for death. The writing sent from Proetus to the king of Lycia is described as σήματα λυγρά (*Il.* 6.168); but they brought suffering to Bellerophon, not mourning. We cannot conclude on the basis of this adj. whether the song tells of the death of Odysseus rather than just his grievous sufferings.

αἰεί See 340 n.

342 τείρει Probably cognate (*DELG* 1098) with τετραίνω ('pierce') and τιτρώσκω ('wound'); cf. Lat. *tero* ('rub', 'wear away'). This is a strong word and does not simply mean that the song 'wears her out' in a metaphorical sense. It tends to be used of a physical force operating on somebody: a foul smell (*Od.* 4.441), hunger (*Od.* 7.218), having one's eye gouged out (*Od.* 9.441), exhaustion from plying the oar (*Od.* 10.78), old age (*Od.* 24.233). The noun πένθος ('grief') is often found in association with τείρω or τείρομαι (*Od.* 7.218; 24.233). At *Od.* 2.70-1, Telemachus describes his situation in language strongly redolent of this, saying that the Ithacans must not allow him πένθεϊ λυγρῷ | τείρεσθαι ('to be worn away by baneful grief').

μάλιστα This puts beyond doubt that the song tells of Odysseus in particular, not just the Achaeans in general.

πένθος This is often grief at a death (*Il.* 17.37), but not invariably so (*Il.* 9.3). The point adds to our uncertainty as to whether the song of Phemius purported to recount the death of Odysseus (cf. 340, 343 nn.).

ἄλαστον This word appears only 6× in Homer. Three of these qualify πένθος (this instance plus *Il.* 24.105; *Od.* 24.423); one describes the related ἄχος (*Od.* 4.108). It is also used as a neut. adv. with ὀδύρομαι ('grieve'; *Od.* 14.174). The most likely sense for this curious word is 'which cannot be forgotten', a privative alpha followed by the same root as seen in ἔλαθον (252 n.). This association with misfortune explains its use as a voc. in an insult to Hector (*Il.* 22.261)—we might render it as 'accursed', but the underlying sense is that he is unforgettable because of the harm he has done.

343 κεφαλήν This figure, known as synecdoche or *pars pro toto*, is often (*Il.* 11.55; 18.114; 21.336; S. R. West 1988: 119)—but not always (*Il.* 18.82; 23.94)—used as a synonym for a dead person. In the context, one must wonder whether Penelope thinks of Odysseus as dead. Telemachus says that he has disappeared (241, 242 nn.), not that he is dead. Indeed Mentes has just given a strong indication to the contrary. Penelope does not know: she must use her wits (φρεσὶ σύνθετο, 328 n.; Halliwell 2009: 7). If she does think him dead, it is odd that she continues to express hope for his return (*Od.* 18.254). More intriguingly, the suitors cannot know the fate of Odysseus. Perhaps they want to hear a song that suggests that he is dead; it might endear Phemius to them if he sings such. But equally there is dramatic irony because the audience knows better (Thomas 2014: 97 n. 32).

πoθέω Etymologically, the word goes back to a root *$g^wh^e/_odh$– (*DELG* 922; Rix 2001: 217) meaning 'ask for' or 'pray for'; cf. θέσσασθαι (Hes. fr. 231 MW). As early as Hesiod (*Sc.* 41) πoθέω and πόθος can have an erotic sense. The same is true in later Greek. We might expect something of the kind in the present context; but in Homer πoθέω has no such necessary connotation (Kloss 1994: 66–77). It may denote simple feelings of loss: troops that lack their leader (*Il.* 2.703), horses that lack their charioteers (*Il.* 11.161), a fish that is out of water (*Od.* 22.387), or the more affective sense of missing someone or something that has been a constant companion (*Il.* 24.6; *Od.* 9.452–3). It is striking by contrast that Odysseus' longing to die if he cannot return to Ithaca is described in a much more sexualized language (59 n.).

344 ἀνδρός Depends on μεμνημένη in the previous line and not on κεφαλήν. ἀνήρ may mean man as opposed to woman (*Il.* 17.435), man as opposed to a god (*Il.* 1.544), or (here) man as husband (*Il.* 19.291; *Od.* 24.196). The word gains emphasis from being enjambed and coming before a slight pause in sense before the rel. clause begins.

κλέος εὐρύ This looks like the sort of expression that ought to be part of the Indo-European poetic repertoire; but there is in Vedic no attested phrase that exhibits a precise etymological correspondence. The personal name *Uruśravas* ('wide glory') is found in the Purāṇas, and the expression *urugāyám…śrávas* ('wide-going glory') occurs in the Rig Veda (*RV* 6.65.6). We might assume that these and κλεὸς εὐρύ sprang from a common source. Vedic *urú*– was lexically replaced quite early by *pṛthú*– ('wide'; cf. Gk. πλατύς): the expression *pṛthú śrávas* is already found in the Vedas (*RV* 1.9.7). We can thus be confident that the general idea was part of the common inherited Indo-European tradition (M. L. West 2007: 78–9, 407).

κάθ' Ἑλλάδα καὶ μέσον Ἄργος In the *Iliad*, Ἕλλας narrowly denotes the domain of Peleus in Southern Thessaly (cf. Thuc. 1.3). By contrast, Hesiod (*Op.* 653) uses the word to denote Greece in general. Ἄργος is a place in the Peloponnese but it appears here to stand for the whole of the Peloponnese. This expression is apparently meant compendiously for the whole country, north and south. Aristarchus athetized the line on the ground that the usage is not Homeric. It is perhaps not Iliadic, but it need not be out of place in a late part of the *Odyssey*. If the line were deleted, it would leave μεμνημένη without an object. That would be unusual: of the eleven attestations of the ptcp. in Homer, only that at *Od.* 4.151 lacks a direct object.

346 ταρ αὖ MSS give τ' ἄρ αὖ. Most editors since Wolf have printed τ' ἄρα, except for West who has ταρ αὖ. The objection to τ' ἄρ(α) is that τε does not belong in questions (M. L. West 1998a: xxix). Watkins (1995: 150–1) points to a Luwian emphatic particle *tar* that has some affinity for the interrogative pronoun. A freestanding Greek particle ταρ is mentioned by Herodian (*Gr.* 2.22) and attested by Venetus A (*Il.* 1.8; 2.761); it has nothing to do with τ' ἄρ. For the following αὖ, cf. *Od.* 23.264. See also 225 n.

μῆτερ ἐμή That Telemachus should address Penelope as μῆτερ is unremarkable; the force of the possessive adj. is harder to determine. It is strictly speaking unnecessary, unlike examples in the acc. where it indicates whose mother is referred to (e.g. *Od.* 1.248; 15.522; 16.125). Telemachus addresses his mother as μῆτερ ἐμή 6× and only once as just μῆτερ. There need be no special socio-linguistic significance in this. The possessive adj. need be no more than a slightly ornamental turn, such as Fr. *ma mère* or Eng. *brother mine*.

ἐρίηρον This term is probably to be analysed as a compound of the intensifying prefix ἐρι- (cf. ἐριαύχην 'long-necked', ἐρίγδουπος 'loud-thundering') and the root otherwise seen in the word ἦρα, which is probably cognate with Hitt. *warr(a)-* ('help'; Melchert 1984: 11 n. 7). This would fit with the phrase ἐπὶ ἦρα φέρων, where it appears to mean something like 'doing service' (*Il.* 1.572; 14.132; Pulleyn 2000: 266). If this is correct, then the compound ἐρίηρος probably meant originally something like 'helpful'. Used of comrades and bards, it probably denotes something like 'faithful' or 'trusty' in the sense of a person who always helps and does not let one down.

347 τέρπειν Telemachus' tone is oddly detached (cf. 354 n.) and authoritative, in marked contrast to Penelope's emotional reaction: the young man is to some extent able to step back from the particular and make general judgements about art and life (Peponi 2012: 37). He has just had some reassurance that his father will be returning to Ithaca and so might well relish the discomfort that the song will cause to the suitors who do not know whether Odysseus is alive or dead (cf. 340, 342, 343 nn.).

ὅππῃ οἱ νοῦς ὄρνυται A very similar expression is used of Demodocus (*Od.* 8.45) who is said to delight his hearers ὅππῃ θυμὸς ἐποτρύνῃσιν ἀείδειν ('in whichever way his spirit urges him to sing'). The difference between the two is what impels the bard to sing: with Phemius it is his *νοῦς*, with Demodocus his *θυμός*. We tend to think of the former as relating to reasoning and the latter to passion, but there is no such absolute distinction in practice (294 n.). It is also noteworthy that, whilst we are told that it is the Muse that impelled Demodocus to sing of a particular episode (*Od.* 8.73–4), both he and Phemius are also said to be motivated by forces interior to themselves. We may suppose that Phemius is likewise divinely inspired (cf. *θέσπιν* 328 n.). Perhaps in poetry, as in other fields of activity, divine motivation operated simultaneously with human to produce 'over determination' of actions (Dodds 1951: 16, 26 n. 101; cf. *Il.* 16.849–50).

347–8 οὔ νύ τ᾽ ἀοιδοί | αἴτιοι, ἀλλά ποθι Ζεὺς αἴτιος These words echo the famous 'apology' of Agamemnon in the *Iliad* who blamed Zeus and Fate and the Erinys for his conduct (*Il.* 19.86–7) but acknowledged his own guilt as well (*Il.* 19.137–8). Plainly the bard cannot be blamed for causing the ills of which he sings; Penelope's complaint relates to the choice of so painful a theme. But perhaps Penelope is just closing her ears to the truth of the human condition. In the *Iliad* Helen says that Zeus gives men an evil fate precisely so that they may be the subject of song for future generations (*ἀοίδιμοι ἐσσομένοισι*, *Il.* 6.357–8). That tragic outlook is not altogether alien to the *Odyssey*: see next n. and 353 n.

348–9 ὅς τε δίδωσιν | ὅπως ἐθέλησι It is not said that ill fortune is the only kind that Zeus dispenses; but plainly this is part of his dispensation and will. This recalls the memorable passage in the *Iliad* where Achilles tells Priam (*Il.* 24.526–33) that Zeus keeps two jars, one full of good things and one of bad. Nobody receives unalloyed good fortune: the best one may hope for is an unpredictable mixture of good and bad, whereas some people receive only woe. Helen likewise says that Zeus deliberately gives an evil fate to men (see foreg. n.). It has been said that the *Odyssey* has a moralizing strain and a happy ending that differ markedly from the tragic outlook of the *Iliad* (Lloyd-Jones 1983: 31). Zeus may declare that humans suffer by their own fault (*Od.* 1.32 n.), but Telemachus' remark here recalls the more ambiguous theodicy of the *Iliad*. What Zeus wants (*ἐθέλησι*) is left inscrutable in a way that echoes the *Διὸς βουλή* ('will of Zeus') of the *Iliad* (1.5).

349 ἀλφηστῇσιν This peculiar word was explained in antiquity as meaning 'energetic', 'go-getting', and was taken to be derived from the same root as *ἀλφάνω*, *ἀλφεῖν* ('get') and a suffix allegedly seen in *τευχ–ηστής* ('armed') and *ἑρπ–ηστής* ('creeping'). But that is doubtful on formal grounds (Fraenkel 1910: I 38 n. 2). The suffix probably arose by false segmentation of *ὠμηστής* ('eating raw flesh'), which word surely points to the correct etymology. Rather than being a simply agential ending, -ησ-τής means 'eater', being a compound of the full grade of the root *H₁d- ('eat'; Rix 2001: 230–1) and the common agential suffix -τής. The change of δ to σ before τ is regular (Sihler 1995: 202). The first element would appear to be ἀλφός ('white': cf. Hes. fr. 133.4 MW; Lat. *albus*) rather than ἄλφι ('barley groats') since the loss of iota in such a compound would be without parallel. But the two words are surely related, cf. λευκ' ἄλφιτα (*Il.* 18.560; *DELG* 67). The compound thus describes men who eat grain and corresponds to the *hapax* σιτόφαγος (*Od.* 9.191) which distinguishes humans from the monstrous Cyclops. Here the contrast is with gods, whose food is more rarefied than mere bread (cf. 25 n.).

350 νέμεσις See 119, 228 nn.

Δαναῶν In the *Iliad*, the Achaeans are the inhabitants of Achaea and the Hellenes come from Hellas: neither term is a simple description for the entire Greek host (but see 344 n.). There is, however, no toponym to which Δαναοί can plausibly be made to correspond (cf. 344 n.). The name suggests rather a descent from the mythical king Danaus who was believed to have taken refuge in Argos with his daughters the Danaids. The Δαναοί are likely the same as the Danaja who appear in documents from Egypt from around the fifteenth century BC (Latacz 2004: 128–36). Homer uses Δαναοί much less often (155×) than Ἀργεῖοι (612×). This might be because it lacked geographical certainty and so was not felt to be a useful identifier for the Greek host; alternatively, or in addition, it reflects metrical convenience (Adam Parry 1971: 100).

οἶτον This word frequently appears in the formula κακὸν οἶτον and reflects an inherent pessimism about the human condition and divine justice (cf. 32, 348–9 nn.). The attempt (Beekes 1969b: 128) to link οἶτος with αἶσα ('portion') as both derived from a root *H₂it- founders on the lack of attestation of such a root. οἶτος was once compared with an alleged Avestan *aeta* ('debt', 'punishment'; Bartholomae 1901: 136–41); but *aeta* has been shown to be a figment (Fischer and Ritter 1991). The best analysis sees in οἶτος an o-grade of the root seen in Gk. εἶμι ('I shall go') with a -to-suffix (Brugmann 1916–17: 244). The pair εἶμι: οἶτος is formally and semantically parallel to Gk. φέρω: φόρτος. Just as φόρτος is 'that which one carries', so οἶτος is 'that which one goes (i.e. the way)'. The thought is of a person's movement along a path towards destiny.

351 ἀοιδήν See 340, 352 nn.

ἐπικλείουσι See 338 n. (κλείουσιν).

352 ἀκουόντεσσι Masc. dat. pl. pres. ptcp. act. In Attic participial *-ont-* + dat. *-si-* > *-onssi* > *-onsi* > -ονσι > -ουσι (Sihler 1995: 71–2, 204). In epic, an Aeolic ending -εσσι (Morpurgo Davies 1976) has been added so that there is no contact between -ντ- and -σ- and thus no triggering of the kind of changes seen in Attic. Plato (*R.* 424 bc) cites a variant ἀειδόντεσσι which, we might suppose, was a self-serving invention of the rhapsodes of his day to focus on the singer rather than the song. See next n.

νεωτάτη Phemius' song is not new in the sense of a freshly minted, discrete composition that nobody has heard before. Archaic epic song was not like that. What is indicated by ἀοιδή is a general theme or 'path of song' (340 n.). What is novel is Phemius' choice of (and/or approach to) the Ἀχαιῶν νόστον (326) as a broad topic. He has pursued it before— Penelope says that his singing *always* causes her suffering (αἰεί, 341 n.)— but it is νεωτάτη in the sense that people are still saying something like, 'Have you heard that Phemius is doing something different? It's not about what happened at Troy, it's about what happened to our people on the way home'.

ἀμφιπέληται The simple verb πέλομαι often means little more than 'to be' or 'to become' (Neuberger–Donath 1980). But this compound with ἀμφι- tends to suggest motion. The root is *$*k^welH_1$- (Rix 2001: 386–8) whose basic sense is 'turn' or 'go about'; cf. κύκλος (*DELG* 597, 878). The meaning here is likely to be 'circulate' or 'do the rounds' (Dietz 2000: 97). The notion of epic song being diffused in this way is linked with the idea of the spread of a singer's renown: the prefix in περικλυτός (325 n.) and περίφρων (329 n.) has a similar function to ἀμφι- here.

353 ἐπιτολμάτω The PIE *$*telH_2$- (Rix 2001 622–3) probably had the basic sense of 'to take upon oneself' (*DELG* 1088); cf. Gk. τλῆναι, Lat. *tollo*. In one sense, τολμάω means 'endure'; in another, perhaps by way of 'bring oneself to', it means 'dare'. The former is meant here: by enduring listening to tragic song, Penelope will learn what the world is like and the position of humankind within it (Griffin 1980: 143). Cf. 347–8 n.

κραδίη καὶ θυμός See 316 n.

354 Ὀδυσσεύς This is the first time in the poem that Telemachus uses his father's name. During his meeting with Mentes it was striking how Telemachus went to some lengths precisely to avoid using this name (163 n.). Athena-Mentes, by contrast, mentioned it half a dozen times (196 n., 207, 212, 253, 260, 265). That contrast was plainly not accidental. It is a mark of the psychological subtlety of the poet that we now see how Telemachus has been emboldened by the example of his divine visitor to utter Odysseus' name and thereby declare a new closeness to his father.

οἶος Given his recent conversation with Mentes, we might assume that Telemachus is cool about his father's fate. But rather he is standing back from the position of his one family to evaluate their situation as part of the overall sweep of human suffering; this recalls the words of Achilles to Priam in the last book of the *Iliad* (Macleod 1982: 131–2). Certainly Telemachus is finding a new and authoritative voice; having glimpsed the larger picture from Mentes and from Phemius' song, he is keen to impress his newfound insight and maturity upon his mother (cf. 359 n.).

354 νόστιμον ἦμαρ See 9 n.

355 φῶτες Telemachus was described earlier as an ἰσόθεος φώς (324 n.), using a formula rare and unique to him in the *Odyssey* but which commonly denotes in the *Iliad* the vital élan of a warrior in motion. Without the epithet, as here, the word is more or less equivalent to ἀνήρ (*Il.* 17.377–8; *Od.* 8.159; 20.227).

356–9 Σ tells us that Aristarchus athetized these as unsuitable. They recur later in the epic with one small but very significant modification when Telemachus tells his mother that she ought to return to her weaving whilst the men attend to archery (*Od.* 21.350–3). Hector uses practically identical words to Andromache (*Il.* 6.490–3), telling her that the menfolk will attend to the fighting. Such close and, we may presume, deliberate imitation of the *Iliad* invites comparison and contrast. In the mouth of Hector we might detect not so much the tetchy tone of an eager warrior irked by his fussing wife as a subtle and tender attempt to reassure her that all will be well if she returns to her natural sphere of activity and he to his. In the case of Telemachus, it seems odd to speak to Penelope like this. Whatever their status at other times and places, aristocratic women in the *Odyssey* are not excluded from the sphere of men. Helen (*Od.* 4.121–46) and Arete (*Od.* 7.141–52) are fully involved in the public discourse and doings of their respective houses. Some are tempted to see these lines as an interpolation (S. R. West 1988: 120). But there is both psychological credibility and dramatic pathos in the presentation of the adolescent puppy testing the extent of his powers.

356 οἶκον This word, which normally denotes an entire house, is used along with δόμος (330 n.) as a synonym for ὑπερῷα (328 n., 362).

  ἰοῦσα The action of the ptcp. presumably precedes the action of the main verb. But the use of the pres. is not a problem since it indicates not time relative to the main verb but the duration of the act of going (122, 336, 372 nn.; cf. *Od.* 17.45). At Hdt. 3.38.13, Darius asks who would be willing τοὺς πατέρας ἀποθνῄσκοντας κατασιτέεσθαι. He is plainly not suggesting that fathers be eaten whilst in the actual process of dying (cf. Hdt. 2.41.11; 4.190.1).

τὰ σ' αὐτῆς = τὰ σά αὐτῆς. Whilst σά by itself would have been enough to denote a possessive, the gen. αὐτῆς reinforces the sense ('your own'). Cf. 7 n.; *Od.* 2.45 (Chantraine 1953: 158).

ἔργα The content of this '(sc. women's) work' is explained in the next line—weaving. But the idea is so deeply ingrained that it scarcely needs to be spelt out (357 n.).

κόμιζε The sense of 'carry' that is familiar from classical Greek is a later development. The original connotation of words of this family (cf. κομέω, κάμνω) was 'attend to', 'take care of' (*DELG* 560).

357 ἱστόν This name for the loom also denotes the mast of a ship. The root is the same as in ἵστημι—'that which stands'. Weaving was quintessentially an activity for women. An early indication comes from Linear B tablets from Pylos, where the women undertake the weaving and the men the fulling and finishing of the cloth (Morpurgo Davies 1979: 100 n. 46). It occupies not only servants (*Il.* 1.31) but women of high rank: we thus find it occupying Penelope (*Od.* 2.94; 17.97), Helen (*Od.* 4.130–1), Arete (*Od.* 6.306), and Andromache (*Il.* 22.440). The stereotype is so potent that it extends to the goddesses Calypso (*Od.* 5.62) and Circe (*Od.* 10.222). The occupation plainly involves some status, since weaving is a common metaphor in many Indo-European languages for the skilled business of poetical production by men (M. L. West 2007: 36–8).

ἠλακάτην This word of uncertain etymology refers to the distaff. There are no convincing cognates in other PIE languages. The Mycenaean *a-ra-ka-te-ja* (= *ālakateiai*, 'distaff women' (Chadwick and Baumbach 1963: 200)) shows only that the word is old within Greek.

358 ἐποίχεσθαι Although some instances of this verb have a warlike connotation (see 324 n.), this tends to apply to the specific form ἐπῴχετο in the *Iliad*; in other forms, and in the *Odyssey* in general, it has a more ordinary meaning of 'to go about'.

μῦθος See 28 n.

359 πᾶσι, μάλιστα δ' ἐμοί cf. *Od.* 21.353. These words are found at *Il.* 6.493 in the mouth of Hector, where they are as apposite as here they are jarring. At *Od.* 11.353, the claim to power sits rather better. M. L. West (2014: 151 n. 17) suspects a concordance interpolation; but the line is in all surviving MSS and likely reflects a very early written archetype. See also 373 n.

τοῦ This is a demonstrative pron. referring back to ἐμοί. Telemachus is referring to himself. In Attic tragedy, the equivalent expression would be ἀνδρὸς τοῦδε (Soph. *Ant.* 1034, *Tr.* 1113; Eur. *Hel.* 551).

κράτος Although this word etymologically belongs with Eng. *hard*, it would seem that a more 'soft' domestic power is referred to here. κράτος in Homer basically denotes superiority; whether that is physical or political depends on the context (Breuil 1989). Cf. 70, 71 nn.

360–4 Penelope's first appearance was brief but dramatic. This section takes her back upstairs so that the audience's attention may turn to Telemachus and the suitors. Visually there is a sort of ring composition, with Penelope disappearing back whence she came.

360 θαμβήσασα See 323 n.

οἶκόνδε See 356 n.

βεβήκει This is an (unaugmented) pluperf. The perf. denotes a state, not 'she went' but 'she is gone'; the pluperf. is the same idea projected one step into the past: 'she was gone'. Used as it is here, it portrays the action as having been accomplished almost at once (Chantraine 1953: 199–200; Pulleyn 2000: 187).

361 πεπνυμένον See 230 n. It would appear that Telemachus' words were taken to heart by his mother, whatever their apparent oddity to us (356–9 n.).

ἔνθετο The med. of τίθημι with θυμῷ is uncommon but usually indicates the storing up of anger or resentment (*Il.* 6.326; *Od.* 11.102; 13.342; 24.248). The expression with μῦθον is even less common, but recurs exactly at *Od.* 21.355.

362 This reverses the action of 330 (see n.).

363 κλαῖεν See 336 n.

φίλον Surely her 'dear' husband rather than her 'own' husband; see 60 n.

364 ἡδύν Sleep is 'sweet' and is elsewhere described as γλυκερός (*Il.* 24.636), μελιηδής (*Od.* 19.551), and μελίφρων (*Il.* 2.34). Wine is likewise described as ἡδύς (*Od.* 2.350), γλυκερός (*Od.* 14.194), μελιηδής (*Od.* 3.46), and μελίφρων (*Il.* 6.264). That the pleasures of sleep and wine should be reflected in shared epithets is scarcely surprising—wine leads to sleep and brings forgetfulness (cf. Eur. *Ba.* 282). Sleep is said to be not only most sweet but also most like death (*Od.* 13.80); but death itself is never described as sweet in Homer (contrast Hor. *Carm.* 3.2.13; Ach. Tat. 3.22.1).

βάλε This formula recurs three times (*Od.* 16.451; 19.604; 23.462). The verb might at first blush seem out of keeping with a sleep that has just been described as sweet. Elsewhere χέω is used of pouring sweet sleep (*Od.* 2.395). But βάλλω describes letting fall a tear (*Od.* 4.198) or a poppy letting its head droop (*Il.* 8.306). The word plainly has a broader semantic range than 'throw' or 'hit' and extends to 'shed' or 'let fall'. Cf. 201, 438 nn.

γλαυκῶπις See 44 n.

365–416 With his mother returned to her quarters and asleep, Telemachus turns his attention to the suitors. Later on, he and his father will kill the suitors whilst she is likewise asleep (*Od.* 23.5–9). We perceive at once from the manner of his speech and the reaction of the other characters that his meeting with Mentes has boosted his confidence. He also lays the ground for the assembly that follows the next morning. The exchanges with the suitors show something of the individuation of their character and of the political situation on Ithaca.

365 ὁμάδησαν The suitors were initially noisy but in the ordered way of song (152); then they listened in silence to Phemius (325); now their attention span has been exhausted and they turn instead to the disordered noise denoted by this verb. Cf. 369.

σκιόεντα It has been argued (Bremer 1976: 87 n. 110) that this word means 'dark' rather than 'shadowy' because it is used of clouds (*Il.* 5.525). But a cloud gives rise to shadow, albeit not well defined, when it moves athwart the sun. The image is surely of darting shadows cast in the light of the flickering oil lamps (cf. *Od.* 18.307–10). The noun σκία, Ionic σκίη, combined with the adjectival suffix -ϝεισ-, ought to yield *σκιήεις not σκιόεις. The latter was likely the result of metrical adaptation by analogy with σκιόωντο to make it fit more places in the hexameter (Debrunner 1923: 28–30; Chantraine 1958: 75–6).

366 ἠρήσαντο It is conceivable that the suitors are engaged in the unusual act of silent prayer (*Il.* 23.769; *Od.* 5.444; Pulleyn 1997: 184–8), but that seems unlikely in this context. More probably this is a metaphorical usage, an emphatic way of saying 'very much wanted to'.

παραί An epic form of παρά. When used with a dat., the preposition παρά usually denotes 'beside' or 'next to' (e.g. *Il.* 1.358; *Il.* 2.775; Chantraine 1953: 121). But it is not the bed that the suitors want to lie next to but Penelope. So παραί must be a preverb in tmesis with κλιθῆναι; the following dat. denotes place.

ἤρχετο μύθων For the thought, one might compare μύθων ἦρχε (28)—a common formula in Homer to denote beginning a speech. The use of the med., as here, is much rarer (5× *Od.*; never *Il.*). Apart from Telemachus, it is used twice of Arete (*Od.* 7.233; 11.335) and once of Nestor (*Od.* 15.166).

368 μητρὸς ἐμῆς Telemachus' last speech was addressed to his mother; this one is about his mother. Here the possessive adj. is not redundant; contrast 346 n.

μνηστῆρες There is a verbal jingle here with the preceding μητρὸς ἐμῆς.

ὑπέρβιον This compound adj. denotes βίη ('strength') that is beyond the usual (ὑπερ-). The sense is pejorative (e.g. 'violent'), as when applied to Achilles' θυμός (*Il.* 18.262), which Polydamas fears will make him leave the fighting in the plain of Troy and attack the city itself.

ὕβριν In Homer, this is probably a morally neutral term referring to exuberant physical strength (227 n.); words of this family thus often have a qualifier to denote how they are to be taken.

369 δαινύμενοι τερπώμεθα The meal, apparently over at 150 (n.), is now to be resumed as though it had somehow only been interrupted by the suitors' song and dance and their listening to Phemius.

βοητύς A unique form in Greek, an epic coinage on the model of the common ἐδητύς. These words, whilst not *hapaxes*, are nevertheless not part of the formulaic repertoire of the epics; probably this novel ending had to be contrived to fit an otherwise unique line. On noise and shouting, cf. 365, 378 nn.

370–1 Probably a stock description of a bard; cf. *Od.* 9.3–4. It is also used of the herald Talthybius (*Il.* 19.250).

371 θεοῖς ἐναλίγκιος Although followed here by an acc. of respect, θεοῖς ἐναλίγκιος is also found alone (*Od.* 19.267) as a virtual synonym for θεῖος ('godlike'). Phemius does not have a voice *like that* of a god; rather he is *like a god*—i.e. excellent—on account of his voice. Fine voice is not a generalized attribute of divinity in Homer. Some goddesses sing ὀπὶ κάλῃ ('in a beautiful voice'): the Muses (*Il.* 1.604; *Od.* 24.60), Circe (*Od.* 10.221), and Calypso (*Od.* 5.61). But θεοῖς must denote the gods as a whole, not just a subset of minor ones. Several Homeric expressions equate heroes with gods (Griffin 1980: 81–102). This is especially common in battle (e.g. δαίμονι ἶσος, *Il.* 5.438; ἀντίθεος, *Il.* 16.321)—and not because all gods are warriors but because all gods are excellent and some humans approach that when in battle. So it is with a bard when he exercises his skill.

αὐδήν There are other words for voice in Homer. Those of the root *ὄψ are used (in the sg. only) of deities (*Il.* 2.182), animals (*Il.* 3.152), and humans (*Od.* 3.221). φωνή has the same range of application (*Il.* 13.45; *Od.* 10.239; *Il.* 3.161). ὄσσα has a specialized meaning of 'rumour' (282 n.). αὐδή alone is confined to the human voice. But there is a puzzle in the related adj. αὐδήεσσα used of Circe (*Od.* 11.8) and Calypso (*Od.* 12.449). This cannot really mean that they speak the language of humans as well as gods (*pace DELG* 137); other gods do this, but are not so described. If αὐδήεσσα connotes a beautiful singing voice (*Od.* 5.61; 10.221), it is not clear why it is found together with δεινή. Perhaps this combination involves a glance at some magical use of the voice for spells (cf. Old Church Slavonic *vada* = 'calumny'). This would fit with the idea of poetry being connected with incantation (328 n.; cf. Hes. fr. 310 MW; Fournier 1946: 229), but not with the use of αὐδή for the ordinary human voice (e.g. *Il.* 13.757). Perhaps αὐδή began with a specialized, quasi-magical meaning but then became more general in application.

372 ἠῶθεν The suffix –θεν is freely added to nouns to form a sort of ablative denoting motion away from something or somewhere (Chantraine 1958: 242). We naturally say 'at dawn'; the literal thought is presumably, '*From the instant* it gets light, we must be ready to go…'.

ἀγορήνδε The suffix –δε denotes motion towards something. In the overwhelming majority of cases (Chantraine 1958: 247), it denotes a concrete location or thing so that Telemachus most likely means 'to the place of assembly'. But more abstract expressions such as βουλυτόνδε ('towards the time for unyoking oxen; *Od.* 9.58) mean that we cannot entirely exclude the sense 'to a gathering'.

κίοντες The action of going is prior to that of sitting down. The pres. ptcp. here does not denote time but aspect: Telemachus is thinking of the unfolding in time of the act of going to the assembly (cf. 356 n.).

373 πάντες Cf. πᾶσι (359). In both occurrences, the word gains emphasis from being in first position after a run-over. Telemachus declared at 359 that *all* the men would attend to μῦθος whilst Penelope took herself off to her weaving. This is the kind of μῦθος he had in mind.

ὔμιν so accented when unemphatic (Probert 2003: 150–1).

ἀπηλεγέως This would appear (Szemerényi 1964: 160) to be a compound where ἀλέγω ('to concern oneself with') is negated with the prefix ἀπ– to denote an idea such as 'bluntly'. The lengthening of the second syllable is quite regular at the point of junction in Greek compounds (cf. γαμψῶνυξ < ὄνυξ).

374 ἐξιέναι In all likelihood this inf. is epexegetic, explaining the content of μῦθον (373). Alternatively, but much less likely, it could be imperatival (291 n.).

ἀλεγύνετε This is an extended form of ἀλέγω (cf. 373 n.). The choice of word is prompted by the related ἀπηλεγέως in the preceding line. The change of syntax is sharp if the preceding inf. is imperatival.

δαῖτας Telemachus' preoccupation with food (cf. 160) might seem rather comical when his whole inheritance is at stake. But in an archaic society food animals were a significant part of a person's wealth (M. I. Finley 1977: 67), even if one also had precious metals and other goods stored up as treasure (*Od.* 4.71–5). The suitors are killing these animals at their pleasure (108 n.) and so bringing ruin upon the house (*Od.* 17.534–8). Presumably they were not attending to their replacement by breeding or purchase.

375 ἀμειβόμενοι This image of the suitors making a kind of medieval progress from one house to the next, exhausting the resources of each in turn, is just wishful thinking and a bitter joke. It is more likely that the young men would stay in their own houses (*Od.* 16.390–3; cf. 1.250–1 n.). In any event, that would be better than the current situation.

376 λωΐτερον A comparative whose positive form does not exist: λώϊον (*Od.* 17.417) is itself comparative (Leumann 1959: 220–1), perhaps built to the root of the verb λῆν ('want'; Theoc. 5.77). Its use beside ἄμεινον is pleonastic.

377 ἀνδρὸς ἑνός Is this Telemachus or his father? In favour of the former is that Telemachus has already referred to himself as an ἀνήρ (*Od.* 1.358–9) and to the suitors as eating him personally out of house and home (*Od.* 1.250–1). On the other hand, he has also spoken of them as consuming the livelihood of a man (ἀνέρος, *Od.* 1.160–1) whose white bones were rotting on the seashore, by which he meant Odysseus. See next n.

   νήποινον This was the word that Telemachus used (*Od.* 1.160) to describe how the suitors were consuming the livelihood of Odysseus. Its appearance here is surely a deliberate echo. It also suggests that ἀνδρὸς ἑνός (foreg. n.) refers to Odysseus rather than himself. See also 380 n.

378 κείρετ᾽ A word whose root meaning is 'cut' is being used in an extended sense to mean 'devour'. We may detect the bridge between the senses in those passages where the verb is used of non-human animals greedily 'tearing into' crops or flesh: *Il.* 11.560 (a donkey), *Il.* 21.204 (fish), *Od.* 11.578 (vultures). The suitors are being described as animals.

   ἐπιβώσομαι Telemachus has already told the suitors not to shout (369 n.). His shout, unlike theirs, would come not from drunken excess but as a call for the gods to come to his aid. In later Greek, the βοή ('shout') denotes the hue and cry that was raised for public help (Aesch. *Ag.* 1349). βοηθέω ('help') presumably meant originally to come in response to a cry for help. The verbal form here is hypercontracted; Attic would have ἐπιβοήσομαι.

   αἰὲν ἐόντας The deathlessness of the gods is a fundamental characteristic that distinguishes them from humans and is often stressed in the epics (e.g. *Il.* 5.339–42). This formula could mean that their existence was as boundless in the past as it will be in the future; but that idea is absent from archaic and classical Greek religion, which gives definite moments of birth to its various gods.

379 αἴ Epic for εἰ.
   κέ The subj. may be used with or without this modal particle (e.g. *Il.* 9.117; *Od.* 14.85–6) but more commonly with it (Chantraine 1953: 245).

The particle can mark an idea as potential, counterfactual, or habitual (Colvin 2016: 65 n. 1). Here we are dealing with potentiality: 'if perhaps Zeus will grant…'.

Ζεύς Although the appeal was to the gods as a group, the thought changes to Zeus specifically giving redress. The link between Zeus and justice is explicit in the *Odyssey* (22–95, 32 nn.) but not new to it. Already in the *Iliad*, he is appealed to as enforcer of oaths (*Il.* 3.276; 19.258) and is said to care for the treatment of strangers (*Il.* 13.625) and the public administration of justice (*Il.* 16.384–8 with Janko 1992: 365–6). In the *Odyssey* he has a special concern for beggars, strangers, suppliants (*Od.* 6.207–8; 9.270–1; 14.57–8). It is likely that Telemachus thinks of Zeus as punishing the suitors' breach of hospitality rather than intervening in a general capacity as a universal regulator of human conduct.

δῶσι For this spelling, see 167 n.

παλίντιτα This rare word (3× Hom.) looks like a pass. in -τος derived from the verb τίνω. If so, the sense is 'if Zeus grants that *your* deeds meet with requital'. But related formulae at *Il.* 24.213–14 (ἄντιτα ἔργα γένοιτο | παιδὸς ἐμοῦ) and *Od.* 17.51 (αἴ κέ ποθι Ζεὺς ἄντιτα ἔργα τελέσσῃ) tell against this, as does Empedocles' use of παλίντιτα in an active sense (31 B 111.5 DK) to mean 'making requital'. The meaning here is thus 'if Zeus grants deeds of requital (*sc.* to me)'. The idea of τίσις was mentioned in the significant context of the vengeance of Orestes on Aegisthus (40 n.) and Mentes explicitly used this story to motivate Telemachus (298 n.).

380 νήποινοι This word has appeared before (160, 377 nn.) to mean that the suitors were acting without anyone taking vengeance *on* them. Here the sense is that the suitors will die without anyone taking vengeance *for* them. The ironic reversal is palpable. It has been said that oral poetry operates at the level of the formula or line and does not deal in fine ironies at the level of the individual word (Adam Parry 1971: xxiv–xxvi, repr. 1989: 216–18). The placement and use of these words suggests otherwise.

381 ὀδάξ It has been suggested (Heubeck 1971) that this is a compound of an Aeolic ὀ- (said to mean 'together'; < PIE *sm-) and δάκνω ('to bite'). But there is no convincing parallel for ὀ- meaning 'together' in quite this sense (Szemerényi 1972: 88). It seems more likely that ὀδάξ derives from *ὀδάσσι, the conjectured proto-Gk. dat. pl. of ὀδών ('tooth'), remodelled in the same way as γνύξ beside *γνύσι: γόνυ (Szemerényi 1967: 24). The dat. would be instrumental in sense ('with the teeth').

ἐν One cannot tell whether this simply goes with the following dat. or is a preverb in tmesis with φύντες (cf. ἐμπεφύασι: *Il.* 8.84). The first construction is not to be ruled out merely because it is the simpler (cf. *Od.* 10.397).

φύντες This difficult expression is made no easier to interpret by the use of a verb which, in the strong aor., is always intransitive in Homer and generally means 'grew'. The weak aor. means 'plant' (*Od.* 22.348) as does the extended form φυτεύω (*Od.* 5.340). It has been suggested that the strong aor. could also have this transitive sense, so that the expression would mean literally 'planting in their lips with their teeth' (Burger 1925: 3). But such a usage is without parallel in Homer; it would be as surprising as a transitive instance of the strong aor. of ἵστημι. The related expression ἔν...οἱ φῦ χειρί (e.g. *Il.* 6.253) denotes taking the hand, the literal sense presumably being 'grew into him with her hand'. χειρί here is probably instrumental (*pace* Garvie 1994: 299) and ἐν can denote movement into a space (Chantraine 1953: 101–2). By analogy, the current expression must mean 'growing into their lips with their teeth'. We would say that they 'bit their lips'. The thought presumably involves some transference: the teeth grow more prominent, not the suitors.

382 θαύμαζον This verb, denoting astonishment, has a marked affinity for visual spectacle (Mette 1960). Its use here for a primarily aural phenomenon must be a later development. Cf. 323 n.

ὅ This neut. rel. pron. is used to mean 'because' in the same way as Lat. *quod* (Chantraine 1953: 285).

383–411 In reply to these bold words of Telemachus, the two leading suitors Antinous and Eurymachus (cf. *Od.* 4.629) challenge him. Antinous attempts simply to belittle him and so neutralize his attempts to assert authority over the house. Eurymachus adopts a more cautious and perhaps conciliatory tone.

383 Ἀντίνοος...Εὐπείθεος These are speaking names (cf. 14, 71, 154, 180, 259 nn.). Real people did not typically have names of this kind. We may take the son's name to mean 'Contrary-minded'. The father is presumably 'Good-at-persuading', although the advice that he gives is not so good (*Od.* 24.422, 465, 469). Antinous and Eurymachus are the most prominent suitors and are described as the leaders (*Od.* 4.629).

384 διδάσκουσιν θεοί This jibe is truer than Antinous knows since Athena is the proximate cause of Telemachus' new confidence. We see, not for the first time (cf. 343 n.), how dramatic irony operates against the suitors in the poem.

385 ὑψαγόρην This word is found only in the mouth of Antinous to describe Telemachus (*Od.* 2.85, 303; 17.406). Telemachus makes reasonable points; but Antinous cannot really counter these and so has to mock the speaker instead. Thersites in the *Iliad* likewise makes telling points in his

speech to Agamemnon (*Il.* 2.225–42) and is roundly abused by Odysseus (*Il.* 2.246–64). But that is a different world—and Thersites is a low character, not a real hero, and the poet exceptionally tells us in his own voice that he is an unattractive figure whose speech is a breach of good order that makes him hated by all (*Il.* 2.212–23).

386 βασιλῆα Antinous takes the implications of Telemachus' speech to go beyond a criticism of the suitors' conspicuous consumption. For him, the true question is who shall be βασιλεύς. The word does not mean 'monarch' in Homer: Telemachus himself tells us that there are other βασιλῆες in Ithaca (394). It means something like 'chief' or 'headman'. Zeus is an undoubted sovereign (*Il.* 8.17–27), but is never described as βασιλεύς in Homer, only as ἄναξ. Agamemnon is described both as ἄναξ (*Il.* 1.7; 2.441) and as βασιλεύς (*Il.* 1.231, 279); but there are other ἄνακτες (*Il.* 2.405, 777) and βασιλῆες (*Il.* 2.445). In Mycenaean times, there appears to have been one *wa–na–ka* = ἄναξ (Chadwick and Baumbach 1963: 172) who was over-lord in a given territory and under him various local chiefs called *qa–si–re–u* = βασιλεύς (Baumbach 1971a: 160; Morpurgo Davies 1979: 96–8). Homer has somewhat blurred this picture but a βασιλεύς is always one among many. It is revealing that a person (*Il.* 9.160) or family (*Od.* 15.533) may be described as βασιλεύτερος or even βασιλεύτατος (*Il.* 9.69). This suggests a scale of proximity to power and influence. Various families will have been in the competition for ascendancy and fortunes will have fluctuated over time. That we cannot go beyond this to give any neater scheme for the political structure on Ithaca is not surprising. The epics conflate the realities of different periods from the Trojan War to the eighth century; furthermore, those realities at any given time might have been vaguer than we should expect nowadays. Cf. 397 n.

387 ὅ The expectation or fact of becoming βασιλεύς; cf. 391 n.

γενεῇ πατρώϊον This chiefdom is said to belong to the patrilineal line of this family (cf. *Od.* 15.533). That is not to say that there were not other chiefs in other lordly families. It is never made clear how an external suitor might hope to acquire this chiefdom if it passes by inheritance: Telemachus would always be the natural heir. But then it is left equally vague how Odysseus came to rule with Laertes still alive. It has been suggested that women such as Penelope and Clytemnestra were the real king-makers and that it was marriage to them that conferred power (Hughes 2005: 78–9). Cf. 395 n.

389 The thought recalls 158 (n.): the speaker anticipates a negative reaction on the part of the listener ('You might not like this…') and says so, hoping to diminish the impact of the very reaction that he anticipates. The syntax does not exactly mirror l. 158 since here the apodosis of the condition is made explicit.

ἀγάσσεαι Either 2 sg. fut. ind. med. or 2 sg. aor. subj. med. (158 n.). There is a parallel for εἰ + fut. ind. in the protasis followed by an opt. with κε in the apodosis (*Il.* 24.56–7); but the construction is rare. If the protasis contains εἰ + aor. subj. and the apodosis an opt. with κε, one would expect the protasis also to have κε (Chantraine 1953: 279; Goodwin 1965: 191). The fut. ind. thus seems more likely; but the sense will be more or less the same in either case. The verb denotes being struck for good (*Il.* 3.181) or ill (*Od.* 2.67) by the immensity of a thing (*DELG* 5). The latter sense is in play here.

390 τοῦτο i.e. being βασιλεύς; cf. ὅ (387 n.).

Διός γε δόντος Zeus is elsewhere said to be the giver of rule (*Il.* 2.205). He is also said to nurture rulers and to give them honour and friendship (*Il.* 2.196–7). It is perhaps not surprising if mortals seek to validate their power as derived from the supreme ruler among the gods. This gen. absolute is conditional in sense (Chantraine 1953: 324).

ἀρέσθαι Aor. inf. med. of ἄρνυμαι (cf. *Il.* 16.88; *Od.* 22.353); *not* from ἀείρω or the (in Homer) uncommon αἴρω. Both of these would exhibit a weak aor. ending in –ασθαι. The former would have the weak aor. stem ἀειρ– (cf. *Il.* 6.293) and the latter, unattested in Homer, would have initial ἀ̓– not ἀ̓– (cf. Aesch. *Supp.* 342).

391 φῄς What one 'says' is commonly an expression of what one thinks or supposes (cf. *Il.* 2.37).

391–2 κάκιστον…|…κακόν Telemachus treats with heavy irony the wish expressed at 386–7. He pretends to suppose that Antinous spoke as he did in the mistaken belief that kingship was a curse.

392 οἱ i.e. the βασιλεύς.

δῶ This nom. is unique; of the twenty-three occurrences of δῶ in Homer, the others are all acc. This monosyllable was not easy to modify transparently when other parts of the paradigm were needed; that job was done by the newer δῶμα (Lejeune 1976: 79–80; cf. 176 n.).

393 ἀφνειόν The riches of the house would presumably accrue from other nobles offering gifts. The treasure of Menelaus appears to have accrued at least partly in that way (*Od.* 4.613–19).

τιμηέστερος The translation 'more honoured' obscures the basic meaning. τιμήεις indicates worth and may apply to a thing ('valuable'; *Od.* 4.614) as well as a person ('esteemed').

394 βασιλῆες See 386 n.

395 πολλοί There are twelve suitors from Ithaca (*Od.* 16.251). They are probably coextensive with these βασιλῆες. It is unlikely that anyone who was a βασιλεύς would not also be a suitor; to be a suitor without being a βασιλεύς likewise seems a waste of time. Twelve is not a large number in conventional language; but on a smallish island, it might still seem a lot.

νέοι ἠδὲ παλαιοί This is a common expression of a polar type (338 n.). We see from Nestor and Agamemnon in Books 3 and 4 that the office of βασιλεύς is not lost with age. That said, we are never told why the chiefdom passed to Odysseus while his elderly father was still alive (cf. 387 n.).

396 τόδ' The office of βασιλεύς. See next n.

ἐπεὶ θάνε On the question of inheritance, see 387 n. In any event, this statement is a deliberate lie (in the light of *Od.* 1.196–9) and shows Telemachus growing up to be like his father, who is a master of deceit. He raises the suitors' hopes, presumably to put them off guard in the event that Odysseus returns—a possibility that he had himself discounted (*Od.* 1.161–2, 241–3) before the visit of Athena. However the chiefdom passed from Laertes to Odysseus, the suitors plainly suppose that it could potentially fall to one of them upon his death. This is peculiar since the rule was said by Antinous to run in Telemachus' family (387 n.). It is pointless to attempt to reconstruct the intricacies of succession on Ithaca since we cannot be sure that the epic reflects a real society at a single place and time.

397 ἄναξ Even though the Mycenaean record distinguishes between *wa-na-ka* (ἄναξ) and *qa-si-re-u* (βασιλεύς), Homer conflates the picture (see 386 n.). At *Od.* 20.194, both terms are applied to one and the same person (the disguised Odysseus). Telemachus means that, whatever the position regarding the office of chief, he will be lord and master in his own house.

398 δμώων There is a 3rd-declen. masc. noun δμώς (gen. pl. δμώων) and a 2nd-declen. fem. δμῳή (gen. pl. δμῳῶν). The earliest texts will have had no accents, but it seems likely that Telemachus is talking about all the slaves rather than merely the female ones. The masc. is apt to cover both sexes (Chantraine 1953: 21). These words are never found in prose and only rarely in later verse as a stylistic archaism. After Homer, δμώς and δμῳή were replaced wholesale by δοῦλος and δούλη. δοῦλος is absent from Homer and δούλη appears only twice; but the root is plainly old, cf. Myc. *do-e-ro*.

δμώς is generally taken to mean 'slave'. Its etymology is uncertain. If related to δόμος (*DELG* 289–90; Gschnitzer 1976: 71–2), it does not necessarily denote slavery, merely 'house people'. This invites comparison with οἰκεύς which sometimes denotes menial status (*Od.* 4.245; 14.4) but by no means always (*Il.* 6.366; *Od.* 17.533). An alternative etymology (Eustathius 1336.9) sees a connexion with δάμνημι, δαμάω ('conquer') and would make a δμώς a 'conquered' person. This would fit better with the mention here of their acquisition as booty (see on ληΐσσατο below) and with the fact that a δμώς may be bequeathed (*Od.* 4.736) or purchased (*Od.* 14.449–50). This suggests real chattel slavery rather than mere bonded labour. To conclude otherwise (e.g. Beringer 1961) requires one to believe that plunder, bequeathal, and sale were mere accidents that befell people who were already δμῶες in the sense of non-servile domestic staff. That stretches credibility. Whatever is true of the δμῶες, not all the staff in the household are slaves (see 109, 331 nn.).

οὕς The rel. pron. does not necessarily mean that Telemachus is only referring to the male slaves. The masc. can refer to groups of mixed sex (Chantraine 1953: 21). We know from earlier in the book that the house contains female δμωαί too (147 n.).

μοι Telemachus sees the household slaves as undoubtedly his by right from his father (cf. *Od.* 4.736). The slaves are chattels as much as the cups, plates, and furniture.

ληΐσσατο Whatever the true root of δμώς, its collocation with ληΐζομαι (cf. *Il.* 18.28) suggests that it was popularly taken to mean 'conquered people'. Human beings were carried off from the site of a conquest in the same way as chattels. Thus, in the *Iliad*, Chryseis and Briseis were awarded to Agamemnon and Achilles as part of the general distribution of booty after a battle (*Il.* 1.118–26, 182–5). In the same way, Hector imagines his beloved wife being dragged off into slavery by the Greeks (*Il.* 6.450–63). It is sobering to think that the fifty (*Od.* 22.421) maidservants in Odysseus' house would have been acquired in a similar way. Telemachus says that those twelve (*Od.* 22.424) condemned to a 'filthy death' (*Od.* 22.462) by hanging deserved it on account of their rank insubordination and sexual licence with the suitors (*Od.* 22.463–4). Snatched from home, robbed of their freedom (*Il.* 16.381), compulsorily put to work (*Il.* 6.456), expected to submit to sexual relations with their master (*Il.* 1.31; cf. 433 n.), they were finally hanged for disloyalty. One might question whether the *Odyssey* is, as sometimes claimed, more concerned with justice than the *Iliad*.

399–411 Eurymachus speaks for the first time. Neither his name ('Wide-Fighter') nor that of his father ('Of Many Oxen') seems particularly meaningful in the context. His tone is apparently more conciliatory than that of Antinous. Telemachus later describes him as the best (ἄριστος) of the suitors (*Od.* 15.521). But that term need not denote any moral goodness, so much as bravery. His interests are certainly aligned with those of the rest (408 n.).

400 θεῶν ... κεῖται This expression was used earlier by Mentes (see 267 n.) about whether or not Odysseus would return and take vengeance. At that point the audience knew that Zeus himself was actively promoting the return of Odysseus (76–9). So when Eurymachus uses these words here we might detect an undertone. He imagines that the new chief will emerge from the current contest for the hand of Penelope; we know that there will be no new chief because the old one is not dead.

402 ἔχοις ... ἀνάσσοις These optatives are probably mildly concessive in force: 'you can keep your property...' (Chantraine 1953: 216). This admission cannot have come easily to one who, with the other suitors, has been eating Telemachus out of house and home (250–1).

We began with a question about whether Telemachus would be βασιλεύς (386, 401); but in describing his power over the household, the verb ἀνάσσω is used. This is another instance where the bards blur the distinction that existed in the Mycenaean period between the roles of ἄναξ (overlord) and βασιλεύς ('a truly local official, not appointed by the palace, but recognized by the community', Bennet 1997: 521). See 386 n.

οἷσιν Most MSS read σοῖσιν but that is the *lectio facilior*. ὅς (< *σϝός; cf. Lat. *suus*) was originally a reflexive possessive not just for the third person but also for the first and second persons. Aristarchus thought this usage un-Homeric, but it is well attested in Gk. (Leaf 1900: 559–65), in line with that of the cognate Vedic *svás–* (Macdonell 1916: 112), and also found in Slavonic (Unbegaun 1962: 125–6).

403 μὴ γὰρ ὅ γ' ἔλθοι The opt. with μή expresses a negative wish (Chantraine 1953: 213). The particle γάρ here is not short for αἰ γάρ, even though that combination is often used to introduce wishes both positive (e.g. *Il.* 2.371–2) and negative (*Il.* 16.97–9). The sense is rather the normal connective one: 'I say this, because I hope that nobody...' (Denniston 1954: 94–5).

404 ἀπορραίσει' The MSS all have ἀπορραίσει, fut. ind. act. Whilst this is possible, it fits poorly with the preceding opt. Bentley saw that one need write no more than an apostrophe to have an aor. opt. ἀπορραίσειε with elision before the following vowel. The simple verb ῥαίω means 'strike'; the compound must mean 'knock out of (*sc.* possession of something)'. The double acc. is regular in cases where someone is being deprived of something (*Il.* 1.182; 15.462; Chantraine 1953: 43).

ναιεταώσης This word embodies two puzzles. First, its meaning is pass. but its form act. It has been ingeniously suggested (Leumann 1950: 191–4) that this arose from passages such as *Od.* 9.21–3: ναιετάω Ἰθάκην

('I live on Ithaca')... ἀμφὶ δὲ νῆσοι | πολλαὶ ναιετάουσι ('many islands live (i.e. lie) round about'), cf. *Il.* 2.626. It is a short confusion of thought from this to, 'There are many islands round about where people live'. Second, all MSS at this point transmit ναιεταώσης. Plainly a fully contracted *ναιετώσης would be unmetrical; one would thus expect either –αουσ– (uncontracted) or –οωσ– (with contraction and diectasis) but not –αωσ–, which paradoxically exhibits both contraction and the preservation of the stem vowel. Although the unanimous reading here appears to be 'wrong', it probably reflects a confusion among the bards themselves. Chantraine refers to this delicately as a *flottement* (1988: 79).

405 φέριστε This superlative is used beside φέρτατος. It has been conjectured to belong beside a lost adj. *φερύς, cf. τάχιστος beside ταχύς (Neumann 1973: 163 n. 12). A precisely parallel Avestan *bairišta* (voc.) is built directly to the verbal stem and it is possible that the Greek word is a relic of the same process (Tucker 2009). To judge from the contexts of its use, it means 'strongest' or 'best' (*Il.* 1.581; 16.21). How it comes to mean that is a puzzle. To see here a reference to the carrying off of booty in war (Bader 1999: 43–5) depends on privileging a very narrow sense of the verb φέρω. Most likely the field of meaning is rather broad (*DELG* 1188–9), ranging from carrying off a prize (*Il.* 23.259), to getting the advantage (*Il.* 13.486; 18.308), to putting up bravely with misfortune (*Il.* 17.105).

406–9 At 119 (n.), Telemachus felt indignation that a stranger should be left standing at the door. He welcomed Mentes and asked these kinds of questions, albeit not in these precise words (170–2 n.). That Eurymachus asks them now is partly because he wants to know the answer. But we might also feel that these are the questions that the suitors ought to have asked for themselves had they been proper hosts (cf. 120 n.). It is never made clear why these interlopers owe a duty of hospitality since the house is not strictly theirs and Eurymachus has just admitted as much. Nevertheless, their failings in hospitality are a recurring theme (e.g. *Od.* 7.160; 16.108; 17.375–9, 398–9, 483–7; 18.416–17). Another structural irony is that, just as Mentes lied to Telemachus in answer to these questions, so Telemachus now lies to Eurymachus.

406 εὔχεται εἶναι See 172 n.

407 γαίης... γενεὴ... πατρὶς ἄρουρα Just as πόθεν (170 n.) refers to familial rather than geographical origins, so these words probably have less to do with place than with kinship. Old Iranian evidence suggests that Indo-European thought recognized four levels of belonging (Benveniste 1969: 1.293–319): *nmāna–* ('house'), *vīs* ('clan'), *zantu* ('tribe'), and *dahyu* ('country', 'nation'). Whilst γενεή is cognate with Avestan *zantu*, there are no other etymological correspondences here. We are probably dealing with lexical replacement: γαῖα (not γαίη in the nom., Chantraine 1958: 198) corresponds with *dahyu* and πατρὶς ἄρουρα with *nmāna-* (by reference to the ancestral turf). The Homeric terms are arranged in descending order of magnitude and there are three rather than four. Nevertheless, they likely reflect a traditional PIE constellation of ideas.

408 This question interests the suitors most closely. It is perhaps significant that Eurymachus puts it first in his pair of alternatives, leaving the second less disturbing contingency until last (409), where it lingers in the ear of the listener and gives the impression that the speaker hopes that this is the most likely explanation.

ἐρχομένοιο The alternative reading οἰχομένοιο is possible but poorly attested and probably results from contamination with οἴχεται a few lines later (410).

409 χρεῖος This neut. noun, related to χρή, sometimes denotes the abstract idea of 'making use', e.g. *Od.* 11.479 ἦλθον Τειρεσίαο κατὰ χρέος ('I have come to consult (*lit.* make use of) Teiresias'). Here it refers more concretely to a 'business' or 'matter' (Redard 1953: 74–7).

ἐελδόμενος The verb in this form has no obvious cognate outside Gk. Nevertheless, it might an expanded form of the root seen in Lat. *volo, velle*. If so, it might be that ἔλ-π-ομαι is to be analysed in a similar way: ἐέλδομαι denotes wishing as a process whereas ἔλπομαι denotes expectant waiting (*DELG* 334). But it is hard to think of other cases where –δ– and –π– are used as expansions in this way.

τόδε 'hither'—an adv. qualifying ἱκάνει.

410 οἴχεται A pres. with the stative meaning of the perf.: not 'he is going away', nor 'he went', but rather 'he is gone'. The Homeric paradigm of the verb 'to go' contains three different stems: ἔβην (aor.), οἴχομαι (pres. functioning as perf.), εἶμι (pres. functioning as fut.) (Létoublon 1985: 97–109, 237).

411 γνώμεναι Aor. act. inf.—the subject ('us') has been omitted, cf. *Od.* 4.196.

εἰς ὦπα ἐῴκει It is taken for granted in Homer that moral qualities may be read in a person's face or general appearance. The idea is commonly expressed in direct speech to a second person using ἔοικας (*Od.* 1.208; 6.187; 8.164, 166; 19.381; 20.227). The baseness of Thersites at Troy is plainly connected by the narrator with his ignoble appearance (*Il.* 2.217–19). To judge from contemporary visual culture, the idea is not limited to the vanished societies of the distant past.

412–19 The overall tone of this speech artfully reflects Telemachus' mood before the visit from Mentes. This is a deliberate piece of misdirection so that the suitors are not alerted to the possibility that Odysseus might return within the year.

413 See 168 n.

414 ἀγγελίη The majority of MSS read ἀγγελίης (dat. pl.); but this does not sit with the following sg. ἔλθοι and is probably the result of confusion with θεοπροπίης in the line below.

πείθομαι...εἴ ποθεν ἔλθοι The change of mood from ind. to opt. is striking. The pres. ind. probably has an ingressive sense here (Chantraine 1953: 191), pointing to the future and underlined by ἔτι: 'I am no longer believing.' He then repents of this formulation since it prompts the question of whether he has recently received any such message. The opt. is chosen so as to paint the arrival of news as a remote contingency (Chantraine 1953: 278). This is apt for the misdirection that Telemachus intends.

415–16 ἐμπάζομαι...|...ἐξερέηται A similar kind of manipulation of moods is taking place here as in the foreg. n. except that the subj. is used as part of an indefinite clause: 'that my mother should ask about' (cf. Chantraine 1953: 245–6). These lines closely recall *Il.* 16.50, where Achilles denies any special revelation from his mother but, in keeping with his more direct manner, goes on to use the ind. in the rel. clause (οἶδα).

415 θεοπροπίης An abstract noun compounded of the roots in θεός and πρέπω. Although πρέπω is almost always intransitive ('appear'), with the notable exception of Aesch. *Ag.* 1328, the o-grade in a noun suggests transitive action: σκοπίη is thus the act of keeping watch (*Od.* 8.285) or the place where watch is kept (*Il.* 5.771). θεοπροπίη is thus an act of making plain (i.e. declaring) things divine. In this case a goddess has brought news to Telemachus. Although divine intervention is plainly in his mind (cf. 323, 420 nn.), he is careful to maintain the misdirection by suggesting that the only source of such news that he could imagine would be a seer summoned (not by himself but) by his mother.

ἥν τινα Some MSS read here ἤν τινα but that is a poorly attested, minority reading. The choice is between a rel. pron. that is functioning as part of an indefinite clause (Chantraine 1953: 245–6) or the more pedestrian conjunction ἤν. The latter is a late and somewhat doubtful item in Homer and suspect here as elsewhere (Chantraine 1953: 281–2).

416 μέγαρον See 328 n.

θεοπρόπον This is an agential noun indicating a person who makes a θεοπροπίη; see 415 n.

ἐξερέηται 3 sg. pres. subj. med. of ἐξερέομαι, an epic form of ἐξέρομαι ('ask'), cf. ἐρεείνω.

417–19 These lines recall, *mutatis mutandis*, 180–1. On ἔγνω, see 420 n.

420 ἀθανάτην The first vowel is phonetically long, as the metre makes plain. This is not normal for a privative alpha. *Pace* Wyatt (1969: 79–80), the form is unlikely to rest on an earlier Gk. *ἀθϝάνατος, cf. Skt. *á-dhvanīt* (Wyatt 1969: 79–80). More plausible is lengthening by analogy with forms like ἀννέφελος > ἀνέφελος, which latter is the reading of the vulgate at *Od.* 6.45 (Ruijgh 1971: 272). In Attic, an adj. compounded with privative alpha would almost always exhibit only two terminations; in Homer, it is quite usual to find three. It is peculiar that the fem. is used since Telemachus does not know which god or goddess has visited him. The explanation is probably that we are seeing things through the eyes of the omniscient narrator.

θεόν This apparently masc. form is regularly used for both 'god' and 'goddess' in Ionian and Attic (Chantraine 1958: 20), the gender being indicated by any qualifiers that are present. Epic also has an Aeolic form θεά that is also found in tragedy, lyric, and later prose (cf. *Il.* 1.1).

ἔγνω What had begun as mere suspicion (323 n.) has now hardened into recognition. Telemachus now knows that Mentes was in fact an immortal god in disguise but is shrewd enough to tell Eurymachus the same lie that Mentes had told (180–1). This marks a considerable change in his posture, but maybe not in his nature. Penelope and Odysseus are both tricky and they have a son who can be equally tricky when roused. This foreshadows the deceptions in which he and Odysseus will collude in the second half of the poem to bring death to the unwary suitors.

421–3 = *Od.* 18.304–6, likewise said of the suitors, when Odysseus has returned and is planning their death. By Book 18, the audience knows that their pleasure is to be very brief.

421 ἱμερόεσσαν ἀοιδήν The suitors had already turned to song and dance earlier in the evening (152 n.). But there, the song was their own, described as μολπή; here, ἀοιδή is likely the song of Phemius resumed (cf. 159 n.; Thomas 2014: 97). This might seem to sit ill with the fact that the dancing mentioned in this line is surely that of the suitors. But the verb ἀείδω and the noun ἀοιδή in the overwhelming majority of cases denote epic song. Other uses do occur: the hymn to Apollo sung by the Greek soldiers at Chryse (*Il.* 1.473); the Linus song on the Shield of Achilles (*Il.* 18.570); the weaving songs of Calypso and Circe (*Od.* 5.61; 10.227); the song of the Phaeacians in which they excel as much as they do at sport (*Od.* 8.253); and the beguiling song of the Sirens (*Od.* 12.44). These examples all involve divine or quasi-divine persons and might fit with the divine inspiration of heroic song (cf. 328 n.). The epithet ἱμερόεσσα strongly suggests the beguiling qualities of bardic song (cf. 337 n.) rather than the raucous karaoke of the suitors.

422 τρεψάμενοι τέρποντο There is an apparent jingle between these two words. It is enough to note this and the texture that it gives to the verse; there is no need to search for any deeper connexion between the two words.

422–3 μένον… ἐλθεῖν | …ἦλθεν Homer may abbreviate or dilate time to suit the pace of his narrative. At *Il.* 1.53–4, nine days are made to pass in two lines—this in a poem whose narrated action covers only fourteen days and whose central day extends from Book 11 to Book 18 (Taplin 1992: 15–18). In the present case, Mentes arrived at an hour consistent with δεῖπνον—which denotes the main meal taken at some time during the day (134 n.). Everything that passes between Mentes and Telemachus does so between that meal and the coming of darkness.

422 μέλας The equation between ἕσπερος and darkness is found at *Il.* 22.318–19, when the star of evening is seen in the depth of night.

424 This expression for people going their separate ways to bed occurs 6× in Homer. At *Il.* 23.58, we find κλισίηνδε instead of οἶκόνδε, unsurprisingly given the martial context. All other instances begin οἱ μέν; the substitution of δὴ τότε here is a novelty and shows the adaptation of an older formula to a new setting. Σ reports a variant reading δὴ τότε κοιμήσαντο καὶ ὕπνου δῶρον ἕλοντο (cf. *Od.* 19.427) attributed to Aristophanes of Byzantium but also said to be found in the Argive text. This presumably commended itself to an over-fastidious critic who wondered whether all the suitors were in easy reach of home.

κακκείοντες The preverb κατά has been reduced to κατ-, whose final τ assimilates to the following κ of κείοντες (Sihler 1995: 199). It is likely that κείων was originally a desiderative (Hollifield 1981); but the participial forms indicate future purpose rather than desire (cf. *Od.* 7.342).

ἔβαν Attic would have ἔβησαν. There are two quite discrete roots: *g^wem-* ('come'; cf. Vedic *ágman*) and *g^weH₂-*—('go'; cf. Vedic *ágāt*). They became associated in Greek so that the paradigm of βαίνω contains elements of both (Sihler 1995: 484). ἔβαν comes from the second root: see 211 n.

ἕκαστος The sg. subject with a pl. verb is not uncommon (Chantraine 1953: 17). It brings out both collective action and singularity: they went to bed, each and every one.

425–44 Telemachus retires to bed. This is a change of pace involving calm and domesticity. We are introduced to the maid Eurycleia, who will play an important part in the story once Odysseus returns home.

425–7 ὅθι...αὐλῆς |...| ἔνθ᾽ The rel. adv. ὅθι ('where') has been brought to the front of the sentence and looks forward to the demonstrative adv. ἔνθα ('there'): 'where his bedchamber was built…there he went…'. Within the first limb, there are two ways to construe the gen.: either it is partitive (*Od.* 4.639–40) and governed by ὅθι ('where in the beautiful courtyard his bedchamber was built…there he went…') or it is a free-standing gen. of place (*Il.* 9.219; *Od.* 3.251) and ὅθι is in apposition ('where his bedchamber was built, in the beautiful courtyard…there he went…'). It is hard to decide this either way (Chantraine 1953: 58–9); but the sense is clear in any event.

425 θάλαμος In later Greek, the θάλαμος is usually the bedchamber. In Homer it denotes simply a domestic room usually kept locked and not automatically open to visitors (Wace 1951: 207–9). It might be used as a bedroom (cf. *Od.* 4.802; 19.53), but equally well for the storage of goods and/or weapons (*Od.* 21.8–14). Here the context makes plain that this is Telemachus' bedroom, away from the main house, in the courtyard. We may suppose that the infant Telemachus slept with his parents; when he got older, a separate chamber will have been constructed for him in the courtyard (Bassett 1919: 291).

αὐλῆς *Il.* 6.316 suggests that a house could be described compendiously as consisting of αὐλή, δῶμα, and θάλαμος. Most likely δῶμα is a synonym there for μέγαρον whilst θάλαμος encompasses the private rooms. αὐλή denotes the courtyard: it would have been walled (*Od.* 17.266) and stood between the entrance to the compound and the public rooms (Gray 1955: 7–9). The αὐλή might itself contain some rooms, as in the present case.

426 ὑψηλός The most natural interpretation of this adj. is that the overall structure is tall (cf. *Il.* 3.384); it does not tell us that the room was on an upper storey. It might or might not have been, but this line tells us nothing either way.

δέδμητο An unaugmented pluperf. denoting a continuing state of affairs in the past: this is where the room 'was built', i.e. *had been* built and *was still* there.

περισκέπτῳ ἐνὶ χώρῳ The apparent sense is that the room is built somewhere that can be seen from all around. That would suggest elevated ground, but not necessarily an upper storey. The house of Circe is described in the same way (*Od.* 10.211). Since it was in a wood, its conspicuousness must have been limited—perhaps it stood in a clearing. It has been suggested that the poet connected περισκέπτῳ with σκέπας ('protection'), meaning that the structure was 'protected on all sides' (S. R. West 1988: 125–6). But the pig-farm of Eumaeus is also described as περισκέπτῳ ἐνὶ χώρῳ (*Od.* 14.6), and it appears to have been sheltered only on the north side by a cliff (*Od.* 14.533). The sense of 'conspicuous' is the only plausible one for the pig-farm and so presumably applies equally to other instances (Diggle 2005: 522).

427 ἔνθ' Refers back to ὅθι (425 n.).

εὐνήν The word may indicate an actual structure (*Od.* 10.335) but can also denote a place of rest in the broadest sense including animals' lairs (*Il.* 11.115; *Od.* 4.338; 14.14). λέχος by contrast is always a bedstead. Both λέχος (*Il.* 1.31) and εὐνή (*Il.* 3.441, 445; 15.32) may have sexual connotations; these are not present here. Cf. 437, 440 nn.

μερμηρίζων This verb often denotes the anxious pondering of alternatives (e.g. *Il.* 1.189). It can also have an extended sense of 'plan' or 'devise' (*Od.* 2.325; 4.533). That would seem to be appropriate here, with πολλά as the object. Telemachus is mulling over how to execute his mission (cf. 444).

δαΐδας Of the various Homeric terms for things that give light—cf. λαμπτήρ (*Od.* 18.306–12), λύχνος (*Od.* 19.33–4)—these are from their context plainly hand-held torches (Jantzen and Tölle 1968: 83–98).

428 ἅμ' Functions here not as an adv. ('at the same time'; in which case τῷ would be dat. of advantage) but as a preposition ('together with') following its pron. in the dat. case (cf. *Il.* 12.372; 17.494; *Od.* 6.105).

κέδν' εἰδυῖα The expression describes not Eurycleia's knowledge but her temperament (H. Fränkel 1975: 82). For the meaning of κεδνός, see 335 n. The MSS here all read κέδν' εἰδυῖα. In spite of this, some editors print κεδνὰ ἰδυῖα. The original fem. of this ptcp. was *ϝιδυῖα (Chantraine 1958: 421: M. L. West 1966: 241–2). The MSS reading suggests a later stage, with remodelling by analogy with the masc. Since εἰδυῖα is guaranteed by the metre at *Il.* 17.5, we may suppose that this evolution had begun when the poems were being composed. There is thus no need to dismiss the MSS reading as a post-Homeric innovation and write κεδνὰ ἰδυῖα instead.

429 Εὐρύκλει' This is the first mention of this important character. Her name means 'of wide renown'. In Homer, slaves whose names are given at all had names like those of free persons (cf. Ἀντίκλεια (*Od.* 11.85), Διοκλέης (*Il.* 5.542)); in later Greek, they often had names that described their place of origin or ethnic characteristics (Fragiadakis 1988: 13–21, 39–41). Her name and epithets are emphasized by being made to fill the entire line; cf. 329 n.

Ὦπος ... Πεισηνορίδαο We know nothing of these persons; it is quite possible that they were called into being purely for this context. Patronymics are common in the heroic world of the *Iliad* but are much sparser in the *Odyssey* (J. A. Scott 1912: 301). In giving a patrilineal pedigree for two generations to a woman, Homer is conferring on Eurycleia the sort of dignity normally reserved for aristocratic warriors. The inference is that she was originally of free and high birth but later abducted and sold into slavery. In this respect she resembles that other important slave, Eumaeus (*Od.* 15.455–75).

430 Λαέρτης Laertes has already been mentioned as an absent figure who no longer frequents the city (189 n.). He is distinguished throughout the poem by his absence, a figure of pathos. There is lively debate over whether the ending of the *Odyssey* as we have it is genuine or whether it originally ended at 23.296 or 299 (M. L. West 2014: 294–7). Whatever else might be said, it is not unreasonable to think that the meeting between Laertes and Odysseus in Book 24 is adumbrated by these oblique references in Book 1. The figure of the absent father is not to be ignored in a male-dominated society; we cannot conclude that all loose ends have been tied up once Odysseus is back in bed with Penelope.

πρίατο κτεάτεσσιν ἑοῖσιν The dat. is instrumental: the shocking reality of chattel slavery is made especially plain when we see that persons are routinely bought in exchange for things.

431 πρωθήβην The root seen in the noun ἥβη indicates youth not so much lacking adulthood as possessing the vigour of growing maturity (see 41 n.). So Eurycleia was young when bought as a slave; she is now an old woman (*Od.* 23.1) and so has spent most of her life in slavery.

ἔτ' With this one small adverb, the narrator delicately tells us that Eurycleia is no longer young. Here is the same wistful evocation of a lost past that we find in the narrator's voice when he recalls how the Trojan women used to do the washing at the springs, τὸ πρὶν ἐπ' εἰρήνης, πρὶν ἐλθεῖν υἷας Ἀχαιῶν ('before, when there was peace, before the Greeks arrived'; *Il.* 22.156).

ἐεικοσάβοια This is a neut. pl. adj.: Laertes did not give twenty oxen but rather articles (κτεάτεσσι, 430) to that value. Cattle were routinely used as a measure of worth (e.g. *Il.* 6.236). In the funeral games for Patroclus, a skilled woman is offered as a prize and is said to be valued at four oxen (*Il.* 23.705): that Eurycleia was valued at five times that is an arresting comparison, but it is sobering to note that a large tripod could be valued at twelve oxen (*Il.* 23.703). Although it has been argued that there is no evidence in the epics of the direct use of cattle as currency (M. I. Finley 1977: 67), Iphidamas is said to have given a large number of oxen in exchange for his wife and to have promised many sheep and goats beside (*Il.* 11.244–5).

432 τίεν Does Laertes *value* or *honour* her? Is there a difference? In a society where even wives were part of a system of exchange in terms of bride-price or dowry (cf. 277 n.), we might think that all women were possessions and thus susceptible to being ranked in terms of value. That would be accurate up to a point (cf. *Il.* 11.241–5), but not the whole story. The poem presents the relationship between Penelope and Odysseus as mature and deep. Odysseus longs to see Penelope again and prefers death to unending life on an island as the husband of the nubile Calypso (*Od.* 1.13, 15, 59). Penelope weeps whenever she thinks of Odysseus (336 n.) and employs her cunning intelligence to postpone for as long as she can having to marry another man (*Od.* 2.88–105).

433 εὐνῇ Here as often, but not always (cf. 427 n.), the word operates as a synonym for sexual relations. It was taken as part of the settled order of things (θέμις) that a man had a right to sexual enjoyment of an unfree woman (*Il.* 9.276–7). The epics do not seem to question the morality of this kind of rape. Achilles says of Briseis that he felt deep love and care for her, taken as she was by the spear; but he does not actually speak her name, referring to her only by the demonstrative τήν (*Il.* 9.341–3). We are not told what Briseis felt about the arrangement; but her mourning over Patroclus (*Il.* 19.287–300) suggests that any gentleness she ever knew came from that quarter rather than from the man with whom she was obliged to sleep.

ἔμικτο 3 sg. aor. ind. med.

χόλον . . . γυναικός In the context of the *Odyssey*, one need think only of Clytemnestra who murdered Agamemnon in part, at least, for his adultery with Cassandra (*Od.* 11.422–3).

434 δαῖδας An example of ring composition, taking up the story from 428 (n.) after the brief excursus on the history of Eurycleia.

435 φιλέεσκε See 264 n.

436 ὤιξεν The change of subject seems jarring but (a) it is perhaps signalled by ἑ in l. 434 and (b) it would be even more peculiar if the subject of ὤιξεν differed from that of ἕζετο in the next verse.

πύκα ποιήτοιο See 333 n.

437 λέκτρῳ The word is cognate with λέχος. The suffix –τρο– denotes the place where the action in λέχομαι occurs (Risch 1974: 42). The various terms for 'bed' in Homer overlap to a degree where it is often impossible to tell them apart (*pace* Laser 1968: 1–34). That said, animals never have λέχος or λέκτρον. Both of these may denote the bed as a piece of furniture; λέχος may have overtones of sex (*Il.* 1.31). Cf. 427, 440 nn.

χιτῶνα is a short tunic worn by men next to the skin (*Od.* 15.60). The equivalent for women in Homer is a πέπλος (Σ D *ad Il.* 2.42). The same word also describes a corselet worn by warriors (Marinatos 1967: 7). The word appears to have been borrowed into Greek from a Semitic language, probably Phoenician (Lewy 1895: 82; *DELG* 1261). If so, this took place before the period of the Linear B tablets (Chadwick and Baumbach 1963: 257).

438 τὸν μέν More often than not in Homer, there is no answering δέ (Chantraine 1953: 159). The expectation that μέν must look forward to an answering δέ, whilst normal in Attic prose, does not apply in Homer. In this case, μέν has been said to be emphatic (Denniston 1954: 359–60).

γραίης This is a *hapax* in Homer but not later Greek (Eur. *Hcld.* 584). The related γρηῦς is common enough in the *Odyssey* and used for Eurycleia (*Od.* 2.377; 23.1). Its gen. γρηός, although of the correct metrical shape here, is not attested until Agathias in the sixth century AD (*Anthologia Graeca* 16.109.1).

πυκιμηδέος Homeric references to μήδεα πυκνά (*Il.* 3.208), πυκιναὶ φρένες (*Il.* 14.294), and πυκινὴ βουλή (*Il.* 2.55) make it clear that this compound adj. refers to the quality of having wise counsel. The relationship between πυκινός or πυκνός in the sense of wisdom and the use of πύκα to refer to tightly built structures is difficult to explain (see 333 n.). πυκιμηδής is a *hapax*, like the noun it qualifies (foreg. n.).

ἔμβαλε Not 'threw' but 'put'—an attenuated sense (cf. *Il.* 14.218), to be sure, but one that finds parallels in the description of putting an idea into another's mind (201 n.) and shedding sleep onto another's eyelids (364 n.).

439 ἥ μέν See 438 n.; if there is an opposition here, it is marked by ἔνθα ὅ γε (443).

τὸν...χιτῶνα Homer generally uses ὅ, ἥ, τό as a demonstrative pron. ('that one'). This was the meaning of the PIE *so, *seH₂, *tod from which it is derived (Sihler 1995: 388–90). Instances such as this might be taken as examples of fronting ('that thing...namely the tunic'). It is sometimes said that the development of ὅ, ἥ, τό into a definite article was unknown in Homer; but there are instances where it is hard to construe it as anything else (*Il.* 1.33, 185; Chantraine 1953: 165). See 4, 9, 157 nn.

ἀσκήσασα This verb in the aor. ptcp. is normally coordinated with a finite verb to show that some creative process was done carefully (*Il.* 4.110; 14.179; *Od.* 3.438; 23.198). The construction here is different: the action of folding and of ἀσκέω are both participial so that each appears to be an independent action. An attractive explanation in synchronic terms (S. R. West 1988: 127) is to equate ἀσκέω with κομίζω in the sense of 'take care of' (cf. *Il.* 2.183); but this presupposes that we more or less know the semantic field into which ἀσκέω used by itself must fall. If ἀσκέω and ἀσκός were originally connected with the working of skins into clothes (cautiously *DELG* 124–5 and Linear B *a-ke-ti-ra2-o* (= *askētriāhōn*, PY Ad 666) suggests 'finishers'), it might be that ἀσκέω here denotes smoothing the cloth as though finishing a skin.

440 πασσάλῳ undoubtedly denotes a hook (cf. πήγνυμι; *DELG* 860). But on the few other occasions where it is used, it refers to the suspension of a solid item such as a bow (*Il.* 5.209; *Od.* 21.53), a lyre (*Od.* 8.67, 105), or a yoke (*Il.* 24.268). It seems odd to fold (πτύξασα, 439) and smooth a soft garment only to hang it on a hook; any folding would surely be spoilt.

ἀγκρεμάσασα The verb is not otherwise found in Homer but in the Ionic prose of Herodotus refers to temple offerings (5.77.3, 95.1) and crucifixion (9.120.4). The simple verb is used with κατά in tmesis for taking a lyre down from its peg (*Od.* 8.67).

τρητοῖσι That the word means 'bored' (i.e. with holes in it) is not in doubt (cf. τετραίνω; Rix 2001: 632–4). *Etymologicum Magnum* conjectures παρὰ τὸ τετρῆσθαι κατὰ τὰ ἐνήλατα, εἰς ἃ ἐμβάλλεται ἡ σπάρτος ('from being pierced along the rails, into which the cord is set'). In other words, holes are bored into sides of the bedstead; through these holes are passed cords; on top of these cords lies the mattress (Laser 1968: 23).

λέχεσσιν The application of this word to what has just been called a λέκτρον (437 n.) suggests the lack of real distinction between the terms (Snodgrass 1970: 160).

441 βῆ ... ἴμεν The inf. is completive, denoting the goal of the action. This is common after verbs of motion (Chantraine 1968: 301). There appears to be an element of pleonasm when the inf. is ἴμεν ('she went to go'); but the original sense of ἔβη was probably that of taking of a step (cf. 211 n. and μακρὰ βίβας *Il.* 7.213)—thus 'she took a step to go out'.

ἐπέρυσσε This compound is a Homeric *hapax* (but refers in Herodotus (4.8.3) to pulling on a garment). It was probably an ordinary item in the Ionic vocabulary.

κορώνη The noun denotes a sea-bird of some kind (*Od.* 5.66; 12.418). By extension, it may describe anything curved such as the tip of a bow (*Il.* 4.111) or a door-handle as here. The adj. κορωνίς is frequently used, especially in the *Iliad*, to describe the curved beak of a ship.

442 ἀργυρέη The use of precious metals for a door-handle was presumably an aristocratic luxury. King Alcinous of Scheria, egregious in this respect as in so many others, has a golden handle for the door of his palace (*Od.* 7.90).

κληῖδ' In later Greek, this word routinely means 'key'. In Homer, it may have a range of meanings including collar bone (*Il.* 8.235) or rowing bench (*Od.* 2.419). In the domestic context, it may refer to a hook that serves as a key, being inserted through a hole in the door to manipulate the strap (ἱμάς) attached to the bolt (ὀχεύς) that kept the door locked. Here, however, it refers to the bolt itself: Eurycleia closes the door after her by the handle and then *pulls* on a leather strap that passes through the keyhole so as to shoot the bolt into the keep and lock the door. This is a one-way operation. Because of the positioning of the keyhole relative to the point where the strap is attached to the bolt, once the bolt is in the keep it cannot be withdrawn by pulling on the strap from outside. The operation of opening a door is described at *Od.* 21.46–50. One passes through the keyhole a curved hook designed to catch the strap, allowing one to *push* on it and so move the bolt in the opposite direction out of its keep (Diels 1897: 127–9). Telemachus can leave at any time since he is on the inside and can move the bolt directly without a hook.

443 παννύχιος Of the seventeen instances of this adj., only four refer to persons getting a good night's sleep (*Il.* 2.2, 24, 61; 10.2; 24.678). Elsewhere and, it would seem, normatively it refers to spending the night awake, often while bad things are happening (*Il.* 7.476, 478; 8.508, 554; 18.315, 354; 23.105, 217; *Od.* 2.434; 7.288; 12.429).

οἰὸς ἀώτῳ This expression has caused much puzzlement and has been taken to mean 'finest wool' on the (unprovable) basis that ἄωτος in Homer means 'flower' or some such. Whatever the case in later Greek, there is surely a formal parallelism in Homer between λίνοιο...ἄωτος (*Il.* 9.661) and οἰὸς ἄωτος (here and 4× elsewhere). ἄωτος might mean no more than 'that which lies on the surface': the nap of linen and the wool of a sheep (Raman 1975). It would thus be a poetic expression for wool with no connotations as to quality. There is no need to suppose that Telemachus slept under a raw fleece; ἄωτος can refer to wool that has been worked into a sling (*Il.* 13.599) and so, presumably, also into a blanket (S. R. West 1988: 127).

444 πέφραδ' An unaugmented reduplicated 3 sg. aor. ind. act. of φράζω; see 273 n. The type is very common (Chantraine 1958: 395–8). A sigmatic aor. φράσε is also found (*Od.* 11.22). Both forms are old.

Bibliography

Allan, R. J. (2010), 'The *infinitivus pro imperativo* in Ancient Greek: The Imperatival Infinitive as an Expression of Proper Procedural Action', *Mnemosyne* 63: 203–28.

Allen, T. W. (1910), 'The Homeric Catalogue', *JHS* 30: 292–322.

Allen, T. W. (1912), *Homeri Opera: Tomus V Hymnos, Cyclum, Fragmenta, Margiten, Batrachomyomachiam, Vitas Continens* (Oxford: Oxford University Press).

Allen, T. W. (1917–19), *Homeri Opera: Odyssea*, 2nd edn. (Oxford: Oxford University Press).

Allen, W. S. (1947), 'The Name of the Black Sea in Greek', *CQ* 41: 86–8.

Allen, W. S. (1948), 'Supplementary Note on the Name of the Black Sea', *CQ* 42: 60.

Allen, W. S. (1987), *Vox Graeca*, 3rd edn. (Cambridge: Cambridge University Press).

Amory, A. (1966), 'The Gates of Horn and Ivory', *YClS* 20: 3–57.

Anderson, Ø. and Haug, D. (eds.) (2012), *Relative Chronology in Early Greek Epic Poetry* (Cambridge: Cambridge University Press).

Arnott, W. G. (2007), *Birds in the Ancient World from A to Z* (London: Routledge).

Artelt, A. (1937), *Studien zur Geschichte der Begriffe 'Heilmittel' und 'Gift': Urzeit, Homer, Corpus Hippocraticum* (Leipzig: Barth).

Assaël, J. (2000), 'Poétique des étymologies de μοῦσα (mousa), la muse', *Noesis* 4: 11–53.

Austin, J. N. (1972), 'Name Magic in the *Odyssey*', *ClAnt* 5: 1–19.

Bader, F. (1974), *Suffixes grecs en –mi–: Recherches comparatives sur l'hétéroclisie nominale* (Paris: Champion).

Bader, F. (1999), 'Homère et le pélasge', in Blanc and Christol 1999: 15–56.

Bakker, E. J. (1988), *Linguistics and Formulas in Homer: Scalarity and the Description of the Particle Per* (Amsterdam: Benjamins).

Bakker, E. J. (2002), 'Polyphemus', in Roisman and Roisman 2002: 135–50.

Bakker, E. J., De Jong, I. F. J., and Van Wees, H. (eds.) (2002), *Brill's Companion to Herodotus* (Leiden: Brill).

Balsdon, J. P. V. D. (1966), *Roman Women: Their History and Habits* (London: History Book Club).

Bannert, H. (1978), 'Zur Vogelgestalt der Götter bei Homer', *WS* n.s. 12: 29–42.

Barringer, J. M. (1991), 'Europa and the Nereids: Wedding or Funeral?', *AJA* 95: 657–67.

Bartholomae, C. (1901), 'Arica XIV', *IF* 12: 95–150.

Barton, C. R. (1993), 'τέθηπα etc.', *Glotta* 71: 1–9.

Bassett, S. E. (1919), 'The Palace of Odysseus', *AJA* 23: 288–311.

Bassett, S. E. (1923), 'The Proems of the *Iliad* and the *Odyssey*', *AJPh* 44: 339–48.

Baumbach, L. (1971a), 'The Mycenean Greek Vocabulary II', *Glotta* 49: 151–90.

Baumbach, L. (1971b), 'Further Thoughts on PY Vn 46', *Minos* 12: 383–97.

Beazley, J. D. (1956), *Attic Black-Figure Vase Painters* (Oxford: Clarendon Press).

Bechtel, F. (1908), *Die Vocalcontraction bei Homer* (Halle: Niemeyer).

Beekes, R. S. P. (1969a), 'ἔτος and ἐνιαυτός in Homeric Formulae', *Glotta* 47: 138–43.

Beekes, R. S. P. (1969b), *The Development of the Proto-Indo-European Laryngeals in Greek* (Hague: Mouton).

Beekes, R. S. P. (ed.) (1992), *Rekonstruktion und relative Chronologie* (Innsbruck: Institut für Sprachwissenschaft).

Beekes, R. S. P. (2010), *Etymological Dictionary of Greek*, Vol. 1 (Leiden: Brill).

Benedict, R. (1947), *The Chrysanthemum and the Sword: Patterns of Japanese Culture* (London: Secker & Warburg).

Bennet, J. (1997), 'Homer and the Bronze Age', in Powell and Morris 1997: 511–34.

Benveniste, E. (1954) 'Formes et sens de μνάομαι', in Debrunner 1954: 13–18.

Benveniste, E. (1969), *Le Vocabulaire des institutions indo-européennes*, 2 vols. (Paris: Éditions de Minuit).

Beringer, W. (1961), 'Zu den Begriffen für "Sklaven" und "Unfreie" bei Homer', *Historia* 10: 259–91.

Bierl, A. and Latacz, J. (eds.) (2015), *Homer's Iliad: The Basel Commentary. Prolegomena*, tr. B. W. Millis and S. Strack, ed. S. D. Olson (Berlin and Boston: De Gruyter).

Bierl, A., Schmitt, A., and Willi, A. (eds.) (2004), *Antike Literatur in neuer Deutung: Festschrift für Joachim Latacz anlässlich seines 70. Geburtstag* (Munich and Leipzig: Walter De Gruyter).

Bittlestone, R., Diggle, J., and Underhill, J. (2005), *Odysseus Unbound* (Cambridge: Cambridge University Press).

Blanc, A. (1999), 'πέπνῦμαι' (= *Chroniques d'étymologie grecque* 4, 1999), *RPh* 73: 100.

Blanc, A. and Christol, A. (eds.) (1999), *Langues en contact dans l'antiquité: aspects lexicaux. Actes du colloque Rouenlac III* (Paris: de Boccard).

Boedeker, D. (2002), 'Epic Heritage and Mythical Patterns in Herodotus', in Bakker et al. 2002: 97–116.

Bolling, G. M. (1923), 'A Peculiarity of Homeric Orthography', *CPh* 18: 170–7.

Bonifazi, A. (2009), 'Inquiring into *Nostos* and its Cognates', *AJPh* 130: 481–510.

Bonifazi, A. (2012), *Homer's Versicolored Fabric: The Evocative Power of Ancient Greek Epic Wordmaking* (Washington, DC: Center for Hellenic Studies).

Boraston, J. M. (1911), 'The Birds of Homer' *JHS* 31: 216–50.

Bowra, C. M. (1934), 'Homeric Words in Cyprus', *JHS* 54: 54–74.

Bowra, C. M. (1960), 'Homeric Epithets for Troy', *JHS* 80: 16–23.

Bowra, C. M. (1964), *Pindar* (Oxford: Clarendon Press).

Bremer, D. (1976), *Licht und Dunkel in der frühgriechischen Dichtung: Interpretationen zur Vorgeschichte der Lichtmetaphysik* (Bonn: Bouvier).

Bremer, J. M., De Jong, I. F. J., and Kalff, J. (eds.) (1987), *Homer: Beyond Oral Poetry* (Amsterdam: Grüner).

Breuil, J.-L. (1989), '*ΚΡΑΤΟΣ* et sa famille chez Homère: Étude sémantique', in M. Casevitz (ed.), *Études homériques: séminaire de recherche 1984–1987* (Lyon: Maison de l'Orient), 17–53.

Brugmann, K. (1903/4), 'Beiträge zur griechischen, germanischen und slavischen Wortforschung', *IF* 15: 87–104.

Brugmann, K. (1911/12), 'Zur griechischen und italischen Wortforschung', *IF* 29: 200–14.

Brugmann, K. (1916/17), 'Griech. χρῆται u. lat. ūtitur', *IF* 37: 239–49.

Buchholz, E. (1871–85), *Die Homerischen Realien* (Leipzig: Engelmann).

Buck, C. D. (1910), *Greek Dialects*, rev. edn. (Boston: Ginn).

Burger, A. (1925), *Les mots de le famille φύω en grec ancien* (Paris: Champion).

Burkert, W. (1983), *Homo Necans* (Berkeley: University of California Press).

Burkert, W. (1985), *Greek Religion* (Oxford: Blackwell).

Buttmann, P. (1836), *Lexilogus*, tr. J. R. Fishlake (London: John Murray).

Cairns, D. L. (1990), 'Mixing with Men and Nausicaa's Nemesis', *CQ* 40: 263–6.

Cairns, D. L. (1996), 'Hybris, Dishonour and Thinking Big', *JHS* 116: 1–32.

Calhoun, G. (1962), 'Polity and Society (i) The Homeric Picture', in Wace and Stubbings 1962: 431–52.

Carpenter, R. (1950), 'Argeiphontes: A Suggestion', *AJA* 54: 177–83.

Carruba, O. (1968), 'Athena ed Ares Preellenici', *Atti e memorie del Iº congresso internazionale di Micenologia* (Rome: Ateneo), 932–44.

Carter, J. B. and Morris, S. P. (eds.) (1995), *The Ages of Homer* (Austin: University of Texas Press).

Caswell, C. P. (1990), *A Study of Thumos in Early Greek Epic* (Leiden: Brill).

Chadwick, J. and Baumbach, L. (1963), 'The Mycenean Greek Vocabulary', *Glotta* 41: 157–271.

Chadwick, J. (1996), *Lexicographica Graeca* (Oxford: Oxford University Press).

Chandler, H. W. (1881), *A Practical Introduction to Greek Accentuation* (London: Oxford University Press), repr. 1983 (New York: Caratzas).

Chantraine, P. (1933), *La formation des noms en grec ancien* (Paris: Honoré Champion).

Chantraine, P. (1953), *Grammaire homérique*, Vol. 2: *Syntaxe*, repr. 1986 (Paris: Klincksieck).

Chantraine, P. (1958), *Grammaire homérique*, Vol. 1: *Phonétique et morphologie*, repr. 1988 (Paris: Klincksieck).

Chantraine, P. et al. (1999), *Dictionnaire étymologique de la langue grecque. Nouvelle édition avec un Supplément sous la direction de: Alain Blanc, Charles de Lamberterie, Jean-Louis Perpillou* (Paris: Klincksieck).

Chittenden, J. (1948), 'Diaktoros Argeiphontes', *AJA* 52: 24–33.

Clackson, J. (1994), *The Linguistic Relationship between Armenian and Greek*, Publications of the Philological Society 30 (Oxford: Blackwell).

Clackson, J. (2007), *Indo-European Linguistics: An Introduction* (Cambridge: Cambridge University Press).

Clarke, M. (1995), 'The Wisdom of Thales and the Problem of the Word *IEPOΣ*', *CQ* 45: 296–317.

Clarke, M. (1997/8), 'πινύσκω and its Cognates: A Note on Simonides fr. 508 Page', *Glotta* 74: 135–42.

Clarke, M. (1999), *Flesh and Spirit in the Songs of Homer* (Oxford: Oxford University Press).

Cohen, B. (ed.) (1995), *The Distaff Side* (New York: Oxford University Press).

Colvin, S. (2007), *A Historical Greek Reader* (Oxford: Oxford University Press).

Colvin, S. (2016), 'The Modal Particle in Greek', *Cambridge Classical Journal* 62: 65–84.

Coulter, G. and McCullaugh, M. (eds.) (2007), *Greek and Latin from an Indo-European Perspective* (Cambridge: Cambridge Philological Society).

Craik, E. (ed.) (1990), *Owls to Athens: Essays on Classical Subjects for Sir Kenneth Dover* (Oxford: Oxford University Press).

Crane, G. (1988), *Calypso: Backgrounds and Conventions of the Odyssey* (Frankfurt: Athenäum).

Currie, B. (2016), *Homer's Allusive Art* (Oxford: Oxford University Press).

D'Angour, A. (1997), 'How the Dithyramb Got its Shape', *CQ* 47: 331–51.

Davies, M. and Finglass, P. (2014), *Stesichorus: The Poems, Edited with Introduction, Translation and Commentary* (Cambridge: Cambridge University Press).

Debrunner, A. (1923), 'Metrische Kürzung bei Homer', in Wackernagel 1923: 28–40.

Debrunner, A. (ed.) (1954), *Sprachgeschichte und Wortbedeutung* (Bern: Francke).

De Decker, F. (2015), *A Morphosyntactic Analysis of Speech Introductions in Homer* (Diss. Munich).

Dee, J. H. (2004), *Homer: Repertorium Homericae Poiesis Hexametricum*, Vol. 1 (Hildesheim: Georg Olms).

De Jong, I. J. F. (2001), *A Narratological Commentary on the Odyssey* (Cambridge: Cambridge University Press).

Delatte, A. (1936), *Herbarius: recherches sur le cérémonial usité chez les anciens pour la cueillette des simples et des plantes magiques* (Paris: Belles Lettres).

Denniston, J. D. (1952), *Greek Prose Style* (Oxford: Oxford University Press).

Denniston, J. D. (1954), *The Greek Particles*, 2nd edn. (Oxford: Oxford University Press).

Deroy, L. (1946), 'Le pays de Taphos et l'humour homérique: contribution à l'étude du calembour dans la toponymie et l'anthroponymie', *AC* 15: 227–39.

Dickie, M. (1978), 'DIKE as a Moral Term in Homer and Hesiod', *CPh* 73: 91–101.

Diels, H. (1897), *Parmenides Lehrgedicht: griechisch und deutsch mit einem Anhang über griechischen Türen und Schlösser* (Berlin: Reimer).

Diels, H. and Kranz, W. (1964), *Die Fragmente der Vorsokratiker* (Berlin: Weidmann).

Dietz, G. (2000), *Menschenwürde bei Homer* (Heidelberg: Winter).

Diggle, J. (2005), 'A Philologist Reflects', in Bittlestone et al. 2005: 505–29.

Dirlmeier, F. (1966), *Die Giftpfeile des Odysseus* (Heidelberg: Winter).

Dirlmeier, F. (1967), *Die Vogelgestalt homerischer Götter* (Heidelberg: Winter).

Dirlmeier, F. (1970), 'Die "schreckliche" Kalypso' in id. *Ausgewählte Schriften zu Dichtung und Philosophie der Griechen*, ed. H. Görgemanns (Heidelberg: Winter), 79–84.

Dodds, E. R. (1951), *The Greeks and the Irrational* (Berkeley: University of California Press).

Doherty, L. E. (1995), 'Sirens, Muses and Female Narrators in the *Odyssey*', in Cohen 1995: 81–92.

Donlan, W. (1997), 'The Homeric Economy', in Powell and Morris 1997: 649–67.

Drewitt, J. A. (1908), 'Some Differences Between Speech Scansion and Narrative Scansion in Homeric Verse', *CQ* 2: 94–109.

Drewitt, J. A. (1912), 'The Augment in Homer I, II', *CQ* 6: 44–59.

Duchesne-Guillemin, J. (1937), 'Gr. ἱερός —skr. iṣirá–', in Leroy 1937: 333–8.

Duhoux, Y. and Morpurgo Davies, A. (eds.) (2014), *A Companion to Linear B: Mycenean Greek Texts and their World*, Vol. 3 (Louvain-la-Neuve: Peeters).

Dunkel, G. E. (1982/3a), 'πρόσσω καὶ ὀπίσσω', *Zeitschrift für vergleichende Sprachforschung* 96: 66–87.

Dunkel, G. E. (1982/3b), 'IE Conjunctions: Pleonasm, Ablaut, Suppletion', *Zeitschrift für vergleichende Sprachforschung* 96: 178–99.

Dunkel, G. E. (1985), 'IE Hortatory *éy, *éyte: Ved. éta . . . stávāma: Hitt. ehu=wa it: Hom. εἰ δ' ἄγε', *MSS* 46: 47–9.

Durante, M. (1962), 'Richerche sulla preistoria della lingua poetica greca', *Rendiconti Lincei* 17: 25–43 = Schmitt 1968: 291–323.

Durante, M. (1970), 'Etimologie greche', *SMEA* 11: 42–57.

Durante, M. (1976), *Sulla preistoria della tradizione poetica greca*, Vol. 2: *Risultante della comparazione indoeuropea* (Rome: Ateneo).

Edgeworth, R. J. (1983), 'Terms for "Brown" in Ancient Greek', *Glotta* 61: 31–40.

Edwards, C. M. (1984), 'Aphrodite on a Ladder', *Hesperia* 53: 59–72.

Edwards, M. W. (1991), *The Iliad: A Commentary*, Vol. 5: *Books 17–20* (Cambridge: Cambridge University Press).

Edwards, M. W. (1997), 'Homeric Style and "Oral Poetics"' in Powell and Morris 1997: 261–83.

Emlyn-Jones, C. J. (1967), 'ἔτος and ἐνιαυτός in Homeric Formulae', *Glotta* 45: 156–61.

Engels, R. (1977), 'Bemerkungen zum Aithiopenbild der vorhellenistichen Literatur', in Lippold and Himmelmann 1977: 7–53.

Erbse, H. (1972), *Beiträge zum Verständnis der Odyssee* (Berlin: De Gruyter).

Erbse, H. (1980), 'Homerische Götter in Vogelgestalt', *Hermes* 108: 259–74.

Etter, A. (ed.) (1986), *O-o-pe-ro-si: Festschrift für Ernst Risch zum 75. Geburtstag* (Berlin: De Gruyter).

Fehling, D. (1969), *Die Wiederholungsfiguren und ihre Gebrauch bei den Griechen vor Gorgias* (Berlin: De Gruyter).

Felson-Rubin, N. (1987), 'Penelope's Perspective: Character from Plot', in Bremer et al. 1987: 61–83.

Fenik, B. (1974), *Studies in the Odyssey*. Hermes Einzelschriften, Heft 30 (Wiesbaden: Steiner).

Fernandez-Galliano, M. (1992), 'Books XXI–XXIV', in Russo et al. 1992: 131–418.

Finkelberg, M. (2000), 'The *Cypria*, the *Iliad* and the Problem of Multiformity in Oral and Written Tradition', *CPh* 95: 1–11.

Finley, J. H. (1978), *Homer's Odyssey* (Cambridge, Mass.: Harvard University Press).

Finley, M. I. (1955), 'Marriage, Sale and Gift in the Homeric World', *Revue Internationale des Droits de l'Antiquité*, IIIème série, 2: 167–94, repr. in M. I. Finley 1981: 233–45.

Finley, M. I. (1977), *The World of Odysseus*, 2nd edn. (London: Book Club Associates with Chatto and Windus).

Finley, M. I. (1981), *Economy and Society in Ancient Greece* (London: Chatto and Windus).

Fischer, H. and Ritter, R.-P. (1991), 'Zu Bartholomaes (jungavest.) aeta- "das gebührende Teil"', *MSS* 52: 9–13.

Fisher, N. R. E. (1992), *Hybris: A Study in the Values of Honour and Shame in Ancient Greece* (Warminster: Aris & Phillips).

Floyd, E. D. (1992), 'Who and Whose Are You? An Indo-European Poetic Formula', *Word* 43: 399–409.

Fögen, T. (ed.) (2009), *Tears in the Graeco-Roman World* (Berlin: De Gruyter).

Föllinger, S. (2009), 'Tears and Crying in Archaic Greek Poetry', in Fögen 2009: 17–36.

Forster, E. M. (1972), *Maurice* (London: Penguin).

Fortson, B. W. (2009), *Indo-European Language and Culture: An Introduction*, 2nd edn. (Oxford: Wiley-Blackwell).

Fournier, H. (1946), *Les verbes 'dire' en grec ancien* (Paris: Klincksieck).

Fowler, R. (ed.) (2004), *The Cambridge Companion to Homer* (Cambridge: Cambridge University Press).

Fraenkel, E. (1910), *Geschichte der griechischen Nomina agentis auf -τηρ,-τωρ, -της* (Strassburg: Trübner).

Fragiadakis, C. (1988), *Die attischen Sklavennamen* (Athens: Fragiadakis).

Frame, D. (1978), *The Myth of Return in Early Greek Epic* (New Haven, Conn.: Yale University Press).

Fränkel, H. (1975), *Early Greek Poetry and Philosophy* (Oxford: Blackwell).

Frisk, H. (1940), 'Zur griechischen Wortkunde', *Eranos* 38: 36–46.

Frisk, H. (1943), 'Zur griechischen Wortkunde', *Eranos* 41: 48–64.

Frisk, H. (1954–70), *Griechisches etymologisches Wörterbuch*, 2 vols. (Heidelberg: Winter).

Furtwängler, A. (1882), 'Schüssel von Aegina', *Archäologische Zeitung* 40: 196–208.

García-Ramón, J. (1992), 'Griechisch ἱερός und seine Varianten, vedisch iṣirá–', in Beekes 1992: 188–91.

Garvie, A. F. (1994), *Homer: Odyssey Books VI–VIII* (Cambridge: Cambridge University Press).

Gaskin, R. (1990), 'Do Homeric Heroes Make Real Decisions?', *CQ* 40: 1–15.

Geiger, W. and Kuhn, E. (eds.) (1904), *Grundriss der iranischen Philologie Bd. II* (Strasbourg: Trübner).

Geldner, K. F. (1904), 'Awestalitteratur', in Geiger and Kuhn 1904: 1–53.

George, A. (1999), *The Epic of Gilgamesh: A New Translation* (London: Allen Lane).

Georgiev, V. (1960), 'Creto-Mycenaean and Homeric', *Klio* 38: 69–74.

Gérard-Rousseau, M. (1968), *Les mentions religieuses dans les tablettes mycéniennes* (Rome: Ateneo).

Gilchrist, K. E. (1997), *Penelope: A Study in the Manipulation of Myth* (Diss. Oxford).

Ginouvès, R. (1962), *Balaneutiké: recherches sur le bain dans l'antiquité* (Paris: de Boccard).

Godart, L. (2001), 'La Terre Mère et le monde égéen', in Laffineur and Hägg 2001: 463–6.

Goldmann, H. (1942), 'The Origin of the Greek Herm', *AJA* 46: 58–68.

Gonda, J. (1954), 'The Nature of the Indo-European Relative io–', *Lingua* 4: 1–41.

Gonda, J. (1976), *Triads in the Veda* (Amsterdam: North-Holland Publishing Company).

Goodwin, W. W. (1965), *Syntax of the Moods and Tenses of the Greek Verb, Rewritten and Enlarged* (London: Macmillan).

Goold, G. P. (1960), 'Homer and the Alphabet', *TAPhA* 91: 272–91.

Goukowski, P. (1974), 'Les juments du roi Érythras', *REG* 87: 111–37.

Gould, J. (1973), 'Hiketeia', *JHS* 93: 74–103.

Gould, J. (1989), *Herodotus* (London: Weidenfeld and Nicolson).

Gray, D. H. F. (1954), 'Metal-working in Homer', *JHS* 74: 1–15.

Gray, D. H. F. (1955), 'Houses in the *Odyssey*', *CQ* 5: 1–12.

Griffin, J. (1976), 'Homeric Pathos and Objectivity', *CQ* 26: 161–87.

Griffin, J. (1980), *Homer on Life and Death* (Oxford: Oxford University Press).

Griffin, J. (1987), *The Odyssey* (Cambridge: Cambridge University Press).

Griffin, J. (1995), *Homer, Iliad Book Nine: Edited with an Introduction and Commentary* (Oxford: Oxford University Press).

Gschnitzer, F. (1976), *Studien zur griechischen Terminologie der Sklaverei*, Vol. 2: *Forschungen zur antiken Sklaverei* (Wiesbaden: Steiner).

Güterbock, H. G. (1951), 'The Story of Ullikummi: Revised Text of the Hittite Version of a Hurrian Myth', *Journal of Cuneiform Studies* 5: 135–61.

Gwynne, N. M. (2013), *Gwynne's Grammar* (Ebury Press: London).

Haakh, H. (1959), 'Der Schleier der Penelope', *Gymnasium* 66: 374–80.

Hainsworth, J. B. (1962), 'The Homeric Formula and the Problem of its Transmission', *BICS* 9: 57–68.

Hainsworth, J. B. (1964), 'Structure and Content in Epic Formulae: The Question of the Unique Expression', *CQ* 14: 155–64.

Hainsworth, J. B. (1988), 'Books V–VIII', in Heubeck et al. 1998: 3–143.

Hainsworth, J. B. (1993), *The Iliad: A Commentary*, Vol. 3: *Books 9–12* (Cambridge: Cambridge University Press).

Hajnal, I. (2004), 'Die Tmesis bei Homer und auf dem mykenischen Linear B-Tafeln: ein chronologisches Paradox?', in Penney 2004: 146–78.

Halliwell, S. (2009), 'Odysseus's Request and the Need for Song', *Anais de Filosofia Clássica* 3: 1–14.

Harđarson, J. A. (1993), *Studien zum urindogermanischen Wurzelaorist und dessen Vertretung im Indoiranischen und Griechischen* (Innsbruck: Institut für Sprachwissenschaft).

Harrison, S. J. (ed.) (1990), *Oxford Readings in Vergil's Aeneid* (Oxford: Oxford University Press).

Haslam, M. W. (1976), 'Words and Homeric Metre: Two Doublets Examined (λείβω/εἴβω, γαῖα/αῖα)', *Glotta* 54: 201–11.

Haslam, M. W. (1997), 'Homeric Papyri and the Transmission of the Text', in Powell and Morris 1997: 55–100.

Haug, D. (2012), 'Tmesis in the Epic Tradition', in Anderson and Haug 2012: 96–105.

Heath, J. (2001), 'Telemachus *ΠΕΠΝΥΜΕΝΟΣ*', *Mnemosyne* 54: 129–57.

Heer, C. de (1969), *MAKAP—ΕΥΔΑΙΜΩΝ—ΟΛΒΙΟΣ—ΕΥΤΥΧΗΣ: A Study of the Semantic Field Denoting Happiness in Ancient Greek to the End of the 5th Century BC* (Amsterdam: Hakkert).

Heiden, B. (1998), 'The Placement of "Book Divisions" in the *Iliad*', *JHS* 118: 68–81.

Heiden, B. (2000), 'The Placement of "Book Divisions" in the *Odyssey*', *CP* 95: 247–59.

Heiden, B. (2006), 'Review of B. Graziosi and J. Haubold, *Homer: The Resonance of Epic* (London: Duckworth, 2005)', *CR* 56: 2–4.

Heubeck, A. (1970), Review of Gérard-Rousseau (1968), *Gnomon* 42: 810–14.

Heubeck, A. (1971), 'Grieschisch ὀδάξ', in Schmitt-Brandt 1971: 123–9.

Heubeck, A. (1987a), 'Zu den griechischen Verbalwurzeln *nes– und *neu–', in Killen et al. 1987: 227–38.

Heubeck, A. (1987b), 'ἀμύμων', *Glotta* 65: 37–44.

Heubeck, A., West, S. R., and Hainsworth, J. B. (eds.) (1988), *A Commentary on Homer's Odyssey*, Vol. 1: *Books I–VIII* (Oxford: Oxford University Press).

Heubeck, A. and Hoekstra, A. (eds.) (1989), *A Commentary on Homer's Odyssey*, Vol. 2: *Books IX–XVI* (Oxford: Oxford University Press).

Hill, G. (1940), *A History of Cyprus*, Vol. 1 (Cambridge: Cambridge University Press).

Hoekstra, A. (1989), 'Books XIII–XVI', in Heubeck and Hoekstra 1989: 147–287.

Hoffmann, M. (1914), *Die ethische Terminologie bei Homer, Hesiod und den altern Elegikern und Jambographen*, Vol. 1: *Homer* (Tübingen: Kloeres).

Hölkeskamp, K.-J. (2002), 'Ptolis and Agore: Homer and the Archaeology of the City State', in Montanari and Ascheri 2002: 297–342.

Hollifield, H. (1981), 'Homeric κείω and the Greek Desideratives', *IF* 86: 161–89.

Hooker, J. T. (1967), 'Homeric Nominatives in –ΤΑ', *Glotta* 45: 14–23.

Hooker, J. T. (1975), 'The Original Meaning of ΥΒΡΙΣ', *ABG* 19: 125–37.

Hooker, J. T. (1980), ἱερός *in Early Greek* (Innsbruck: Institut für Sprachwissenschaft).

Hooker, J. T. (1987), 'Homeric φίλος', *Glotta* 65: 44–65.

Horrocks, G. (1997), 'Homer's Dialect', in Powell and Morris 1997: 193–217.

Horsfall, N. M. (1990), 'Dido in the Light of History', in Harrison 1990: 127–44, repr. from *PVS* 13 (1973–4): 1–13.

Humbert, J. (1954), *Syntaxe grecque* (Paris: Klincksieck).

Immerwahr, H. R. (1990), *Attic Script: A Survey* (Oxford: Oxford University Press).

Irwin, E. (1974), *Colour Terms in Greek Poetry* (Toronto: Hakkert).

Jacobson, H. (2000). 'Homer, *Odyssey* 1.132–3', *CQ* 50: 290.

Jacoby, F. (1923–58), *Fragmente der griechischen Historiker* (Leiden: Brill).

Jacquinod, B. (1989), *Le double accusative en grec d'Homère à la fin du Ve siècle avant J.-C.* (Louvain-le-Neuve: Peeters).

Jahn, T. (1987), *Zum Wortfeld 'Seele-Geist' in der Sprache Homers* (Munich: Beck).

Janda, M. (2010), *Die Musik nach dem Chaos: Der Schöpfungsmythos der europäischen Vorzeit* (Innsbruck: Institut für Sprachen und Literaturen).

Janda, M. (2014), *Purpurnes Meer: Sprache und Kultur der homerischen Welt* (Innsbruck: Institut für Sprachen und Literaturen).

Janko, R. (1978), 'A Note on the Etymologies of διάκτορος and χρυσάορος', *Glotta* 56: 192–5.

Janko, R. (1982), *Homer, Hesiod and the Hymns* (Cambridge: Cambridge University Press).

Janko, R. (1992), *The Iliad: A Commentary*, Vol. 4: *Books 13–16* (Cambridge: Cambridge University Press).

Janko, R. (2012), 'πρῶτόν τε καὶ ὕστατον αἰὲν ἀείδειν: Relative Chronology and the Literary History of the Early Greek *epos*', in Anderson and Haug 2012: 20–43.

Jantzen, U. and Tölle, R. (1968), 'Beleuchtungsgerät', *Archaeologia Homerica* Bd. 3. *Kap. P* (Göttingen: Vandenhoeck & Ruprecht), 83–98.

Jeffery, L. H. (1990), *The Local Scripts of Archaic Greece*, 2nd edn. rev. A. W. Johnston (Oxford: Oxford University Press).

Jones, B. (2012), 'Relative Chronology and an "Aeolic" Phase of Epic', in Anderson and Haug 2012: 44–64.

Jones, P. V. (1991), *Homer: Odyssey 1 & 2* (Warminster: Aris & Phillips).

Joseph, B. D. (1982), 'The Source of Ancient Greek τολύπη', *Glotta* 60: 230–4.

Kahane, A. (1992), 'The First Word of the *Odyssey*', *TAPhA* 112: 115–31.

Kahane, A. (2005), *Diachronic Dialogues: Authority and Continuity in Homer and the Homeric Tradition* (Lanham: Lexington).

Kahane, A. (2012), *Homer: A Guide for the Perplexed* (London: Bloomsbury).

Kamptz, H. P. von (1982), *Sprachwissenschaftliche und historische Klassifikation der homerischen Personennamen* (Göttingen: Vandenhoeck & Ruprecht).

Kanavou, N. (2015), *The Names of Homeric Heroes: Problems and Interpretations*, Sozomena 15 (Berlin: De Gruyter).

Kardara, C. (1960), 'Problems of Hera's Cult Images', *AJA* 64: 352–8.

Katz, J. T. (2007), 'The Epic Adventures of an Unknown Particle', in Coulter and McCullaugh 2007: 65–79.

Katz, J. T. (2010), 'Nonne lexica etymologica multiplicanda sunt?', in Stray 2010: 25–48.

Kerényi, C. (1976), *Dionysos: Archetypal Image of Indestructible Life*, tr. R. Manheim, repr. 1996 (Princeton: Princeton University Press).

Killen, J. T., Melena, J. L., and Olivier, J.-P. (eds.) (1987), *Studies in Mycenean and Classical Greek Presented to John Chadwick* (Salamanca: Ediciones Universidad de Salamanca).

Kirk, G. S. (1960), 'Objective Dating Criteria in Homer', *MH* 17: 189–205.

Kirk, G. S. (1981), 'Pitfalls in the Study of Sacrifice', in Rudhardt and Reverdin 1981: 41–90.

Kirk, G. S. (1985), *The Iliad: A Commentary*, Vol. 1: *Books 1–4* (Cambridge: Cambridge University Press).

Kirk, G. S. (1990), *The Iliad: A Commentary*, Vol. 2: *Books 5–8* (Cambridge: Cambridge University Press).

Kloss, G. (1994), *Untersuchungen zum Wortfeld 'Verlangen/Begehren' im frühgriechischen Epos* (Göttingen: Vandenhoeck & Ruprecht).

Knapp, A. B. and Kassianidou, V. (2008), 'The Archaeology of Late Bronze Age Copper Production: Politiko Phorades on Cyprus', in Yalçin 2008: 135–48.

Knox, M. O. (1970), ' "House" and "Palace" in Homer', *JHS* 90: 117–20.

Knox, M. O. (1973), 'Megarons and *ΜΕΓΑΡΑ*: Homer and Archaeology', *CQ* 23: 1–21.

Kober, A. E. (1932), *The Use of Colour Terms in the Greek Poets, Including All the Poets from Homer to 146 BC except the Epigrammatists* (New York: Humphrey).

Koch, H. J. (1976), '*αἰπὺς ὄλεθρος* and the Etymology of *ὄλλυμι*', *Glotta* 54: 216–22.

Koller, H. (1965), '*ΘΕΣΠΙΣ ΑΟΙΔΟΣ*', *Glotta* 43: 277–85.

Kratz, R. G. and Sprechermann, H. (eds.) (2008), *Divine Wrath and Divine Mercy in the World of Antiquity* (Tübingen: Mohr Siebeck).

Kraus, W. (1955), 'Die Auffassung des Dichtersberuf im frühen Griechentum', *WS* 68: 65–87.

Kretschmer, P. (1909a), 'Zur Geschichte der griechischen Dialekte', *Glotta* 1: 9–59.

Kretschmer, P. (1909b), 'Zur griechischen und lateinischen Wortforschung', *Glotta* 1: 323–33.

Kretschmer, P. (1913), 'Mythische Namen', *Glotta* 4: 305–9.

Kretschmer, P. (1916), 'Literaturbericht für das Jahr 1913', *Glotta* 7: 321–5.

Kretschmer, P. (1919), 'Mythische Namen', *Glotta* 10: 38–62.

Kretschmer, P. (1927), 'Griech. *φίλος*', *IF* 45: 267–71.

Kretschmer, P. and Skutsch, F. (1909), 'Literaturbericht für das Jahr 1907', *Glotta* 1: 349–416.

Kühner, R. and Gerth, B. (1898), *Ausführliche Grammatik der griechischen Sprache, Zeiter Teil: Satzlehre*, Vol. 1 (Hannover: Hahnsche Buchhandlung).

Kumpf, M. (1984), *Four Indices of the Homeric Hapax Legomena* (Hildesheim: Olms).

Kurke, L. (1999), 'Ancient Greek Board Games and How to Play Them', *CPh* 94: 247–67.

Lacey, W. K. (1966), 'Homeric *ΕΔΝΑ* and Penelope's *ΚΥΡΙΟΣ*', *JHS* 86: 55–68.

Laffineur, R. and Hägg, R. (eds.) (2001), *Potnia: Deities and Religion in the Aegean Bronze Age*, Aegeum 22 (Liège: Université de Liège).

Lamberterie, Ch. de (1997), '*φώς*' (= *Chroniques d'étymologie grecque* 2, 1997), *RPh* 71: 177–8.

Laser, S. (1968), 'Hausrat', *Archaeologia Homerica Bd. 3. Kap. P* (Göttingen: Vandenhoeck & Ruprecht).

Laser, S. (1987), 'Sport und Spiel', *Archaeologia Homerica Bd. 3. Kap. T* (Göttingen: Vandenhoeck & Ruprecht).

Latacz, J. (2004), *Troy and Homer*, tr. K. Windle and R. Ireland (Oxford: Oxford University Press).

Leaf, W. (1886), *The Iliad: Edited, with English Notes and Introduction*, Vol. 1 (London: Macmillan).

Leaf, W. (1888), *The Iliad: Edited, with English Notes and Introduction*, Vol. 2 (London: Macmillan).

Leaf, W. (1900), *The Iliad: Edited, with Apparatus Criticus, Prolegomena, Notes and Appendices*, 2nd edn., Vol. 1 (London: Macmillan).

Lehrs, K. (1865), *De Aristarchi Studiis Homericis* (Leipzig: Hirzel).

Lejeune, M. (1963), 'Noms propres de boeufs à Cnossos', *REG* 76: 1–9.

Lejeune, M. (1976), 'ΔΩ Maison', *SMEA* 17: 79–84.

Lenz, J. R. (1993), *Kings and the Ideology of Kingship in Early Greece (c.1200–700 BC): Epic, Archaeology, History* (Diss. Columbia).

Leroy, M. (ed.) (1937), *Mélanges E. Boisacq*, Vol. 1 = *Annuaire de l'Institut de Philologie et d'Histoire*, 5: 333–8 (Brussels: Secrétariat des éditions de l'Institut).

Lesky, A. (1947), *Thalatta: Der Weg der Griechen zum Meer* (Vienna: Rohrer).

Lesky, A. (1950), 'Hethitische Texte und griechischer Mythos', *Anzeiger der phil.-hist. Klasse der Österreichischen Akademie der Wissenschaften* 9: 148–55.

Lesky, A. (1959), 'Aithiopika', *Hermes* 87: 29–38.

Lessing, G. E. (1767), *Laokoon*, cited from the German text edited by A. Hamann, revised 1901 with introduction by L. E. Upcott (Oxford: Clarendon Press).

Létoublon, F. (1985), *Il allait, pareil à la nuit: les verbes de mouvement en grec: supplétisme et aspect verbal* (Paris: Klincksieck).

Leukart, A. (1986), 'Homerisch ἀτρύγετος', in Etter 1986: 340–5.

Leumann, M. (1950), *Homerische Wörter* (Basel: Reinhardt; repr. 1993 Darmstadt: Wissenschaftliche Buchgesellschaft).

Leumann, M. (1959), *Kleine Schriften* (Zurich and Stuttgart: Artemis).

Lewy, H. (1895), *Die semitischen Fremdwörter im Griechischen* (Berlin: Gaertner).

Lillo, A. (1992), 'Zur griechisch τίπτε', *Glotta* 70: 15–19.

Lippold, A. and Himmelmann, N. (eds.) (1977), *Bonner Festgabe Johannes Straub* (Bonn: Rheinland Verlag).

Lloyd-Jones, H. (1983), *The Justice of Zeus*, 2nd edn. (Berkeley: University of California Press).

Lord, A. B. (1960), *The Singer of Tales*, 2nd edn. (2000) ed. S. Mitchell and G. Nagy (Cambridge, Mass.: Harvard University Press).

Lorimer, H. L. (1950), *Homer and the Monuments* (London: Macmillan).

Macdonell, A. A. (1916), *A Vedic Grammar for Students*, 12th Indian repr. 1990 (Delhi: Oxford University Press).

MacDowell, D. M. (1976), 'Hybris in Athens', *G&R* 23: 14–31.

Macleod, C. W. (1982), *Homer: Iliad, Book XXIV* (Cambridge: Cambridge University Press).

Macleod, C. W. (1983), 'Homer on Poetry and the Poetry of Homer' in *Collected Essays* (Oxford: Oxford University Press), 1–15.

Marinatos, S. (1967), 'Kleidung', *Archaeologia Homerica Bd. 1. Kap. A* (Göttingen: Vandenhoeck & Ruprecht).

Martin, R. P. (1989), *The Language of Heroes* (Ithaca: Cornell University Press).

Maslov, B. (2009), 'The Semantics of ἀοιδός: Towards a Historical Poetics of Solo Performance in Archaic Greece', *ClAnt* 28: 1–38.

Matthews, V. J. (1978), 'Atlas, Aietes and Minos ΟΛΟΟΦΡΩΝ', *CPh* 73: 228–32.

Maurice, N. (1991), '*Τολύπη*: ou les écheveaux de l'étymologie', *RPh* 65: 161–7.

Mead, M. (1937), *Co-operation and Competition among Primitive Peoples* (New York: McGraw-Hill).

Meiggs, R. and Lewis, D. (1988), *A Selection of Greek Historical Inscriptions, Revised Edition with Addenda and Concordance* (Oxford: Clarendon Press).

Meillet, A. (1926), 'De la prothèse vocalique en grec et en arménien', *BSL* 27: 129–35.

Meillet, A. (1935), *Introduction à l'étude comparative des langues indo-européennes* (Paris: Hachette).

Meissner, T. (2006), *S-Stem Nouns and Adjectives in Greek and Proto-Indo-European: A Diachronic Study in Word Formation* (Oxford: Oxford University Press).

Meister, K. (1921), *Die Homerische Kunstsprache* (Lepizig: Teubner).

Melchert, H. C. (1984), *Studies in Hittite Historical Phonology* (Göttingen: Vandenhoeck & Ruprecht).

Melena, J. L. (2014), 'Mycenean Writing', in Duhoux and Morpurgo Davies 2014: 1–186.

Merkelbach, R. (1967), 'Ein Alkaios-Papyrus', *ZPE* 1: 81–95.

Merkelbach, R. and West, M. L. (1967), *Fragmenta Hesiodea* (Oxford: Clarendon Press).

Metcalf, C. (2015), *The Gods Rich in Praise* (Oxford: Oxford University Press).

Mette, H. J. (1960), 'Schauen und Staunen', *Glotta* 39: 49–71.

Mondi, R. (1983), 'The Homeric Cyclopes: Folktale, Tradition and Theme', *TAPhA* 113: 17–38.

Monro, D. B. (1891), *Homeric Grammar*, 2nd edn. (Oxford: Oxford University Press).

Monsacré, H. (1984), *Les larmes d'Achille: le héros, la femme et la souffrance dans la poésie d'Homère* (Paris: A. Michel).

Montanari, F. and Ascheri, P. (eds.) (2002), *Omero tremila anni dopo* (Rome: Edizioni di Storia e Letteratura).

Moorhouse, A. C. (1940), 'The Name of the Euxine Pontus', *CQ* 34: 123–8.

Moorhouse, A. C. (1941), 'IE *PENT and its Derivatives', *CQ* 35: 90–6.

Moorhouse, A. C. (1948), 'The Name of the Euxine Pontus Again', *CQ* 42: 59–60.

Morpurgo Davies, A. (1964), ' "Doric" Features in the Language of Hesiod', *Glotta* 42: 138–65.

Morpurgo Davies, A. (1976), 'The -εσσι Datives, Aeolic -ss- and the Lesbian Poets', in Morpurgo Davies and Meid 1976: 181–97.

Morpurgo Davies, A. (1979), 'Terminology of Power and Terminology of Work in Greek and Linear B', in E. Risch and H. Mühlestein (eds.),

Colloquium Mycenaeum VI (Neuchâtel: Neuchâtel Faculté des Lettres), 87–108.

Morpurgo Davies, A. and Meid, W. (eds.) (1976), *Studies in Greek, Italic and Indo-European Linguistics Offered to Leonard R. Palmer on the Occasion of his Seventieth Birthday* (Innsbruck: Innsbrucker Beiträge zur Sprachwissenschaft).

Morris, I. (1987), *Burial and Ancient Society: The Rise of the Greek City-State* (Cambridge: Cambridge University Press).

Morris, I. (1997), 'Homer and the Bronze Age', in Powell and Morris 1997: 535–59.

Morris, S. (1997) 'Homer and the Near East', in Powell and Morris 1997: 599–623.

Morrison, J. S. and Williams, R. T. (1968), *Greek Oared Ships: 900–322 BC* (Cambridge: Cambridge University Press).

Most, G. W. (ed.) (1998), *Editing Texts/Texte edieren*, Aporemata: Kritische Studien zur Philologiegeschichte Band 2 (Göttingen: Vandenhoeck & Ruprecht).

Motte, A. (1986), 'L'expression du sacré dans la religion grecque', in Ries 1986: 109–256.

Muehll, P. von der (1962), *Homeri Odyssea*, 3rd edn. (Stuttgart: Teubner).

Muellner, L. (1996), *The Anger of Achilles* (Ithaca: Cornell University Press).

Muller, F. (1929), '*ΑΛΑΣΤΩΡ*', *Mnemosyne* 57: 116–24.

Murnaghan, S. (1995), 'The Plan of Athena', in Cohen 1995: 61–80.

Murray, O. (1993), *Early Greece*, 2nd edn. (London: Fontana).

Mylonas, G. (1962), 'Burial Customs', in Wace and Stubbings 1962: 478–88.

Nadeau, J. Y. (1970), 'Ethiopians', *CQ* 20: 339–49.

Nagy, G. (1995), 'An Evolutionary Model for the Making of Homeric Poetry', in Carter and S. P. Morris 1995: 163–79.

Nagy, G. (1996), *Homeric Questions* (Austin: University of Texas Press).

Nagy, G. (1997), 'Homeric Scholia', in Powell and Morris 1997: 101–22.

Neuberger-Donath, R. (1980), '*ΠΕΛΩ*—Syntaktischer Gebrauch und Diathesenunterschied', *Grazer Beiträge* 9: 1–10.

Neumann, G. (1973), 'Kyprisch *mo-ne-mi-si-ta*', *Kadmos* 12: 159–65.

Nikolaev, A. S. (2004), 'Die Etymologie von altgriechischem ὕβρις', *Glotta* 80: 211–30.

Nilsson, M. (1967), *Geschichte der griechischen Religion*, 3rd edn. (Munich: C. H. Beck).

Nordheider, H. W. (2004), '*πολύς, πουλύς, πολλός, πλε(ί)ων, πλεῖστος*', in Snell et al. (1955–2010) *Lfg. 20*: 1405–28.

Notopoulos, J. A. (1960), 'Homer, Hesiod and the Achaean Heritage of Oral Poetry', *Hesperia* 29: 177–97.

Novikov, N. V. (1977), 'Baba-Jaga', in K. Ranke et al. (eds.), *Enzyklopädie des Märchens*, Vol. 1 (Berlin: De Gruyter), 1121–3.

Nünlist, R. (2011), Review of F. Pontani, *Scholia Graeca in Odysseam, I* in *Mnemosyne* 64: 140–4.

Olson, S. D. (1990), 'The Stories of Agamemnon in Homer's *Odyssey*', *TAPhA* 120: 57–71.

Olson, S. D. (1992), 'Name-Magic and the Threat of Lying Strangers in the *Odyssey*', *ICS* 17: 1–7.

Onians, R. B. (1924), 'On the Knees of the Gods', *CR* 38: 2–6.

Onians, R. B. (1951), *The Origins of European Thought* (Cambridge: Cambridge University Press).

O'Nolan, K. (1978), 'Doublets in the *Odyssey*', *CQ* 28: 23–37.

Osborne, R. (2004), 'Homer's Society' in Fowler 2004: 206–19.

Osthoff, H. (1883), 'μνάομαι, ich freie', *KZ* 26: 326.

O'Sullivan, J. N. (1990), 'Nature and Culture in *Odyssey* 9', *SO* 65: 7–17.

Page, D. (1955), *The Homeric Odyssey* (Oxford: Clarendon Press).

Page, D. (1966), *History and the Homeric Iliad* (Berkeley and Los Angeles: University of California Press).

Pagliaro, A. (1961), *Saggi di critica semantica*, 2nd edn. (Messina: G. d'Anna).

Palm, J. (1969), 'Lag die Zunkunft der Griechen hinter ihnen?', *Annales Academiae Regiae Scientiarum Upsaliensis* 13: 5–13.

Palmer, L. R. (1963), *The Interpretation of Mycenaean Texts* (Oxford: Oxford University Press).

Palmer, L. R. (1980), *The Greek Language* (London: Faber).

Parker, R. (2011), *On Greek Religion* (Ithaca: Cornell University Press).

Parkinson, R. B. (1997), *The Tale of Sinuhe and Other Ancient Egyptian Poems 1940–1640 BC* (Oxford: Oxford University Press).

Parry, Adam (1966), 'Have We Homer's *Iliad*?', *YClS* 20: 177–216.

Parry, Adam (1971), *The Making of Homeric Verse: The Collected Papers of Milman Parry* (Oxford: Oxford University Press).

Parry, Adam (1989), *The Language of Achilles and Other Papers* (Oxford: Oxford University Press).

Parry, Anne (1973), *Blameless Aegisthus* (Leiden: Brill).

Parry, M. (1928), *L'Épithète traditionelle dans Homère: Essai sur un problème de style homérique* (Paris: Belles Lettres).

Parry, M. (1933), 'Whole Formulaic Verses in Greek and Southslavic Heroic Song', *TAPhA* 64: 179–97 = A. Parry (1971): 376–90.

Penney, J. H. W. (ed.) (2004), *Indo-European Perspectives: Studies in Honour of Anna Morpurgo Davies* (Oxford: Oxford University Press).

Peponi, A.-E. (2012), *Frontiers of Pleasure: Models of Aesthetic Response in Archaic and Classical Greek Thought* (Oxford: Oxford University Press).

Peradotto, J. and Sullivan, J. P. (eds.) (1984), *Women in the Ancient World: The Arethusa Papers* (Albany: SUNY Press).

Perysinakis, I. N. (1991), 'Penelope's ΕΕΔΝΑ Again', *CQ* 41: 297–302.

Pfeiffer, R. (1949–53), *Callimachus*, 2 vols. (Oxford: Clarendon Press).

Pfeiffer, R. (1968), *History of Classical Scholarship from the Beginnings to the End of the Hellenistic Age* (Oxford: Clarendon).

Platt, A. (1891), 'The Augment in Homer', *Journal of Philology* 19: 211–37.

Platt, A. (1899), 'Notes on the *Odyssey*', *CR* 13: 382–4.

Pontani, F. (2005), *Sguardi su Ulisse: la tradizione esegetica greca all'Odissea* (Roma: Edizioni di Storie e Letteratura).

Pontani, F. (2007), *Scholia graeca in Odysseam*, Vol. 1 (Roma: Edizioni di Storie e Letteratura).

Poulengeris, A. C. (2001), *Studies in the Text of Iliad 3–5* (Diss. London: Royal Holloway).

Powell, B. (1991), *Homer and the Origin of the Greek Alphabet* (Cambridge: Cambridge University Press).

Powell, B. and Morris, I. (eds.) (1997), *A New Companion to Homer* (Leiden: Brill).

Prévot, A. (1935a), 'Verbes grecs relatifs à la vision et noms de l'oeil (suite)', *RPh* 9: 233–79.

Prévot, A. (1935b), 'L'expression en grec ancien de la notion "entendre"', *REG* 48: 70–8.

Pritchard, J. B. (1974), *Solomon & Sheba* (London: Phaidon).

Probert, P. (2003), *A New Short Guide to the Accentuation of Ancient Greek* (Bristol: Bristol Classical Press).

Probert, P. (2015), *Early Greek Relative Clauses* (Oxford: Oxford University Press).

Pucci, P. (1979), 'The Song of the Sirens', *Arethusa* 12: 121–32.

Puhvel, J. (1964), 'The Meaning of Greek Βουκάτιος', *Zeitschrift für vergleichende Sprachforschung* 79: 7–10.

Pulleyn, S. J. (1997), *Prayer in Greek Religion* (Oxford: Oxford University Press).

Pulleyn, S. J. (2000), *Homer, Iliad Book One: Edited with an Introduction, Translation, and Commentary* (Oxford: Oxford University Press).

Pulleyn, S. J. (2006), 'Homer's Religion', in M. J. Clarke, B. G. F. Currie, R. O. A. M. Lyne (eds.), *Epic Interactions* (Oxford: Oxford University Press), 47–74.

Raaflaub, K. (1997), 'Homeric Society', in Powell and Morris (1997), 624–48.

Radt, S. (1999), *Tragicorum Graecorum Fragmenta*, Vol. 4: *Sophocles*. 2nd edn. corrected and expanded (Göttingen: Vandenhoeck & Ruprecht).

Raman, R. (1975), 'Homeric ἄωτος and Pindaric ἄωτος', *Glotta* 53: 195–207.

Redard, G. R. (1953), *Recherches sur ΧΡΗ, ΧΡΗΣΘΑΙ: étude sémantique* (Paris: Champion).

Reden, S. von (1995), *Exchange in Ancient Greece* (London: Duckworth).

Redfield, J. (1994), *Nature and Culture in the Iliad: The Tragedy of Hector*, expanded edn. (London and Durham: Duke University Press).

Reece, S. (1992), *The Stranger's Welcome: Oral Theory and the Aesthetics of the Homeric Hospitality Scene* (Ann Arbor: University of Michigan Press).

Reece, S. (1994), 'The Cretan Odyssey: A Lie Truer Than Truth', *AJPh* 115: 157–73.

Reiner, E. and Roth, M. T. (1999), *Chicago Akkadian Dictionary*, Vol. 14: *R* (Chicago Illinois: Oriental Institute).

Richardson, N. J. (1973), *The Homeric Hymn to Demeter* (Oxford: Oxford University Press).

Richardson, N. J. (1980), 'Literary Criticism in the Exegetical Scholia to the *Iliad*: A Sketch', *CQ* 30: 265–87.

Richardson, N. J. (1987), 'The Individuality of Homer's Language', in Bremer et al. 1987: 165–84.

Richardson, N. J. (1993), *The Iliad: A Commentary*, Vol. 6: *Books 21–24* (Cambridge: Cambridge University Press).

Richardson, N. J. (2010), *Three Homeric Hymns* (Cambridge: Cambridge University Press).

Richter, G. (1966), *Furniture of the Greeks, Etruscans and Romans* (London: Phaidon).

Richter, W. (1968), 'Die Landwirtschaft im homerischen Zeitalter', *Archaeologia Homerica, Bd. 2, Kap. H* (Göttingen: Vandenhoeck & Ruprecht).

Ries, J. (ed.) (1986), *L'expression du sacré dans les grandes religions*, Vol. 3 (Louvain-la-Neuve: Centre d'histoire des religions).

Rijksbaron, A. (2002), *The Syntax and Semantics of the Verb in Classical Greek*, 2nd edn. (Amsterdam: Gieben).

Risch, E. (1974), *Wortbildung der homerischen Sprache* (Berlin and New York: De Gruyter).

Rix, H. (2001), *Lexikon der indogermanischen Verben* (Wiesbaden: Reichert).

Robinson, D. (1990), 'Homeric φίλος: Love of Life and Limbs, and Friendship with One's θυμός', in Craik 1990: 97–108.

Roisman, H. and Roisman, J. (eds.) (2002), 'Essays in Homeric Epic', *ColbyQ* 38.2.

Roller, D. (2015), *Ancient Geography: The Discovery of the World in Classical Greece and Rome* (London: Tauris).

Romm, J. S. (1992), *The Edges of the Earth in Ancient Thought: Geography, Exploration and Fiction* (Princeton, NJ: Princeton University Press).

Roth, C. P. (1974), 'More Homeric "Mixed Aorists"', *Glotta* 52: 1–10.

Rudd, N. (1990), 'Dido's *Culpa*', in Harrison 1990: 145–66, repr. from id. (1976) *Lines of Enquiry* (Cambridge: Cambridge University Press), 32–53.

Rudhardt, J. and Reverdin, O. (eds.) (1981), *Le Sacrifice dans l'Antiquité*, Entretiens sur l'antiquité classique 27 (Geneva: Fondation Hardt).

Ruijgh, C. J. (1957), *L'Élement achéen dans la langue épique* (Assen: Van Gorcum).

Ruijgh, C. J. (1967a), *Études sur la grammaire et le vocabulaire du grec mycénien* (Amsterdam: Hakkert).

Ruijgh, C. J. (1967b), 'Sur le nom de Poséidon et sur les noms en -α-ϝων, -ι-ϝων', *REG* 80: 6–16.

Ruijgh, C. J. (1968), 'Les noms en -won- (-āwon-, -īwon-), -uon- en grec alphabétique et en mycénien', *Minos* 9: 109–55.

Ruijgh, C. J. (1970), 'L'origine du signe *41 (si) de l'écriture Linéaire B', *Kadmos* 9: 172–3.

Ruijgh, C. J. (1971), Review of Wyatt (1969), *Lingua* 27: 263–76.

Russo, J. (1992), 'Books XVII–XX', in Russo et al. 1992: 3–127.

Russo, J., Fernandez-Galliano, M., and Heubeck, A. (eds.) (1992), *A Commentary on Homer's Odyssey*, Vol. 3: *Books XVII–XXIV* (Oxford: Oxford University Press).

Rüter, K. (1969), *Odyseeinterpretationen: Untersuchungen zum ersten Buch und zur Phaiakis* (Göttingen: Vandenhoeck & Ruprecht).

Rutherford, R. B. (1986), 'The Philosophy of the *Odyssey*', *JHS* 106: 145–62.

Rutherford, R. B. (1992), *Homer: Odyssey Books XIX and XX* (Cambridge: Cambridge University Press).

Rutherford, R. B. (2013), *Homer*, 2nd edn., Greece and Rome New Surveys in the Classics No. 41 (Cambridge: Classical Association).

Sacks, R. (1987), *The Traditional Phrase in Homer* (Leiden: Brill).

Schenk, P. (2008), 'Darstellung und Funktion des Zorns der Götter in antiker Epik', in Kratz and Sprechermann 2008: 153–75.

Schmiedeberg, O. (1918), *Über die Pharmaka in der Ilias und Odyssee*, Schriften der Wissenschaftlichen Gesellschaft in Straßburg 36. Heft (Strasburg: Trübner).

Schmitt, R. (1968), *Indogermanische Dichtersprache* (Darmstadt: Wissenschaftliche Buchgesellschaft).

Schmitt-Brandt, R. (ed.) (1971), *Donum Indogermanicum: Festgabe für Anton Scherer zum 70. Geburtstag* (Heidelberg: Winter).

Schneider, P. (2004), *L'Éthiopie et l'Inde: interferences et confusions aux extrémités du monde antique* (Rome: École Française de Rome).

Schulze, W. (1892), *Quaestiones Epicae* (Gutersloh: Bertelsmann).

Schwyzer, E. (1939), *Griechische Grammatik: auf der Grundlage von Karl Brugmanns Griechischer Grammatik*, Vol. 1 (Munich: C. H. Beck).

Schwyzer, E. (1950), *Griechische Grammatik: auf der Grundlage von Karl Brugmanns Griechischer Grammatik*, Vol. 2 (Munich: C. H. Beck).

Scott, J. A. (1912), 'Patronymics as a Test of the Relative Age of Homeric Books', *CPh* 7: 293–301.

Scott, W. C. (1971), 'A Repeated Episode at *Od.* 1.125–48', *TAPhA* 102: 541–55.

Scott, W. C. (1974), *The Oral Nature of the Homeric Simile* (Leiden: Brill).

Seaford, R. (1994), *Reciprocity and Ritual* (Oxford: Oxford University Press).

Segal, C. (1971), *The Theme of the Mutilation of the Corpse in the Iliad* (Leiden: Brill).

Segal, C. (1974), 'Eros and Incantation: Sappho and Oral Poetry', *Arethusa* 7: 139–60.

Shelmerdine, C. W. (1995), 'Shining and Fragrant Cloth in Homeric Epic', in Carter and S. P. Morris 1995: 99–107.

Shipp, G. P. (1961), *Essays in Mycenean and Homeric Greek* (Parkville: Melbourne University Press).

Shipp, G. P. (1972), *Studies in the Language of Homer*, 2nd edn. (Cambridge: Cambridge University Press).

Sihler, A. (1995), *New Comparative Grammar of Greek and Latin* (Oxford: Oxford University Press).

Smyth, H. W. (1956), *Greek Grammar* (Cambridge, Mass.: Harvard University Press).

Snell, B. (1953), *The Discovery of the Mind*, tr. T. G. Rosenmeyer (Oxford: Blackwell).

Snell, B. et al. (1955–2010), *Lexikon des frühgriechischen Epos* (Göttingen: Vandenhoeck & Ruprecht).

Snell, B. (1978), *Der Weg zum Denken* (Göttingen: Vandenhoeck & Ruprecht).

Snell, B. (1986), *Tragicorum Graecorum Fragmenta*, Vol. 1: *Didascaliae Tragicae, Catalogi Tragicorum et Tragoediarum, Testimonia et Fragmenta Tragicorum Minorum*, 2nd edn. corrected and expanded by R. Kannicht (Göttingen: Vandenhoeck & Ruprecht).

Snodgrass, A. M. (1970), Review of Laser et al. (1968), *Gnomon* 42: 157–66.

Snodgrass, A. M. (1974), 'An Historical Homeric Society', *JHS* 94: 114–25.

Snowden, F. M. (1970), *Blacks in Antiquity: Ethiopians in the Greco-Roman Experience* (Harvard: Belknap Press).

Solmsen, F. (1905), *Inscriptiones Graecae ad Inlustrandas Dialectos Selectae* (Leipzig: Teubner).

Sommer, F. (1934), *Ahhijavafrage und Sprachwissenschaft* (Munich: Verlag der Bayerischen Akademie der Wissenschaften).

Spyropoulos, T. G. and Chadwick, J. (1975), *The Thebes Tablets II, Including Indexes of the Thebes Tablets by José L. Melena* (Salamanca: Universidad de Salamanca).

Stanford, W. B. (1952), 'The Homeric Etymology of the Name Odysseus', *CPh* 47: 209–13.

Stanford, W. B. (1959), *ΟΜΗΡΟΥ ΟΔΥΣΣΕΙΑ: The Odyssey of Homer, Edited with General and Grammatical Introduction, Commentary and Indexes*, 2nd edn., Vol. 1 (London: Macmillan).

Steele, P. M. (2013), *A Linguistic History of Ancient Cyprus: The Non-Greek Languages and their Relations with Greek c.1600–300 BC* (Cambridge: Cambridge University Press).

Stefanelli, R. (2009), 'Νόος ovvero la "via" del pensiero', *Glotta* 85: 217–63.

Steiner, D. (1995), 'Stoning and Sight: A Structural Equivalence in Greek Mythology', *ClAnt* 14: 193–211.

Steiner, G. (1989), *Real Presences* (London: Faber).

Stray, C. (ed.) (2010), *Classical Dictionaries: Past, Present and Future* (London: Duckworth).

Strunk, K. (1957), *Die sogennanten Äolismen der homerischen Sprache* (Diss. Düsseldorf and Köln).

Stubbings, F. H. (1962), 'Arms and Armour', in Wace and Stubbings 1962: 504–22.

Sundermann, W., de Blois, F., and Hintze, A. (eds.) (2009), *Exegisti Monumenta: Festschrift in Honour of Nicholas Sims-Williams* (Wiesbaden: Harrasowitz).

Szemerényi, O. (1951), 'Greek μέλλω: A Historical and Comparative Study', *AJPh* 72: 346–68.

Szemerényi, O. (1954), 'Greek ταφών—θάμβος—θεάομαι', *Glotta* 33: 238–66.

Szemerényi, O. (1964), *Syncope in Greek and Indo-European and the Nature of the Indo-European Accent* (Naples: Istituto Universitario di Napoli).

Szemerényi, O. (1966), 'The Labiovelars in Mycenean and Historical Greek', *SMEA* 1: 29–52.

Szemerényi, O. (1967), 'The Perfect Participle Active in Mycenean and Indo-European', *SMEA* 2: 7–26.

Szemerényi, O. (1972), Review of Schmitt-Brandt 1971 in *Kratylos* 17: 86–90.

Szemerényi, O. (1979), 'Etyma Graeca IV: Homerica et Mycenaica', *SMEA* 20: 207–26.

Szemerényi, O. (1999), *Introduction to Indo-European Linguistics* (Oxford: Oxford University Press).

Taplin, O. (1992), *Homeric Soundings* (Oxford: Oxford University Press).

Thieme, P. (1952), 'Studien zur indogermanischen Wortkunde und Religionsgeschichte', *Berichte der Sächischen Akademie*, Phil.-Hist. Klasse 98/5 (Berlin).

Thomas, O. (2014), 'Phemius Suite', *JHS* 134: 89–102.

Thompson, D. W. (1936), *A Glossary of Greek Birds* (London: Oxford University Press).

Thornton, A. (1970), *People and Themes in Homer's Odyssey* (London: Methuen).

Thornton, A. (1984), *Homer's Iliad: Its Composition and the Motif of Supplication* (Göttingen: Vandenhoeck & Ruprecht).

Thumb, A. (1932), *Handbuch der griechischen Dialekte: Erster Teil*, 2nd edn., ed. E. Kieckers (Heidelberg: Winter).

Thumb, A. (1959), *Handbuch der griechischen Dialekte: Zweiter Teil*, 2nd edn., ed. A. Scherer (Heidelberg: Winter).

Tichy, E. (1983), *Onomatapoetische Verbalbildungen des Griechischen* (Vienna: Österrreiche Akademie der Wissenschaften).

Tièche, E. (1945), 'Atlas als Personifikation der Weltachse', *MH* 2: 65–86.

Toy, C. H. (1907), 'The Queen of Sheba', *Journal of American Folklore* 20: 207–21.

Tracy, S. V. (1997), 'The Structures of the *Odyssey*', in Powell and Morris 1997: 360–79.

Trümpy, C. (2001), 'Potnia dans les tablettes mycéniennes: quelques problèmes d'interpretation', in Laffineur and Hägg 2001: 411–21.

Tsitsibakou-Vasalos, E. (1999), 'Modern Etymology versus Ancient. Nestor: Comparisons and Contrasts', *Glotta* 74: 117–32.

Tucker, E. (2009), 'Old Iranian Superlatives in –išta–', in Sundermann et al. 2009: 509–26.

Unbegaun, B. O. (1962), *Russian Grammar*, corrected repr. (Oxford: Clarendon Press).

Usener, H. (1896), *Götternamen* (Bonn: Cohen).

Ustinova, Y. (2009), *Caves and the Ancient Greek Mind* (Oxford: Oxford University Press).

Valk, M. van der (1949), *Textual Criticism of the Odyssey* (Leiden: Sijthoff).

van Leeuwen, J. (1885), 'Disquisitiones de pronominum personalium formis Homericis: I. De pronominum personalium numero singulari', *Mnemosyne* 13: 188–221.

van Leeuwen, J. (1886), 'Homerica', *Mnemosyne* 14: 335–65.

van Leeuwen, J. (1894), *Enchiridium Dictionis Epicae* (Leiden: Sijthoff).

Van Thiel, H. (1991), *Homeri Odyssea* (Hildesheim: Bonn).

Vendryes, J. (1904), *Traité d'accentuation grecque* (Paris: Klincksieck).

Vergados, A. (2012), 'ἐρίηρος ἀοιδός (θ 62/3). Etymologisches Wortspiel in der *Odyssee*', WS 125: 7–22.

Vernant, J.-P. (1991), *Mortals and Immortals: Collected Essays*, ed. F. Zeitlin (Princeton: Princeton University Press).

Villoison, J. B. G. d' (1788), *Homeri Ilias ad veteris codicis Veneti fidem recensita* (Venice: Fratres Coleti).

Vine, B. (1998), *Aeolic ὄρπετον and Deverbative -*eto- in Greek and Indo-European* (Innsbruck: Institut für Sprachwissenschaft).

Wace, A. J. B. (1951), 'Notes on the Homeric House', *JHS* 71: 203–11.

Wace, A. J. B. (1962), 'Houses and Palaces', in Wace and Stubbings 1962: 489–97.

Wace, A. J. B. and Stubbings, F. H. (eds.) (1962), *A Companion to Homer* (London: Macmillan).

Wachter, R. (1998), 'Griechisch χαῖρε: Vorgeschichte eines Grusswortes', *MH* 55: 65–75.

Wachter, R. (2015), 'Grammar of Homeric Greek', in Bierl and Latacz 2015: 65–115.

Wackernagel, J. (1916), 'Sprachliche Untersuchungen zu Homer', *Glotta* 7: 161–319.

Wackernagel, J. (1923), *Antidoron: Festschrift J. Wackernagel zur Vollendung des 70. Lebensjahres am 11 Dezember 1923, gewidmet von Schülern, Freunden und Kollegen* (Göttingen: Vandenhoeck & Ruprecht).

Wackernagel, J. (1926), *Vorlesungen über Syntax*, 2nd edn. (Basel: Birkhäuser).

Wackernagel, J. (1957), *Kleine Schriften*, 3 vols. (Göttingen: Vandenhoeck & Ruprecht).

Ward, M. (forthcoming), 'Glory and Nostos: The Ship-Epithet ΚΟΙΛΟΣ in the *Iliad*', *CQ*.

Watkins, C. (1995), *How to Kill a Dragon: Aspects of Indo-European Poetics* (Oxford: Oxford University Press).

Watkins, C. (2007), 'The Golden Bowl: Thoughts on the New Sappho and its Asianic Background', *ClAnt* 26: 305–24.

Weiss, M. (1998), 'On the Prehistory of Greek Desire', *HSCP* 98: 31–61.

Werner, K. (1993), *The Megaron during the Aegean and Anatolian Bronze Age* (Jonsered: P. Anströms Verlag).

Werner, R. W. (1948), *H und ει vor Vokal bei Homer* (Freiburg in der Schweiz).

West, M. L. (1965), 'Comparisons between Homer and Hesiod', Review of Fritz Krafft, *Vergleichende Untersuchungen zu Homer und Hesiod*, *CR* 15: 158–9.

West, M. L. (1966), *Hesiod: Theogony, Edited with Prolegomena and Commentary* (Oxford: Oxford University Press).

West, M. L. (1971), *Sing Me, Goddess* (London: Duckworth).

West, M. L. (1978), *Hesiod: Works and Days, Edited with Prolegomena and Commentary* (Oxford: Oxford University Press).

West, M. L. (1982a), *Greek Metre* (Oxford: Oxford University Press).

West, M. L. (1982b), 'Three Topics in Greek Metre', *CQ* 32: 281–97.

West, M. L. (1989), 'An Unrecognized Injunctive Usage in Greek', *Glotta* 67: 135–8.

West, M. L. (1989–92), *Iambi et Elegi Graeci ante Alexandrum Cantati*, 2nd edn. (Oxford: Oxford University Press).

West, M. L. (1992), *Ancient Greek Music* (Oxford: Oxford University Press).

West, M. L. (1997a), *The East Face of Helicon* (Oxford: Oxford University Press).

West, M. L. (1997b), 'Homer's Meter', in Powell and Morris 1997: 218–37.

West, M. L. (1998a), *Homerus: Ilias, Volumen Prius Rhapsodiae I–XII* (Leipzig: Teubner).

West, M. L. (1998b), 'The Textual Criticism and Editing of Homer', in Most 1998: 94–110.

West, M. L. (2002), *West on Rengakos (BMCR 2002.11.15) and Nagy (Gnomon 75, 2003, 481–501)*, at http://bmcr.brynmawr.edu/2004/2004-04-17.html, accessed 20 June 2018.

West, M. L. (2004), 'An Indo-European Stylistic Feature in Homer', in Bierl et al. 2004: 33–49.

West, M. L. (2007), *Indo-European Poetry and Myth* (Oxford: Oxford University Press).

West, M. L. (2011), *The Making of the Iliad* (Oxford: Oxford University Press).

West, M. L. (2013), *The Epic Cycle* (Oxford: Oxford University Press).

West, M. L. (2014), *The Making of the Odyssey* (Oxford: Oxford University Press).

West, M. L. (2017), *Homeri Odyssea* (Berlin: de Gruyter).

West, S. R. (1967), *The Ptolemaic Papyri of Homer* (Opladen: Westdeutscher Verlag).

West, S. R. (1981), 'An Alternative *Nostos* for Odysseus', *LCM* 6 (July): 169–75.

West, S. R. (1988), 'Books I–IV', in Heubeck et al. 1988: 51–245.

West, S. R. (1989), 'Laertes Revisited', *PCPhS* 35: 113–43.

Wilamowitz-Moellendorff, U. von (1884), *Homerische Untersuchungen* (Berlin: Weidmann).

Willi, A. (2007), 'Demeter, Gē and the Indo-European Word(s) for "Earth"', *HSF* 120: 169–94.

Wilson, H. (2003), *Wine and Words in Classical Antiquity and the Middle Ages* (London: Duckworth).

Wilson, N. G. (1984), 'Scoliasti e Commentatore', *SCO* 33: 83–112.

Windekens, A. J. van (1982/3), 'Grec νύμφη < "femme enceinte"', *Zeitschrift für vergleichende Sprachwissenschaft* 96: 93–4.

Witte, K. (1911), 'Zur homerischen Sprache', *Glotta* 3: 105–53.

Wyatt, W. F. (1969), *Metrical Lengthening in Homer* (Rome: Ateneo).

Yalçin, U. (ed.) (2008), *Anatolian Metal IV* (Bochum: Deutsches Bergbau Museum).

Zeitlin, F. (1995), 'Figuring Fidelity in Homer's *Odyssey*', in Cohen 1995: 117–52.

Zerdin, J. (1999), *Studies in the Ancient Greek Verbs in –sko* (Diss. Oxford).

Glossary

Words are generally cited here in their dictionary form (1 sg. pres. ind. act. for verbs, nom. sg. for nouns and adjectives). This extends to irregular forms, so that ἔδωκα and ἑσπόμην are not listed but δίδωμι and ἕπομαι are. The exceptions are where there is no dictionary form in use or where the form appearing in the text makes it difficult to establish the dictionary form. Where the epic dialect has a different form from Attic, only the epic form is given. With proper nouns, the oblique cases are not always attested and cannot be predicted with certainty; only the nom. is given. Since the gen. of common nouns of the 1st and 2nd declen. is predictable, together with that of neut. *s*-stems of the 3rd declen., none of these genitives is given below. Exceptions are made where the gen. is unpredictable or where some other complexity arises. The reader is further referred to the introductory section on Dialect and Grammar (pp. 51–60). The meanings given here are specifically meant to explain the way(s) in which the word is used in *Odyssey*, Book 1. This is not meant to be an exhaustive lexicon of epic Greek. For example, although εὔχομαι often means 'to pray' in the epics, it is not used in this way in Book 1 and so that sense is not listed.

ἀγαθός, -ή, -όν	good, brave
Ἀγαμεμνονίδης, -αο (*masc.*)	son of Agamemnon (Orestes)
ἀγάσσομαι	to wonder at, (*bad sense*) feel angry
ἀγγελίη (*fem.*)	message
ἄγε, ἄγετε	(*with following command*) come now!
ἀγήνωρ	haughty, arrogant
ἀγκρεμάννυμι	to hang up
ἀγόρευω	to speak (in public)
ἀγορή (*fem.*)	assembly
ἄγριος, -η, -ον	savage
ἀγρός (*masc.*)	country
ἄγχι	near
Ἀγχίαλος (*masc.*)	Anchialus
ἄγω	to lead, lead, take
ἀδήσειεν	*see 134 n.*
ἀδινός, -ά, -όν	abundant, dense
ἀέθλον (*neut.*)	trial, struggle
ἄειδω	to sing
ἀείρω	to lift up; to win
ἀέκητι	(+ *gen.*) against the will of
ἀέκων, -ουσα, -ον	unwilling
ἀθάνατος, -ον	immortal
Ἀθήν(αι)η (*fem.*)	Athena
ἀθρόος, -α, -ον	together, assembled

αἰ	if
Αἴγισθος (*masc.*)	Aegisthus
αἰδοῖος, –η, –ον	worthy, having a claim to regard
αἰεί, αἰέν	always, continually
ἀΐω	to hear
αἶα (*fem.*)	land
Αἰθίοπες (*masc. pl.*)	Ethiopians
αἴθομαι	to blaze
αἴθων	? dark (*184 n.*)
αἱμύλιος, –η, –ον	wheedling
αἰνῶς	strangely, terribly
αἰπύς, –εῖα, –ύ	sheer, steep, high
αἱρέομαι	to take up
αἱρέω	to take, grasp
ἀΐσσω	to dart
ἄϊστος, –ον	unseen, obscure
αἴσχεα (*neut. pl.*)	disgraceful deeds
αἴτιος, –η, –ον	responsible, culpable
αἰτιάομαι	to censure, blame
αἶψα	suddenly, forthwith
ἀκαχμένος, –η, –ον	pointed
ἀκαχοίμην	*1 sg. aor. opt. med.* < ἀχέω
ἀκλειῶς	ingloriously
ἄκοιτις (*fem.*)	wife
ἀκούω	hear, listen
ἄλαστος, –ον	unforgettable
ἀλαόω	to blind
ἄλγος (*neut.*)	pain
ἀλεγύνω	to heed, care about
ἀλεείνω	to avoid
ἄλκιμος, –ον	strong, brave
ἀλλά	but
ἄλλος, –η, –ον	other; as well
ἄλληλος, –η, –ον	one another, each other
ἀλλόθροος, –ον	speaking a different language
ἀλλότριος, –η, –ον	belonging to another
ἄλοχος (*fem.*)	wife
ἅλς, ἁλός (*fem.*)	sea
ἀλφηστής	grain-eating
ἀλωή (*fem.*)	prepared ground
ἅμα	at the same time, (+ *dat.*) together with
ἀμβρόσιος, –η, –ον	immortal, divine
ἀμείβομαι	to answer, respond
ἀμείνων, –ον	better
ἄμμι	Att. ἡμῖν
ἀμόθεν	from some point or other
ἀμοιβή (*fem.*)	return
ἀμύμων, –ον	extraordinary (*29 n.*)
ἀμφαδόν	openly
ἀμφί(ς)	apart, asunder; (+ *dat.*) about
ἀμφιάλος, –ον	sea-girt
ἀμφιπέλομαι	to go about, do the rounds

ἀμφίπολος (*fem.*)	waiting-woman, handmaid
ἀμφίρυτος, -ον	sea-girt
ἄν	(*modal particle*)
ἀνά	(+ *acc.*) throughout, all over
ἀναβαίνω	to go up; (*med.*) to go on board ship
ἀναβάλλομαι	to begin (playing or singing)
ἀναγιγνώσκω	to know for certain
ἀνάγκη (*fem.*)	necessity
ἀνάθημα (*neut.*)	adornment
ἀναιδής, -ές	shameless
ἀναΐσσω	to jump up, get up suddenly
ἄναξ, ἄνακτος (*masc.*)	lord, master
ἀνάσσω	(+ *dat.*) to rule over, be master of
ἀνδροφόνος, -ον	murderous
ἄνειμι	to rise, go up
ἀνείρεαι	2 sg. pres. ind. med. < ἀνέρομαι
ἄνεμος (*masc.*)	wind
ἀνέρομαι	to ask
ἀνέρχομαι	to return
ἀνήρ, ἀνδρός, ἀνέρος (*masc.*)	man, husband
ἀνηρέψαντο	*see 241 n.*
ἄνθρωπος (*masc.*)	man, human being
ἀνιάω	to distress
ἄνειμι	to return; (of sun) to rise
ἀνοπαῖα	up through a hole in the roof (*321 n.*)
ἄντα	(+ *gen.*) in front of
ἀντία	(*neut. pl. acc. as adv.*) (*also* + *gen.*) against
ἀντίθεος, -η, -ον	godlike
Ἀντίνοος (*masc.*)	Antinous
ἀντίον	(*neut. sg. acc. as adv.*) in reply
ἀντιάω	(+ *gen.*) to partake of
ἄνωγα	urge, bid
ἄξιος, -η, -ον	worthy
ἀοιδή (*fem.*)	song
ἀοιδός (*masc.*)	singer, bard
ἀπαμείβομαι	to answer
ἀπάνευθεν	far away
ἅπας, ἅπασα, ἅπαν	all
ἀπείρων, -ον	boundless
ἀπηλεγέως	outright, bluntly
ἀπό	(+ *gen.*) from
ἀποβαίνω	to go away
ἀπ(ο)εῖπον	(*aor. only*) (*intr.*) to make a declaration; (*tr.*) to declare
ἀποθρῴσκω	to spring up from
ἀποίχομαι	to be absent
ἀπόλλυμαι	to perish (*med.*)
ἀπόλλυμι	to lose (*act.*)
ἀπόλωλα	(*perf. med. of ἀπόλλυμι*)
ἀποπαύω	stop (*tr.*)
ἀπορραίω	to deprive (*sb. of sth.*)

ἀποτίνω	(*act.*) to pay back; (*med.*) to take vengeance
ἄποτμος, –ον	ill-starred
ἄπυστος, –ον	unheard of
ἀπωθέω	to thrust away
ἄρα	indeed
ἀράομαι	to pray; wish earnestly
ἀραρίσκω	to fit out
Ἀργειφόντης (*masc.*)	(*an epithet of Hermes; 38 n.*)
Ἀργεῖοι (*masc. pl.*)	the Argives (= Greeks)
Ἄργος (*neut.*)	Argos > the Peloponnese (*344 n.*)
ἀργύρεος, –η, –ον	silver
Ἀρέπυιαι (*fem. pl.*)	*see 241 n.*
ἀρέσθαι	*aor. med. inf.* < ἄρνυμαι
ἄριστος, –η, –ον	best
ἀρνέομαι	to refuse
ἀρνειός (*masc.*)	ram
ἄρνυμαι	to get, gain, win
ἄρουρα (*fem.*)	land
ἄρσας	*masc. sg. nom. aor. ptcp. act.* < ἀραρίσκω
ἀρτυνέω	to prepare, put in order
ἀρχή (*fem.*)	beginning
ἄρχω	(+ *gen.*; *also med.*) to make a beginning of
ἀσκελής, –ές	tough, stubborn
ἀσκέω	to smooth (*239 n.*)
ἀσπερχές	(*neut. adj. as adv.*) furiously
ἀσπίς, –ίδος (*fem.*)	shield
ἄστυ (*neut.*)	city, town
ἀσχαλάω	(+ *acc.*) to be aggrieved at
ἀτάρ	(*transitional particle, 181 n.*)
ἀτασθαλίη (*fem.*)	wickedness
Ἄτλας, –αντος (*masc.*)	Atlas
Ἀτρείδης, –αο (*masc.*)	son of Atreus (here = Agamemnon)
ἀτρεκέως	accurately, exactly
ἀτρύγετος, –ον	which cannot be dried out (*72 n.*)
αὖ	in turn, again
αὐδάω	to speak
αὐδή (*fem.*)	voice
αὐλείος, –η, –ον	belonging to the courtyard
αὐλή (*fem.*)	courtyard
αὔριον	tomorrow
αὐτάρ	but; and so (*9 n.*)
αὖτε	in turn
αὐτίκα	at once
αὖτις	(back) again
αὐτός, –ή, –όν	self; (*in obl. cases*) him, her, it; (*with art.*) same
ἀφαιρέω	to take away
ἄφαρ	suddenly
ἀφικνέομαι	to arrive
ἀφνειός, –όν	rich, abundant

Ἀχαιοί (*masc. pl.*)	the Achaeans (= Greeks)
ἀχέω	to mourn, grieve
ἄψ	back again
ἄωτον (*neut.*)	wool (*443 n.*)
βαίνω	to go, take a step
βάλλω	put, place (*of thoughts*)
βασιλεύς, –ῆος (*masc.*)	chieftain
βασιλεύω	be chief; (+ *gen.*) rule over
βένθος (*neut.*)	depth
βίη (*fem.*)	power, force
βίοτος (*masc.*)	substance, livelihood
βλάπτω	(+ *gen.*) hinder from
βλέφαρα (*neut. pl.*)	eyelids
βοητύς, –ύος (*fem.*)	shout, cry
βουλεύω	to deliberate
βουλή (*fem.*)	will, determination
βοῦς, βοός (*masc.*)	ox
βριθύς, –εῖα, ύ	heavy
βροτός (*masc.*)	mortal
βρῶσις (*fem.*)	food, meat
γαῖα (*fem.*)	land, earth
γαιήοχος, –ον	riding on the earth (*68 n.*)
γαμέομαι	(+ *dat.*) to marry (*only with fem. subject*)
γάμος (*masc.*)	marriage
γάρ	for
γε	(*emphatic particle*)
γείνομαι	to bring forth, give birth to
γενεή (*fem.*)	lineage; family
γέρων, –οντος (*masc.*)	old man
γῆρας, –αος (*neut.*)	old age
γίγνομαι	to become, be
γιγνώσκω	to get to know, recognize
γλαυκῶπις, –ιδος	owl-eyed
γλαφυρός, –ή, –όν	hollow
γνώμεναι	*aor. inf. act.* < γιγνώσκω
γόνος (*masc.*)	descent, stock
γόος (*masc.*)	weeping, wailing
γόνυ, γούνατος (*neut.*)	knee
γουνός (*masc.*)	high ground
γραῖα (*fem.*)	old woman
γρηῦς, γρηός (*fem.*)	old woman
γυῖα (*neut. pl.*)	limbs
γυνή, γυναικός (*fem.*)	woman, wife
δαιδάλεος, –η, –ον	embellished
δαίνυμαι	to have a feast
δαίς, δαιτός (*fem.*)	meal, banquet
δαΐς, δαΐδος (*fem.*)	torch
δαίω	to divide; to tear apart
δαιτρός (*masc.*)	carver
δαΐφρων, –ον	cunning, prudent
δακρύω	to weep
δάμνημι	subdue, kill

Δαναοί (*masc. pl.*)	the Danaans (= Greeks)
δάτεομαι	to share out, distribute
δέ	(*connective or adversative particle*)
δεδαίαται	3 *pl. perf. ind. pass.* < δαίω
δεῖπνον (*neut.*)	main meal (*134 n.*)
δέμω	to build
δενδρήεις, -εσσα, -εν	wooded
δεξιτερός, -ή, -όν	right (hand)
δέομαι	to tie
δέσμα (*neut.*)	bond, fetter
δεύομαι	(+ *gen.*) need, miss
δεύτατος, -η, -ον	last
δέχομαι	take, accept
δή	indeed
δηθά	for a long time
δῆμος (*masc.*)	land
δήν	for a long time
δηρόν	for a long time
διάκτορος (*masc.*)	messenger (*84 n.*)
διαρραίω	to destroy
διδάσκω	to teach
δίδωμι	to give; to dispense
διαπέτομαι	to fly through
διζήμαι	to seek
δῖος, -α, -ον	illustrious (*14 n.*)
διχθά	in two
δμωαί (*fem. pl.*)	female slaves
δμῶες (*masc. pl.*)	male slaves
δοκέω	to seem
δολόμητις	wily
δόλος (*masc.*)	trickery, stratagem
δόμος (*masc.*)	house
Δουλιχίον (*neut.*)	Dulichium
δόρυ, δουρός (*neut.*)	spear
δουροδόκη (*fem.*)	spear-stand
δύναμαι	to be able
δύο	two
δύομαι	to go down, sink, set
δύσμορος, -ον	ill-fated
δύστηνος, -ον	wretched
δῶ (*indecl.*)	house
δῶμα (*neut.*)	house
δῶρον (*neut.*)	gift
ἑ	him (her, it) (-self)
ἐβόλοντο	willed, determined (*234 n.*)
ἐγγύθι	(*adv.*) near
ἔγκος (*neut.*)	spear
ἐγώ(ν)	I
ἐδητύς, -ύος (*fem.*)	food
ἔδω	consume, devour
ἔεδνα (*neut. pl.*)	dowry (*277 n.*)
ἐεικοσάβοια	worth twenty oxen (*431 n.*)

ἐείκοσι(ν)	twenty
ἐέλδομαι	to desire
ἕζομαι	to seat oneself
ἐθέλω	to want, wish
εἰ	if
εἵατο	*3 pl. imperf. ind. act.* < ἧμαι
εἶδαρ, –ατος (*neut.*)	food
εἴδομαι	(+ *dat.*) to look like
εἰδῶ	*1 sg. pres. subj. act.* < οἶδα
εἰλαπίνη (*fem.*)	feast
εἰλίπους, –οδος	shambling
εἰμί	to be
εἶμι	I shall go (*inf.* ἴμεν)
εἰν	(+ *dat.*) in
εἴρομαι	to ask
εἰς	(+ *acc.*) into, to
εἷς, μία, ἕν	one
εἷσα	*1 sg. aor. ind. act.* < ἵζω
εἰσοράω	to look upon, see
ἐκ, ἐξ	(+ *gen.*) from, out of
ἕκαστος, –η, –ον	each
ἑκάτερθε	on each side
ἑκατόμβη (*fem.*)	sacrifice (*25 n.*)
ἐκδύνω	to take off
ἔκτα	*3 sg. aor. ind. act.* < κτείνω
ἔκτανε	*3 sg. aor. ind. act.* < κτείνω
ἔκτοθεν	(+ *gen.*) apart from
ἐλαφρός, –ή, –όν	nimble, light
ἐλέαιρω	to take pity
ἕλιξ, –ικος	black (*92 n.*)
Ἑλλάς, –άδος (*fem.*)	Hellas (*344 n.*)
ἐμβάλλω	to put into
ἔμικτο	*3 sg. aor. ind. pass.* < μίγνυμι
ἐμός, –ή, –όν	my
ἐμπάζομαι	(+ *dat.*) to take heed of
ἐν(ί)	(+ *dat.*) in
ἐναλίγκιος, –ον	like
ἔνθα	(*time*) then; (*place*) there, where
ἐνθάδε	hither
ἐνιαυτός (*masc.*)	year; anniversary (*16 n.*)
ἐνναίω	to inhabit, dwell in
ἐννέπω	to tell
ἐνοσίχθων, –ονος	earth-shaker
ἐντίθημι	to place in; take to, lay up in
ἔντο	*3 pl. aor. ind. med.* < ἵημι
ἔντοσθεν	(+ *gen.*) within
ἐντρέπομαι	to have regard to
ἐξείης	in order, in a row
ἔξειμι	I shall go out
ἐξερέομαι	to ask about (*416 n.*)
ἐξιέμαι	to put off from oneself
ἔοικα	(+ *dat.*) to look like, seem

ἔοικε	it is fitting
ἐοικώς, -υῖα, -ός	fitting, appropriate
ἑός, -ή, -όν	his own
ἐπαλαστέω	? to feel indignation (252 n.)
ἐπεί	when
ἐπείγομαι	(+ gen.) to be eager for
ἔπειτα	in such a case (65 n.); next, then; now (106 n.)
ἐπεκλώσαντο	3 pl. aor. ind. act. < ἐπικλώθω
ἐπερύω	to pull to
ἐπέρχομαι	to go to, to come upon
ἐπέχευε	epic 3 sg. aor. ind. act. < ἐπιχέω
ἐπήν	when
ἐπιτέλλω	to enjoin, command; to direct
ἐπί	(+ acc.) over, across, to, among; (+ gen.) with, on board; (+ dat.) upon, on; in possession of
ἐπιβοάομαι	to call upon
ἐπιδήμιος, -ον	resident
ἐπικλείω	praise, extol
ἐπικλώθω	(lit.) to spin (sc. the web of destiny) for (17 n.)
ἐπικρατέω	(+ dat.) to rule over
ἐπιλήθομαι	(+ gen.) to forget
ἐπιμένω	to wait, remain
ἐπιμιμνήσκομαι	(+ gen.) to remember
ἐπιστέφομαι	to fill to the brim
ἐπίστροφος, -ον	(+ gen.) going about among
ἐπιτίθημι	to set out
ἐπιτολμάω	(+ inf.) to endure (doing something)
ἐπιχέω	to pour over
ἐπιχθόνιος, -ον	on earth
ἔπλετο	3 sg. aor. ind. med. < πέλομαι
ἐποίχομαι	to go about among; to set about
ἕπομαι	to follow, accompany
ἔπος (neut.)	word
ἐποτρύνω	to urge on
ἔρανος (masc.)	potluck meal (226 n.)
ἔργον (neut.)	deed, action, work
ἔρδω	to do
ἐρεείνω	to ask
ἐρέτης (masc.)	rower
ἐριδαίνω	to quarrel
ἐρίηρος, -ον	faithful, trusty (346 n.)
ἕρκος (neut.)	barrier, enclosure
Ἑρμείας	Hermes
ἔρξῃς	2 sg. aor. subj. act. < ἔρδω
ἔρομαι	to ask
ἔρος (masc.)	desire
ἑρπύζω	to creep (infirm with old age)
ἐρυκανάω	to detain, restrain
ἐρύκω	to detain, restrain

ἐρύομαι	to rescue, save
ἔρχομαι	to come; to go
ἐς	*see* εἰς
ἐσέρχομαι	to go to
ἐσθής, –ῆτος (*fem.*)	clothing
ἐσθίω	*see* κατεσθίω
ἐσθλός, –ή, –όν	noble, good
ἕσπερος (*masc.*)	evening
ἔσχατος, –η, –ον	farthest, remotest
ἕτα(ι)ρος (*masc.*)	comrade, companion
ἑτέρως	otherwise
ἔτετμον	(*aor. only*) to overtake, find
ἐτήτυμον	(*neut. sg. as adv.*) truly
ἔτι	still
ἑτοῖμος, (–η), –ον	ready
ἔτος (*neut.*)	year
ἔΰ	well
εὐνή (*fem.*)	bed
ἐΰξόος, –ον	well-polished
Εὐπειθής, –εος	Eupeithes
ἐϋπλόκαμος, –ον	with beautiful hair
εὑρίσκω	to find
Εὐρύκλεια (*fem.*)	Eurycleia
Εὐρύμαχος (*masc.*)	Eurymachus
εὐρύς, –εῖα, –ύ	wide, broad
ἐΰσκοπος, –ον	keen-sighted
εὖτε	when
εὐχετάομαι	*epic expansion of* εὔχομαι
εὔχομαι	declare, claim, maintain
ἐφίημι	to lay (*sc.* hands) on
ἐφεστάμεν	*epic aor. 2 inf. act.* (*intr.*) ἐφίστημι = to stand by
ἐφορμάομαι	to be eager
Ἐφύρη (*fem.*)	Ephyra
ἔχω	to have
Ζάκυνθος (*fem.*)	Zacynthus
Ζεύς, Ζηνός/Διός (*masc.*)	Zeus
ζωός, –ή, –όν	alive
ἤ, ἠέ, ἦε	or
ἦ	indeed
ἡβάω	to reach puberty, manhood
ἡγέομαι	to lead the way
ἡγήτωρ, –ορος (*masc.*)	leader
ἠδέ	and
ἤδη	forthwith
ἡδύς, –εῖα, –ύ	sweet
Ἥλιος (*masc.*)	the Sun
ἠλακάτη (*fem.*)	distaff
ἠμαθόεις, –εσσα, –εν	sandy
ἧμαι	to sit
ἦμαρ, –ατος (*neut.*)	day
ἠμέν … ἠδέ	both … and

ἡμέτερος, -η, -ον	our
ἤν	if
ἤπειρος (*masc.*)	dry land
ἤρατο	3 sg. aor. ind. med. < ἀείρω
ἥρως, -ωος (*masc.*)	warrior, champion, lord (*189 n.*)
ἤτοι	indeed
ἦτορ (*nom./acc. only*) (*neut.*)	heart
ἠῶθεν	as soon as it is dawn
θάλαμος (*masc.*)	(bed)room
θάλασσα (*fem.*)	sea
θαλπωρή (*fem.*)	warmth, comfort
θαμά	often, repeatedly
θαμβέω	to be astonished
θαρσαλέως	confidently
θάρσος (*neut.*)	courage
θαυμάζω	to marvel at
θεά (*fem.*)	goddess
θεῖος, (-η), -ον	godlike, excellent
θέλγω	to cozen, beguile
θελκτήριον (*neut.*)	charm, spell
θεοειδής, -ές	godlike
θεός (*masc.*)	god
θεοπροπίη (*fem.*)	prophecy, oracle
θεοπρόπος (*masc.*)	prophet
θεράπων, -οντος (*masc.*)	servant
θέσπις, -ιος	inspired
θνήσκω	to die
θνητός, -ή, -όν	mortal
θοός, -ή, -όν	swift
Θόωσα (*fem.*)	Thoösa
θρῆνυς, -υος (*masc.*)	footstool
θρόνος (*masc.*)	seat (*130 n.*)
θυγάτηρ, -τ(έ)ρός (*fem.*)	daughter
θυμός (*masc.*)	spirit; life
θύρα (*fem.*)	door
ἰάλλω	thrust forth (*149 n.*)
ἵεμαι	(< ἵημι) to be eager
ἱερός, -ή, -όν	vital > sacred (*2 n.*)
ἵζω	to seat (somebody)
Ἰθάκη (*fem.*)	Ithaca
ἰθύς, -εῖα, -ύ	(+ *gen.*) straight towards
ἱκάνω	to come
Ἰκάριος	Icarius
ἵκομαι	to come to, reach
Ἶλος (*masc.*)	Ilus
ἱμάς, -άντος (*masc.*)	strap, thong
ἱμείρομαι	(+ *gen.*) to long for, desire
ἴμεν	Att. ἰέναι
ἱμερόεις, -εσσα, -εν	lovely
ἵνα	in order that
ἰός (*masc.*)	arrow
ἱρα (*neut. pl.*)	sacrifices, offerings (*see* ἱερός)

ἴσα (*neut. pl. as adv.*)	equally
ἰσόθεος, –ον	godlike
ἵστημι	(*tr.*) to put, cause to stand; (*intr.*) to stand
ἱστός (*neut.*)	loom
καθέζομαι	to seat oneself
καθικνέομαι	to reach, touch
καί	and; even
κακκείοντες	in order to lie down (*424 n.*)
κακός, –ή, –όν	bad, evil; base, ill-born
καλέω	to summon, call
κάλλιπεν	3 *sg. aor. ind. act.* < καταλείπω
καλός, –ή, –όν	beautiful, handsome; good, fine
καλύπτω	to cover
Καλυψώ, –οῦς (*fem.*)	Calypso
κάματος (*masc.*)	weariness
κάνεον (*neut.*)	bread-basket
καπνός (*masc.*)	smoke
κάρη, –ητος (*neut.*)	head
κάρηνα (*neut. pl.*)	peaks
κατά	(+ *acc.*) in, throughout
καταβαίνω	to descend
κατακτείνω	to kill
καταλαμβάνω	to overtake
καταλείπω	to leave behind
καταλέγω	(*aor.* –λεξ–) recount, tell
κατερύκω	to hold back, detain
κατέρχομαι	to go down, come down
κατεσθίω	to eat up, devour
κατήλυθον	= κατῆλθον
κε(ν)	*potential particle*
κεδνός, –ή, –όν	trusty, worthy (*335 n.*); κεδνὰ εἰδυῖα, well-disposed (*428 n.*)
κεῖθεν	from there
κειμήλιον (*neut.*)	treasure, heirloom
κεῖνος, –η, –ον	that
κείρω	cut > devour, ravage
κεῖσε	thither
κελεύω	to order, bid
κέλευθος (*fem.*)	path, road
κεφαλή (*fem.*)	head; (*part for whole*) person
κῆδος (*neut.*)	trouble, grief
κῆρ, κῆρι (*neut.*)	heart
κῆρυξ, –υκος (*masc.*)	herald (*109 n.*)
κίθαρις, –ιος (*fem.*)	lyre; playing on the lyre
κίων, –ονος (*masc.*)	pillar
κίω	to go
κλαίω	to weep for
κλείω	to make famous, celebrate
κλέος (*neut.*)	fame, renown
κληΐς, κληΐδος (*fem.*)	key
κλῖμαξ, –ακος (*fem.*)	stair

κλίνομαι — to recline

κλισμός (*masc.*) — chair with sloping back (*132 n.*)

κλυτός, -όν — renowned, glorious

κοίλος, -η, -ον — hollow

κοιρανέω — to be lord

κομάω — to have long hair

κομίζω — to take care of, attend to

κορώνη (*fem.*) — door-handle

κοτέσσεται — to be angry (*101 n.*)

κοτέω — (+ *dat.*) to be angry with

κούρη (*fem.*) — daughter

κοῦρος (*masc.*) — lad, male servant

κραδίη (*fem.*) — heart

κραναός, -ή, -όν — rocky, rugged

κράτος (*neut.*) — might, power

κρέας (*neut.*), *pl.* κρέα — meat

κρείων, -οντος (*masc.*) — ruler

κρειῶν — *gen. pl.* < κρέας

κρήδεμνον (*neut.*) — head-dress, mantilla

κρητήρ, -ῆρος (*masc.*) — mixing bowl

Κρονίδης (*masc.*) — son of Cronus > Zeus

Κρονίων, -ωνος (*masc.*) — son of Cronus > Zeus

κτεάτεσσιν (*neut. pl. dat.*) — goods, property

κτείνω — to kill

κτέρεα (*neut. pl.*) — funeral gifts

κτερεΐζω — to bury with due honours

κτήματα (*neut. pl.*) — property, possessions

Κύκλωψ, -ωπος (*masc.*) — Cyclops

κυλίνδω — to roll

κῦμα (*neut.*) — wave

κύπελλον (*neut.*) — goblet

Λαέρτης (*masc.*) — Laertes

λανθάνομαι — (+ *gen.*) to forget

λέβης, -ητος (*masc.*) — basin

λέκτρον (*neut.*) — bed

λευκός, -ή, -όν — white

λέχος (*neut.*) (*often pl.*) — bed, couch

ληΐζομαι — to carry off as booty

λίην — exceedingly; καὶ λίην = Yes, surely …

λιλαίομαι — to long to *or* that (+ *inf.*), for (+ *gen.*)

λιμήν, -ένος (*masc.*) — harbour

λιπαρός, -ή, -όν — bright, brilliant

λῖτα — linen cloths (*130 n.*)

λόγος (*masc.*) — word

λοέομαι — to have a wash

λοεσσάμενος — *epic aor. med. ptcp.* < λοέομαι

λυγρός, -ή, -όν — baneful

λωΐτερος, -ον — preferable, better

μακάρ, -αρος — (*gods*) blessed; (*humans*) fortunate, wealthy

μακρός, -ή, -όν — tall, high

μάλα — (+ *adj.*) very; (+ *verb*) indeed

μαλακός, –ή, –όν	soft
μάλιστα	most of all
μᾶλλον	more
μαντεύομαι	foretell
μάντις, –ιος (*masc.*)	prophet
μάρτυρος (*masc.*)	witness
μέγας, μεγάλη, μέγα	big, large
μέγα (*neut. as adv.*)	greatly, very
μέγαρον (*neut.*)	house (27 *n.*)
μέγιστος, (–η,) –ον	greatest
μέδων, –οντος (*masc.*)	lord, ruler
μεθέπω	to come to visit
μέθημαι	(+ *dat.*) to sit among
μεθίημι	to put aside, let go
μέλας, μέλαινα, μέλαν	black, dark
μέλλω	(+ *inf.*) to be destined to, likely to
μέλω (*usu. 3 sg.*)	(+ *dat.*) to be a matter of concern; to occupy the mind
μεμήλει	*epic 3. sg. perf. ind. act.* < μέλω
μέμνημαι	to remember
μέν	*correlative particle, often contrasts with following* δέ
μενεαίνω	to be angry, to rage
Μενέλαος (*masc.*)	Menelaus
μένος (*neut.*)	force, power, passion
μένω	to wait
Μέντης (*masc.*)	Mentes
μερμηρίζω	to plan, devise
Μερμερίδης (*masc.*)	son of Mermerus > Ilus
μέσος, –ή, –όν	central
μετά	(+ *dat.*) in company with; (+ *acc.*) in quest of
μετακιάθω	(*pres. not in use*) to visit
μεταλλάω	to ask (+ *acc. pers.* + *gen. thing*)
μεταυδάω	to address (+ *acc. of word spoken*, + *dat. of addressee*)
μετέρχομαι	to come among
μή	*negative particle for commands, prohibitions, conditions*
μῆλα (*neut. pl.*)	sheep *or* goats; small animals, *contrasted with* βοῦς
μήτε	μή + τε (*qvv.*)
μήτηρ, –τ(ε)ρός (*fem.*)	mother
μητιάω	to plan, devise
μίγνυμι	to mix; (*med./pass.*) to have intercourse (*social or sexual*)
μιμνήσκομαι	(+ *gen.*) to remember, have in mind
μίσγω	*pres./imperf.* < μίγνυμι
μνάομαι	to woo, pay suit to
μνήσατο	*3 sg. aor. ind. med.* < μιμνήσκομαι
μνηστός, –ή, –όν	wooed and won > lawfully wedded
μνηστήρ, –ῆρος (*masc.*)	suitor, wooer

μολπή (*fem.*)	song (*152 n.*)
μόρος (*masc.*)	fate; apportioned lot
Μοῦσα (*fem.*)	Muse (*1 n.*)
μυθέομαι	to tell of, recount
μῦθος (*masc.*)	word, speech
ναίω	see ἐνναίω
ναιετάω	to be inhabited (*404 n.*)
ναύτης (*masc.*)	sailor
νέομαι	to return
νεμεσάω	to feel indignation (*119 n.*)
νεμεσίζετο	(+ *acc.*) to fear the indignation of (*263 n.*)
νέμεσις	cause for indignation
νέος, -η, -ον	young
νέον (*adv.*)	newly; only just now
Νέστωρ, -ορος (*masc.*)	Nestor
νεφεληγερέτα, -αο (*masc.*)	cloud-gatherer
Νήϊον	Neium (*185-6 n.*)
νημερτής, -ές	infallible; which will definitely happen
νηπιάας	*acc. pl.* < νηπιέη (*297 n.*)
νηπιέη (*fem.*)	childishness
νήπιος, -ον	foolish, childish
νήποινος, -ον	without compensation; unavenged (*380 n.*)
νῆσος (*fem.*)	island
νηῦς, νηός (*fem.*)	ship
νίζω	to wash, cleanse
νίπτω	*epic for* νίζω
νοέω	to see
νόος (*masc.*)	mind; disposition
νοστέω	to return home
νόστιμος, -ον	of return
νόστος (*masc.*)	safe return home
νόσφι	apart from, except
νυ	*emphatic particle*
νύμφη (*fem.*)	nymph (*14 n.*)
νῦν	now
νώνυμνος, -ον	without a name; inglorious
ξανθός, -ή, -όν	fair, golden
ξεῖνος (*masc.*)	stranger; guest, guest-friend (*175-6 n.*)
ξεστός, -ή, -όν	planed
ξύν	(+ *dat.*) with
ξυνίημι	to hear, pay attention
ὁ, ἡ, τό	that person, that one; it (*9 n.*)
ὅ	(*neut. of foreg.*) because
ὀβριμοπάτρη	having a mighty father
ὀδάξ (*adv.*)	with the teeth
ὅδε, ἥδε, τόδε	this
ὁδός (*fem.*)	way, journey
ὀδούς, -όντος (*masc.*)	tooth
ὀδύνη (*fem.*)	pain, grief
ὀδύρομαι	to lament, mourn
Ὀδυσσεύς, -ῆος (*masc.*)	Odysseus

ὅθι (*rel. adv.*)	where
οἴγω	to open
οἶδα	to know
οἴκοι (*adv.*)	at home
οἴκόνδε (*adv.*)	homewards
οἶκος (*masc.*)	house; household (goods), substance
οἶνος (*masc.*)	wine
οἴνοπα, –ι	wine-dark (*183 n.*)
οἰνόπεδον (*neut.*)	vineyard
οἰνοχοεύω	to pour out wine for drinking
ὀΐομαι	to think, reckon
ὄϊς, ὄϊος/οἰός (*masc.*)	sheep
οἶος, –η, –ον	alone
οἷος, –η, –ον	such as; (*neut. adv.*) how
οἶτος (*masc.*)	doom
οἴχομαι	to have gone, departed; to be away
ὀΐω	to think
οἰωνός (*masc.*)	bird (of omen)
ὄλεθρον (*neut.*)	ruin, destruction; death
ὄλλυμαι	to perish
ὀλοόφρων, –ον	baleful
Ὀλύμπιος, –ον	Olympian
ὀμαδέω	to make a din
ὄμβρος (*masc.*)	rain
ὁμιλέω	to associate with; to join (battle) with
ὅμιλος (*masc.*)	throng
ὄμμα (*neut.*)	eye
ὀμφαλός (*masc.*)	navel
ὀνείατα (*neut. pl.*)	food, victuals
ὀξύς, –εῖα, –ύ	sharp
ὀπίσσω	hereafter (*222 n.*)
ὅππῃ	in whatever way
ὁππόθεν	(*ind. qn.*) whence; from where
ὁπποῖος, –η, –ον	what sort of…?
ὅπποτε	whensoever
ὅ(π)πως	in order that; (*ind. qn.*) how
ὁράω	to see
Ὀρέστης (*masc.*)	Orestes
ὄρνις, –ιθος (*com.*)	bird
ὄρνυμαι	to stir oneself
ὀρχηστύς, –ύος (*fem.*)	dance
ὀρυμαγδός (*masc.*)	din
ὅς, ἥ, ὅ	(*rel.*) who, which; (*dem.*) that one
ὅς, ἥ, ἑόν	his, her, its
ὅς(σ)οι, –αι, –α	as many as; as great as
ὄσσα (*fem.*)	rumour
ὄσσομαι	to see in the mind's eye
ὀστέον (*neut.*)	bone
ὅστις, ἥτις, ὅτι	who, which
ὅτε	when
ὅτις	*epic for* ὅστις
ὀτρηρός, –ή, –όν	busy, nimble

ὀτρύνω	to stir up, urge on
ὅττι	*epic for* ὅτι, *neut. of* ὅστις
οὐ, οὐκ, οὐκί	*negative particle*
οὐδέ	not even; and not
οὐδός (*masc.*)	threshold
οὐκέτι	no longer; not yet
Οὐλύμπος (*masc.*)	Mt. Olympus
οὖν	and so
οὐρανός (*masc.*)	sky; heaven
οὔτε	and not
οὗτος, αὕτη, τοῦτο	this
ὄφελον	(+ *inf.*) would that I had …
ὀφθαλμός (*masc.*)	eye
ὄφρα	in order that; for as long as; until
ὀχέω	to hold fast, keep to
ὀψίγονος, -ον	born later
παῖς, πάϊς, -ιδος (*com.*)	child; son; daughter
παλαιός, -ή, -όν	old
παλάμη (*fem.*)	hand
πάλιν	back
παλίντιτος, -ον	*see 379 n.*
Παλλάς (*fem.*)	Pallas (*sc.* Athena)
Παναχαιοί (*masc. pl.*)	all the Achaeans
παννύχιος, -ον	all night long (*agrees with subject*)
παντοῖος, -η, -ον	of all kinds
παρά, παραί, παρ	(+ *acc.*) beside, by; to the house of; (+ *gen.*) from; (+ *dat.*) beside, at the house of, in the presence of
παρατίθημι	to set before, beside
παρειά (*fem.*)	cheek
πάρειμι	to be at hand, available
παρενήνεον	to pile up (*147 n.*)
παρήμαι	to sit by
παρίσταμαι	to stand beside
πάροιθεν	(+ *art.*) beforehand
πάρος	before
πᾶς, πᾶσα, πᾶν	all; every
πάσσαλος (*masc.*)	peg
πασσάμενος	*epic masc. sg. nom. aor. ptcp.* < πατέομαι
πάσχω	to suffer
πατέομαι	to eat, partake of
πατήρ, -τ(ε)ρός (*masc.*)	father
πατρίς, -ίδος (*adj.*)	of one's fathers
πατροφονεύς, -ῆος (*masc.*)	father-slayer
πατρώϊος, -η, -ον	hereditary
πέδιλα (*neut. pl.*)	sandals
πεζός, -όν	on foot
πείθομαι	(+ *dat.*) to believe, trust, listen to
πείθω	to persuade
Πεισηνορίδης	son of Peisenor
πέλομαι	to become, be
πέμπω	to send

πένθος (*neut.*)	grief, sorrow
πέπνυμαι	to be wise, prudent
περ	*particle (6 n.)*
πέρθω	to sack
περί	(*adv.*) exceedingly; (+ *gen.*) beyond (66 *n.*); about
περικαλλής, –ές	very beautiful
περικλυτός, –όν	very famous (329 *n.*)
περιπέλομαι	to go round
περίσκεπτος, –ον	conspicuous
περιφράζομαι	to think about, consider
περίφρων, –ον	very prudent
πεσσοί (*masc. pl.*)	gaming pieces (107 *n.*)
πεύθομαι	(*intr.*) to hear; (+ *acc./gen.*) to enquire about
πέφραδε	< φράζω; see 273, 444 *nn.*
πήληξ, –ηκος (*fem.*)	helmet
πῆμα (*neut.*)	misery, calamity
Πηνελόπεια (*fem.*)	Penelope
πίθηαι	2 *sg. aor. sub. med.* < πείθομαι
πικρόγαμος, –ον	attaining a bitter kind of marriage
πίναξ, –ακος (*masc.*)	platter
πινυτός, –ή, –όν	prudent
πίνω	to drink
πλάζω	to turn aside; (*pass.*) to wander, rove
πλέω	to sail
πνοιή (*fem.*)	gust
πόθεν	whence?
ποθεν	from somewhere or other
ποθέω	to yearn after, miss
πόθι	where?
ποθι	perhaps
ποιέω	to make
ποιητός, –ή, –όν	made
ποικίλος, –η, –ον	intricate
ποῖος, –η, –ον	of what kind?
πόλεμος (*masc.*)	war
πόλις, πόληος (*fem.*)	city
πολύς, πολλή, πολύ	much
Πολύβος (*masc.*)	Polybus
πολυμήχανος, –ον	resourceful
πολύτρητος, –ον	full of holes
πολύτροπος, –ον	of many turns
Πολύφημος (*masc.*)	Polyphemus
πολύφρων, –ον	ingenious
πόντος (*masc.*)	sea
πόποι	*expression of irritation or disgust* (32 *n.*)
Ποσειδάων (*masc.*)	Poseidon
πόσις, –ιος (*masc.*)	spouse, husband
πόσις, –ιος (*fem.*)	drink
ποτε	at some time or other
πότνια	lady

ποτός (*masc.*)	drink
ποῦ	where?
που	somewhere; I suppose
πούς, ποδός (*masc.*)	foot
πρίατο	3 *sg. aor. ind. act. (suppletive)* < ὠνέομαι
πρίν (*conj.*)	before
πρό (*adv.*)	beforehand
πρόθυρον (*neut.*)	doorway
προκεῖμαι	to lie before
προπάροιθε	(+ *gen.*) in front of
πρός	(+ *acc.*) against
προσαγορεύω	to address, speak to
προσαυδάω	to address, speak to
προσέειπον	3 *sg. aor. ind. act.* < προσαγορεύω
προσέφην	(*aor. only*) to address, speak to
προτίθημι	to set out
πρόχοος (*fem.*)	jug
πρωθήβη	in the prime of youth
πρῶτα (*adv.*)	first
πρῶτον (*adv.*)	first
πρῶτος, –η, –ον (*adj.*)	first; front
πτερόεις, –εσσα, –εν	winged
πτολίεθρον (*neut.*)	citadel, city
πτύσσω	to fold up
πύθομαι	to decay
πύκα	solidly
πυκιμηδής, –ές	shrewd
πυκινῶς	shrewdly
Πύλος (*fem.*)	Pylus
πω	yet
πῶς	how?
ῥα	*emphatic particle*
ῥέζω	to do; to perform
ῥεῖα (*adv.*)	easily
Ῥεῖθρον (*neut.*)	Reithrum (*harbour*)
ῥινός (*masc.*)	hide
Σάμη (*fem.*)	Same (*island*)
σάφα (*adv.*)	clearly
σῆμα (*neut.*)	mound
σιδήρεος, –η, –ον	iron
σίδηρος (*masc.*)	iron
σῖτος (*masc.*)	bread
σιωπή (*fem.*)	silence
σκέδασις (*fem.*)	scattering
σκίδναμαι	to disperse (*intr.*)
σκιόεις, –εσσα, –εν	shadowy
σός, σή, σόν	your
Σπάρτη (*fem.*)	Sparta
σπέος (*neut.*)	cavern
σπόγγος (*masc.*)	sponge
σταθμός (*masc.*)	pillar
στῆθος (*neut.*)	chest, breast

στιβαρός, –ή, –όν	stout
στίχες (*fem. pl.*)	ranks
στοναχίζω	groan
στυγερός, –ή, –όν	hateful
σύ	you
σύν	(+ *dat.*) with
συντίθεμαι	to give heed to
σφάζω	to slaughter
σφέτερος, –η, –ον	their own
σφός, –ή, –όν	their own
σφεῖς	they
σφιν	to them
ταλασίφρων, –ον	stout-hearted
ταμίη (*fem.*)	steward
τανύω	(*aor.* –νσσα) to pull; (long table) to lay out
ταρ	*emphatic particle*
ταῦρος (*masc.*)	bull
Τάφιοι (*masc. pl.*)	Taphians
Ταφός	Taphos
τάχα	soon
τάχιστα	with all speed
τέγος (*neut.*)	roof
τείρω	to distress
τέκνον (*neut.*)	son, child
τελέεσθαι	*fut. inf. med. in pass. sense* < τελέω
τελευτή (*fem.*)	accomplishment, completion
τελευτάω	to accomplish
τελέω	to fulfil, accomplish
Τεμέση (*fem.*)	Temesa
τεός, –ή, –όν	your
τέρπομαι	to enjoy oneself, take delight
τέρπω	(*tr.*) to gladden; (*abs.*) to give delight
τεταρπόμενος	*nom. sg. aor. ptcp. med.* < τέρπω
τετιημένος, –η, –ον	sorrowing
τέτυγμαι	to be; to come into being (*perf. pass.* < τεύχω)
τεύχω	to make
τηλεκλυτός, –όν	far-famed
Τηλέμαχος (*masc.*)	Telemachus
τηλίκος, –ον	of such an age
τηλόθι (*adv.*)	at a distance
τί	why?
τι	at all
τίθημι	to put; to make, cause
τίκτω	to give birth to
τιμή (*fem.*)	esteem, honour
τιμήεις, –εσσα, –εν	valuable, costly; esteemed
τίπτε	why ever?
τίς, τίς, τί	who, what?
τις, τις, τι	some, someone, something
τίσις (*fem.*)	vengeance

τίω	to honour, value
τλάω	(*pres. not used*) endure, hold out
τόδε	hither
τοί	who
τοι	*epic for* σοι; *also* = mark you, indeed, I tell you
τοιοῦτος, τοιαύτη, τοιοῦτο	such as this
τοίγαρ	well then, therefore
τοῖος, τοίη, τοῖον	such
τοιόσδε, τοιήδε, τοιόνδε	such
τοκεύς (*masc.*), –ῆες (*pl.*)	parent
τολυπεύω	see through to the end; endure
τό(σ)σος, –η, –ον	so great, so much; so grown-up (*207 n.*)
τότε	then
τράπεζα (*fem.*)	table
τρέπομαι	to turn (*intr.*)
τρέφω	to rear, bring up
τρητοῖσι	bored, with holes in (*440 n.*)
Τροίη (*fem.*)	Troy
τρύχω	to wear out, consume
Τρῶες (*masc. pl.*)	Trojans
τύμβος (*masc.*)	burial mound
τυτθός, –ον	little, young
τῷ	then, therefore
ὑβρίζω	to behave with high spirits, exuberance (*227 n.*)
ὕβρις	high spirits; exuberance (*227 n.*)
ὑγρή (*fem.*)	sea (*97 n.*)
ὕδωρ, –ατος (*neut.*)	water
υἱός, υἱέος (*masc.*)	son
ὑληέεις, –εσσα, –εν	wooded
ὑμεῖς	you
ὑμός, –ή, –όν	your
ὕπατος, –ον	highest
ὑπέρ	(+ *acc.*) beyond; (+ *gen.*) above
ὑπέρβιος, –ον	violent; overweening
Ὑπερίων	Hyperion; the Sun (*8 n.*)
ὑπερφίαλος, –ον	arrogant
ὑπερφιάλως	arrogantly
ὑπερῷον (*neut.*)	upper storey
ὕπνος (*masc.*)	sleep
ὑπό	(+ *dat.*) under
ὑπό (*adv.*)	underneath
ὑπομένω	to wait behind
ὑπομνήσκω	(+ *gen.*) to remind of
ὑποπέταννυμι	to spread out underneath
ὑποτίθεμαι	(+ *dat.*) to advise
ὑψαγόρης (*masc.*)	boaster
ὑψηλός, –ή, –όν	high
φάρμακον (*neut.*)	poison
φέριστος	very brave (*405 n.*)
φέρω	to carry

φεύγω	to escape, get away from
φημί	to say
Φήμιος (*masc.*)	Phemius
φθινύθω	to waste
φθονέω	to grudge
φιλέεσκε	*epic 3 sg. imperf. ind. act.* < φιλέω
φιλέω	to love, treat kindly
φιλήρετμος, -ον	fond of rowing
φίλος (*masc.*)	friend
φίλος, -η, -ον	dear
Φόρκυς, -υνος	Phorcys
φορμίζω	to play the lyre
φράζομαι	to consider, ponder
φράζω	to show, reveal; to tell
φρήν, φρενός (*fem.*)	mind (*294 n.*)
φρονέω	to think; (+ *adj.*) to be...disposed
φύντες	*see 381 n.*
φωνέω	to speak
φώς, φῶτος (*masc.*)	man; warrior (*324 n.*)
χαῖρε	greetings (*123 n.*)
χαίρω	to rejoice
χαλεπός, -ή, -όν	harsh; cruel
χάλκεος, -είη, -εον	made of bronze
χαλκήρης, -ες	tipped with bronze
χαλκός (*masc.*)	bronze; (*raw material*) copper (*184 n.*)
χαλκοχίτων, -ωνος	bronze-clad
χαρίζομαι	to oblige (*61 n.*); (+ *gen.*) to give generously of (*140 n.*)
χείλος (*neut.*)	lip
χείρ, χειρός (*fem.*)	hand
χέρνιβα (*fem.*)	(*acc., no nom. in epic*) water for washing hands
χέω	(*aor.* χευ-) to pour
χθών, -ονός (*fem.*)	earth
χιτών, -ῶνος (*masc.*)	tunic
χόλος (*masc.*)	anger, wrath
χολόομαι	to be angry (+ *gen.* on account of)
χράομαι	(+ *gen.*) to long for, desire, yearn after
χρεῖος (*neut.*)	business, matter
χρεώ, -οῦς (*fem.*)	need (*225 n.*)
χρή (*impers.*)	(+ *acc. pers., gen. of thing*) to need; (+ *acc. pers., inf.*) to be necessary
χρίομαι	to smear, anoint
χρύσειος, -η, -ον	golden
χρύσος (*masc.*)	gold
χῶρος (*masc.*)	place
ψυχή (*fem.*)	life (*5 n.*)
ὤ	ah!
ὤ	O...!
Ὠγυγίη	Ogygia
ὧδε	thus; hither (*182 n.*)
ὠδυσάμην	(*aor. only*) (+ *dat.*) to hate (*62 n.*)

ὤϊξεν	3 sg. aor. ind. act. < οἴγω
ὠκύμορος, –ον	dying early
ὠλόμην	3 sg. aor. ind. med. < ὄλλυμι
ὠνέομαι	to buy
ὦπα (fem.)	(acc. only) face
Ὤψ, Ὦπος (masc.)	Ops
ὡς	as; when; in order that
ὥς, ὣς	thus

Technical Terms

A number of technical terms and symbols appear in this book. Since these might not be familiar to all readers, explanations are given below. A certain level of knowledge is taken for granted in those who come to a book of this kind, so that concepts such as verb, noun, active, passive, and the like are not explained. Those unfamiliar with such matters could begin by consulting Gwynne (2013); a convenient introduction to Indo-European is Fortson (2009). Terms that are explained as they occur in the text are not explained again here. A superscript [g] indicates that a term used within a definition is itself defined elsewhere in this glossary.

A. Symbols

*	Indicates an unattested or non-existent form. Typically used for reconstructions of PIE[g] or pre-Greek.[g]
$a > b$	Indicates that form a evolved into form b.
$c < d$	Indicates that form c was the result of an earlier form d.
C	Consonant
H_1, H_2, H_3	A group of three sounds called laryngeals, not directly extant in historical Greek but assumed to have existed in PIE[g]. Their precise phonetic qualities are controversial (Clackson 2007: 57). The following developments from PIE to Greek are important: $^*CH_1C > CeC$, $^*CH_2C > CaC$, $^*CH_3C > CoC$, $^*H_1C > eC$, $^*H_2C > aC$, $^*H_3C > oC$, $^*H_1e > e$, $^*H_2e > a$, $H_3e > o$, $^*eH_1 > \bar{e}$, $^*eH_2 > \bar{a}$ ($\bar{e}$ in Attic-Ionic), $^*eH_3 > \bar{o}$.
k^w, g^w, g^wh	A group of sounds called labio-velars, not directly extant in historical Greek but assumed to have existed in PIE[g]. Depending on the following sound, $^*k^w- >$ Gk. p, t, or k; $^*g^w- >$ Gk. b, d, or g; and $^*g^{wh}- >$ Gk. p^h, t^h, or k^h.
V	Vowel

B. Technical Terms

Ablaut	The alternation of vowels between e, o, and *zero* to mark inflexional or derivational categories: e.g. λείπω (e-grade verb), λέλοιπα (o-grade verb), λοιπός (o-grade adjective), ἔλιπον (zero-grade verb).
Apocope	The loss of one or more sounds at the end of a word, e.g. παρά may be reduced to παρ (192 n.).

Apodosis	The second limb of a conditional ('*if…then*') clause.
Aspect	Describes the marking of a verbal action in terms not of the time of its occurrence but of whether it is punctual (perfective) or durative (imperfective) in character. '*He threw*' and '*he was throwing*' both occurred in the past; the difference is one of aspect, not tense. Eng. *arrive* is generally used punctually whereas *walk* is generally durative. But *arrive* may be presented imperfectively (e.g. 'he was just arriving when the fire alarm went off') and *walk* may be used perfectively (e.g. 'he walked to work that morning').
Asyndeton	A lack of explicit connexion between two items which nevertheless belong together, e.g. *Visit Morecambe, die happy*.
Athematic	A verb or noun that lacks the theme vowel.[g]
Caland	A Caland formation is one where an adjective whose stem ends in *-ro-* may substitute an *-i-* for that ending when the adjective appears as the first element in a compound. (Since this rule was formulated by Willem Caland in the nineteenth century, it has been discovered that other adjectival forms are also involved in this phenomenon.)
Cognate	Two or more words are cognate when they are etymologically related, e.g. Skt. *pitar*, Gk. πατήρ, Lat. *pater*, Eng. *father*.
Concordance interpolation	A line weakly attested in the MSS tradition, apparently ill-suited to the context where it is found and thus suspected of being an interpolation, the explanation being that it has been lifted bodily by a scribe from its original context.
Copulative	The copulative alpha at the beginning of a Greek word derives from PIE[g] **sm-* ('one') and typically expresses unity, e.g. ἀ-δελφός ('brother' < 'of the same womb'). It might alternatively just reinforce the basic sense of the word to which it is prefixed, e.g. ἀ-σπερχές ('furiously'; 20 n.). Its opposite is the privative[g] alpha.
Correption	See Introduction, p. 49.
Desiderative	A verbal category specifically marking will or desire on the part of the subject.
Diectasis	See Introduction, p. 52.
Digamma	See Introduction, pp. 47–8.
Dissimilation	Where two sounds of a similar kind occur in quick succession, one or other may lose a distinctive feature such as aspiration or disappear altogether.
E-grade	See ablaut.[g]
Enclitic	A word so closely associated in pronunciation with the one preceding that it has no accent of its own.
Figura etymologica	A figure of speech where two words are juxtaposed which are, or are imagined to be, cognate (e.g. 241 n.).

Grassmann's Law	An instance of dissimilation^g whereby the first of two aspirates in successive syllables loses its aspiration, e.g. the genitive of Gk. θρίξ is realized as τριχός rather than *θριχός.
Hiatus	The occurrence of two distinct vowels in adjacent syllables with no intervening consonant, e.g. between πευθοίατο ἄλλοι.
Hypocoristic	A diminutive or 'pet' name for a person.
Imperfective	See aspect^g.
Inchoative	Indicates an action that is being begun; cf. ingressive.^{g}
Indo-Iranian	A branch of the PIE^g language family that includes Vedic Sanskrit (Indic) and Avestan (Iranian).
Ingressive	A synonym for inchoative.^{g}
Lectio difficilior	Lit. 'the more difficult reading'—refers to the idea that where one has a choice between two different readings at a given point in a manuscript tradition, the more difficult is likely to be correct since scribes tend to airbrush out or 'correct' forms that seem to them unfamiliar or difficult.
Lectio facilior	Lit. 'the easier reading'—see previous entry. The easier reading is not necessarily the correct one.
Lexeme	A unit of meaning that exists irrespective of the inflected forms in which it is found. Thus *will* and *would* belong together as different forms of the same lexeme, conventionally represented as WILL; *am, is, are*, and *were* belong to the lexeme BE; *goose* and *geese* are instances of GOOSE. The headwords in a dictionary are usually lexemes.
Metathesis	The rearrangement of sounds within a word (e.g. 225 n.).
Morpheme	A morpheme is the smallest unit of grammatical meaning in a language. Thus in English the plural ending *–s* or the past tense endings *–ed, –t* are morphemes.
O-grade	See ablaut.^{g}
Osthoff's Law	A sound change whereby, in Greek and possibly some other PIE^g languages, a long vowel is shortened before *l, *m, *n, *r, *i, or *u followed by a consonant.
Perfective	See aspect^g.
PIE	Proto-Indo-European—a hypothetical parent language reconstructed as the ancestor of Latin, Greek, Sanskrit, Armenian, and other languages whose historically attested forms show that they belong together as a family.
Pleonasm	The use of more words than are necessary, e.g. *cod fish*.
Plosive	See p. 46 n. 384.
Pre-Greek	A stage of Greek not attested but assumed to have existed in order to explain the historically attested forms. It represents a phase after the PIE^g parent language broke up and began to be differentiated into its discrete daughter languages.

Privative	A privative alpha at the beginning of a word negates the root sense of the following element, e.g. $\dot{a}$-$\theta\acute{a}\nu a\tau os$ ('not-mortal').
Proclitic	A word so closely associated in pronunciation with the one following that it has no independent accent of its own.
Protasis	The first limb of a conditional ('*if*...*then*') clause.
Prothetic vowel	A vowel of any kind that is neither copulative nor privative but is placed before a known root and whose function as a morpheme^g is often obscure (252 n.).
Sigmatic	Containing a sigma—as in the sigmatic aorist $\check{\epsilon}\lambda v\sigma a$ beside a non-sigmatic aorist such as $\check{\epsilon}\lambda a\beta ov$.
Stative	A verb that indicates a state of affairs ('be heavy', 'be in love').
Suppletion	A verbal paradigm is suppletive if it contains any inflexional forms that are etymologically unrelated to others. Examples are Greek $\phi\acute{\epsilon}\rho\omega$, $\mathring{\eta}\nu\epsilon\gamma\kappa ov$, $o\check{\iota}\sigma o\mu a\iota$; Lat. *fero, tuli*; Eng. *go, went*.
Syncope	The loss, generally of an unstressed vowel, from the interior of a word as a result of the accent falling elsewhere.
Synecphonesis	A phenomenon where the last syllable of a word is slurred together with the first syllable of the following word so as to be pronounced as a single syllabic unit, e.g. $\epsilon\iota\lambda a\pi\acute{\iota}\nu\eta\,\,\mathring{\eta}\acute{\epsilon}$ (226 n.).
Synizesis	See Introduction, p. 49.
Thematic	A noun or verb that has the theme vowel^g.
Theme vowel	A vowel placed between the stem and ending in verbs and nouns: $\lambda\acute{v}$-o-$\mu\epsilon\nu$ and $\lambda\acute{o}\gamma$-o-ν ($\nu < {}^*m$) are thematic whereas $\check{\iota}$-$\mu\epsilon\nu$ and $\check{a}\nu a\kappa\tau$-a ($a < {}^*m$) are athematic.
Tmesis	See Introduction, pp. 57–8.
Zero-grade	See ablaut^g.

Index

References are to page numbers throughout.

Index Verborum

Mycenaean Greek

Proto-Indo-European